MASQUERADE

AND

CARNIVAL:

Their Customs and Costumes.

Fredonia Books
Amsterdam, The Netherlands

Masquerade and Carnival:
Their Customs and Costumes

by
The Butterick Publishing Co.

ISBN: 1-4101-0386-2

Reprinted from the 1892 edition

Fredonia Books
Amsterdam, The Netherlands
http://www.fredoniabooks.com

In order to make original editions of historical works available to scholars at an economical price, this facsimile of the original edition of 1892 is reproduced from the best available copy and has been digitally enhanced to improve legibility, but the text remains unaltered to retain historical authenticity.

Fair ladies mask'd, are roses in their bud"—*Shakespeare.*

To brisk notes in cadence beating,
Glance their many twinkling feet."—*Gray.*

When you do dance, I wish you
A wave of the sea, that you might ever do
Nothing but that." —*Winter's Tale.*

INTRODUCTION.

IN all the collection of books and pamphlets heretofore issued upon the subject of Masquerades and kindred festivities, no single work has contained the condensed and general information sought by the multitude of inquirers who desire to render honor to Terpsichore in her fantastic moods, in the most approved manner and garb.

Continuous queries from our correspondents and patrons indicated this lack, and research confirmed it. A work giving engravings and descriptions of popular costumes and naming appropriate occasions for their adoption, and also recapitulating the different varieties of Masquerade entertainments and their customs and requirements was evidently desired and needed; and to that demand we have responded in a manner that cannot fail to meet with approval and appreciation. In preparing this book every available resource has been within our reach, and the best authorities upon the subject have been consulted. These facts entitle us to the full confidence of our patrons who have only to glance over these pages to decide for themselves that the work is ample and complete, and that everyone may herein find a suitable costume for any festivity or entertainment requiring Fancy Dress, and reliable decisions as to the different codes of etiquette governing such revelries.

Entertainments of this class for young folk are also fully discussed, and a large number of charming costumes for such occasions are illustrated and described in so clear a manner that any mother in the land may easily array her little ones for a Fancy-Dress Party, a School or Church Entertainment, or a Carnival. We have no hesitation in announcing that in this work we offer you the most accurate information, and the largest and best collection of illustrations of Fancy-Dress Costumes that can be obtained either complete in one book or scattered through many.

THE BUTTERICK PUBLISHING CO. [Limited.]

Contents.

ENTERTAINMENTS FOR YOUNG FOLK.

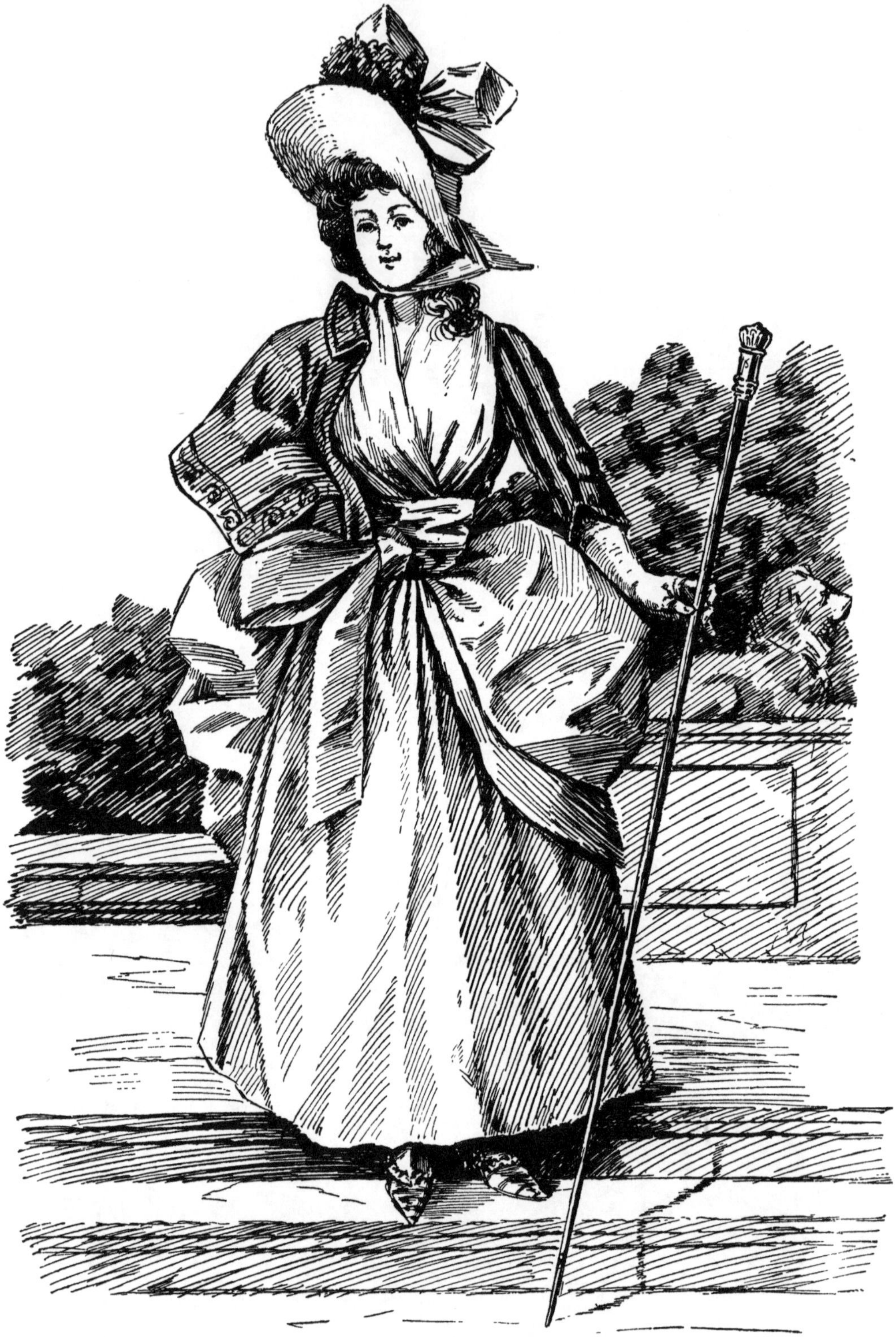

LA TOSCA.

Surplice of white China silk or mull. Panniers and skirt of pale-pink silk. Waist of pale-pink-and-brown striped silk. Sash of pale, yellowish sage-green Jacket of sage-colored cloth trimmed with braid Large yellow straw hat trimmed with yellow ribbons and red flowers. Gray mitts and stockings, gray-and-black striped slippers. Brown staff mounted and tipped with silver.

Masquerade and Carnival:

THEIR

Customs and Costumes.

AMONG the most pleasing forms of entertainment are those festivities which require the adoption of masquerade costumes. Borrowed characters and borrowed plumage have ever possessed a fascination for the multitude, whether upon the stage, at carnivals or in brilliantly lighted ball-rooms. In the latter, however, may be found the real domain of the masquerader. Here the borrowed plumage leads to merry happenings among the maskers; most incongruously assorted pairs whirl in the mazes of the dance or wander about among other grotesquely attired guests, each individual peering inquisitively from behind his mask at his neighbor; and fun and frolic grow apace, leading up to unexpected disclosures and laughable climaxes at the hour of unmasking.

The wearing of masks and fancy dress is not confined, as many suppose, to a ball or dance, although to this class of festivity must be accredited the origin of the custom of character-dressing upon social occasions. House parties are frequently given at the country residences of towns-people, the guests appearing in fancy dress and indulging in quaint games and old-time dances; and frequently a social gathering is arranged at which there is to be an amateur theatrical performance followed by a dance, or a supper given in commemoration of some historical event at which the guests are expected to appear in costume; and there are also Tableaux, Charade and Bal Poudré parties, and Martha Washington and Japanese teas, all requiring, to a greater or less extent, fancy-dress costumes. The Pose Plastique and Plastique Tableaux are among popular fancy-dress entertainments. Two costumes, given as examples of what is required for this class of entertainment are shown on other pages of this book.

An invitation to an affair of this class is usually hailed with pleasure though frequently with perplexity, for the invitation always develops the important question of what costume to wear or what character to select. The giving of a fancy ball or any of the entertainments named, is also often attended by difficulties in case the hostess is not fully informed as to preliminaries and requirements; and our object in preparing this pamphlet is to offer host and guest requisite information regarding the necessary adjuncts in the matter of costume and detail for various fancy-dress entertainments.

MASQUERADE OR FANCY BALLS.

Under this heading we shall give general information and instructions; but throughout the pamphlet will appear illustrations of costumes that may be appropriately worn upon any occasion of this class of entertainment, as well as at any of the other festivities named.

A successful fancy ball is generally the result of careful pre-arrangement. Naturally, the details of such an entertainment are much more elaborate than those of an ordinary ball, and demand proportionate attention from the writing of the invitations to the decorating of the ball room and opening the ball.

Where it is possible, have the invitations engraved instead of writing them, but in any event formulate them so that they will be distinctly understood as to date and requirements, and send them out at least two weeks before the ball is to take place. In the height of the season it is wise to allow even more time than that suggested, in order that hostesses may not clash in their arrangements, and that guests may have ample opportunity for any preparation that may be needed.

As private houses are seldom commodious enough to afford comfortable space for a large fancy ball, it is quite customary for the host or hostess to engage the exclusive use of the ball and supper rooms of some hotel or other public resort, and give the entertainment in them; and the custom is commendable, since it provides more room for the guests and thus insures them a greater amount of enjoyment, besides relieving the hostess of the household confusion which prefaces and follows a ball given at a private dwelling.

On the occasion of a private ball in a public ballroom, the latter may be decorated as far as possible to appear like the parlors of a private house; and as refreshments are served in rooms reserved for the purpose, the affair is as exclusive as if given under one's own roof.

In decorating for a fancy ball, the ballroom is usually festooned with draperies of the national or other colors fastened up under comic masks, or shields upon which are grotesque faces and figures, armorial emblems and mimic instruments of music. Flowers and foliage are banked and grouped in different parts of the room, but foliage should predominate, as its rich green forms a charming background for the brilliant costumes of the maskers. Japanese lanterns also add, by their soft radience, to the effectiveness of the scene.

In many instances the musicians are dressed in fancy costumes; and not infrequently the men servants are habited as were the retainers of olden days, and the women servants are also dressed as were those of ancient times. In this way greater realism is obtained and there are no inharmonious comminglings of the unpicturesque costumes of the present day.

Before touching upon costumes, it may be well to add the information concerning the general programme of a masquerade or fancy ball which is given either by private individuals or societies, in a public ballroom or hall. At a private house, unless there is a large ballroom, the plan can scarcely be followed, though it is the regular custom at the entertainments first mentioned.

A large fancy ball is usually opened with tableaux. For this purpose a stage or platform at one end of the room is necessary. Temporary steps should lead from the floor to the stage at its center. As soon as a sufficient number of guests have arrived to conduct the tableaux as planned, the entertainment begins. The subjects for the tableaux should be comic in character, and may consist of "hits on the times," or upon local politics or institutions; or they may be arranged from some familiar humorous picture or series of pictures. This matter must be left to the host and hostess of a private ball or to the committee of arrangements for a society ball, who will select the subjects and decide upon the number of tableaux to be given. The last tableaux must include all the maskers who have taken part in the tableaux, and also the host and hostess, or at a society ball the president of the society and his lady; and it must be so arranged that at the end of the scene those on the stage, headed by the host and hostess or the president and his lady, will fall into line of march and move down the steps to the floor, where all the other guests are waiting, and also join in the grand march which generally opens every ball. If the first dance is to be a waltz, the guests should at the close of the march, be standing so that the line will form a sort of spiral. But if the first dance is to be a square dance, then the couples should be arranged along the sides of the room, ready to fall into sets at the first bars of the music.

Sometimes the first dance of the evening is conducted by one set dressed in a very grotesque manner. For instance, eight young men will be costumed as bears in real bear-skins easily hired from a costumer, there being four black or brown ones and four white ones, the latter taking the ladies' parts in the dance. The performance is a very laughable one, naturally, as the costumes make the dancers as clumsy as the bears would be themselves.

Among the many quadrilles from which to select a subject for this one dance, which may include other sets of the guests, are the following, and it must be understood that the gentlemen of the set in most of the cases must be dressed alike and the ladies also; and that the costumes must belong to the same period or be naturally associated together: Shepherds and Shepherdesses; the Seasons; Watteau and Poudré periods; Louis Quinze Hunting Quadrille, in the hunting costume of that period; Kings and Queens of various nations; Army and Navy; Holbein Quadrille in Tudor dress; Flowers of the Year; Birds; Pack of Cards; Puritan Maidens and Cavaliers; Noah's Ark; (the animals in pairs); National Games; Politicians and Nuns; Policemen and Nurse Girls; Dudes and Tailor-made Girls; Clowns and Fairies; in fact, anything of the kind that may suggest itself to the hostess or committee of arrangements, who plans when such a dance shall take place and who are to take part in it. In other respects a fancy ball for adults is conducted the same as an ordinary full-dress ball, except that at midnight every guest must unmask. Occasionally, with the aid of wax, grease-paint, cosmetics and the general paraphernalia of a theatrical facial "make-up," a guest may so disguise himself as to require no mask, and at the hour of unmasking may retain his "make-up" but must reveal his identity; and it may here be added that face veils of thick lace, bordered with narrow fringe or edging are often substituted for regular masks, and lend a very piquant effect to the *tout ensemble* of a costume.

And *apropos* of this point, during the arrival of tne guests, the hostess (or reception committee) stands at the entrance to the ball-room, and to her each guest must lift his or her mask just long enough to disclose the face, as this is the only way in which the hostess may protect herself against the intrusion of unbidden guests. Reception commitees at society balls are obliged to be even more strict than this, and may exclude even a bidden guest who wears an objectionable costume.

It must be understood that the conventionally accepted fancy costume of historical periods is far from authentic in many instances, though there is always sufficient foundation in its details to identify it with the epoch which it is supposed to represent. In deliberating over "what to wear," it not infrequently occurs that discussions and research often prove foundations for happy inspirations in the way of costumes, and the more original the idea the more striking will be the result. The inventive genius of a bright woman knows no limitations when it is called into play as the creator of re-inforcements for the ranks of fantastic dress, even though her material resources are restricted; and give her all possible facilities in the matter of money and paraphernalia, and she will work wonders in producing novelties in the way of fancy costumes to add to those already familiar. The costumes illustrated in this pamphlet, as well as the many described, will furnish the unimaginative women or man with sufficient information as to what to wear at a fancy dress ball; and they will, at the same time, suggest many possibilities to the inventive class just mentioned.

Fancy dress affords ample opportunity for effective results, and everyone should study what is individually becoming, and make the selection of a peronal costume on that basis. For instance, a brunette should ordinarily select characters who from their nationality would be of a dark type, while a blonde should follow a similar principle in choosing her character and costume; although by the aid of wigs and stains a blonde may assume a brunette character, and a brunette may to some extent also, change her type, aided by wigs and pigments.

For the brunette there are many characters of which the following are illustrations; Autumn, Carmen, Cleopatra, Egyptian Woman, Gypsy, Esmeralda, Indian Girl, Britannia, Diana, Erin, Italian and Spanish Women, Japanese Women, etc., etc.

For the blonde: Aurora, Canada, Arctic Maiden, Elaine, Fair Maid of Perth, Flora, Marguerite, Ophelia, Moonlight, Titania, Water Nymphs and Naiads, besides many others which will suggest themselves to the reader.

One of the main difficulties is encountered in dressing the hands and feet properly. A student of the art of costuming will object to the use of gloves or mitts, except with costumes belonging to a period when they were worn; but as gloves are almost necessities as protectors of fine fabrics and costumes, and also to prevent the disagreeable contact of perspiring hands during the dance, they are universally worn; but it is well to have them as inconspicuous in color as possible in order that they may not subdue by contrast, the bright hues of the rest of the toilette, and may also preserve, to a moderate extent, the effect produced by uncovered hands or arms. A point in favor of the wearing of gloves is that they also conceal the hands by which a person may often be identified as easily as by the face. When a lady decides to attend a fancy ball with bare hands, she usually exchanges rings with some of her friends or wears none at all; and if her mask does not conceal her neck and ears, she wears borrowed or hired jewelry instead of her own, or omits it altogether.

Where boots and shoes cannot be hired from a costumer to suit various costumes, then the handsomest fancy boots and shoes that can be bought are worn. They may be of white or colored kid, including gilt, silver and bronze; and let it be whispered here, that a pair of ordinary kid boots or slippers that have seen previous service may be gilded or bronzed by liquid preparations sold for such uses, and will serve the purpose intended as well as expensive new ones. In selecting shoes for a historical costume, it should be remembered that those with high heels were not known until Elizabeth was queen.

Then, the hair should be dressed as near as possible after the style worn during the period when the costume selected was fashionable, or as it is worn in the countries whose fashions have been, for the time being, decided upon. It is better not to wear wigs, as they are heavy and generally uncomfortable. Obtain the effect desired, as far as possible, with powder. Dress the hair in the style required, using plenty of pomatum or vaseline, and then dust the powder (violet powder) on with a puff held over the head with one hand and jerking or jarring the elbow with the other hand. The process must be repeated over and over again to produce the desired effect. The next day the head will have to be very thoroughly shampooed to remove the pomatum and powder, but even this trouble is preferable to wearing a wig.

In powdering the hair, however, it is well to avoid very glaring inconsistencies by comparing the date of the costume with that marking the introduction of powder, which was during the reign of James I. At this time it was not generally worn, but it was in the zenith of its popularity during the Georgian period; but in 1795 it was heavily taxed by Pitt, and, therefore, was worn only by those who could afford the guinea-tax. Wigs were first worn in 1529; but a clever hair-dresser will easily copy their effects, aided by curling tongs, puffs, rolls, pomatum and powder, and even the ingenious amateur hair-dresser will not find it so difficult a task as it may seem to the reader, if she is provided with the implements and other assistants above mentioned. For historical characters, up to the reign of Queen Elizabeth, who introduced padding and frizzing, the hair was parted at the middle and allowed to float over the shoulders, or else it was bound up under a coif. During the time of the Stuarts short curls were worn over the forehead and long ones at the back; but Marie Stuart's hair was turned over side-rolls in order to fill up the space under the velvet head-dress. The following general hints will be useful to those who select national costumes, though it is well in dressing the front hair to keep as near as possible to the arrangement ordinarily most becoming to the individual, and make the marked changes at the back.

With classic costumes the hair is worn in a knot at the nape of the neck and bound with a fillet—that is, a narrow band which is passed over the head and under the knot two or three times; and when the knot is raised higher, a few short curls are allowed to escape from it. Almost any book of historical pictures, or the heads upon ancient coins will disclose the classic coiffure. In modern Greek costumes the hair should fall in loose curls over the shoulders or hang in two long braids. With Italian costumes these two braids are tied with colored ribbons, and often interwoven with coins and beads; and sometimes they are coiled round and round and fastened with fancy pins thrust through the twist. With Egyptian costumes the hair is generally flat and smooth in front, but falls in ringlets at the back. Many plaited strands at the back, entwined with coins and jewels, mark the Turkish method of hair-dressing, while at the sides are flat curls of the present Montague style. Scottish costumes require the hair to be flat in front and curled at the back, while the Irish peasant wears her hair in a coil at the nape of the neck. With German peasant costumes the style of hair dressing varies. Some wear the hair flat next the face and in a loose chignon at the back; others wear it plaited in two braids that are tied with ribbons. The peasantry near Dresden who sell their hair, cover their shorn heads with close-fitting caps. Norwegians plait their hair, and either pin it close to the head or allow it to fall in long braids. Swedish women turn it back from the face over a cushion, and allow it to fall in curls at the back. Polish girls dress theirs in two long braids, and the Russians braid and wind theirs about their heads. Normandy peasants dress their hair flatly in front and in broad looped-up braids at the back. A Puritan maiden wears a close coiffure under a cap. In legendary characters the hair is worn floating over the shoulders. Ophelia also adopts this style, entwining her tresses with flowers; while Marguerite wears her hair in two long, fair braids. For Undine, Winter, Snow, Fairies, etc., etc., dampen floating locks with thin white starch and then frost them with powder shaken over the starch.

In dressing the hair to imitate a wig, it may be arranged in the Swedish style just described; or, several rolls or puffs aided by hair pads may cross the crown diagonally; or, one roll may cross the center of the head between a curled bang and falling curls, while tiny rolls are made at the side; or the hair may be arranged in short curls all over the head and then powdered.

In making up costumes of a historical type, endeavor to secure such material as will in the main correspond with the characteristics of those used for the original costumes. A historical dress made of modern and conventional fabrics in most cases would prove a failure, unless the above caution were heeded. As much attention is now given to artistic dressing on ordinary occasions, it is undoubtedly true that this tendency has varied the correct costumes of the sixteenth century for fancy balls; and very quaint they now are with their flowing skirts, low, square bodies and richly broidered, puffed sleeves. Still it will be noticed by the observant, that the most popular costume of a season will be one taken from the last new popular opera or play; or possibly from some picture or book dug from the past and placed in present popularity.

Notable historical characters are Queen Anne, Anne Boleyn, Catherine of Arragon; Catherines de Medici, Howard and Parr, Queen Elizabeth, Marie Antoinette, Marie Stuart, Marguerite de Valois, Elizabeth of York; and men and women of the Georgian, Charles I., James II., and Louis XIII., XIV., XV. and XVI., periods.

Other suitable characters for ladies and gentlemen, as well as for misses, girls, boys and children, will be given upon following pages of this pamphlet, with accompanying descriptions. Many of the costumes illustrated may be easily made at home from an inspection of the engravings and their descriptions. Others may be found at costumers and hired for a moderate sum. Or, any first-class dress-maker or capable costumer will copy any costume desired or develop any individual idea of an original or familiar costume. The composing materials may be as rich or as inexpensive as desired, and represent strong or delicate color-contrasts.

A CARNIVAL SESSION.

A Carnival Session is classed as a Fancy-Dress Ball, although it is not a masquerade and ordinarily, not a costume ball It is conducted, however, upon the general plan of fancy balls, and though character dress is not required, every person attending is obliged to wear a fancy cap like or similar to those seen on the next page. The session is generally given under the auspices of some society, and arranged by an executive committee appointed by the society, there being four or more according to the magnitude of the session. Every person whose presence is desired receives an individual invitation, and the committee provide caps, each of which is equivalent to a ticket of admission, since every individual who accepts his invitation must procure his cap at the door from the committee ; and as he pays for it may carry it away at the end of the ball as a souvenir of the session. These caps are in great variety and each season adds something new in the way of design. The different sections of each cap are of varying bright colors, so arranged that the cap may be red and yellow or white at one side, and blue and yellow, or green and white at the other. The caps are also variously trimmed with silver and gilt braid or paper, and tiny bells ; and birds and animals are also shaped by the different sections of some of them. When the session is given at a residence as a private affair, the hostess provides the caps at her own expense and presents every guest with one at the entrance to the room.

While evening dress is always desirable for either a society or private session, and quite imperative for the latter, the gentlemen may attend in ordinary demi-dress if the affair is not to be very elaborate; but there are no "ifs" and "ands," so far as the cap is concerned—that *must* be worn, as it is really the badge of the Carnival Session.

Of the executive committee, one is President and the others his aides. The President and his aides may be dressed the same as the guests, but the result is more effective if they assume costumes and characters. For instance, the committee may represent the kings of different nations, or Indian chiefs; or a king and his courtiers, or a single chief and his braves. Then there is a clown or jester who *must* be in costume even though no one else is, and he must also be a very bright, witty man.

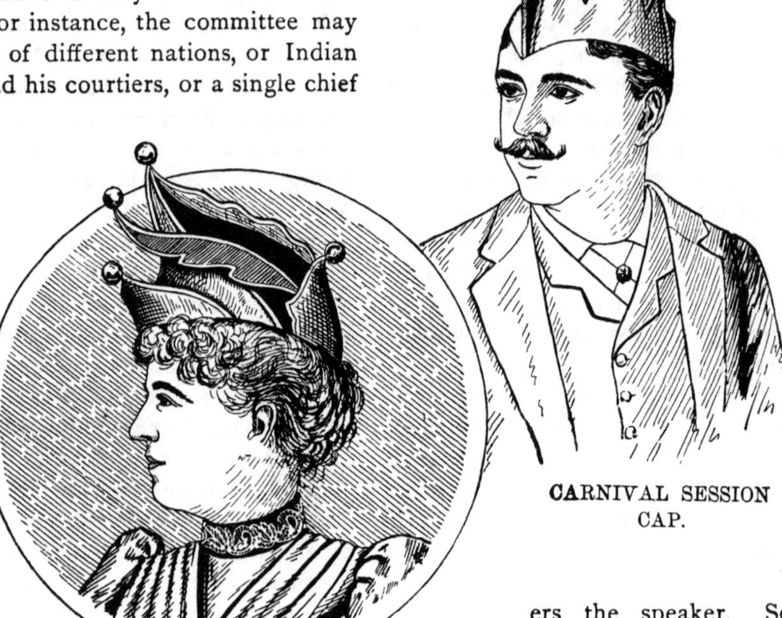

CARNIVAL SESSION CAP.

CARNIVAL SESSION CAP.

A stage or platform at one end of the room is for the following purpose: The President and his suite occupy one end of it, while upon the other is erected another small rostrum which may represent the Eiffel tower, a huge candle in a candle-stick or any absurd structure which suggests itself to the committee of arrangements. Take for instance the candle and candle-stick, which is put to the following use: The President controls the session, and calls upon such guests as have been prepared for it, or even upon the unprepared, to address the session. The man called upon mounts the candle-stick, his head appearing just where the wick would come in a real candle, and begins his remarks, which, of course, are expected to be humorous. Now suspended directly over this candle-stick is a huge extinguisher moved by a pulley and rope, the latter in the hands of the clown. This personage must interrupt the speaker now and then with comic questions and remarks; and when the speaker makes a bad pun, or is confused or becomes personal, or has spoken at some length, the clown must suddenly let the extinguisher down over him, no matter what he is saying. When the clown is inattentive or not quick enough on certain occasions, any guest of the session may rise, and addressing the President, call the speaker to order, whereupon the clown must lower the extinguisher. The latter, of course, is open at the back so that it only apparently covers the speaker. Sometimes in its place a bell is rung or a large rattle is used, or the clown presents him with a basket of huge chestnuts. In fact many laughable substitutes for the extinguisher may be invented. The President and his aides govern the entertainment and settle all discussions. When the addresses have all been made—beginning say at about nine o'clock, and lasting until ten or half-past—the grand march begins, led by the President and his lady, followed then by his aides and their ladies and the clown, who attaches himself to any couple he fancies, or flits from couple to couple, as he sees fit. In fact he is a privileged character and uses his privileges generously. The rest of the entertainment is conducted the same as at an ordinary ball. The addresses and speeches may be upon topics of the day or upon local institutions, politics, etc., etc., but they must be of a humorous character and include no unpleasant or personal allusions. The "hits" must be free from thrusts that might be offensive.

SUGGESTIONS FOR FANCY-DRESS PARTIES.

Some of the most successful fancy-dress parties as to costume, and most fascinating as to the amusement afforded, have been arranged by limitations to books, eras, countries, etc., which have been mentioned by the hostess upon the cards of invitation. For instance, she invites her friends and acquaintances to a Mother-Goose party, or perhaps to a classic party, the latter including both Greeks and Romans, a few of the most presentable of the gods and goddesses and so on down to some of the characters portrayed in Hawthorne's *Marble Faun.*

Both the Greek and Roman costumes of the free men and women are a most interesting study well worth giving a party for, if only that; while following such a research, one's memory of classic times is refreshed, if not newly stored with historic facts, regarding tastes and habits that have influenced all the succeeding generations of civilized peoples. Gentlemen and ladies who carry themselves with dignity can wear these vestments with charming and novel effects, that contrast curiously with the appointments of a modern drawing-room.

As an extreme contrast to a party of Greek and Roman guests, a Mother-Goose entertainment is a decided bliss. The whimsical raiment of its inconsequent personages, with their light laughter or droll tribulations, offers endless possibilities of delight. There are the rôles of "Little Bo-Peep," "Little Boy Blue," "Mary, Quite Contrary," "Mother Hubbard," "Cry, Baby, Cry," "Little Jack Horner," "Little Red Riding-Hood and her Grandmother," and enough more to fill a house, each being very funny when assumed by a grown-up person.

Then there are heroes and heroines of eminent writers of verse, which may be grouped into one entertainment. Keats' "Madeline," Burns' "Highland Mary," Wordsworth's "Meg," Scott's "Ellen Douglass," Spencer's "Una," Herrick's "Corinna," Tennyson's "Elaine," "Enid," and other of his own creation or reproductions from history, Mrs. Browning's "Aurora Leigh," "George Eliot's "Spanish Gypsy," Chaucer's "Griselde," Coleridge's "Genevieve," Longfellow's "Evangeline," and "Minnehaha," Whittier's "Cassandra," etc., are all delightful characters. Each of these, and also many more heroines, which, with their attendant heroes, every reader may think out for him or herself, can be gathered together in proper dresses, with immense pleasure to one's eyes and even more satisfaction to one's intellect.

Then there may be a Shakespearean fancy party, with only the leading characters of this greatest of great poets represented together. It goes without saying that the toilettes of these personages, if historically correct, will present a set of pictures the magnificence of which cannot be portrayed by words or even by pencils of many coloring. There are Juliet in the robe of her time and social station, Cordelia, Rosalind when she was not masquerading as a man, Portia, Ophelia, Jessica, Beatrice, Viola, Lady Macbeth, witches, etc., all of whom wore costumes that can readily be reproduced with a little research.

Another fancy party, even more interesting than that of the heroes and heroines of the poet or dramatist, and which can be arranged with less expense as to raiment, may be made up of the national costumes of the world; of course including those worn on holidays by peasants. There are the Spanish, the Norman, the Breton, the Dutch, among each of which are several styles that are all first cousins to each other as are the differing caps of the women of Normandy and Brittany. The Italian dress varies in different departments; the Trasteverian vestments being only a slightly modernized Roman dress, while the Neapolitan, the Venetian, the North-Italian mountaineer's clothing and the dress of the fisher-folk of Capri, etc., offer a charming variety from which to choose. The Swedish and Norwegian, the Chinese and Japanese, the Russian, Turkish, Persian and Egyptian costumes are all picturesque, and they may be very simple in fabric and completion, as the peasants add ornamental elaborateness only for the sake of announcing their financial status.

The Roumanian peasant's dress is especially attractive, and the Queen of Roumania often wears it wrought after the manner of her rural subjects. Her picture, taken while dressed as a peasant, is one of the most beautiful of all her many exquisite portraits. In her country only the accidents of birth give place and position in society, and no height or depth of cultivation of character elevates or lowers the individual, and, because of this inflexible and pitiless law of custom, the Queen grieves deeply. More than that she wears the garb of the peasantry as an assurance of her respect for all of them who are good and true.

To find the costume of all nations, one has only to visit a public library and look at the pictures of them in its books of reference. A short study of such pictures will be more useful in giving one ideas as to their construction than would any description possible to the pen, no matter how concise or elaborate it may be.

MARTHA WASHINGTON BALLS AND TEA PARTIES.

These festivities are alike in the matter of dress, but each is conducted quite differently from the other. A Martha Washington ball may be an affair at which the guests are masked; the ladies dressed in the Martha Washington and other costumes of the eighteenth century, and with powdered hair; and the gentlemen in the Continental and Revolutionary costumes, with powdered wigs and braided queues, and ruffles and frills of lace at their wrists and necks.

At an ordinary Martha Washington ball the men attend in fashionable evening dress; but all of the ladies are in full Martha Washington costume in all its variations. Long silk mitts are worn in preference to gloves, the hair is dressed as Lady Washington wore hers and heavily powdered to render it snowy white; antique fancy bags are suspended from the arms, and every detail of fashion that can be unearthed from historical records of the Revolutionary period is carried out as far as possible. Of course black patches must appear upon the faces near pretty mouths, seductive dimples, an arching eyebrow or a beautiful eye. The balls are conducted the same as those of the usual type, but the ball room should be decorated with draped American flags, muskets, bayonets, swords and antique emblems. Not infrequently at a Martha Washington fancy ball the host and hostess assume the characters of the Father of his Country and his lady, and receive their guests seated upon a low platform under a dais or canopy of evergreens, flowers and the national colors intermingled. They also open the ball and lead the german or cotillion. Martha Washington balls always take place upon "Washington's Birthday," February 22nd, or in case that date falls upon Sunday, the day selected before or after this date as the one to be celebrated is the one also decided upon for the ball.

Martha Washington tea parties, however, may occur at any time during the season for balls, fairs and general festivities. They may be afternoon affairs, taking the place of "a five o'clock tea" at which a party of ladies may receive, each lady wearing a Martha Washington costume, and the lady guests invited to do so, though not compelled to.

Or, when a tea party is given by a church society for a charitable object, only the ladies of the committee and those serving the refreshments need dress in the Martha Washington costume. If, however, these ladies desire them to do so, the men who are also upon the committee should dress as far as possible in a corresponding fashion. In garrets and trunks and chests in many an old family, may be found ancestral garments that will prove "just the thing" for a Martha Washington tea party or even a ball. Antique looking buckles of pebbles or Rhine stones or silver may be found in almost every fancy store, with which to decorate high-heeled shoes; and scarlet stockings once of the past are now no longer so, but may be obtained almost anywhere.

Lady Washington parties may be given for progressive euchre, and the prizes may include relics of the period of '76, or small boxes of tea which may also contain modern prizes. At the end of the playing, if such boxes form the prizes, tea might be brewed from their contents and served at the different tables by the occupants of each of the latter at the end of the game.

A Lady Washington musicale might include instrumental and vocal musicians dressed in Revolutionary costumes; and as far as possible the music should be such as was popular at that early period.

In fact any fashionable amusement may be the main feature of a Lady Washington party; but the latter is the result of the costumes worn more than of any special amusement.

Upon page 53 of this pamphlet may be seen the popular Martha Washington costume for the gentler sex; while upon other pages are illustrated the Revolutionary and Continental costumes worn by the men of that period.

A BALL POUDRÉ.

A ball of this description is conducted upon the same basis as an ordinary ball, so far as the programme and the general details are concerned. The guests attire themselves as for a full-dress ball, except that the ladies are required to powder their hair white and wear fancy black patches upon their faces; and the gentlemen to wear white vests and small button-hole bouquets. The effect is very pretty, especially with the present artistic style of dressing which closely copies antique fashions.

A CALICO BALL.

As the requirements of calico balls are very generally understood, they will need scarcely more than a passing mention in this pamphlet. Gloves or mitts are seldom used at calico balls, although they are permissible. Regarding materials for calico-ball costumes, the wearers are by no means restricted to a use of all-cotton goods, for satins and velvets having cotton backs may be appropriately selected, and ribbon, net and tinsel trimmings are also allowable. Among the costumes most generally chosen for calico balls are Peasant and Shepherdess dresses, and those for Fish Girls, Flower Girls and Charity Girls; Poudré and Watteau costumes and those for Cinderella, Mother Hubbard, Waiting Maids, Bo-Peep, Dolly Varden, or almost any of those suggested and pictured throughout this pamphlet. The men at such balls wear simply-made character costumes, or full-dress suits made of " calico "; or sometimes ordinary dress suits faced with bright cambric or satin, or flowered fabrics. Original costumes for a ball of this kind usually create the greatest sensation and are often productive of the most fun. Strong color-contrasts are desirable features in costumes of calico or other cotton fabrics.

JAPANESE PARTIES.

In giving a Japanese party which may take the form of a five o'clock tea, or a card party in the evening, or a party in which music, readings and recitations are the main features of the social part of the entertainment, the only imperative requirement relates to the matter of costumes. These *must* be Japanese for the ladies; and a greater zest may also be given when the gentlemen are habited as far as possible like those of Japan. This, however, is a matter for personal decision; and it is also argued that the neat though sombre customary evening dress for men affords an effective contrast for the bright and picturesque Japanese costumes worn by ladies at such parties. At afternoon teas it is not only allowable but advisable that gentlemen attend in street costume or frock coats, since it is now considered better form to don evening attire only for evening occasions. As a compliment to the hostess and other ladies in Japanese dress, gentlemen in ordinary evening toilette wear Japanese decorations or bits of Japanese silk in their button-holes instead of *boutonnieres*. Unless the entertainment is to be of a masquerade or fancy-ball character, a gentleman is not compelled to wear other than the conventional street, afternoon or evening dress as before mentioned.

Ladies' Japanese costumes—kimonos, as they are called—may be made up of China silks, Oriental stuffs found in Japanese stores, or even of sateen, if the latter is of a good quality and of an Oriental pattern. Velvet, silk and satin, and gilt and silver trimmings are occasionally intermingled in Japanese costumes, though as a rule edges of garments are plainly finished.

As regards the room in which the entertainment is held, it should be decorated with Japanese lanterns, parasols or any fancied Oriental decorative hangings or articles that can be obtained. If tea is served it should be offered in Japanese cups and saucers, and the refreshments, if possible, may be Japanese delicacies offered upon lacquered trays or spread upon an Orientally arranged table. Tiny perfumed pastiles may be burned before the receiving hour; and an odor of sandal-wood, that perfume so popular with the inhabitants of the Orient, may add its fragrance to the atmosphere to still further intensify the effect of the illusion.

If tableaux form a part of the entertainment, they should be founded on Japanese life, and can be readily arranged from engravings depicting scenes from the land of the Japanese; or from books of Japanese history or travels. Japanese tales may be read or, if obtainable, translations from Japanese literature.

Upon various pages of this pamphlet may be seen two or three Japanese costumes for ladies and gentlemen's wear. Short descriptions of these garments accompany the engravings and, with the picture, supply sufficient information as to details of construction.

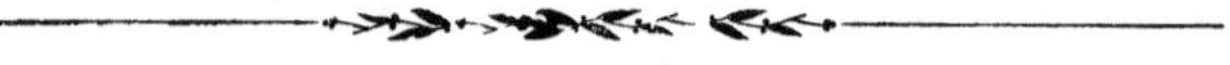

FLORAL ENTERTAINMENTS.

These entertainments are confined to teas and dinners. In giving them the hostess selects some flower—a pink, or a chrysanthemum, for instance—and sends out cards inviting her guests to her pink tea or chrysanthemum dinner. The guests wear full dress, and find the rooms decorated with the flower mentioned in the invitation, special attention in this respect being paid to the dining or supper room. Here everything in the way of carrying out the colors or coloring of the flower selected that can be done is done; and beside the covers are laid small bouquets of the flowers for the ladies and *boutonnieres* for the gentlemen.

The rose, narcissus, jonquil, violet, orchid, chrysanthemum and pink form the most popular list to select from, but the hostess is by no means restricted to it. She may choose any other flower, so long as it is pretty and is suitable for the small bouquets mentioned. Several pretty floral costumes may be seen on other pages of this pamphlet.

TABLEAUX VIVANTS.

Although not strictly belonging to the class of entertainments named in the title of this pamphlet, *tableaux vivants* partake of some of the characteristics of masquerades, inasmuch as they require special costumes for the characters assumed. Tableaux afford excellent amusement at a large party where there is to be no dancing or where amateur theatricals cannot be arranged. The impression, however, that they may be produced with little preparation, in fact, almost on the spur of the moment, is very erroneous. To be successfully represented they require quite as much attention as a dramatic performance; and, as the setting or frame for the living pictures you are to present needs special supervision in its preparation, it is a wise plan, where possible, to secure the services of a good stage manager or some one possessing artistic skill and some knowledge of stage requirements to superintend and direct this part of the preliminaries.

In a double parlor, with sliding doors between, the stage should be erected so that this opening may be utilized in imitating a theatre stage.

Hang a dark curtain at each side, draping it prettily, and suspend a valance of the same material across the top of the opening; and then over the opening stretch and tack a screen of gauze, tarletan or fine mosquito netting, in order to soften the effect of the scenes. Black or white is always used for this purpose, the former preferably, since it absorbs the light and renders the picture more distinct than the white which reflects the light and obscures the effect. When practicable the stage should be raised; but if this cannot be done a board six inches wide and covered with the curtain material should rest on the floor across the opening, just where the footlights would come on a real stage.

The sliding doors may be used in place of draw-curtains, but if the latter are necessary or preferred, the usual domestic arrangement of *portiere* curtains will be found satisfactory. The most artistic effect, however, will be produced by using the regular green baize theatrical curtain.

The "background" is an important point. In dramatic tableaux, where incidents are represented, a special background will be required for each scene; but tableaux portraying merely a picture, statuary, or allegorical and legendary subjects require only a simple background of drapery of a color which will not kill but will accentuate the tints in costumes of the silent actors, and give the actors themselves full prominence. The material should be wool or velvet, so that the light may be absorbed. A glazed background will destroy the life of any picture presented against it.

In tableaux lights and shade must be skilfully managed in order to produce artistic effects. Footlights are not needed—in fact the effect is better without them, or with at least but two or three. The stronger light should come from one side or the other of the stage.

Colored lights greatly enhance the effect of tableaux and may be secured by several methods. The powdered materials used for colored lights may be purchased for a few cents at any druggists. They are placed, as wanted, in a pan or dish at the side, away from the curtains, scenery, etc., etc., and as the curtain is raised, a match is touched to the powder and a green or red light is thus thrown upon the group. But as the odor of this powder is objectionable in a close or small room, colored glass or silk is sometimes placed between the regular lights and the picture to produce the tint desired. A strong white light is produced by burning the end of a magnesium wire in the flame of an ordinary candle.

In tableaux it will not be necessary to use as rich fabrics in constructing costumes as for a fancy ball or theatricals, as the gauze screen softens and harmonizes all effects, and behind it glazed muslin will look as well as satin, cotton velvet as rich as silk, and worsted ermine as royal as the real fur.

The subjects for living pictures are many and may also be originated to satirize or burlesque local events or institutions. Paintings, pictures, illustrated books and celebrated statuary; and books of humor, history, romance and poetry will all supply subjects suited to every occasion; but for those who desire more definite information upon the point we offer a short list of subjects:

Faith, or Rock of Ages.—A large wooden cross whitewashed or covered to represent marble or granite, with a woman dressed in loose brown cloak clinging to its base.

Hope.—A female figure clad in soft gray, posed sideways with right elbow on knee, right hand supporting her chin, face raised heavenward and if possible a single star appearing in a sky background, while at her feet rests the emblematic anchor.

Charity.—A Sister of Mercy bending over a beggar child seated on a block of stone, offering him alms.

Cain and Abel.—A cane standing against a chair on which is *a bell.*

Single Blessedness.—A bachelor's untidy apartment, bachelor seated in arm-chair trying to darn a sock; one of his feet is dressed, the other bare and resting on a foot-stool. Blue light.

The Wooing O't.—Same bachelor pleading his cause with a pretty girl, either in a parlor or a rustic lane. Rosy light.

Married and Happy.—Same bachelor in same room, now tidy; pretty wife at his feet and both gazing happily at a dainty cradle at their side. Red light.

The Fortune Teller.—A gypsy holding the hand of a pretty girl and gazing intently into the palm, or looking smilingly and shrewdly into her face.

Dignity and Impudence.—A pompous-looking individual gazing downward into the saucy upturned face of a street gamin.

Paul and Virginia.—Dark youth and fair maiden dressed in classic costumes and holding over their heads an arched palm leaf. Attitude lover-like.

Prince and Pauper.—A man dressed in prince's costume gazing contemptuously at another man dressed in rags and in a shrinking attitude. Prince might occupy a throne-like seat and be surrounded by men and women in court dress.

Faust and Mephistopheles, with Visions of Marguerite.—Faust in his study listening to Mephistopheles' promises of youth; circular opening cut from background, covered with gauze screen; Marguerite behind the screen at her spinning-wheel in strong light; rest of the picture in subdued light.

A Picture of Bliss.—Small negro boy eating a large slice of watermelon.

Maud Muller.—Pretty girl in Dntch peasant costume, raking hay; portly squire in riding costume looking at her with admiration.

Catherine at the Stake.—Servant girl preparing a large beefsteak for broiling.

The Light of Other Days.—Old-fashioned candlestick with lighted candle in it standing on a plain table.

Whispering Hope.—An imitation window in a pretty room; girl seated at the window gazing shyly out at gentleman who is kissing his hand to her.

Country Cousins.—Man, woman and two children dressed in very rustic style, greeting a mortified city relative in her own handsome parlor, which is filled with friends.

Personal ingenuity, together with remembrances and observations of past occasions must be called upon in working out poses and details of the following subjects which are universally popular among adults: Faith, Hope and Charity; Pocahontas and Captain John Smith; Night and Day; the Blue and the Gray (soldiers); Youth and Old Age; Past, Present and Future; Tempest and Sunshine.

For children there are many pretty subjects to be found in nursery rhymes, fairy tales and story books. The following are always popular and may be supplemented from the sources mentioned: Babes in the Wood; The Old Woman who Lived in a Shoe; A Pyramid of Children; King Cole and His Fiddlers Three; May-Pole Dance; Red Riding-Hood; Little Lord Fauntleroy and His Friends, The Bootblack and Grocer; Fairy Queen and Her Subjects; Robinson Crusoe and His Man Friday; Jack the Giant Killer; Miles Standish and Priscilla the Puritan Maiden; Quaker Courtship; Group of Kate Greenaway Children; Grandfather's Hat and Grandmother's Spectacles; The Two Friends (child and large dog); Passing Under the Rod (mischievous boy in school being punished by teacher.)

Costumes for statuary are made from white muslin. The skin, wherever exposed, is covered with prepared whitening, chalk, flour or starch, and so is the hair. When the pose is arranged the drapery is also dusted with whatever white substance is used for the face. Statuary should be shown in a strong, white light.

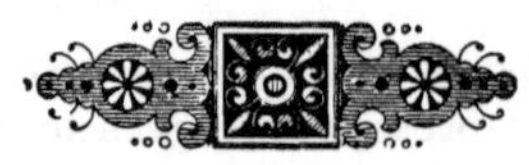

PLASTIQUES AND TABLEAUX D'ART.

These entertainments combine the characteristics of pantomime and tableau, and are very popular whether given privately or publicly, for amusement alone or for some charitable purpose.

Pantomime is the expression of sentiments and emotions by gestures unaccompanied by words; while a tableau is a motionless representation of some picture or incident.

In plastiques or tableaux d'art, some descriptive poem, recitation or short play is selected and its characters costumed and arranged according to the lines of the selection. The curtain rises upon the tableau and after a moment or two a reader who may or may not be out of sight, begins the reading or recitation. As he proceeds the figures in the tableau fall into various attitudes expressive of whatever emotion or sentiment is being described. For instance, if a shipwreck were being described, the tableau might disclose a group of picturesquely dressed people standing as if upon a shore gazing out to sea. Fear, anxiety, hope, horror, despair, grief and every emotion likely to be incited by such a catastrophe must be simulated by expression and gesture as required by the description.

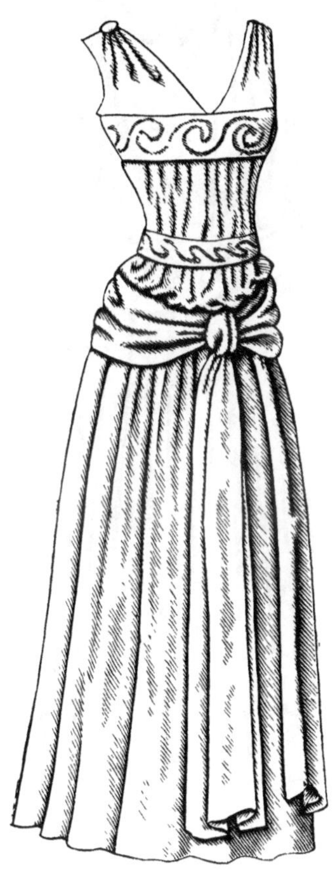

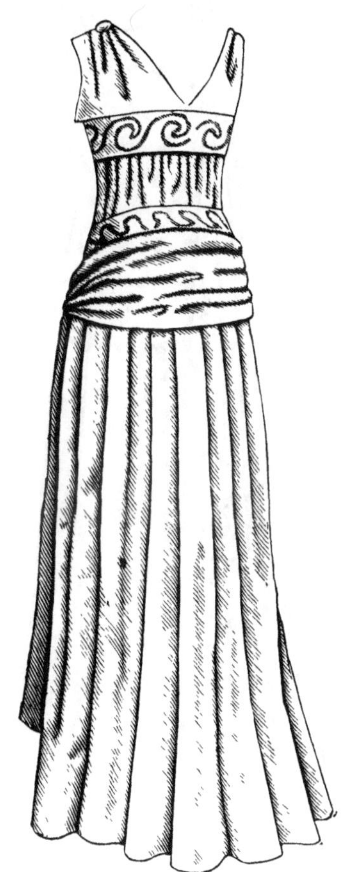

FIGURE NO. 1.—DESIGN OF DRAPERY FOR MASQUERADES, PLASTIQUES AND STATUARY.

THE HERMIONE COSTUME.

(For Description see Page 22.)

It will be easily seen that the literature of all

ages will provide endless material for this species of entertainment. Grecian and Roman costumes are most effective in plastiques and tableaux d'art, and Macaulay's "Lays of Ancient Rome" would provide ample subject matter. From the classics also, as well as from modern works, many beautiful suggestions for these entertainments may be derived. Those well versed in literature will not need assistance in their selections. Those who are not, will find in the works of Dickens, Scott, Irving, Lytton, Blackmore, Bret Harte, Lever, Longfellow, Tennyson, Whittier, Holmes, Heine, Shakespeare, Byron or those of other favorite authors and poets, many dramatic and descriptive bits that will serve as most effective foundations for these pictures.

As in tableaux, it is well to show plastiques behind a black gauze screen; and an authority upon the subject, and after many experiments, has decided that deep red is the best background for them. This should be very tightly drawn so that the movements of the characters will cause no undulations of the background—an occurrence which invariably lessens the effectiveness of the picture. It is not necessary to have the stage draped in red. A background of this color is all that is absolutely needed.

The fabrics chosen for the costumes should be those which drape gracefully and softly—such as cashmere, flannel, cheese cloth, etc., etc.

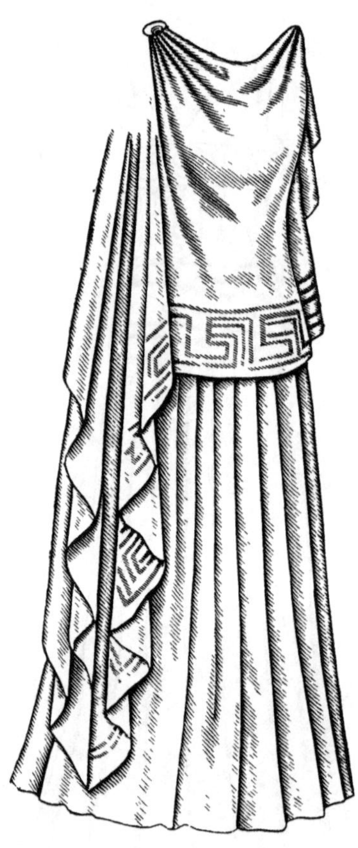

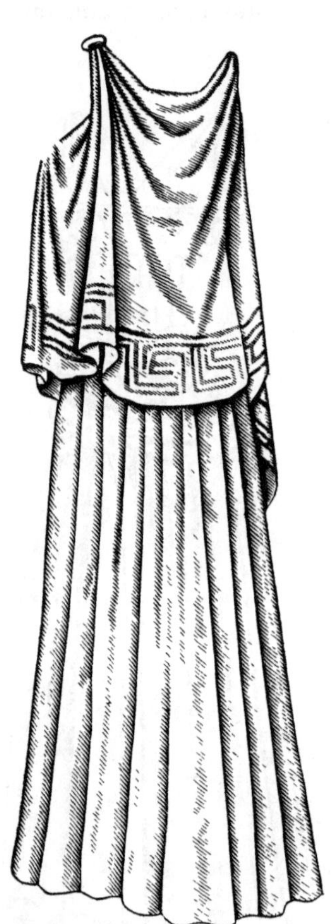

FIGURE No. 2.—DESIGN OF DRAPERY FOR MASQUERADES, PLASTIQUES AND STATUARY.

THE HELEN OF TROY COSTUME.

(For Description see Page 22)

Some of the representations may be humorous, some grave and others a commingling of the two; and in each instance the costuming and pantomime should be in keeping with the characters decided upon.

Some very charming costumes for the characters in ancient literature, or for statues, may be seen upon pages 19 and 20. They may be made up of very simple fabrics or as expensively as desired.

Some of the plastique tableaux become miniature pantomimes. For instance, in "The Coquette Brigade," a number of young ladies will go through a sort of drill with the fan, which, skillfully handled, may express invitation, repulsion, coyness, sentiment, sauciness, anger, mirth, indifference, anxiety, jealousy, etc., etc. "House cleaning" may illustrate the general confusion arising from the use of the broom and feather duster, together with the pertubation and distress of the masculine part of the household on such occasions. "Woman's Rights" may picture the wife preparing a public lecture while the husband washes the dishes, rocks the cradle, and attends to the sweeping and dusting. "The little Schoolmarm" may illustrate the struggles of a youthful teacher in a country school-house filled with mischievous children.

The figures of the minuet performed by a single couple also make a very pretty plastique tableau. Such subjects are endless in number and are always received with approbation by the average audience.

Colored glass may be used to place between the light and the pictures as in the Tableaux Vivants, already described, and footlights are less preferable on this and other accounts than side lights; and a calcium light is better than any other in bringing out the picture, from its intense brilliancy. However, this is a point that must be governed by surroundings and circumstances, except in the matter of footlights; they should be abjured on every possible occasion, as they do not throw a good light upon either plastiques or tableaux.

THE POSE PLASTIQUE.

This popular entertainment differs somewhat from what has just been described. It represents statues who pose without the aid of recitation or reading. Dress, make-up, wigs, will all be quite as important as attitudes. One, two or three moving statues may be seen upon a parlor stage, hung severely in folds of black cambric. The lights are all turned out save the lantern which illuminates the stage, bringing out in sharp relief the *poseur* or *poseuse*, as the case may be.

We will take for granted that you are a Delsartian and accomplished in all the lithe, supple turns of the body and facial expressions conveying all the passions of the soul. If you are of the feminine gender your costume must be a simple little gown of white cashmere or cheese cloth, cut in Parthenia-like fashion, falling loose from the low neck and drawn in a bit at the waist with a loosely knotted white cord. Your wig must be white and the hair caught in a genuine Psyche knot at the back.

Neck, arms, face and hands must be whitened, and then you are ready to pose. A man must wear a sort of Roman toga, white tights and buskins and a white wig. All sorts of beautiful plastiques may be done by a graceful man and woman together. "The Storm," "Paul and Virginia," and "The Carnival" are all suitable subjects for poses, besides hundreds of others, including representations of jealousy, consolation, temptation, protection; in fact all sorts of subjects will easily suggest themselves to the *poseur*. Soft low music accompanies the posing, changing from grave to gay, according to the subject of the plastique. Dresden china effects are specially attractive in these plastiques.

COSTUMES FOR PLASTIQUES.

FIGURE No. 1. (see page 19).—HERMIONE COSTUME.—This costume should be made up in soft wool or silk fabrics, and trimmed with gold or silver embroidery. White, gray and all the soft tints look especially well in this costume, which may be assumed for the character of Hermione or any kindred character. The engravings will be a sufficient guide in making up the garment, inasmuch as it is sleeveless and loose fitting, and is simply drawn in to the figure by a soft girdle. It is especially desirable for plastiques or tableaux, and is charming in representations of either white or colored statuary.

FIGURE No. 2. (see page 20.)—THE HELEN OF TROY COSTUME.—This costume, like that on page 19, is appropriate for plastiques, tableaux and similar entertainments. It looks best made up in white serge, camel's-hair or flannel, or any softly draping fabrics, and should be trimmed with gold or silver braid or embroidery in Grecian design. It may, however, be made up in pale blue, pink, yellow or green tints. A straight skirt, with a toga formed of a long, straight breadth of the goods draped at the shoulders as illustrated, composes the costume. Characters from Shakespeare's plays and Grecian and Roman History may be appropriately garbed in this costume.

When the garments illustrated at figures Nos. 1 and 2 are chosen for the representation of statuary drapery, they may be made up in plain white cotton cloth, and after the *poseuse* has been powdered, the folds of the drapery may also be powdered with excellent effect. Cheese cloth in the many faint shades of red, green, blue, lavender, yellow and cream may be effectively made up into these costumes with velveteen of the same or contrasting tints for the decorations, where groupings of characters and colorings are desirable. Flesh-tinted statuary could be represented by using a pinkish-tinted drapery.

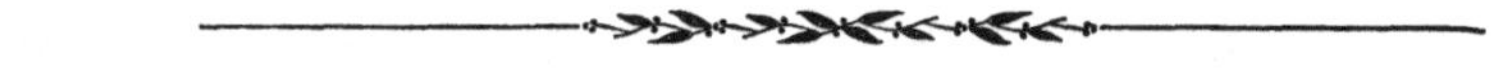

MRS. JARLEY'S WAXWORK COLLECTION.

In their search for new amusements, the Americans are said to have introduced the idea of giving a burlesque exhibition of a waxwork collection with living performers for the "figures"; but the "collection" upon which the burlesque was founded was supposed to be that of Dicken's celebrated character, Mrs. Jarley, in "The Old Curiosity Shop."

The figures are costumed according to their several requirements, and when the curtain rises from the stage on which they are arranged in a semi-circle, they must be perfectly motionless.

Mrs. Jarley may be assisted in the exhibition by "Little Nell" and two servants, John and Peter; but she can also conduct the exhibition alone. Little Nell may have a feather duster for dusting off the figures as the curtain rises; and the two men servants must be provided with a watchman's rattle, a screw-driver, hammer, nails and oil-can. The rattle will be used back of the figures to "wind them up," and the other implements will from time to time be needed to repair the figures that may "purposely" get out of order and refuse to perform.

Mrs. Jarley may be well represented by a stout, smooth-faced man, and should be costumed in a black dress with a gay-flowered shawl and a large scoop-bonnet fantastically trimmed. She stands in front and at one side of the circle and describes each figure in a ridiculous manner, ordering the servants to "set out" each one before she describes it; and the figure should either be carried from and to its place or should be mounted on a small wheel-platform after the usual manner of exhibited figures. The figure is wound up before Mrs. Jarley begins, and as she talks it goes through all of its motions, and sometimes "runs down" and stops suddenly in some grotesque position from which it must be straightened by the servant or servants who then replace it in the semi-circle. A good deal of fun will be created by the defective working of a figure in the midst of its movements which will involve re-winding, oiling of the supposed machinery, tightening of screws, etc., etc. The winding-up may be done with a winch, or a watchman's rattle, and a good imitation of the latter may be produced by drawing a piece of hard wood along a notched stick, which of course must be done behind the scenes by a second party. Sometimes the figure is not wound until Mrs. Jarley has described it; then she looks complacently on while to the slow or rapid music of the piano, the figure goes through its motions. A good deal of fun results from the tendency of any figure to tip over, whereupon the servants try to prop it up with bits of wood, coins or wedges placed under its feet. In fact, any of the mishaps which might occur to mechanical figures may be imitated and will prove provocative of much amusement. At some exhibitions Mrs. Jarley is a figure herself, and the collection is exhibited by some witty man in ordinary evening attire.

After each figure has been separately exhibited and the semi-circle is again complete, the figures are all wound up again, and unanimously go through their motions to the music of the piano or a small orchestra.

Space will not permit us to give more than a list of the characters or "figures" in the exhibition; but a pamphlet published by Samuel French of 28 West 23d Street, New York, will supply all necessary information, from the dressing and motions of the figures to Mrs. Jarley's opening speech and her individual descriptions of the characters. This is one of the most amusing entertainments that can be given with little expense. At quiet Summer or Winter resorts the guests frequently arrange successful waxwork exhibitions at very short notice, using whatever they can find in the way of costumes for the figures.

Some of the favorite characters of Mrs. Jarley's collection are :

The Chinese Giant.
The Serving Woman.
The Siamese Twins.
The Vocalist.
The Cannibal.
Little Red Riding Hood.
Pocahontas and Captain Smith.
The Two-Headed Girl.
Captain Kid and his Victim.
The Welsh Dwarf.
The Yankee.
The Babes in the Wood.
The Dancing Wax Doll.
The Organ Grinder and Monkey.

Many other "figures" may be individually suggested by those in charge of the entertainment.

MAKE-UP MATERIALS AND PIGMENTS.

It may not be amiss just here to give a list of "make-up" materials such as are used for theatricals and for masquerades when masks are not worn:

Prepared Fuller's Earth.—To powder the face with before making up.

Powdered Blue.—For imitating a shaven chin.

Pearl Powder.—To whiten the complexion, hands and arms.

Rouge.—Absolutely indispensable before footlights, which apparently bleach the rosiest complexion to a sickly hue.

Ruddy Rouge.—For imitating tan and sunburn.

Dutch Pink.—For sallow complexions.

Mongolian.—For imitating the complexion of Orientals or North American Indians.

Powdered Antimony.—To produce the effect of hollows under the eyes and in the cheeks.

Chrome.—To imitate a sallow complexion and lighten the natural color of the whiskers or mustache.

Carmine.—To produce a red tint in the same.

Prepared Whitening.—For clowns' faces, statuary, etc.

Prepared Burnt Cork.—For minstrels or other negro characters.

Émail Noir (black enamel).—For applying to a front tooth to produce the effect of being missing.

Joining Paste.—To apply over the edge of a wig across the forehead.

Paste Powder.—For "building up" a nose.

Crape Hair.—Artificial hair sold in plaits for forming wigs, eyebrows, moustaches, etc., etc.

Spirit Gum.—For attaching such hair to the face.

Crayons d'Italie.—Pencils for marking veins.

Eyebrow pencils, camel's-hair brushes, powder puffs, etc.

With these assistants the face may be so made up that no mask will be needed and the disguise will still be complete, especially when the complexion is changed from either blonde or brunette to its opposite.

FANCY-DRESS COSTUMES FOR ADULTS.

FIGURE NO. 1.—COLUMBIA.—Pale-blue satin skirt trimmed with silver braid; epaulet-bodice of silver brocade over a white silk blouse, with short sleeves of the blue satin lined with white silk; bands of ruby velvet on the bodice and epaulets; silver clasps down the front of the bodice and silver braid pendants tipped with silver buttons on the epaulets. White satin cap, blue satin band; word "Liberty" in silver. Blue silk stockings and silvered, fancy shoes. Wide silver bands on wrists.

FIGURE NO. 2.—COLUMBUS.—Shirt of white, fine lawn or silk with ruffle at neck and wrists. Under coat of pale-blue satin overlaid with silver braiding and with sleeves of puffs of the satin and bands of braided satin. Outer coat and cape of light gray embroidered in silver and gold, and lined and faced with pale-yellow. Full trunks to match puffed sleeves and completed with gold bands. Gilt belt with silver clasp, and gilt and silver necklet. Long pale gray or blue silk stockings; gray suéde shoes decorated with silver and gold. Pale-blue cap with white and silver-colored ostrich feathers.

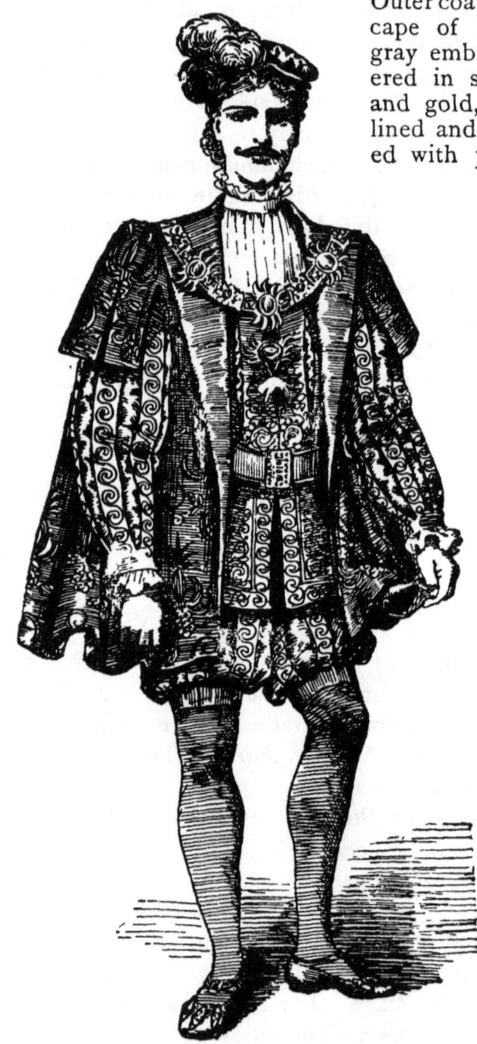

FIGURE NO. 2.—COLUMBUS.

FIGURE NO. 1.—COLUMBIA.

FIGURE NO. 3.—BRITANNIA.—Skirt and classic tunic of white cashmere or any soft white wool fabric, with a golden belt or girdle. Helmet and trident of gold. Golden shield with deep-blue back ground. Gilded shoes, and hair flowing loosely. A scarlet scarf may be fastened to the left shoulder to float over the dress; and, in place of the shield the Union Jack may be draped at one side of the dress.

FIGURE NO. 4.—AUSTRIAN NOBLEMAN OF THE XVI. CENTURY.—This is a very picturesque costume and was copied from the portrait gallery of a noble family. It is made as follows: A tight red silk undervest over which is worn a sleeveless body of light yellow striped alternately with red and blue-green. This body is stuffed with cotton-wool or down, so that it rounds smoothly out as seen in the engraving. The short black velvet mantle is lined with blue-green silk and has a row of gold buttons extending from the top to the bottom. The short, yellow, upper trousers are slashed and puffed out like a roll, over thick wadding. The tight breeches are of blue-green silk and meet yellow stockings. The shoes are made of fine leather. The black velvet cap has a rosette at one side. A ruff is about the neck and wrists, and a short sword completes the costume.

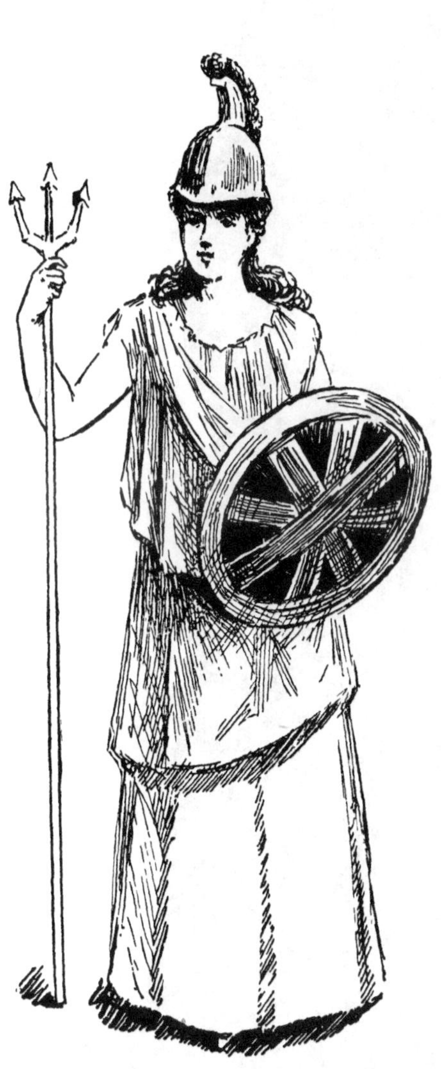

FIGURE NO. 3.—BRITANNIA.

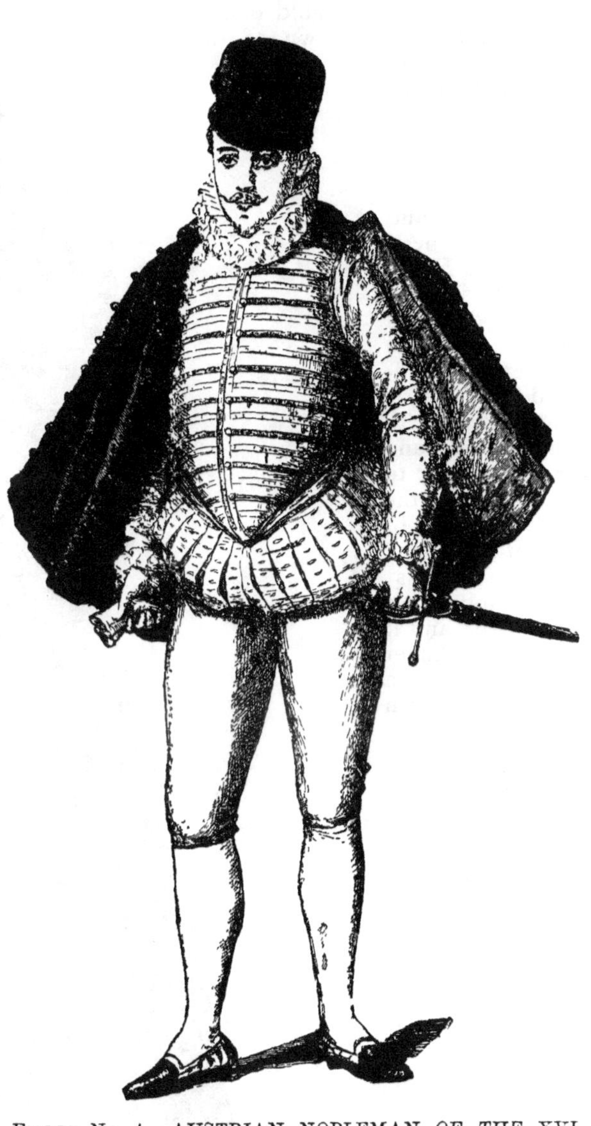

FIGURE NO 4.—AUSTRIAN NOBLEMAN OF THE XVI CENTURY.

Figure No. 5.—Lady of the Harem. Turkish trousers of pale-blue satin striped with silver embroidery; drapery of silver and blue trimmed with silver fringe. Pale-yellow blouse-bodice of satin with white chiffon frills. Turkish Zouave jacket of deep crimson velvet, trimmed with gold embroidery. Long coat or over-gown of dull red camel's hair, sprinkled with silver and gilt spangles. Veil of white chiffon; ornaments, ropes of pearls wound about the head and body. Flesh-colored stockings; deep-red velvet Turkish slippers embroidered with pearls and gold thread. Face, hands and arms made up to resemble the deep rich tints of Oriental complexions; eyes, brows and lashes darkened; and if desired the finger nails stained a deep orange with henna.

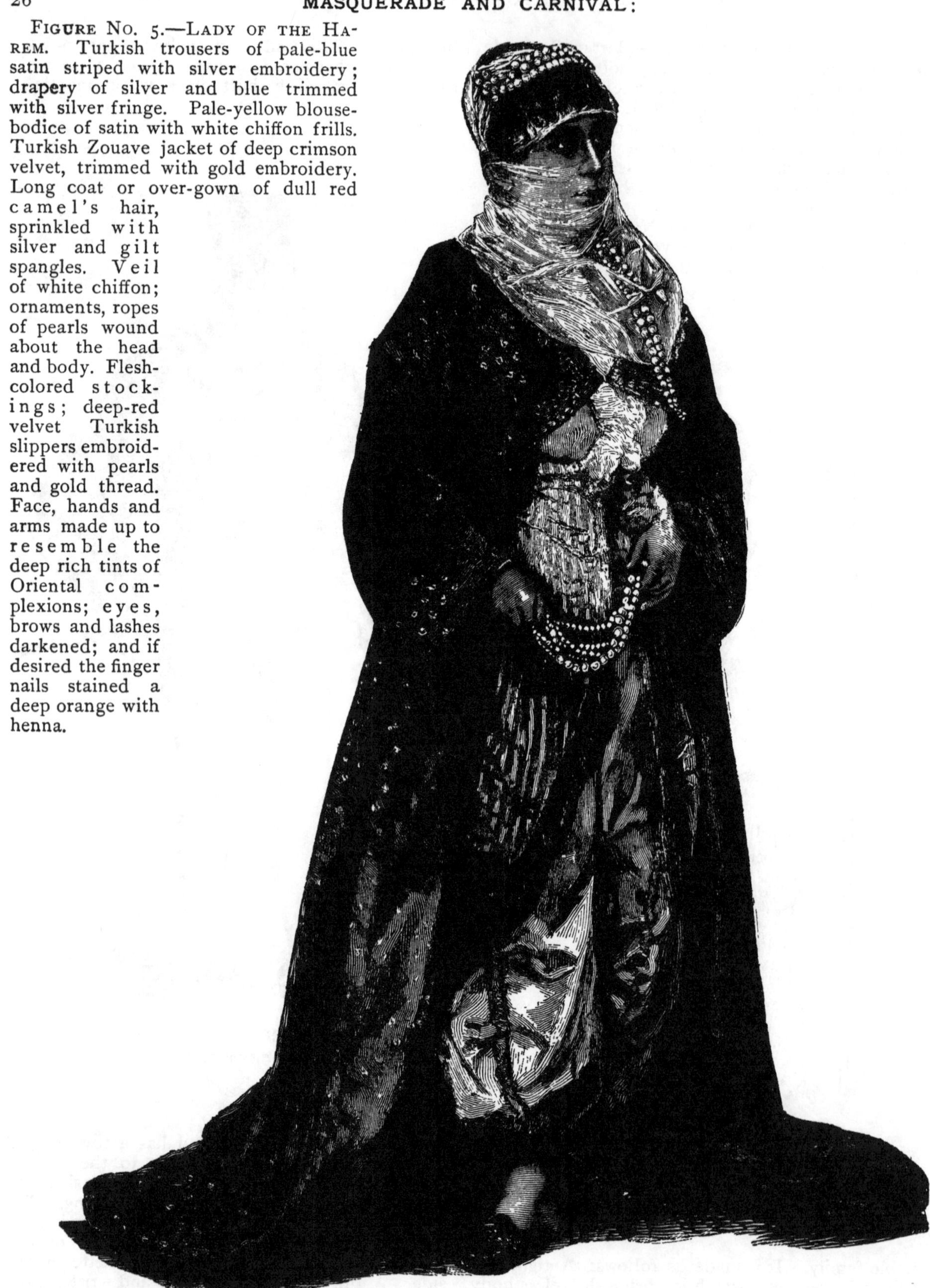

Figure No 5—LADY OF THE HAREM.

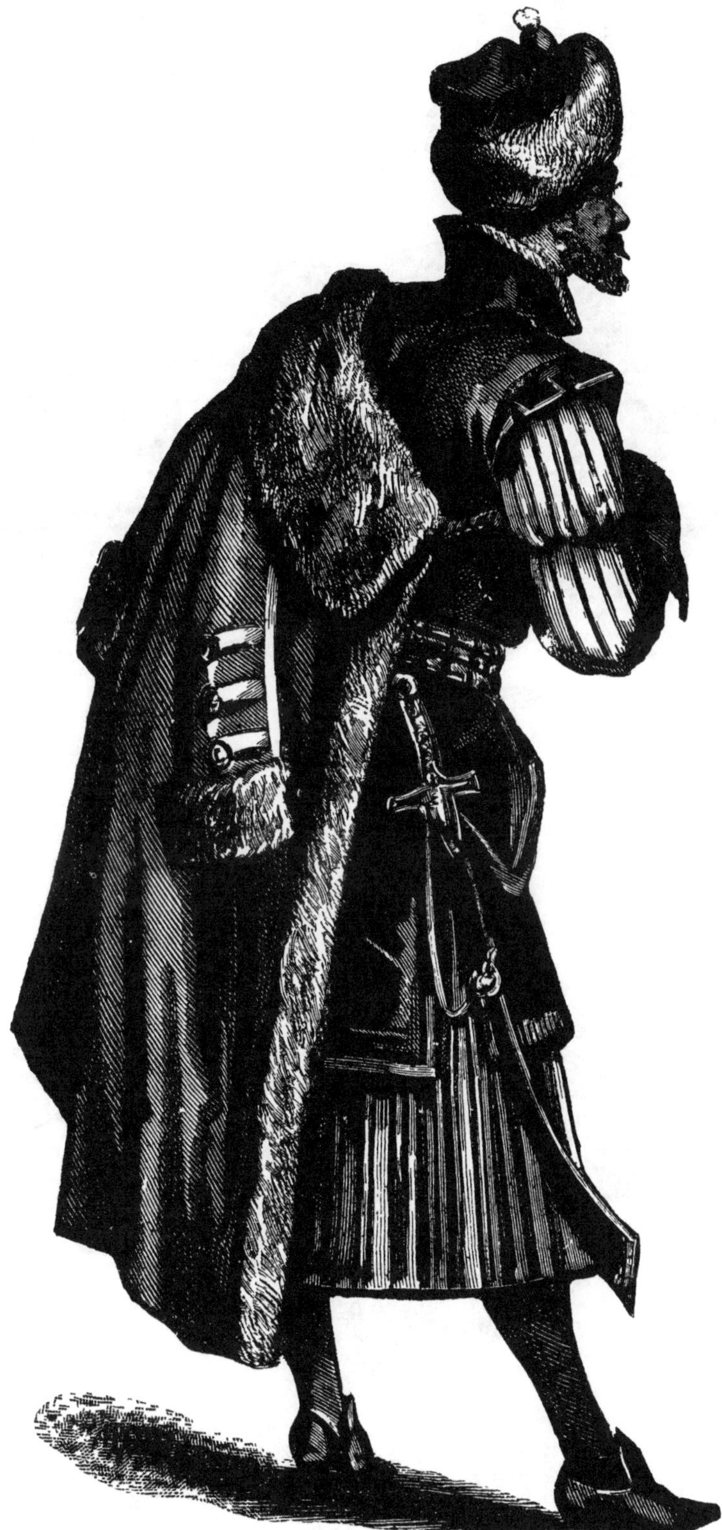

FIGURE No. 6.—POLISH COSTUME.—Skirt and shirt of some white fabric handsomely striped with bright colors. Sleeveless tunic of red velvet trimmed with gold braid and faced and lined with yellow silk or satin. Gold belt with curved sword suspended from it. Coat of rough, brownish wool fabric, lined with dull-red and handsomely trimmed with gold braid and buttons, and long, rough yellowish fur, with a deep collar of the fur; coat suspended from the left shoulder by a heavy cord used for closing it at the throat. Cap of the coat fabric trimmed with the fur. Stockings to match the coat in color, and deep russet-leather shoes edged with gilt.

FIGURE No. 6.—POLISH COSTUME

FIGURE No. 7.—GERMAN GENTLEMEN OF THE XVI. CENTURY.—Jacket, round at the waist, and puffed breeches, both of green stuff, ornamented with silver bands and a huge yellow bow. Ruff about the neck and a "lucky coin" suspended from the latter by a long, colored ribbon. Tight breeches extending to the knee where they are finished with deep gold fringe. Long, violet colored hose, and fancy black shoes bound with gold. Short stiff mantle of cloth or velvet lined with silk and edged with gold braid. Hat of black velvet with a jaunty feather at the left side.

FIGURE No. 8.—FANCY COSTUME. (GERMAN YOUTH OF THE XV. CENTURY).—The upper dress consists of a short, pink stuff doublet scarcely covering the hips, while the long wide sleeves of the same material hang down far below the knees. The doublet has a large, turned-down fur collar, and is likewise lined throughout with fur. It is bordered with green velvet and has a scarf of the same which draws it in at the waist. A dark red undervesture with full sleeves is worn immediately below the doublet. This "Schecke" (jacket) is cut to display the pleated shirt with its black, gold-embroidered bands. The shirt reaches to the collar bones and is like a sailor's jersey. The heavy gold chain is made of single long links, resembling the so-called "steel" in the chains of the order of the Golden Fleece. Gray hose and broad, russet shoes are worn.

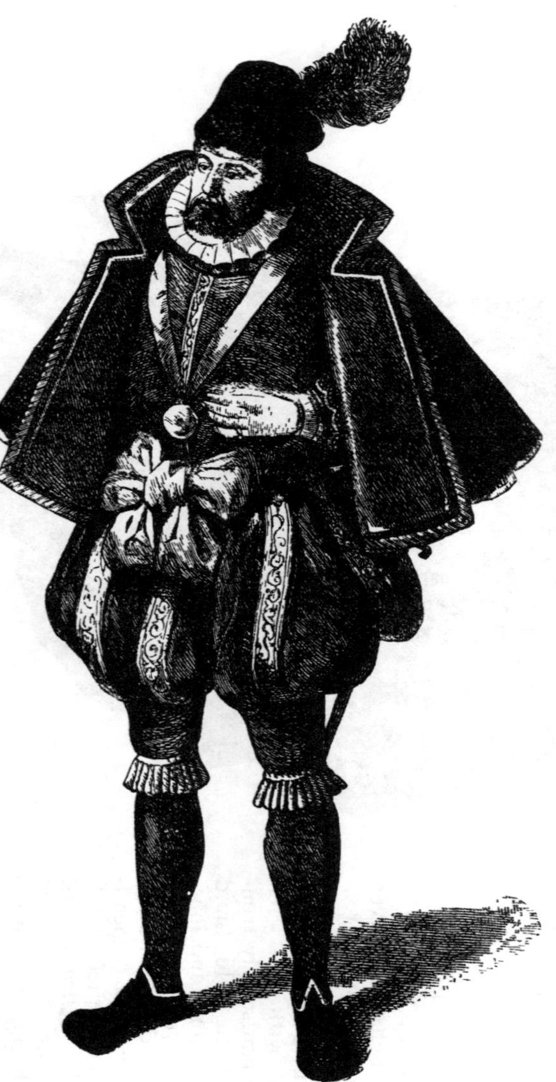

FIGURE No. 7.—GERMAN GENTLEMAN OF THE XVI. CENTURY.

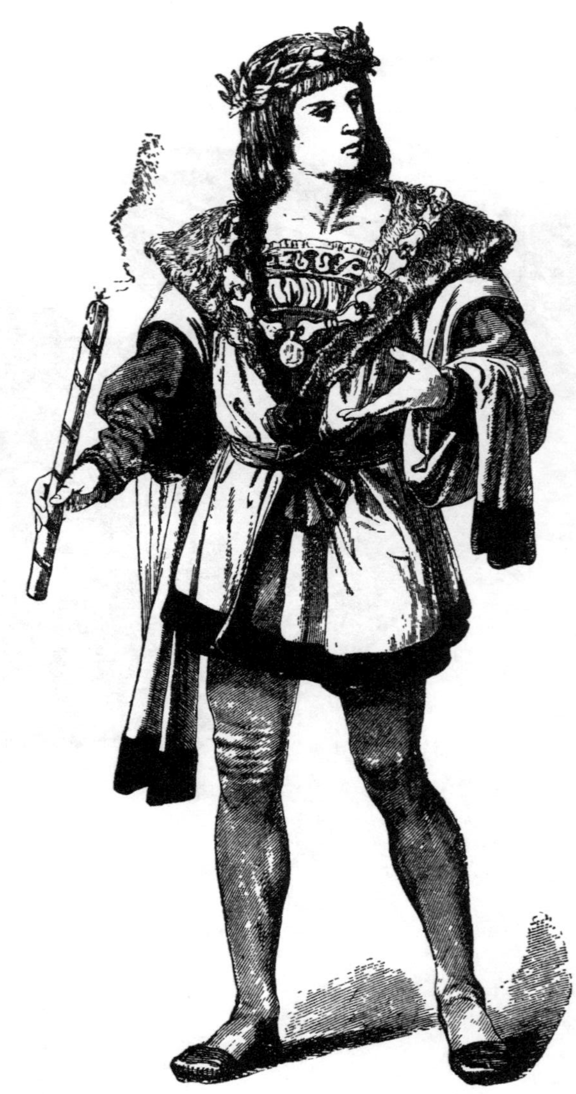

FIGURE No 8.—FANCY COSTUME. (GERMAN YOUTH OF THE XV. CENTURY.

FIGURES NOS. 9 AND 10.—JAPANESE KIMONO.—The ordinary dress of the Japanese lady is shown by these engravings. It is called the "kimono" and may be made of soft silk or wool goods stamped with a Japanese design. The kimono laps over in front in double-breasted style, and has long loose sleeves. It is held in to the figure only by a broad sash of silk tied in a large bow at the back. Under the kimono should be worn one or two gay-colored, straight petticoats of very soft silk. The hair is rolled high in the typical Japanese style.

FIGURE NO. 11.—BAVARIAN PEASANT GIRL. (For illustration see next page.)—This becoming costume is worn on Sundays and festive occasions, in the neighborhood of Tegernsee and Miesbach. A gold cord is twisted several times round the greenish-black hat and ends in gold tassels, which lie on the brim. The neck is adorned with from eight to ten rows of silver chain, its single links, like the cord of the bodice, consisting of small separate globules. The neck chain is held together by an often beautifully-made clasp of stones set in gilt or filagree silver. The half silk-neckerchief is tucked into the bodice in front and allows a corner of the chemise to be seen. It is pinned down behind low enough for the point to cover a great part of the waist. The black richly quilted bodice only reaches to the bottom of the natural waist and it is scalloped out at the top. Silver hooks are set on both sides of it, through which the grand ornament, the cord several metres long, is interwoven. All sorts of trinkets, such as coins, silver hearts, etc., are attached to it. The bodice and neckerchief so far cover the "Spencer" that only the sleeves of the latter are visible. These always reach to the wrists, and they are laid in tiny folds from the shoulder to the elbow, below which they fit tightly. They can be made of the same stuff and color as the colored print skirt; though at the present day, one often also sees silk sleeves of any color the wearer chooses. The skirt reaches to the ankles, and is covered in front by the "Fürtuch," a large apron generally made of flowered print, though now and then silk aprons are worn. The stockings are white. The shoes are made of black stuff or leather and reach over the instep.

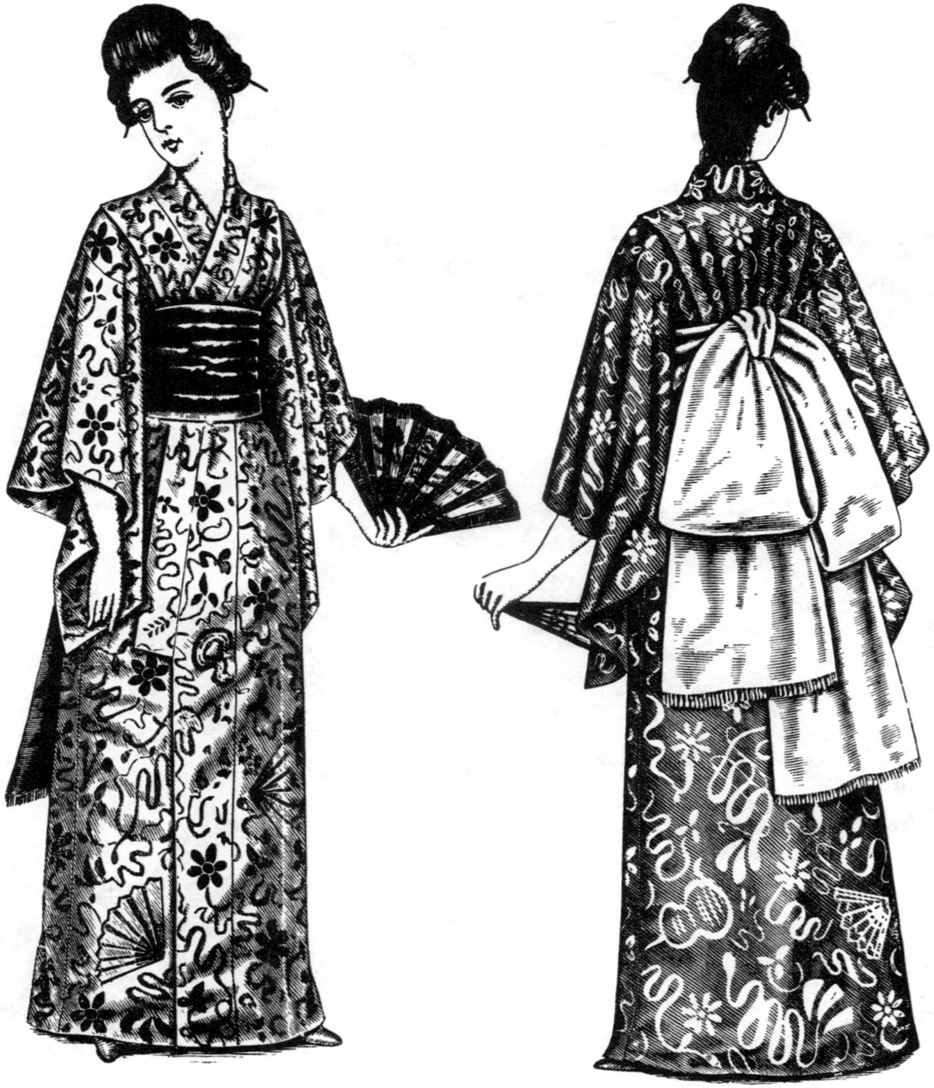

FIGURES NOS. 9 AND 10—JAPANESE KIMONO. (*Front and Back View.*)

FIGURE NO. 12.—TAMBOURINE GIRL. (For illustration see next page.)—Skirt of white cashmere, with a broad band of Oriental embroidery. Wide, red silk scarf, wrought with gold, and loosely knotted round the hips. Full chemise in Algerian gauze, striped with tinsel and red satin. Short vest in white satin, spangled and embroidered with gold. Outlining of gold galoon. Short sleeves, looped up to display bands of gold. Bangles encircle the wrists. Rows of pearls round the neck; large rings in the ears. Strings of sequins are twisted with the long black hair. Tambourine, with multicolor streamers. Red stockings, with gold clocks. White satin shoes and red spangled rosettes.

FIGURE NO. 13.—MOORISH DANCING GIRL.—Trousers of pale-pink satin embroidered in silver; blouse waist of a darker shade of pink embroidered or brocaded with silver and gold and edged with gold lace. Worn over a surplice-chemisette of white gauze spangled with gold. Loose sleeves of fancy Oriental gauze in pink, blue and white. Silver girdle tied with silver, tasseled rope. Head-dress of white gauze and pearls; pearl ornaments about the neck. Gold hoops in ears and on the wrists and ankles. Pointed pink slippers and flesh colored stockings.

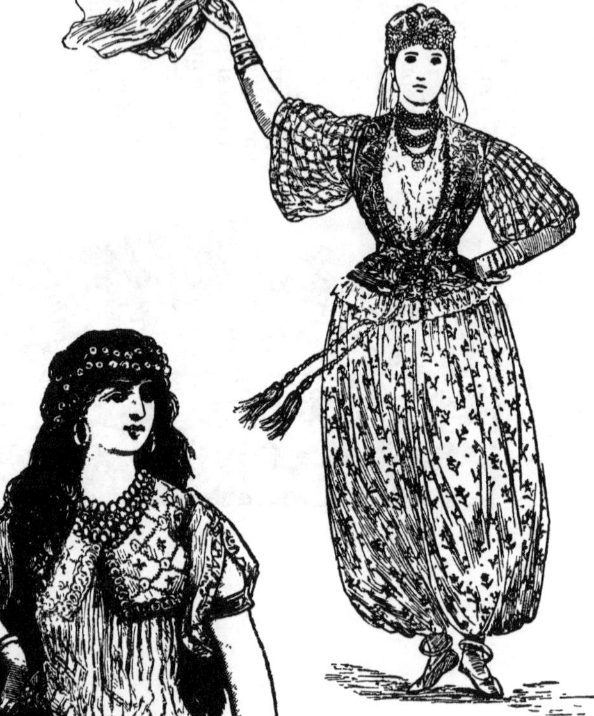

FIGURE NO. 13.—MOORISH DANCING GIRL

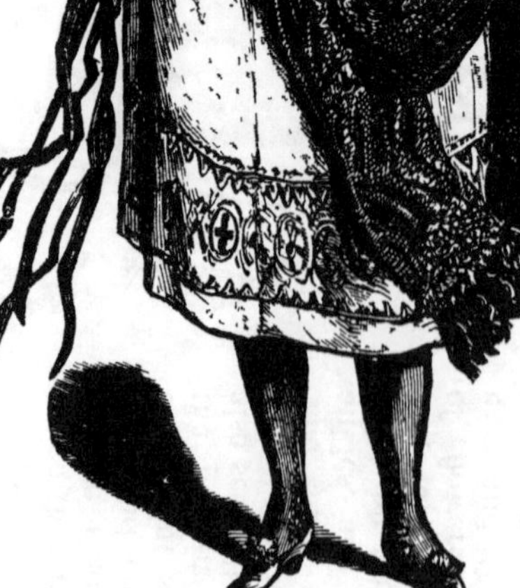

FIGURE NO. 11.—BAVARIAN PEASANT GIRL.
(For description see preceding page.)

FIGURE NO. 12.—TAMBOURINE GIRL.
(For description see preceding page.)

If preferred the trousers may be made of some delicately-wrought, tinted gauze brocaded with gilt or silver and worn over silk under-trousers. Colorings must be selected to suit the natural or made-up complexion of the lady who is to assume the character; but it is well to keep to dainty shades and light fabrics, as they produce more fascinating and graceful costumes for the character than heavy materials and deep tints.

FIGURE NO. 14.—POLISH COSTUME.—Petticoat of pale-blue satin; bodice and draped skirt of white cashmere trimmed with swan's down and silver braid. Polish sleeves of the cashmere lined with blue satin, trimmed with swan's down; silver ropes around the arm-holes and silver beads about the neck. Cap of blue satin with swan's down band and silver aigrette. Pale-blue gloves and silver bracelets. Pale-blue stockings and white shoes with silver buttons and lacing cords.

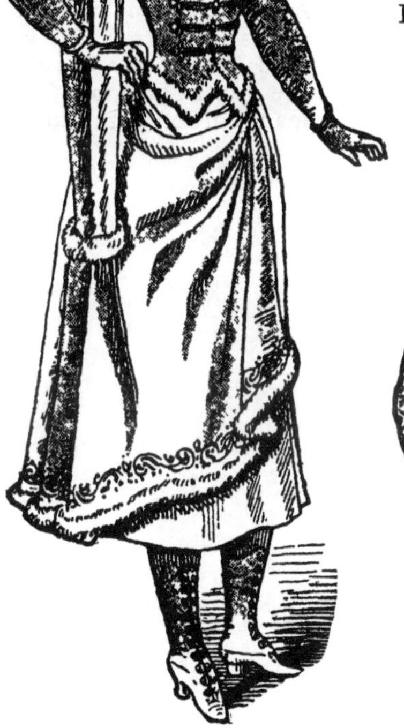

FIGURE NO. 14.—POLISH COSTUME.

FIGURE NO. 15.—ILLYRIAN LADY.—Wool crêpe or merino should be used for this costume. The skirt is trimmed with Turkish borderings in various colorings. The apron is of cotton Algerine and is trimmed with gold lace, black velvet and fancy tassels. Sleeves of India muslin trimmed with scroll gimp. Head wrap of the same material trimmed with tassels. Red velvet cap covered with gold braid and sequins. Stockings of fancy lisle thread, and shoes of leather in two colors.

FIGURE NO. 16.—ALBANIAN COSTUME.—Kemise (or chemise) of white linen, narrow, and reaching to the ankles where it is edged with a colored border. It has wide sleeves, also bordered. Over the kemise is an Albanian sleeveless jacket of soft white woolen goods, tightly fitted, open in front and reaching to below the knees. It is curiously bordered with a colored design which extends up the sides of short openings. A broad woolen sash is picturesquely adjusted about the waist—red being the color worn by girls, and blue, yellow, etc., by married women. A narrow red apron or "futea" is worn over the sash and is tied with long red tasseled cords. The head-dress is similar to the Turkish fez, and the pointed slippers have tassels on their tips. The stockings may be white or flesh colored.

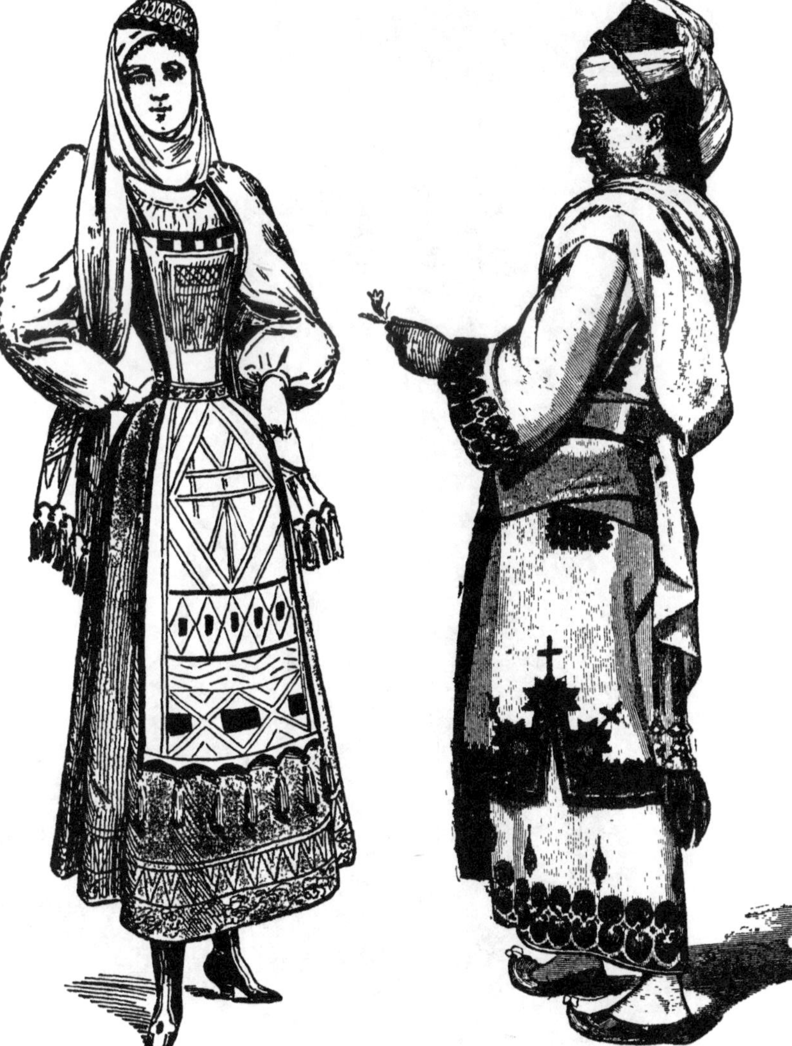

FIGURE NO 15.—ILLYRIAN LADY. FIGURE NO. 16.—ALBANIAN COSTUME.

Figure No. 17.—Domino.—Trained dress of black satin slashed at the left side of the skirt and turned over in *revers* that are faced with gold-colored silk. Panel of plaited white lace set under *revers*. Long open sleeves lined with gold-colored silk. Black gauze veil with yellow aigrette; black and yellow wings on the shoulders; gold and black fan; gold, tasseled girdle. Black gloves and gold bracelets. Gilt braid at the foot of the dress; yellow silk stockings; black satin slippers with golden butterfly buckles. Any other combination of colors preferred may be used; but it is advisable to use black or gray for the main portion of the costume.

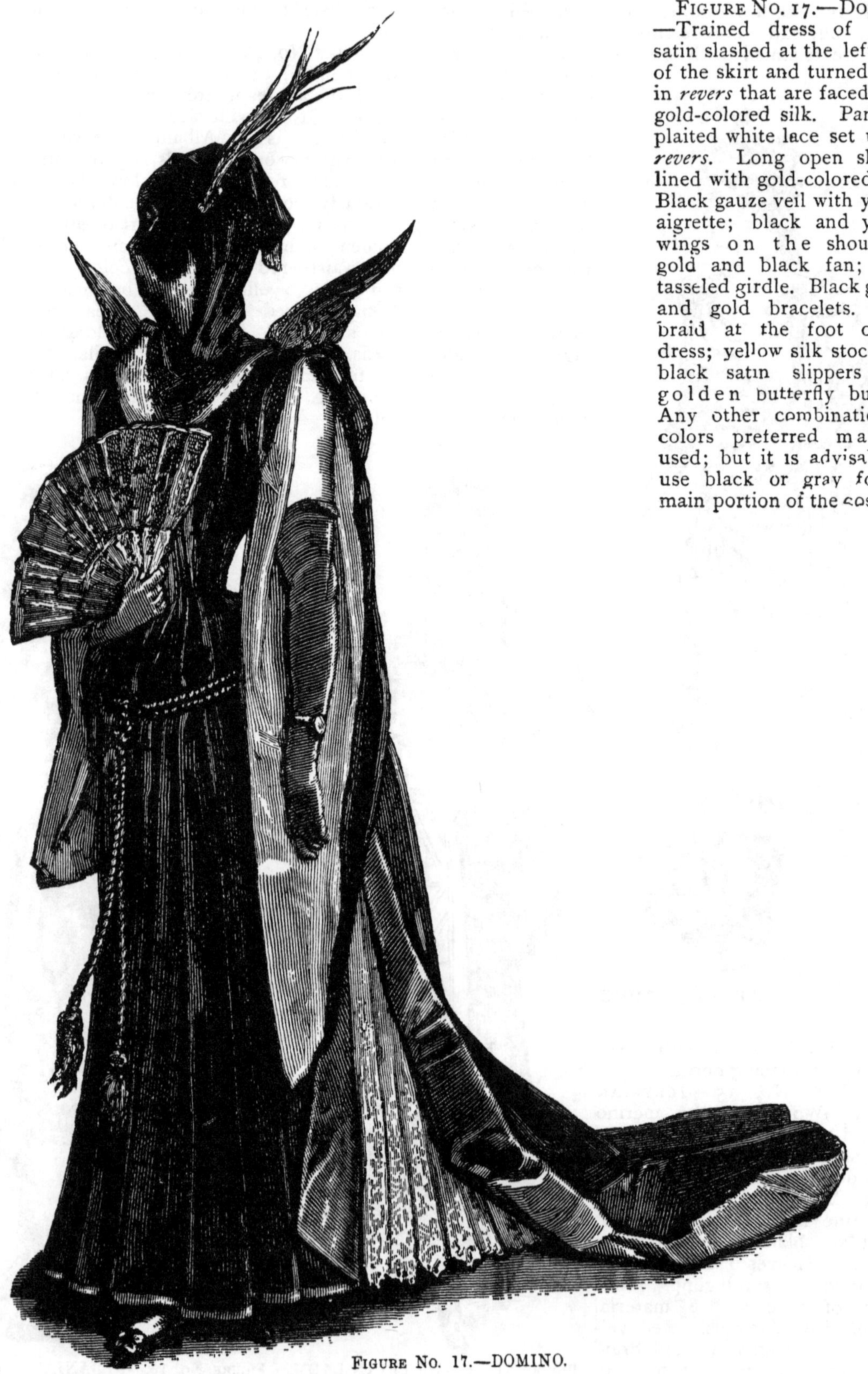

Figure No. 17.—DOMINO.

FIGURE NO. 18.—MEPHISTOPHELES.—This character is usually dressed all in brilliant scarlet from the long feather to the pointed shoes into which the silken-clad feet are thrust. The costume may, however, be varied by having the cloak and hood of black and the rest of the costume red, or *vice versa.*

Soft, clinging, woolen goods is always selected for the upper part of the costume and the cloak. The tights may be of fine wool or of silk, as preferred; and the shoes should be of dull-finished leather or of firmly lined felt. The girdle and sword may be of a dull red or black metal or of old silver.

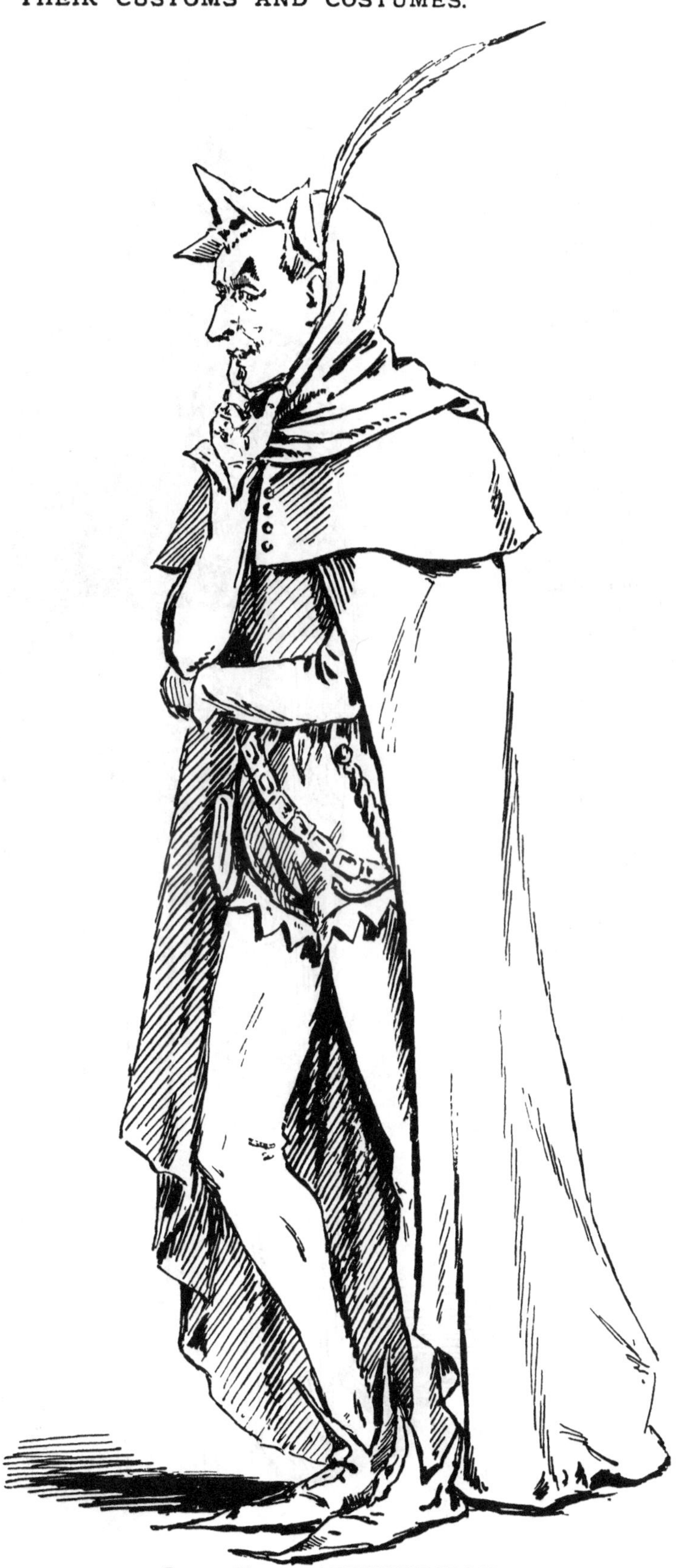

FIGURE NO. 18.—MEPHISTOPHELES.

FIGURE NO. 19.—MARGUERITE.—Skirt of soft, gray cashmere, made plain. Chemisette of white India mull drawn closely about the throat. Stomacher of black velvet decorated with pearl beads. Waist of gray, brocaded silk, with long, flowing sleeves of the same falling over close sleeves of the gray cashmere. Waist and sleeves trimmed with frills of lace. Small closely-fitting cap of gray, edged with pearl beads, worn above two long braids of the yellow hair. Chatelaine of silver holding keys, scissors, etc., etc. Rope of pearl beads falling from waist under a girdle of silver holding the velvet pocket of olden times. This pocket is ornamented with silver embroidery and pearl beads. Sometimes the skirt of the Marguerite costume is caught up through this girdle just where the pocket falls. In this event a handsome silken petticoat should be worn under the dress skirt.

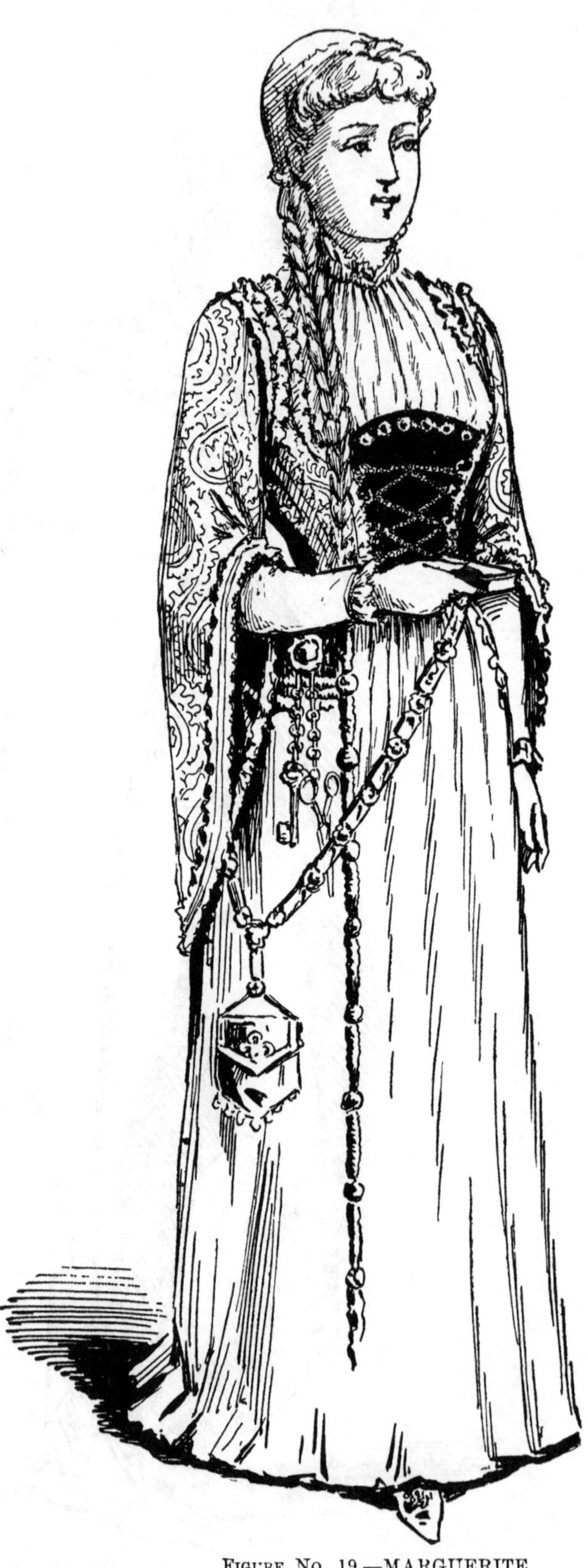

FIGURE NO 19—MARGUERITE.

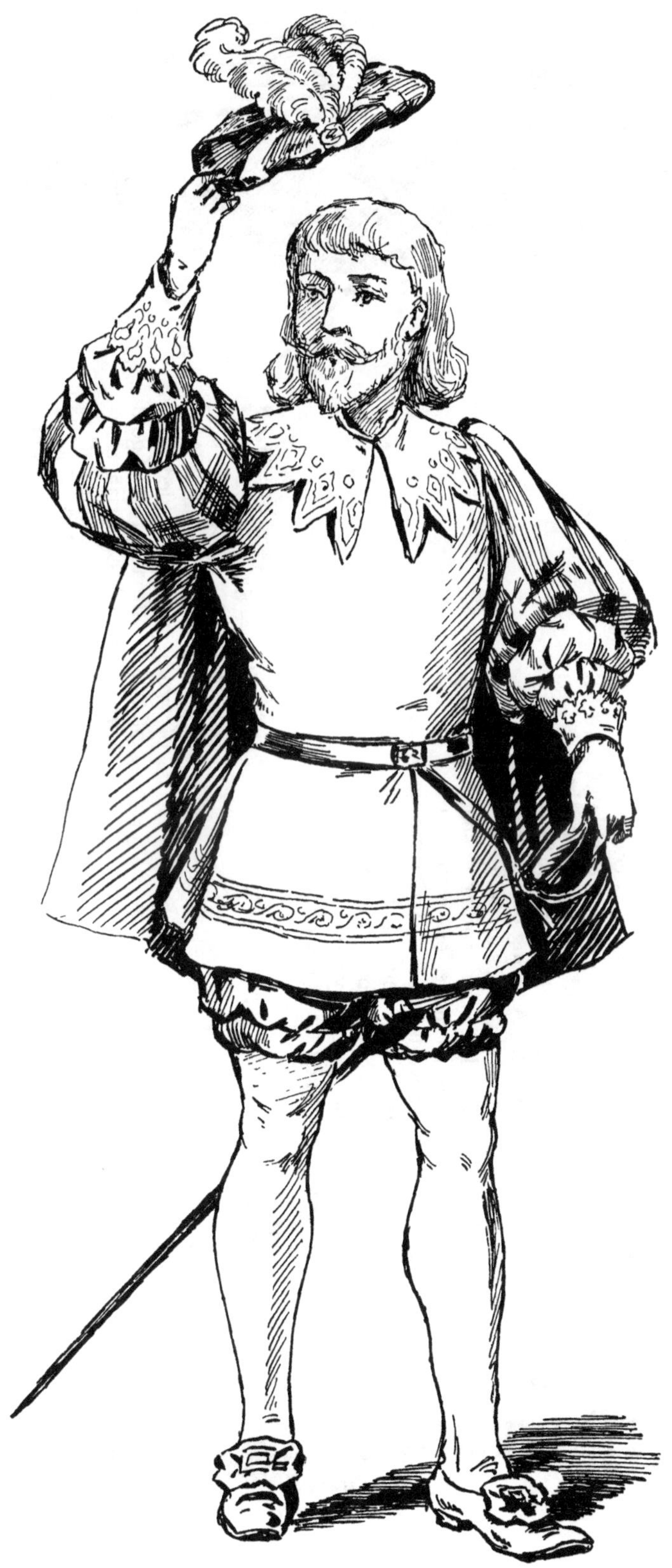

FIGURE No. 20.—FAUST.

FIGURE No. 20.—FAUST.—Tightly fitted waistcoat of white satin fastened at one side; skirt of the same embroidered with silver and fastened under a narrow silver belt from which is suspended a sword. Full trunks and sleeves of blue-and-white striped silk, with lace cuffs and collar. Short cloak of soft, white wool goods lined with pale-blue satin or silk. Pale-blue tights, gray suéde shoes with gray rosettes and silver buckles. Pale-blue cap decorated with silver bands and white ostrich plumes.

This costume may be made up in gray and blue, or in two shades of gray, or in gray and white; or, the wood-brown tints may be chosen for its development.

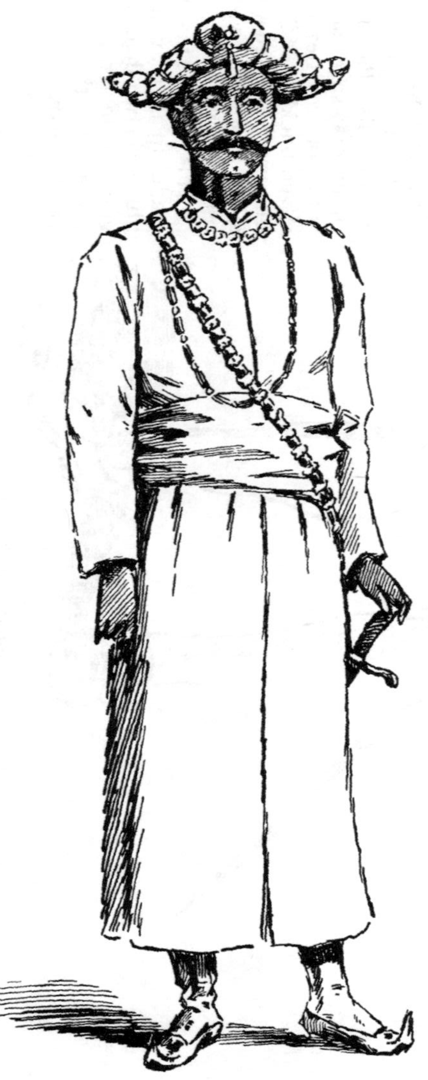

FIGURE NO. 21.—EAST INDIAN COSTUME.

FIGURE NO. 21.—EAST INDIAN COSTUME.—This costume is very simple in construction and inexpensive as to materials. It is made of some soft, white woolen or silken fabric, and consists of loose white trousers tapering down to a close fit at the knees, where the long white stockings end. The robe is a straight loose garment drawn in to the figure by a soft scarf of silk or wool. A decoration of jewel trimming extends about the neck and a long strip of the same forms the support for the sword. A string of many colored beads falls upon the breast. The hat is triangular in shape, and is made of white gauze drawn into puffs under strings of bright-colored beads, in which amber predominates. Slippers of yellow kid sharply turned up at the toes.

FIGURE NO. 22.—EGYPTIAN COSTUME.—Skirt portion of pale-blue or nile-green silk, with upper portion and waist of white gauze sprinkled with gilt tinsel. Broad girdle of gold with enameled Egyptian characters upon it; ornament to correspond over left side of bust. Long cloak of white wool lined with dull, copper-red silk and confined at the neck under a gold-embroidered band. Fillet of gold about the head with golden lotus flower at the front; lotus blossom in the hand. Pale-blue or nile-green stockings with dull red or golden slippers, banded with gold.

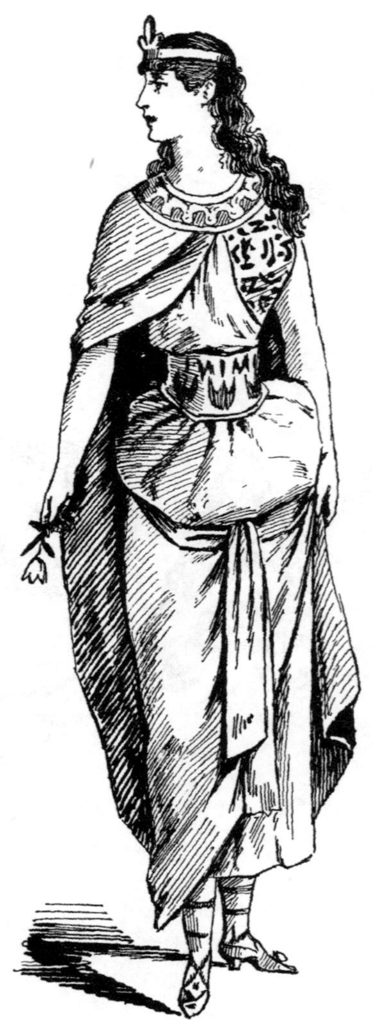

FIGURE NO 22.—EGYPTIAN COSTUME.

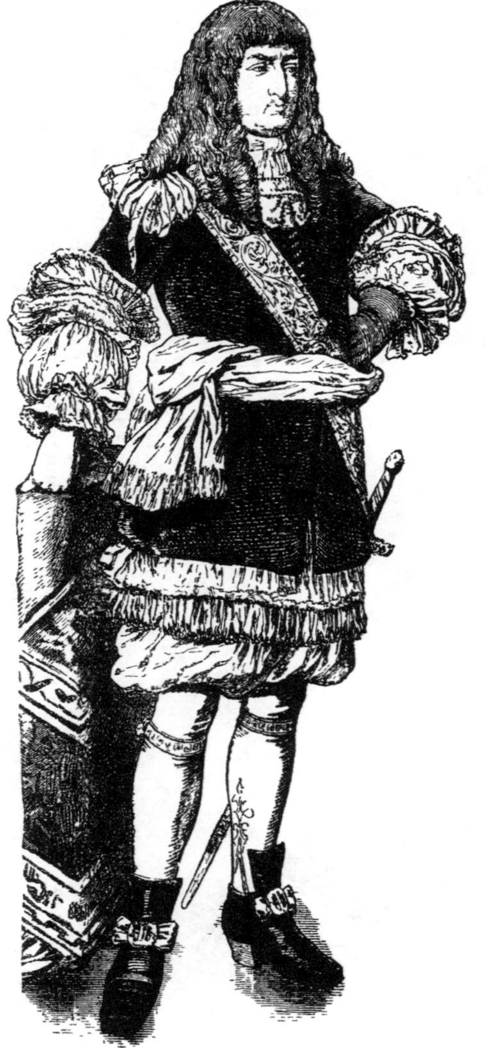

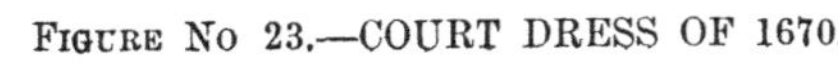

FIGURE No 23.—COURT DRESS OF 1670.

FIGURE No. 23.—COURT DRESS OF 1670.—Coat of some rich, dark-tinted fabric with sleeves reaching only to the elbow. Worn over a shirt or blouse of fine white material elaborately trimmed with frills of lace. Full short trousers of light-colored satin; long fancy stockings to match, gartered with jeweled bands. Shoes with flaps, bows and high red heels. Sword band of gilt, and sash of bright silk. Shoulder knot of ribbon to match sash; necktie or cravat of lace, and gloves of natural leather color. Curled wig of light hair and a tiny, dark mustache. The hat belonging to this costume is a broad-brimmed felt with square crown over which curl backward two feathers of a light color or white.

FIGURE No. 24.—GRETCHEN.—Plain, round skirt of gray woolen goods reaching to just above the ankles. Chemise of fine white muslin, with full sleeves reaching to the elbow. The top of the chemise is gathered to form a little ruffle, and the sleeves are completed to correspond. Bodice of dark-blue velvet or wool forming a short point at the front and back, and laced with a silken string. White, stiffly starched muslin cap, blue woolen stockings and wooden shoes, or wood-colored, broad-toed, suéde slippers. Long gold ear-rings and any other trinket-adornment desired. Carries a daisy from which she apparently plucks the petals in order to read her own future.

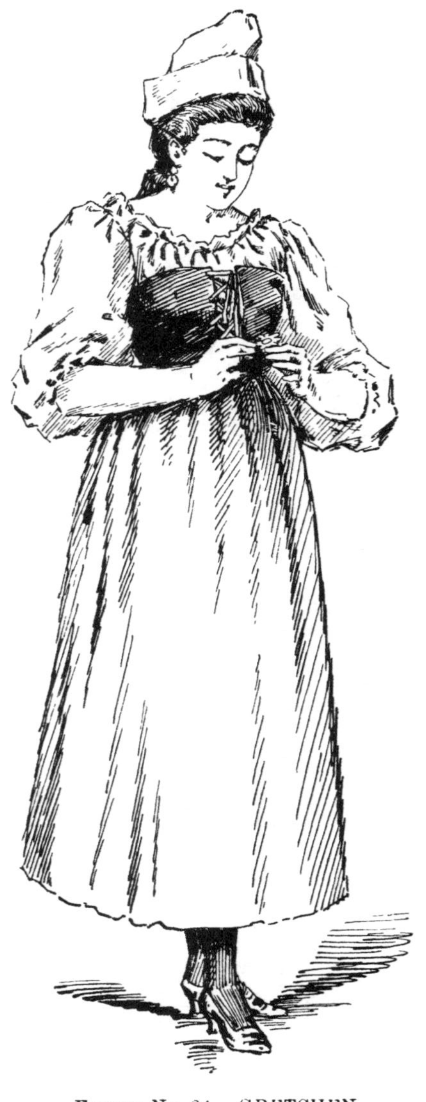

FIGURE No 24.—GRETCHEN.

FIGURE NO. 25.—ORIENTAL COSTUME.—This unique costume is exceedingly simple and may be made at home. It is composed as follows: Shirt of white silk gathered about the neck, and with sleeves of the same extending to the wrists. Low-necked sleeveless tunic of soft white woolen fabric, (or linen or silk,) fastened on the shoulder, and held in to the figure by a silk sash or girdle. Trousers of white wool, silk or linen, and white linen shoes. White gauze wound about the head in turban style.

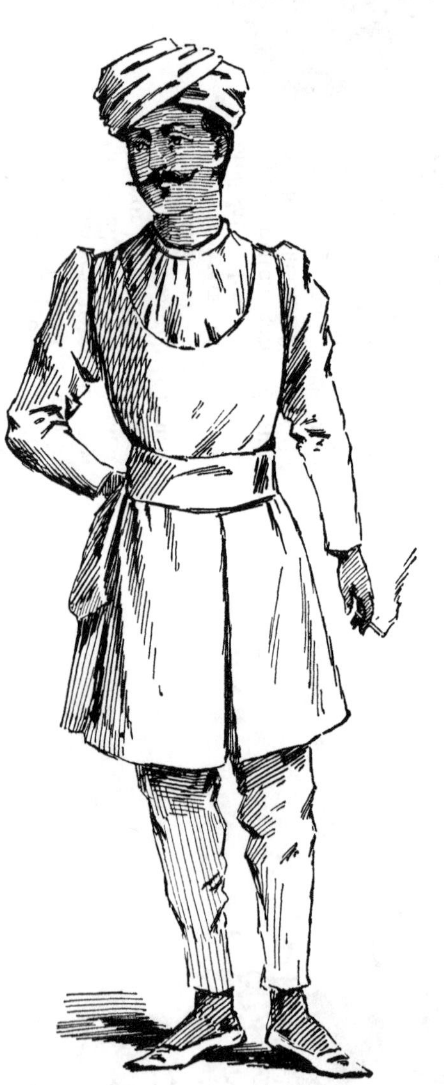

FIGURE NO. 25.—ORIENTAL COSTUME.

FIGURE NO. 26.—EAST INDIAN COSTUME.—This costume is white and gold in its colorings, and the composing materials are soft white wool and silk, and gold embroidery, rope and ornaments. The silk is used for the sleeves and chemisette, and also for the jacket and cap, while the wool is used for the dress. A long, white gauze veil is

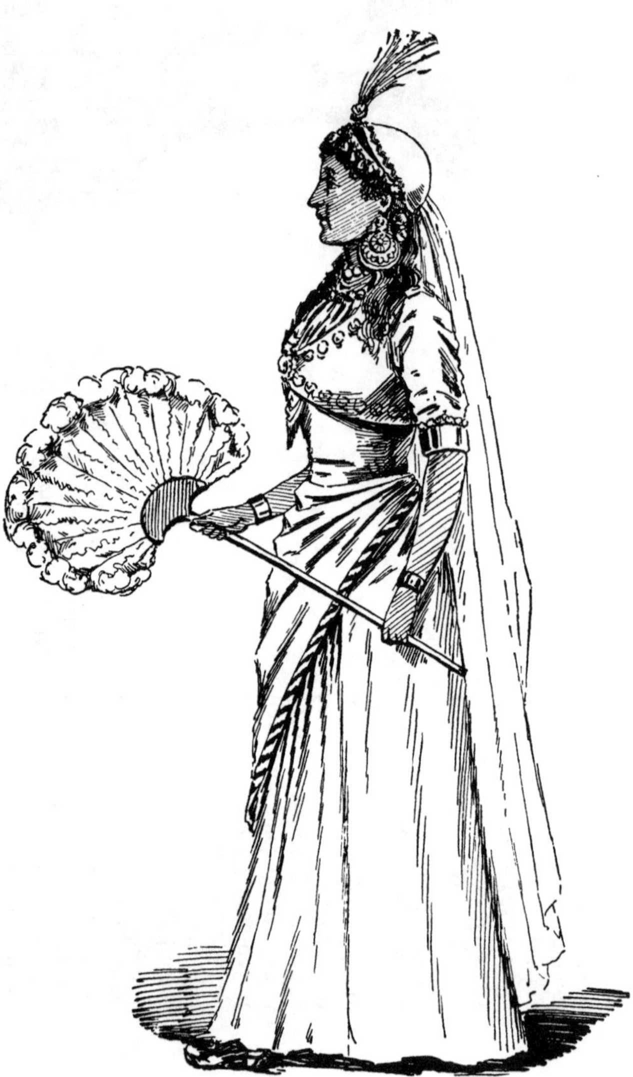

FIGURE NO. 26.—EAST INDIAN COSTUME.

attached to the cap, and the white feather fan has a golden handle. Gold jewelry and golden slippers complete this picturesque costume.

FIGURE NO. 27.—NORTH AMERICAN INDIAN. (For illustration see next page.)—A coat and pair of trousers that show some wear may be used for this suit. The trousers display broad pipings of cloth at the sides, the coat is decorated with colored beads, a brass armlet is worn above the elbow, and a necklace of wolf's teeth encircles the neck. About the waist is a belt or sash, in which are the tomahawk, scalping-knife and other weapons. A wig of long, coarse black hair is worn, and the huge Indian head-dress of feathers

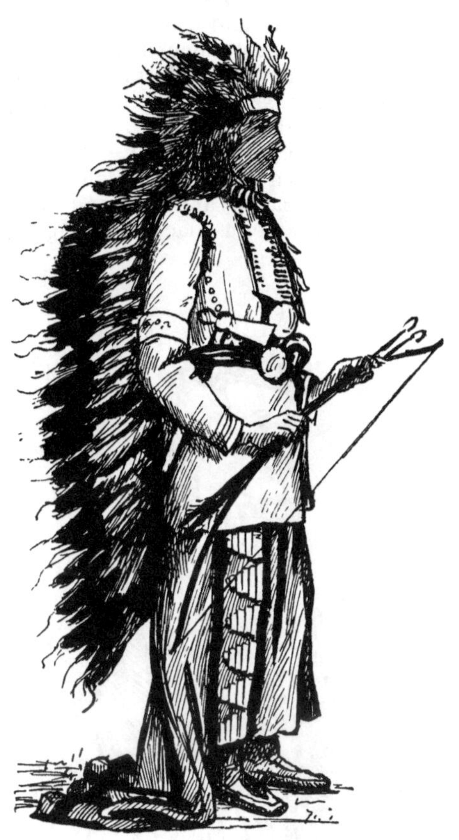

FIGURE No. 27.—NORTH AMERICAN INDIAN.

(For description see preceding page.)

is arranged in characteristic fashion. A flannel blanket is adjusted at the back to trail far behind, leather moccasins are worn and a bow and arrows are carried. Of course, the character demands that the face be stained a reddish-brown or copper color; and in addition the eye-brows may be blackened to meet at the center, and the face may be painted beneath the lower eyelids to produce a properly savage expression.

FIGURE No. 28.—POCAHONTAS.—This is a pretty costume for a dark brunette. The foundation material is smooth woolen goods of light leather color, and the decorations may be embroidered or appliquéed upon the fabric, or applied in any manner that will result effectively. Feathers, beads, Turkish bands or colored passementerie may be used in decorating the costume. The skirt is not hemmed at the bottom, but is cut in narrow strips to form fringe and the fancy decorations are added above it. A wolf skin hangs from the shoulders, and a gayly beaded pouch is suspended from the belt. Strings of beads and the teeth of animals are about the neck, and the hair is decorated to correspond with another string of teeth and an eagle's feather. Fancy stockings decorated to represent leggings, beaded moccasins, a bow and arrows, and a tomahawk complete the costume.

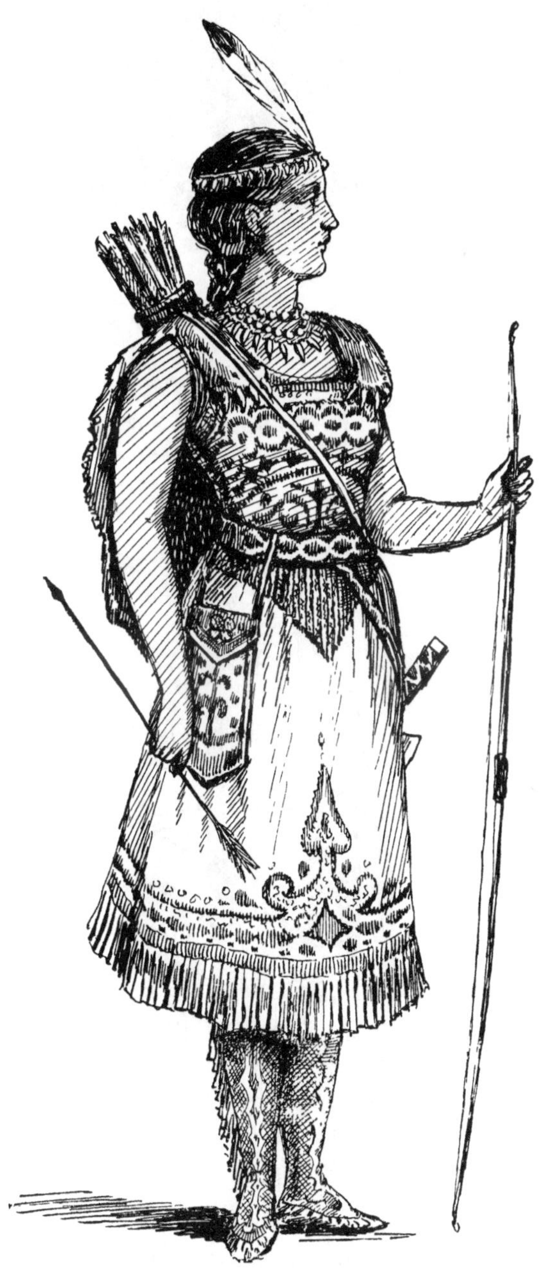

FIGURE No. 28 —POCAHONTAS.

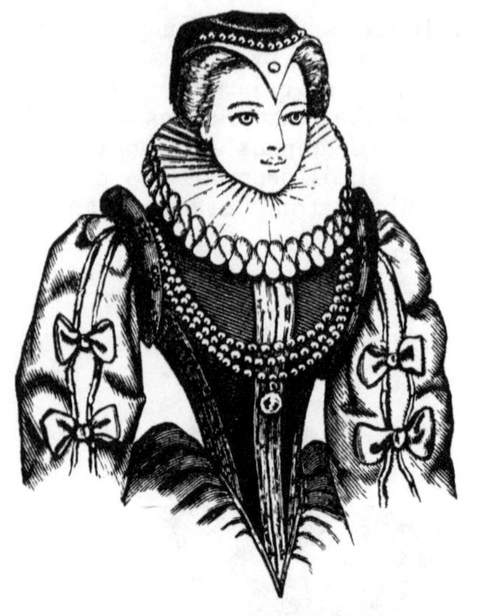

FIGURE No. 29.—MARY, QUEEN OF SCOTS.

FIGURE No. 29.—MARY, QUEEN OF SCOTS.—Bodice of royal-purple silk or velvet, shaped and trimmed to produce the effect of a stomacher, flowered heliotrope ribbon being used for the trimming. Full sleeves of heliotrope silk, trimmed with padded rolls of the ribbon. Ruff of stiffly starched muslin. Hair puffed at the sides and covered with pointed head-dress of velvet and silk trimmed with pearl beads. Pearl necklace and a gold medallion. Any full skirt of purple or any harmoniously contrasting color may be worn with this bodice.

FIGURE No. 30.—PORTIA.—Plain black silk under-gown with a close collar turning over a long cravat, and a broad scarf to hold the garment in place. Over-garment

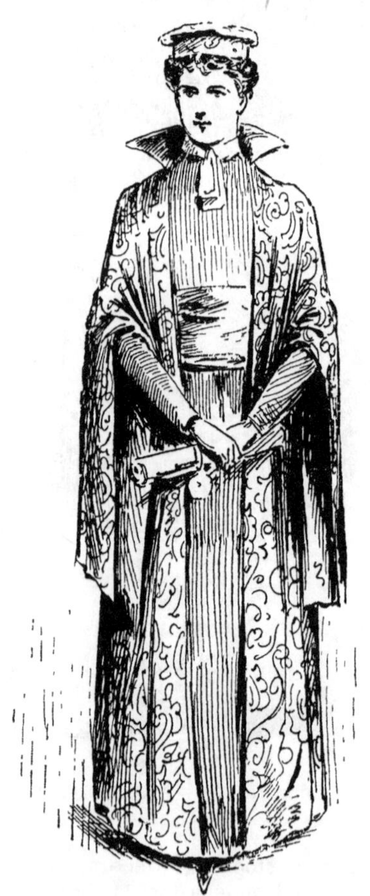

FIGURE No 30.—PORTIA.

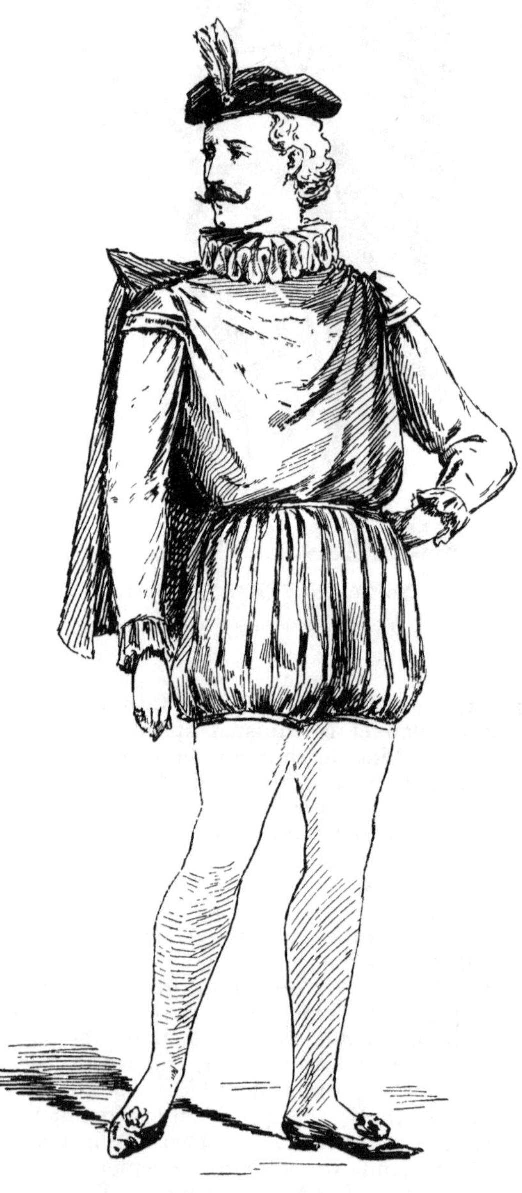

FIGURE No 31.—BASSANIO

(For description see next page.)

of black brocade with large loose sleeves and a high-standing pointed collar. Cap of the brocade.

FIGURE NO. 31.—BASSANIO. (For illustration see preceding page.)—Tunic of gray silk; trunks of gray striped with deep Venetian red; cape of gray cloth lined with Venetian red silk; red velvet cap with gray feather; gray tights and red shoes with gray rosettes. Lace ruffles at the wrists and a muslin ruff about the neck.

FIGURE NO. 32.—BLUEBEARD.—This character may be assumed by young people or adults. The costume is arranged as follows: Red silk or woolen trousers; yellow coat with red embroidery and sash; deep orange-colored cape lined with brown; orange-colored turban trimmed with rainbow gauze and a silver star and crescent; gold fringe and tassels for trimmings; false beard and mustache of jute that has been dyed a deep blue. The scimeter may be made of pasteboard and covered with silver or gilt paper.

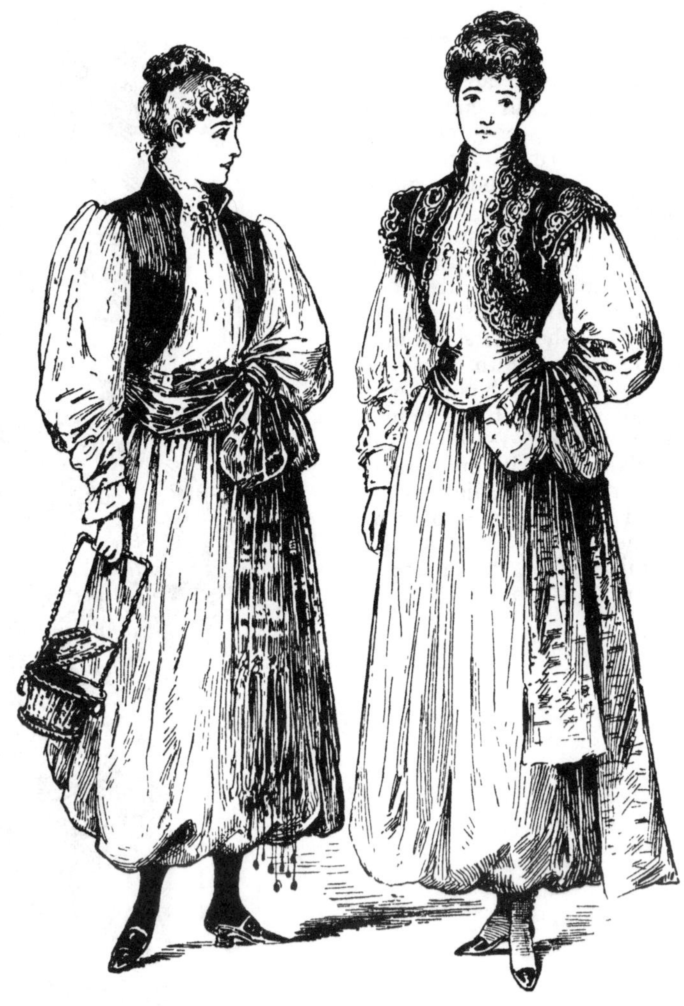

FIGURES NOS. 33 AND 34.—DANCING GIRLS.

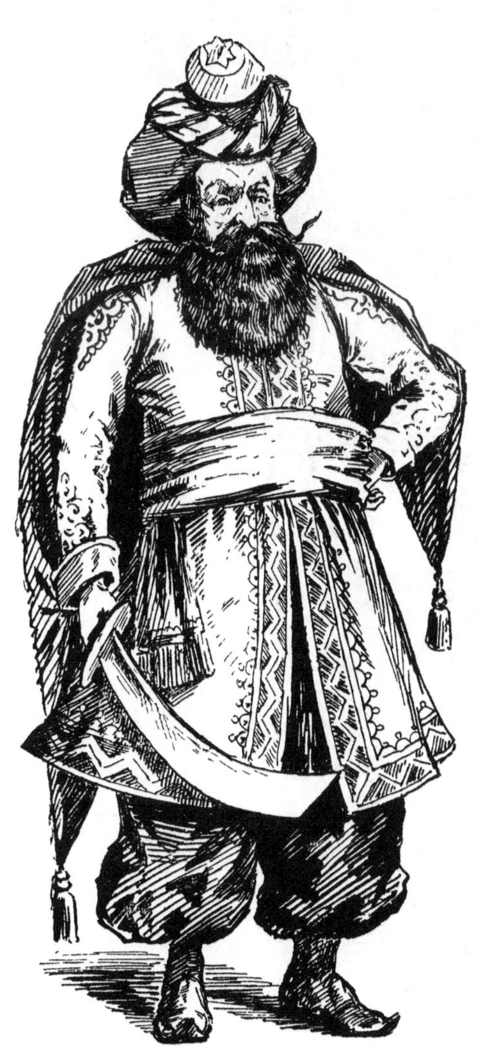

FIGURE NO. 32.—BLUEBEARD.

FIGURES NOS. 33 AND 34.—DANCING GIRLS.—Velvet and a soft thin woolen fabric, or China silk may be used in making these costumes. For the figure at the left use rich green velvet, Nile-green woolen gauze and a soft silk sash striped with the Roman colors and fringed with gold and other colored beads. Green stockings to match the jacket; gilt slippers.

The lower portion of the dress is made like very full Turkish trousers, each section being banded about the ankle. The waists are loose and the sleeves long and full. For the second costume the materials are crimson velvet, cream-colored nun's veiling, a gold-tinsel scarf, and heavy gold embroidery on the jacket. Pale-pink stockings and crimson velvet or satin slippers.

FIGURE NO. 35.—ROMAN SOLDIER. — Under-garment of white linen; cuirasse of white woolen fabric elaborated with gold embroidery and pendants of orange colored silk tipped with gold fringe; blue ribbon girdle about the waist, tied in a knot at the front and looped backward as seen in the picture; epaulets to match pendants, and massive clasps upon the shoulders. Mantle of crimson cloth fastened upon the left shoulder with a gilt clasp. Brass helmet with crimson feathers; gilt sandals tied with orange-colored ribbons. Shield in one hand and insignia of rank in the other. This costume is suitable for the character of Julius Cæsar.

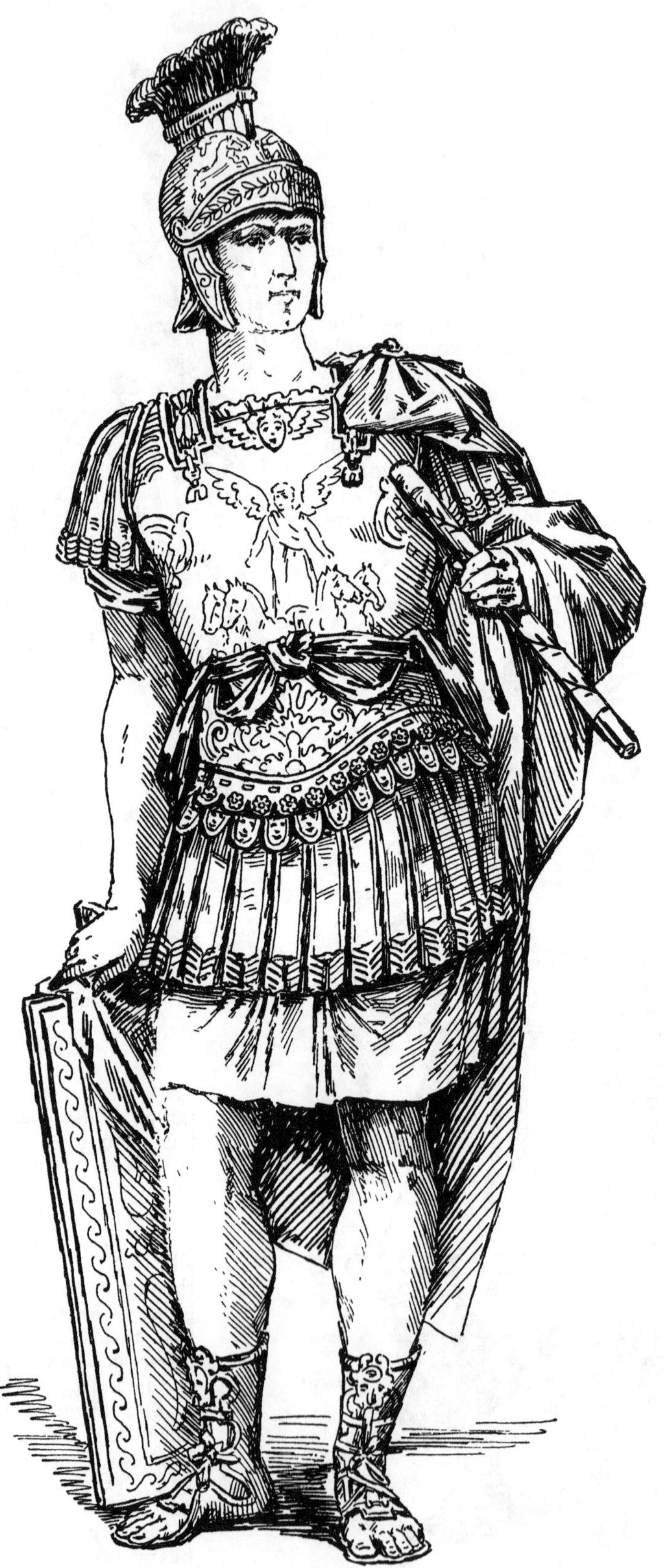

FIGURE NO. 35.—ROMAN SOLDIER.

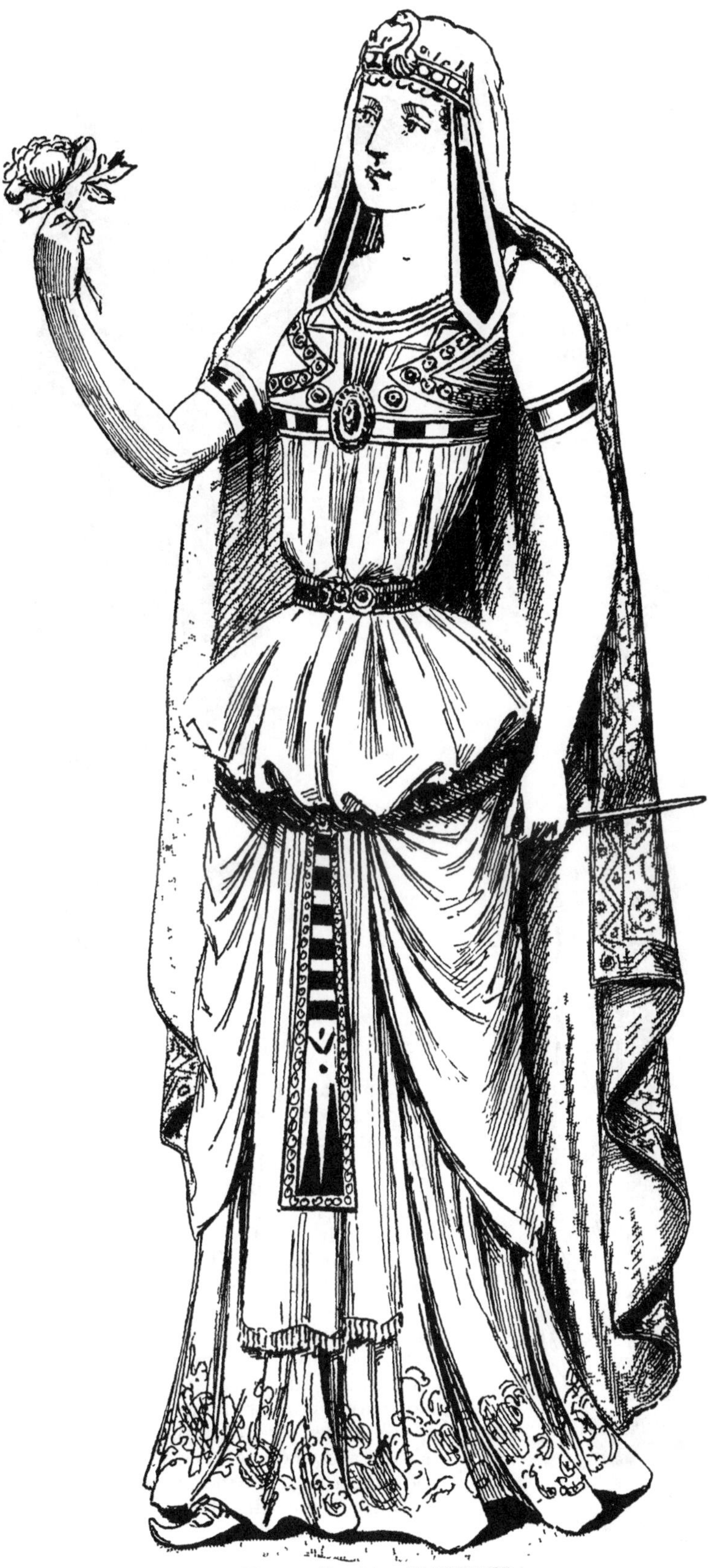

FIGURE NO. 36—CLEOPATRA.

FIGURE NO. 36.—CLEOPATRA.—Princess-shaped foundation of muslin on which is draped the skirt and tunic of soft wool crêpe in yellow or any pale tint desired. Border of lotus blossoms painted or embroidered upon the skirt. Zouave jacket of tinsel brocade in many colorings, with plenty of the gold. Girdle, belt and ornaments of gold braid, and black braid or velvet. Cloak of Oriental gold-printed fabric lined with some rich Egyptian tint. Head-dress of cream-colored India muslin, with stiff lapels of the same and black velvet; golden swan and other ornaments above the brow. Armlets of gold and velvet, and slippers or sandals of gold. Lotus blossom in one hand and a short dagger in the other.

FIGURE NO. 37.—ARAB.—Long, full trousers of dark blue woolen goods; shirt of the same with jacket of lighter blue edged with silver braid; cloak of heavy white wool; head-dress of Algerian striped cotton; broad brown-and-red sash from which are suspended various implements of warfare and defense; red morocco boots sharply pointed at the toes.

FIGURE NO. 38.—ALBANIAN COSTUME.—The chief feature of this becoming dress is a white petticoat, from beneath which either a chemise or an under-skirt with long sleeves is visible; this reaches below the knee and fastens over the bosom in front. A colored woolen scarf or a heavy metal girdle draws it in at the waist, and at the same time serves to fasten on a colored, (mostly red,) narrow apron. Then follows a long, sleeveless jacket made of thick, white woolen material, which is ornamented in the upper part as far as the waist, with colored and gold embroidery. The jacket reaches to the knee and is worn open in front. It fits tightly at the waist and then falls in folds over the skirt. The head is enveloped in a white cotton handkerchief with a colored pattern on the ends. The neck and bosom are adorned with rows of beads, with gold and silver coins hanging from them.

The feet are clad in colored stockings. The shoes are made of red or yellow leather, and the pointed toes are ornamented with red rosettes.

The curious distaff stuck into the girdle so as to leave the hands free for twisting the wool into threads, is a relic of the primitive style of work before spinning wheels of a later day were invented.

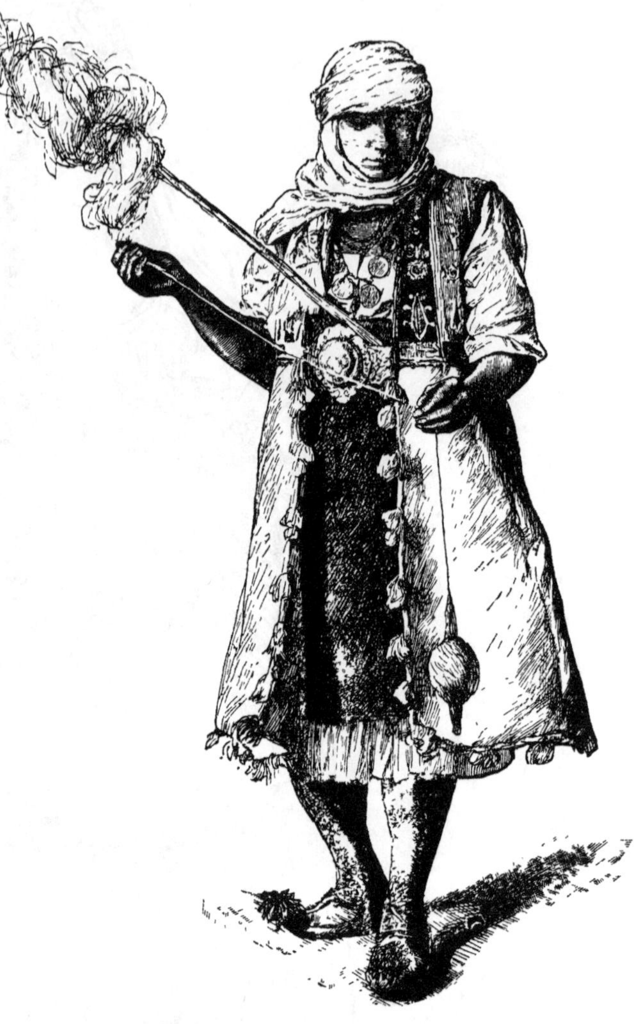

FIGURE NO 38.—ALBANIAN COSTUME

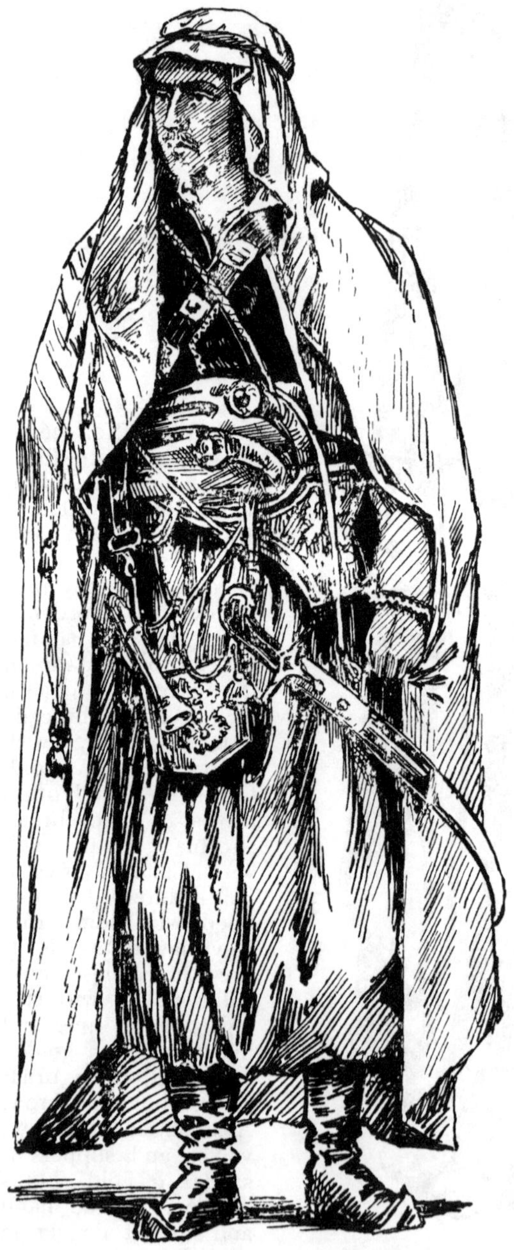

FIGURE NO. 37.—ARAB

FIGURE No. 39.—TURK.—This costume is gorgeous in coloring and elaborate in detail. The robe is of bright yellow silk, figured with green and lined with red, and bordered with white fur.

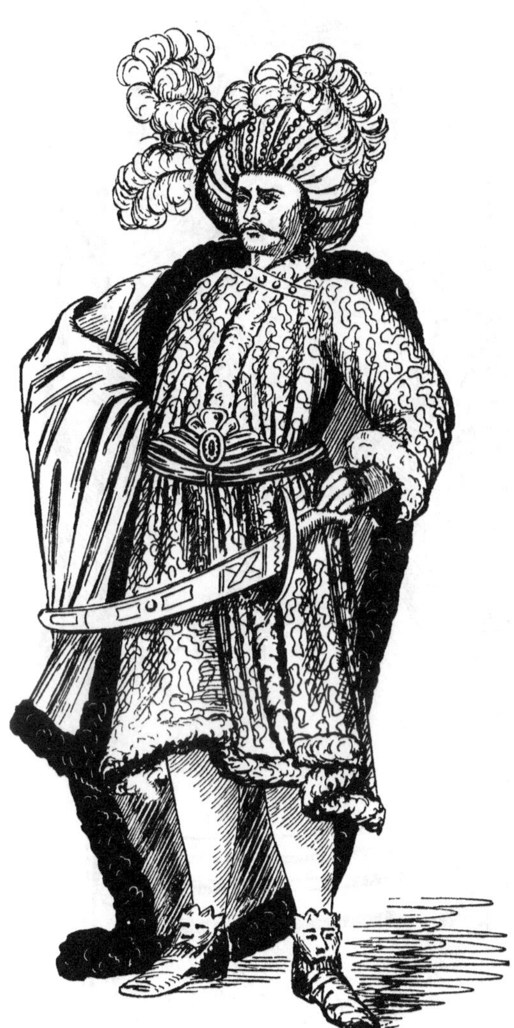

FIGURE No 39.—TURK.

The mantle is of gray woolen goods lined with red silk and bordered with black or brown fur, and is fastened at the back so that it will not slip off. The long stockings are turquoise-blue, and the shoes are of yellow kid decorated with small bright-red masks. The girdle is blue silk of the same tint as the stockings, and has an immense imitation ruby or carbuncle at the center. The turban is of blue gauze made a la Turk, and is heavily decorated with plumes of red, yellow, gray, green and blue, together with strings of glass beads which imitate jewels.

FIGURE No. 40.—HOLLAND PEASANT COSTUME.—Round full skirt of brown or gray woolen goods, with sleeveless bodice of the same decorated with fancy braid or ribbon in some bright contrasting tint. The neck is only slightly low at the back where it is of oval shape. The skirt may also be trimmed with rows of braid or ribbon. Shirt waist or blouse of soft white muslin, with neck and wristbands embroidered with red. Long white apron of white or blue woolen, trimmed with a gay bordering of printed material or embroidery.

The cotton bonnet is made of a very thick cordonette, starched and ironed, and then skilfully folded as represented, and held in shape by long, silver-headed pins. These caps are worn by the peasants of Norway, Finland and the northern part of Holland.

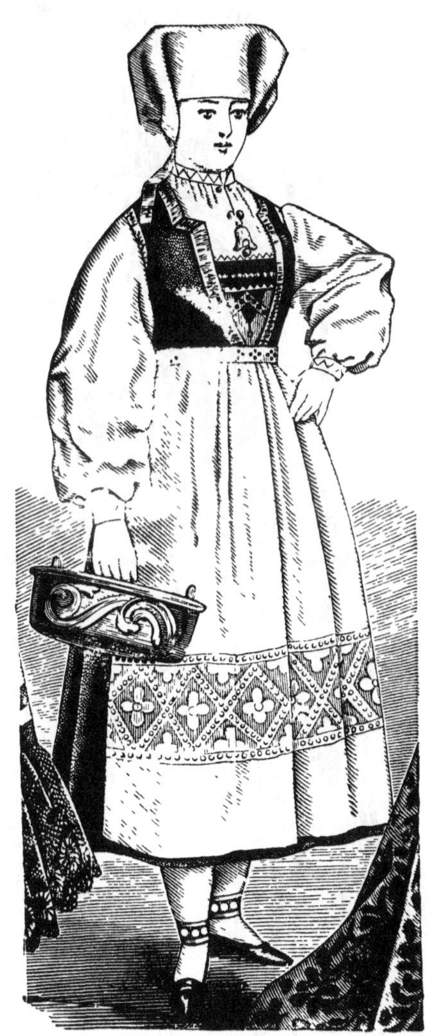

FIGURE No. 40.—HOLLAND PEASANT COSTUME

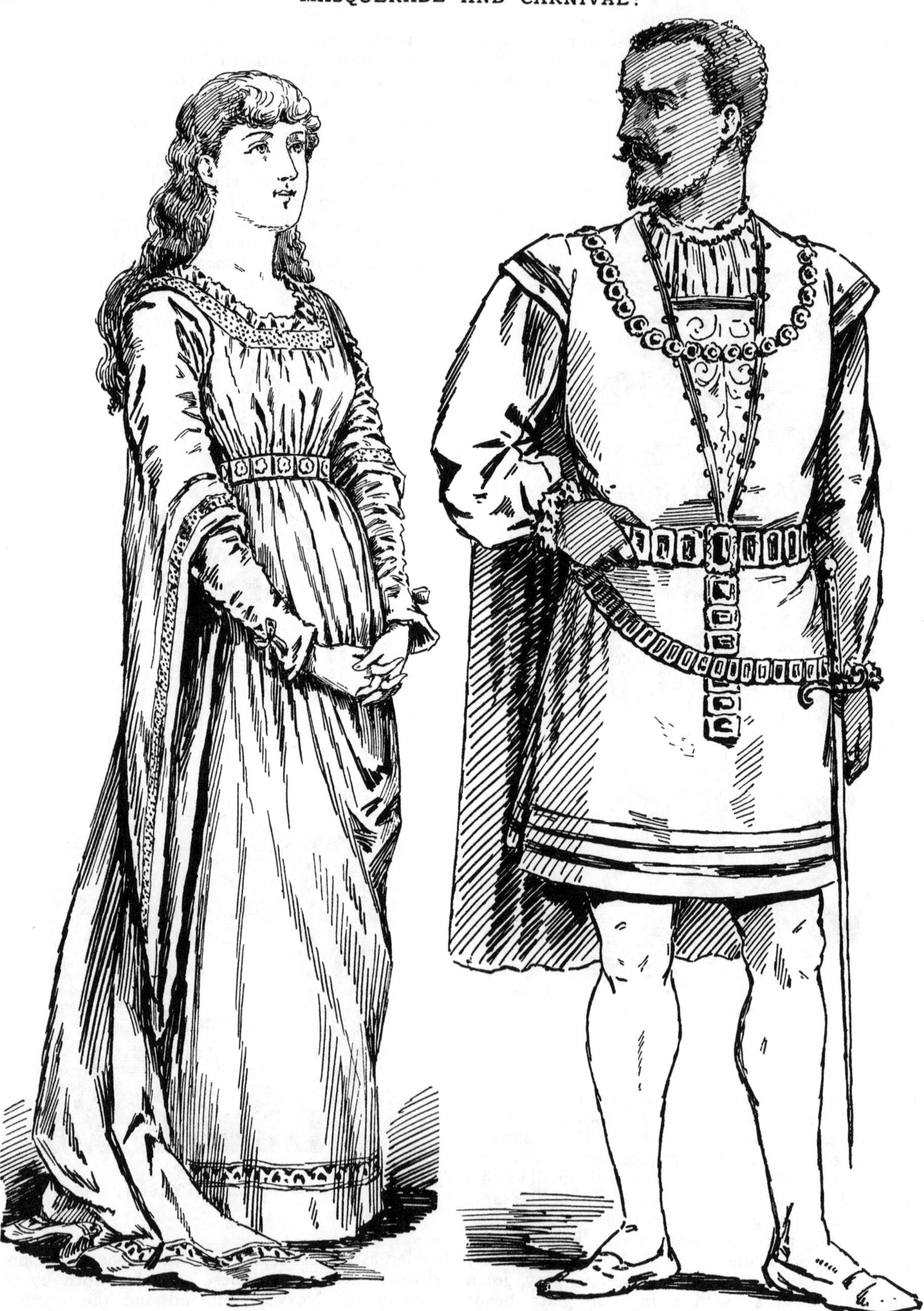

FIGURE No. 41.—DESDEMONA.

FIGURE No. 42.—OTHELLO.

(For descriptions see next page.)

FIGURE No. 41.—DESDEMONA. (For illustration see preceding page.) —Gown of some soft white fabric, trimmed with a delicate embroidery in gold, though dainty shades of green, pink, blue, purple or a deep Venetian red may be used in place of the gold. Long undersleeves of the color of the embroidery tied at the wrists with narrow white ribbons. Hair worn flowing but may be braided and worn under a Venetian cap.

FIGURE No. 42.—OTHELLO. (For illustration see preceding page.)—Shirt of white silk gathered at the neck and wrists; sleeveless tunic of black silk handsomely trimmed with gold bands; gold necklet, belt and sword-band. Full cloak of white cloth which may be lined or not, as desired, with tinted silk. Pale-brown tights, black shoes; face and hands darkened to a brown tint.

FIGURE No. 43.—IAGO.—White silk shirt with long sleeves; ruffles at the neck and wrists and up the backs of the sleeves. Pale-blue vest embroidered or stamped with gold. Tunic of deep wine-colored velvet handsomely trimmed with gold; sleeves lined with pale-blue. Jewelled girdle from which is suspended a dagger and sword. Pale-blue and wine-colored striped tight upon one leg; wine-colored tight with fancy blue and wine-colored top upon the other; deep red shoes or slippers, and wine-colored velvet cap. Drab and pale-blue, or deep-blue and fawn-color, with silver trimmings, combine handsomely in such a costume.

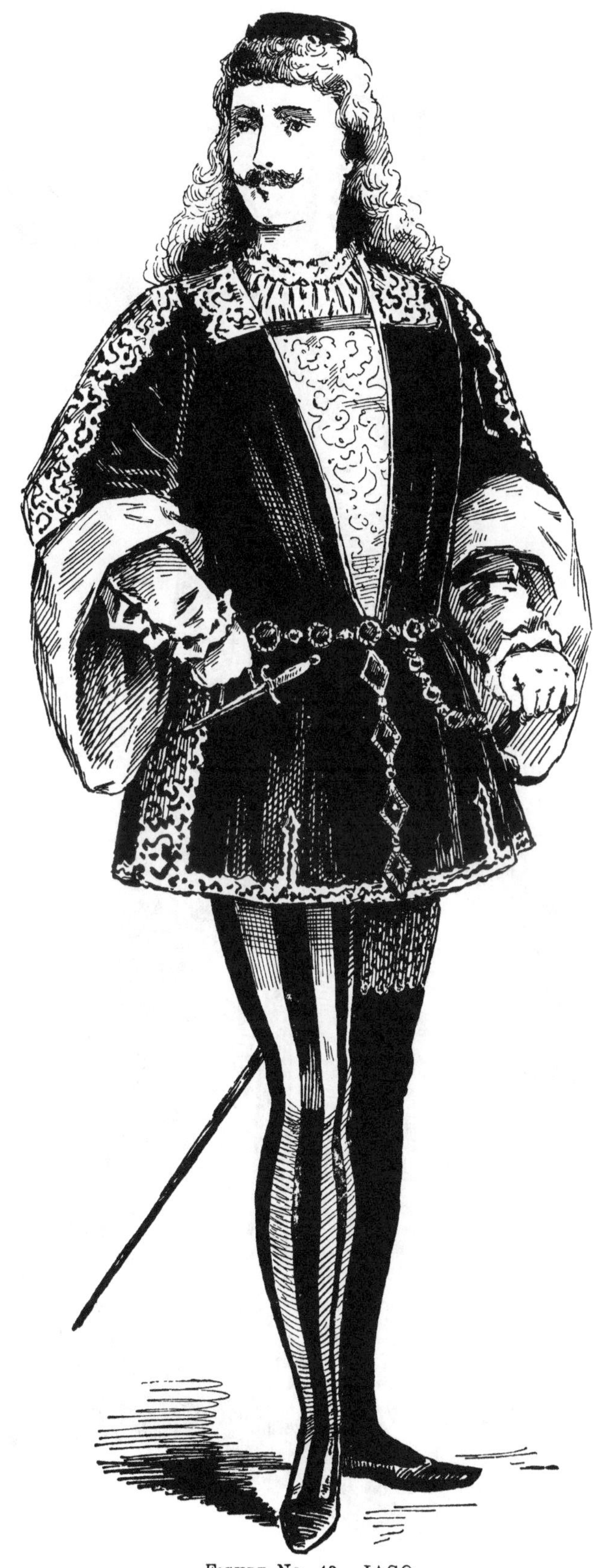

FIGURE No 43.—IAGO.

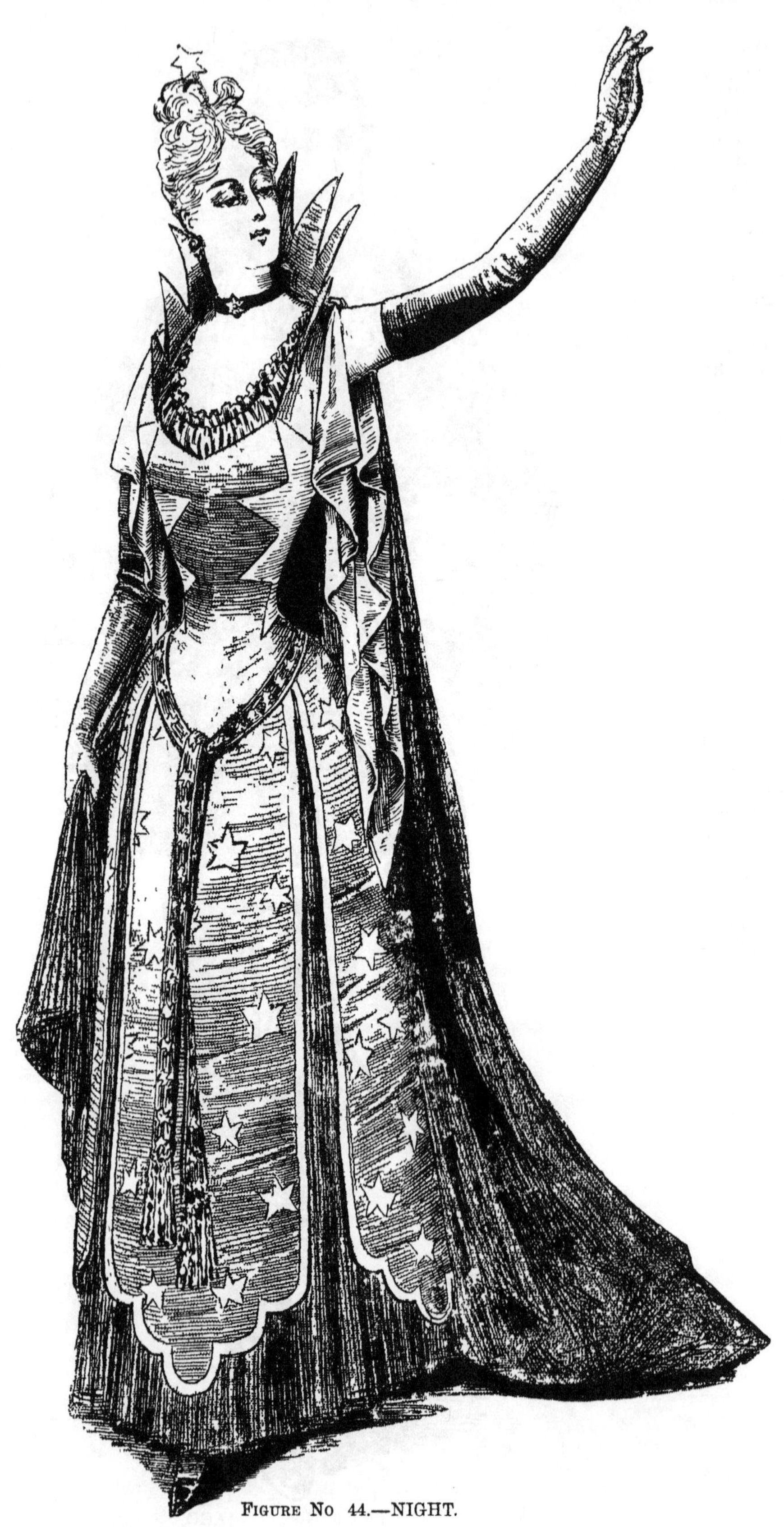

FIGURE No 44.—NIGHT.

FIGURE NO. 44.—NIGHT.—Gown and mantle of black gauze or lace, with the skirt very finely plaited. Bodice and over-dress of indigo-blue satin trimmed with silver and ornamented with silver stars. Large silver star on each side of the bodice and silver-gauze points standing about the neck. Silver-gauze drapery hanging from each shoulder and a puff of the same at the top of the bodice. Girdle of black lace studded with stars. Diamond or silver star in the hair and at the throat, and star ear-rings. Long black suéde gloves fastened with tiny stars The veil is so arranged that it may be thrown over the the whole figure when desired.

FIGURE NO. 45.—BAT.—Gown of black gauze made over a black foundation. Mantle of black satin, made double and whaleboned to represent huge wings cut similarly to an umbrella top. Fichu of black gauze fastened with an artificial bat, and a bat head-dress. Long black gloves, black stockings and slippers with bats upon the latter. A bat-wing mask may be worn if desired.

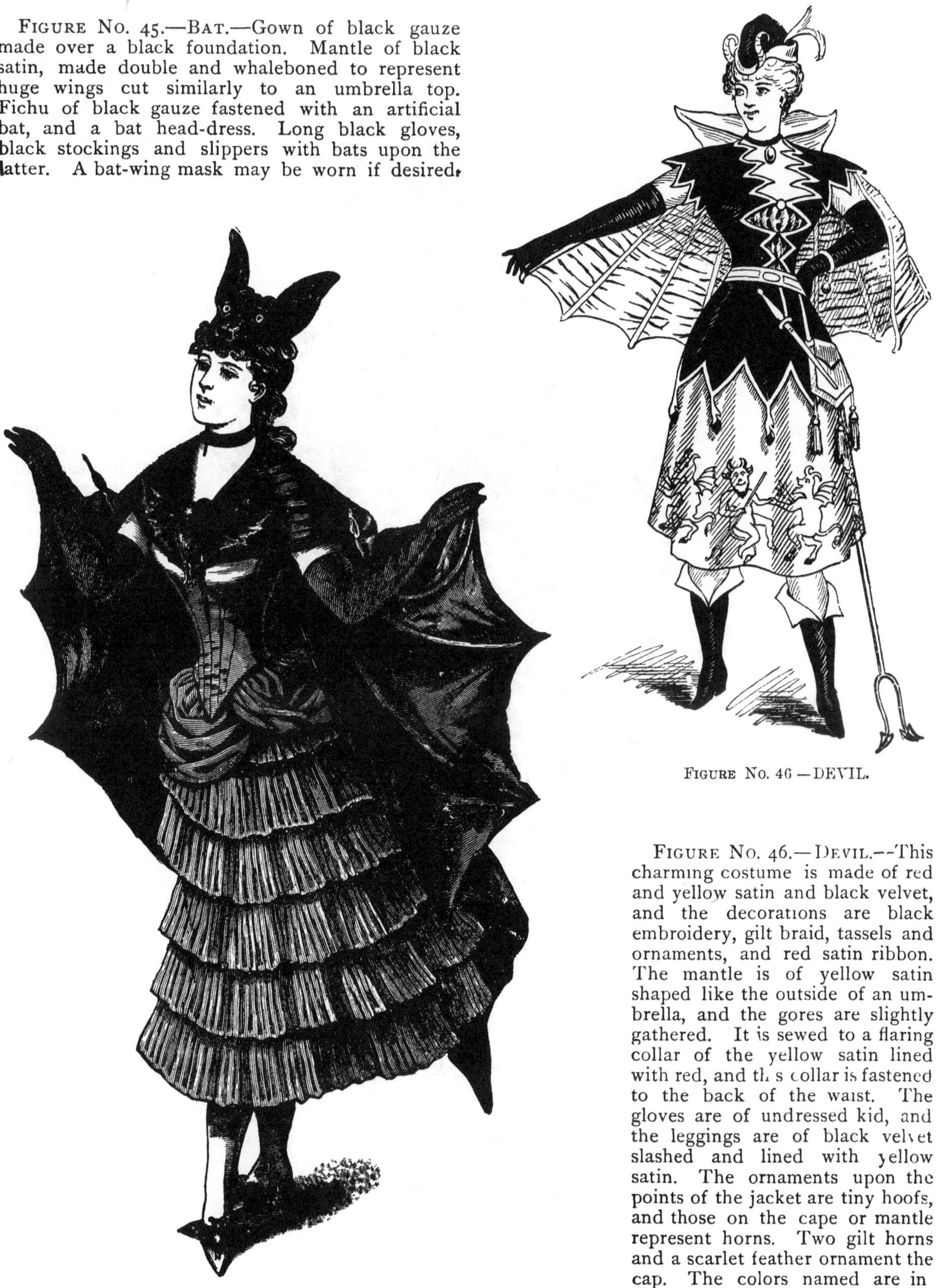

FIGURE NO. 46.—DEVIL.

FIGURE NO. 45.—BAT.

FIGURE NO. 46.—DEVIL.—This charming costume is made of red and yellow satin and black velvet, and the decorations are black embroidery, gilt braid, tassels and ornaments, and red satin ribbon. The mantle is of yellow satin shaped like the outside of an umbrella, and the gores are slightly gathered. It is sewed to a flaring collar of the yellow satin lined with red, and this collar is fastened to the back of the waist. The gloves are of undressed kid, and the leggings are of black velvet slashed and lined with yellow satin. The ornaments upon the points of the jacket are tiny hoofs, and those on the cape or mantle represent horns. Two gilt horns and a scarlet feather ornament the cap. The colors named are in variably used for this costume

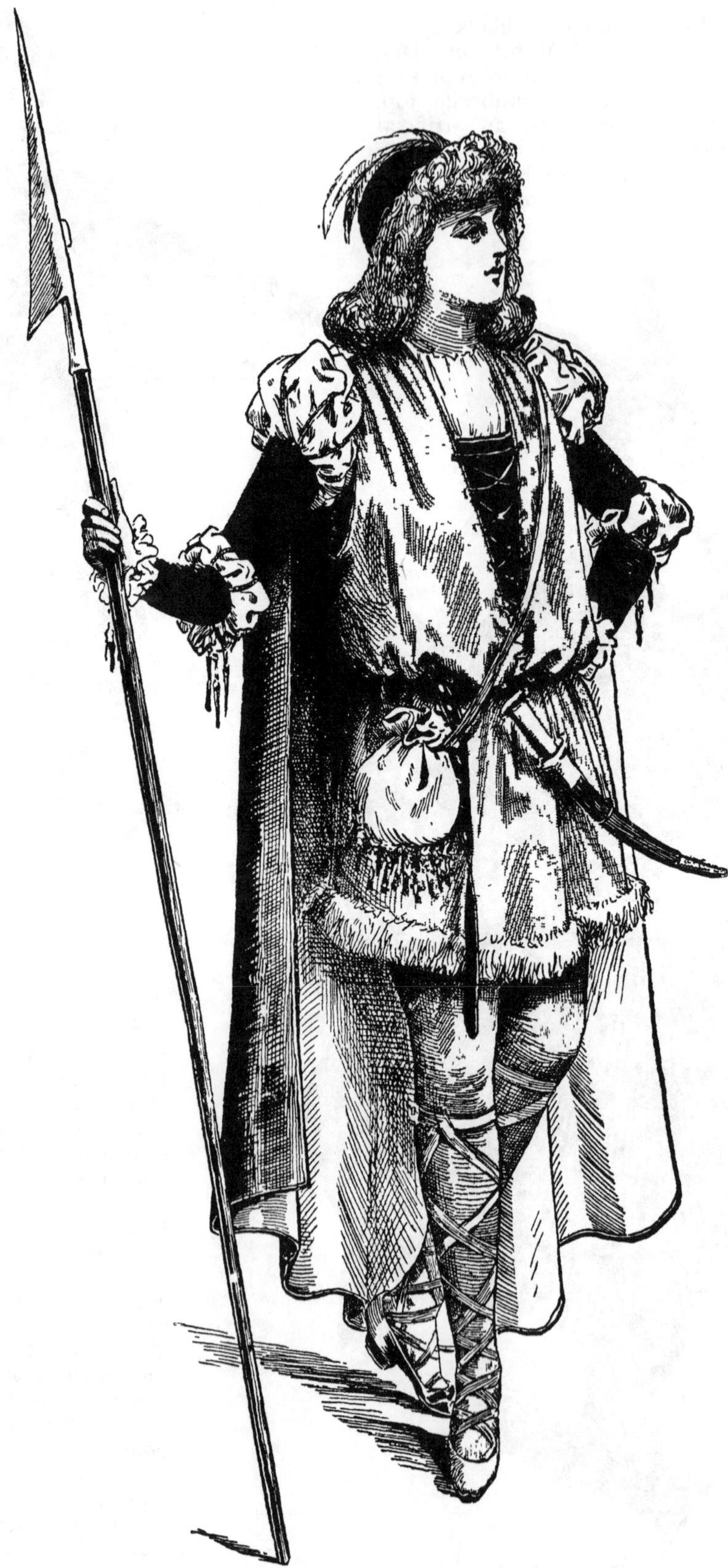

FIGURE NO. 47.—ROSALIND.—(AS DRESSED BY MRS LANGTRY.)

FIGURE NO. 47.—ROSALIND.—Doublet and hose of soft, light gray wool; doublet laced with gray silk cord and trimmed with gray fur; gray slippers and hose banded with gray satin ribbon. Green velvet bodice; chemisette and puffs of Nile-green silk; pouch of the same trimmed with silver. Long gray cloak lined with shell-pink. Velvet cap with pale-green heron's feather. The brown wood-tints combine beautifully with crimson or blue for this costume.

FIGURE No. 48.—ORLANDO.—This costume is very simply made, and is composed of the following colors and fabrics: The tunic is of brown cloth cut square at the neck where it is filled in with soft white cambric. It is fastened about the waist with a leather sword-belt. The sleeves, which are very full from the shoulder to the elbow, are of reddish brown cloth, and are tied at the back with tiny leathern strings. Brown silk hose and low pointed shoes of the same color complete the lower part of the costume. The hat is of brown felt and has a long white ostrich plume.

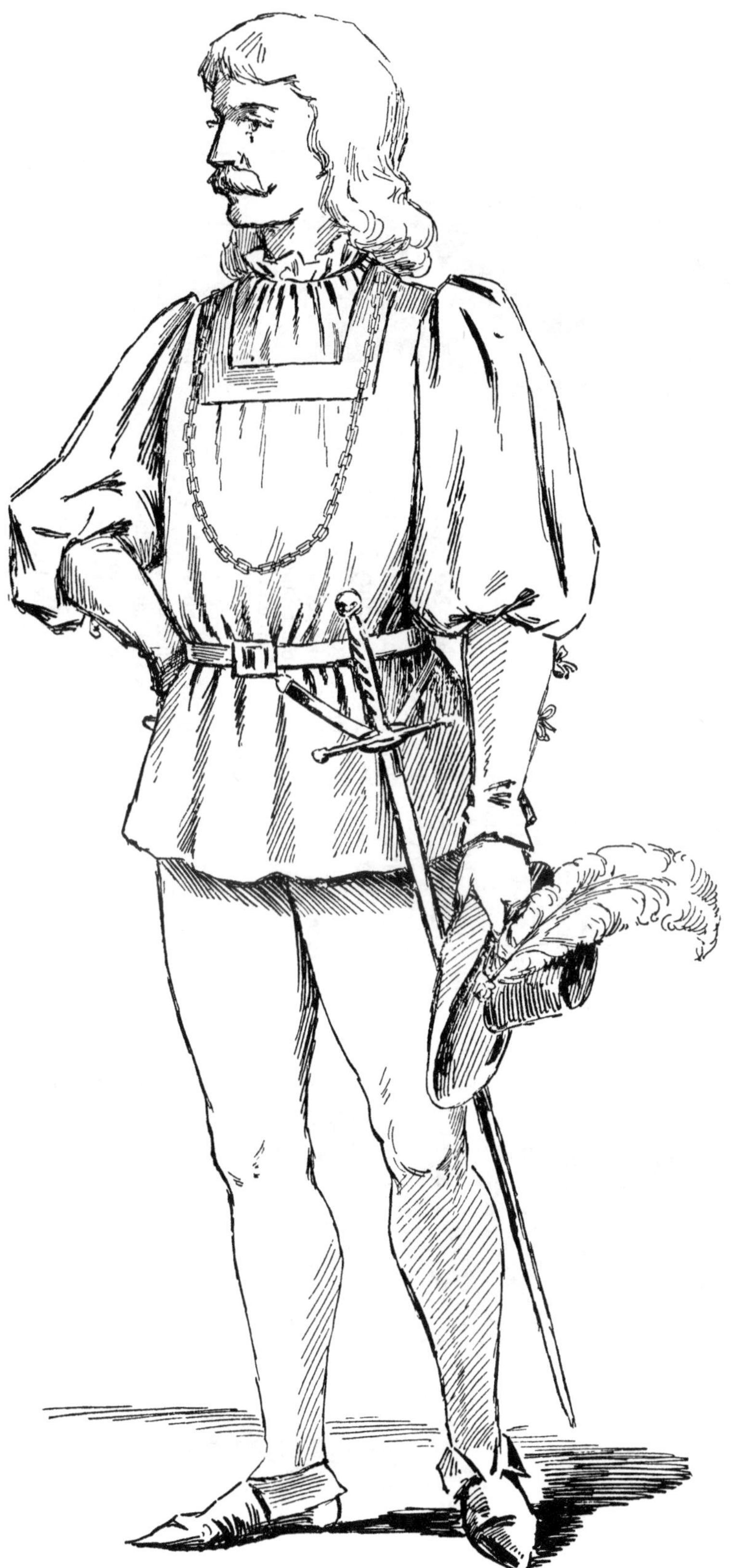

FIGURE No. 48.—ORLANDO.

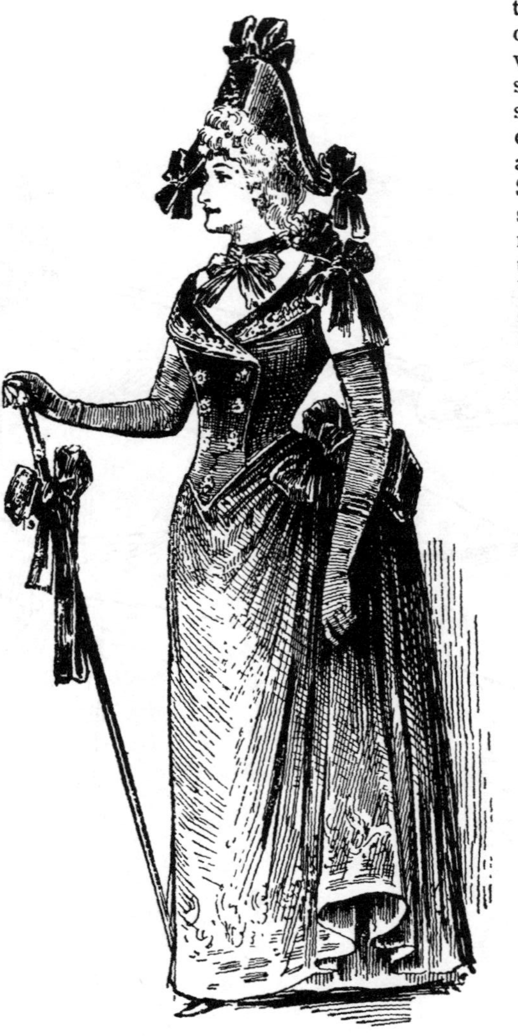

FIGURE NO 49.—INCROYABLE.

FIGURE NO. 49.—INCROYABLE.—Costume of dark green cloth trimmed with silver braid and buttons; skirt draped over a silver-colored petticoat; drapery fastened under a huge satin bow. Satin bows on the shoulders and satin ribbon wound about the neck and tied in a bow in front. Large satin bow at the back of the neck. Hat of dark green felt trimmed with silver braid and satin ribbon. Silver-gray gloves; silver staff decorated with green ribbon. Hair powdered; black patches on the face.

FIGURE NO. 50.—CONTINENTAL BEAU.—A dandy of the XVIII. century is here illustrated. His coat is of snuff-colored satin with collar-lapels and cuffs of green satin; his vest is of white satin and his breeches of pale-blue; his stockings are white silk and his shoes and hat are black. His hair is a powdered queue-wig, and his costume is further completed by lace ruffles, a high cravat, a button-hole bouquet and a cane. His manner should be supercilious and mincing, and frequent resorts to a silver snuff box would be in keeping with the character.

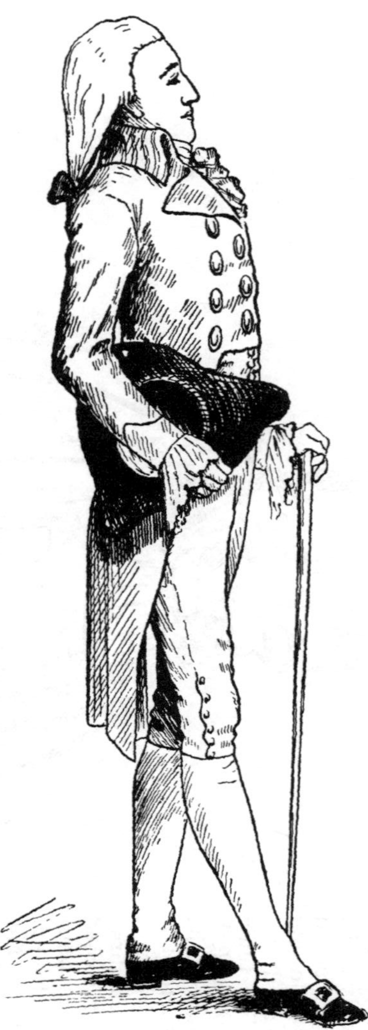

FIGURE NO. 50.—CONTINENTAL BEAU.

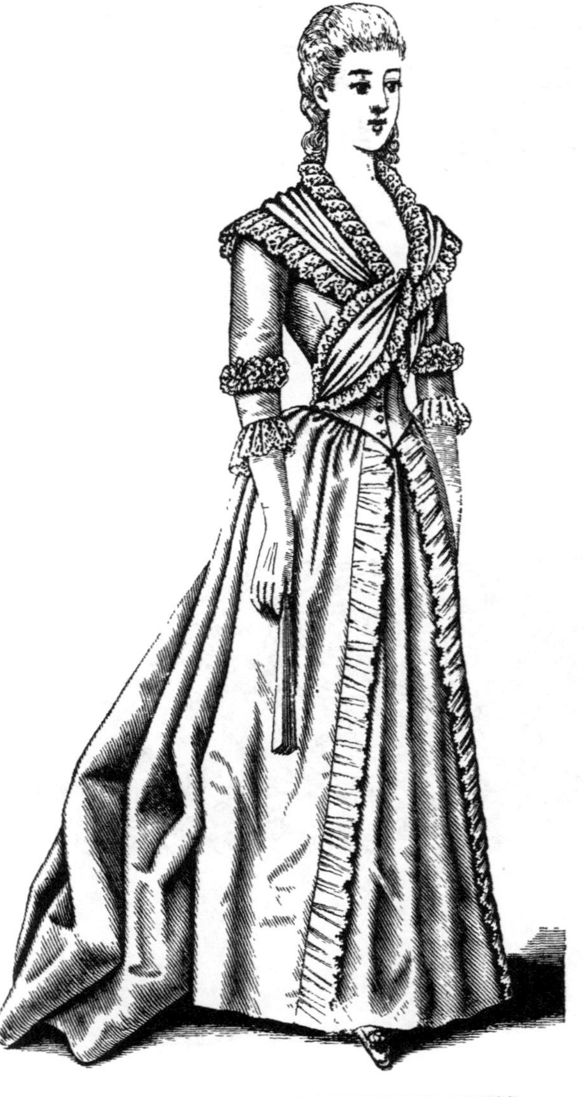

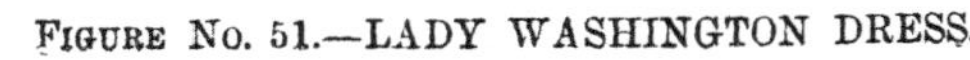

FIGURE No. 51.—LADY WASHINGTON DRESS.

FIGURE NO. 51.—LADY WASHINGTON DRESS.—This figure represents the Martha Washington dress. The dress may be of plain or brocaded silk, or of satin of some rich color, opening over a quilted satin petticoat of white or some delicate tint. At a Martha Washington entertainment when this gown is worn, the hair should be powdered, tiny black patches should be applied to the face, and long silk mitts, scarlet stockings, and slippers with buckles of Rhine stones should be worn.

FIGURE NO. 52.—CONTINENTAL SOLDIER.—In this costume the coat is of light-blue cloth faced and lined with red; gilt buttons and epaulets; vest and straps white; breeches buff color and leggings black. The sash is green, but may be white or blue. The cocked hat is black and has a red ornament at the side. If preferred a "Busby" or tall fur hat may be worn.

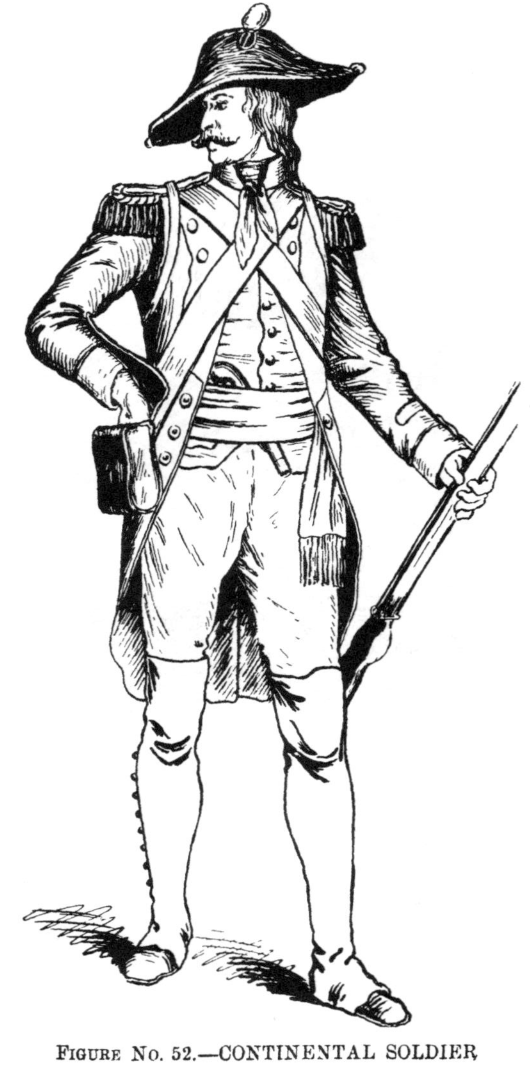

FIGURE NO. 52.—CONTINENTAL SOLDIER.

FIGURE NO. 53.—JULIET.—This charming costume may be made of white, dove-color, pale-blue or any dainty tint suited to the complexion of the wearer. The gown is very simply made, and it and the mantle-like drapery are trimmed with pearl passementerie. The long, puffed, Venetian sleeves are pointed over the hand and draped at the shoulders. A string of pearl beads is about the neck and another rests on the hair. A pointed Venetian cap may be worn if desired.

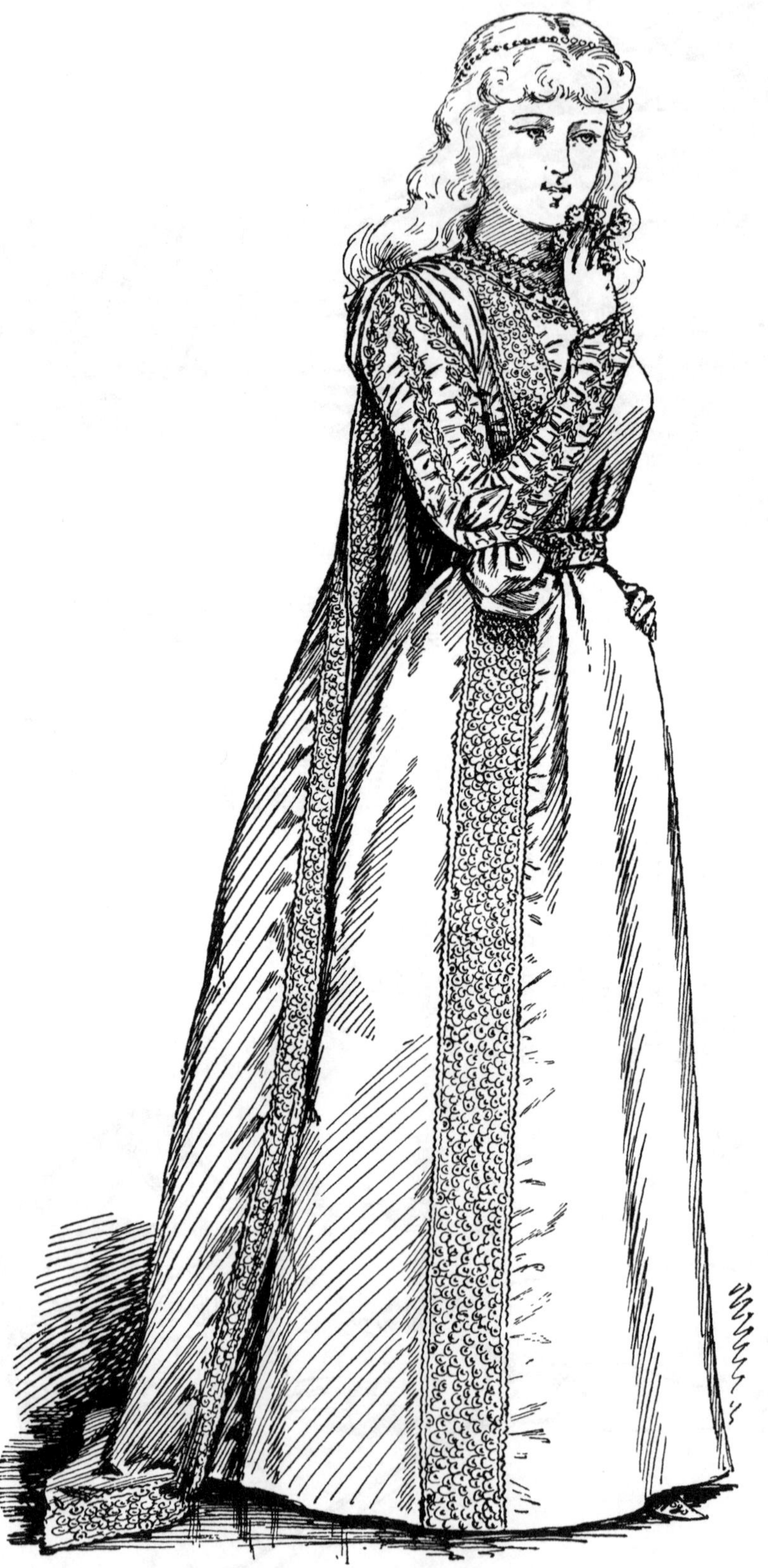

FIGURE NO. 53.—JULIET.

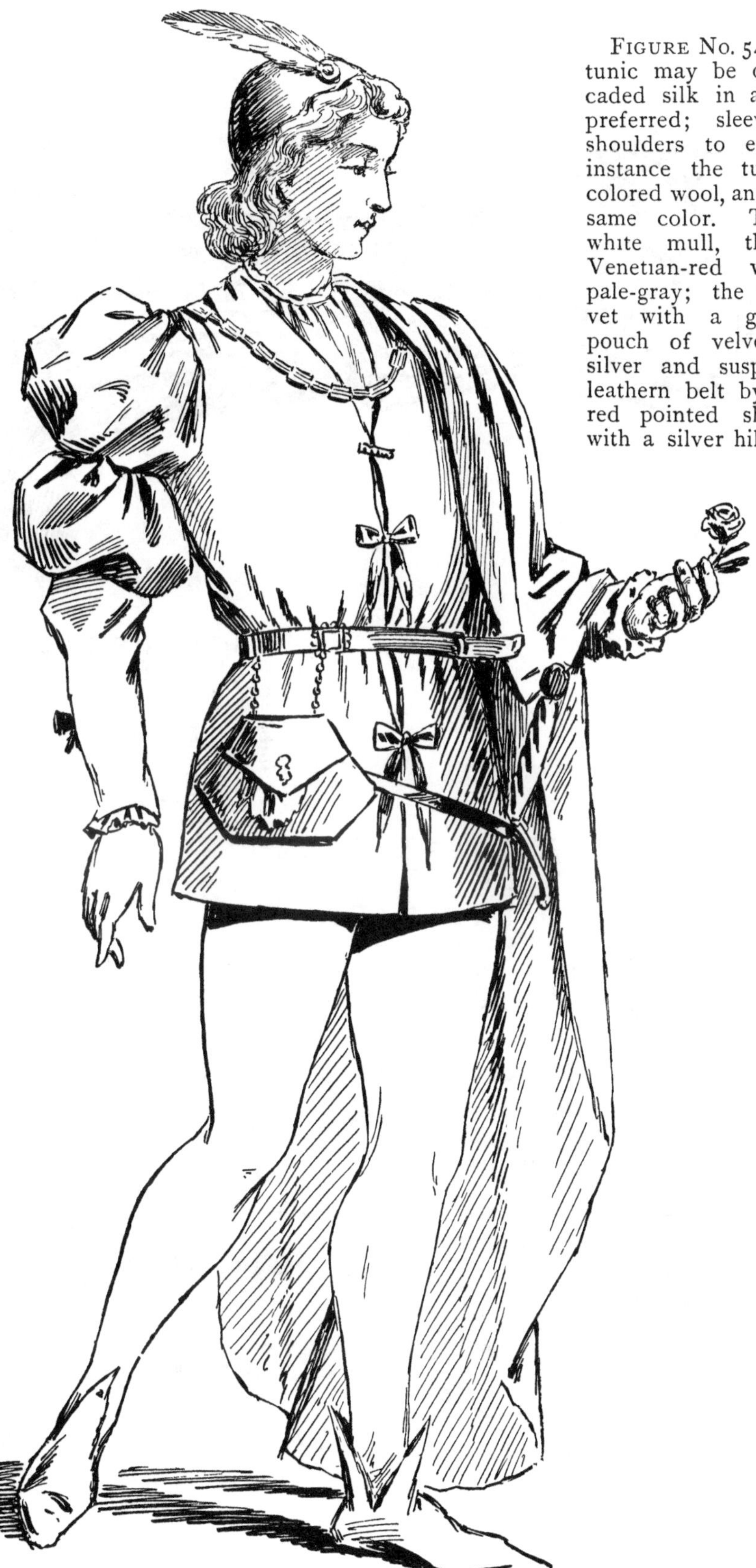

FIGURE No. 54.—ROMEO.—The tunic may be of plain or brocaded silk in any rich coloring preferred; sleeves puffed from shoulders to elbows. In this instance the tunic is of dove-colored wool, and the tights of the same color. The shirt is of white mull, the cloak is of Venetian-red wool lined with pale-gray; the cap of red velvet with a gray plume; the pouch of velvet trimmed with silver and suspended from the leathern belt by a silver chain; red pointed shoes and sword with a silver hilt.

FIGURE No. 54.—ROMEO.

FIGURE No. 55.—BEAU BRUMMEL.

FIGURE No. 55.—BEAU BRUMMEL.—In this costume the tail coat (under coat), is of black satin worn over breeches of black and white striped satin. The "great-coat" is of snuff-colored cloth lined with a lighter shade of satin. A high collar with a white lawn cravat, and a beaver hat of antique shape completes the upper part of the costume; and polished leather boots the lower part. Buff kid gloves and a heavy walking stick are also accesssories.

FIGURE No. 56.—WATTEAU COSTUME.—Bodice and sleeves of plain pale-blue or pale-pink silk with low neck; elbow sleeves finished with frills of lace. Watteau and skirt portion of brocaded-striped silk, draped as seen in the engraving. Round hat of pink or blue trimmed with flowers and ribbon. Blue or pink stockings with slippers to match.

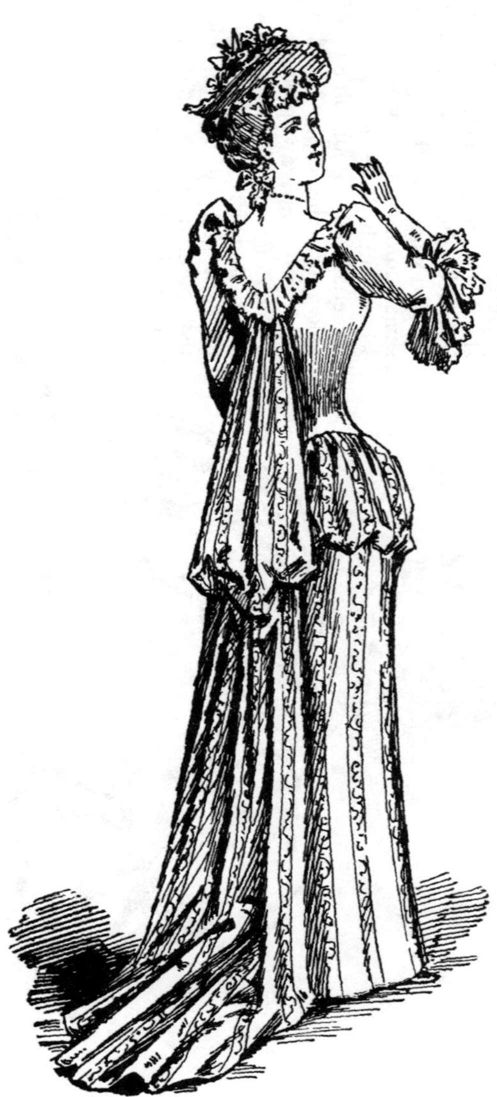

FIGURE No. 56.—WATTEAU COSTUME.

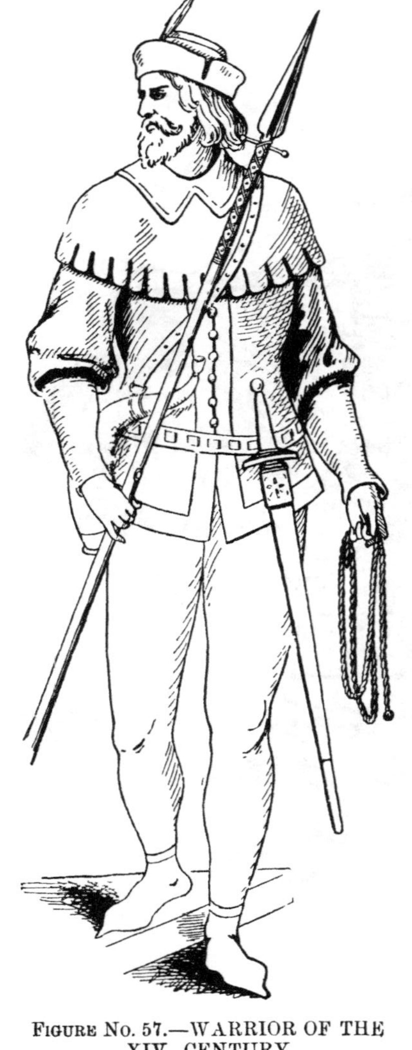

FIGURE No. 57.—WARRIOR OF THE XIV. CENTURY.

FIGURE NO. 57.—WARRIOR OF THE XIV. CENTURY.—Long silk tights of tan color, a tan-colored slashed cape, a green doublet trimmed with white, and a brown felt hat and leather buskins comprise the important details of this costume. The girdle is of gilt and a clarion is suspended from the breast. A spear, sword and sling complete the *tout ensemble*.

FIGURE NO. 58.—EARLY ENGLISH COSTUME.—Pale-gray dress brocaded with pink. Bodice in cuirass shape, low in the neck and with the skirt gathered and sewed to its lower edge under a girdle-band of jeweled passementerie. Passementerie chatelaine-pocket attached to belt. Sleeves tight from shoulder to elbow, and falling from the elbow in long narrow sections that are lined with pink. Under-sleeves of gray silk made tight and falling over the hand. Head-dress of gray silk; gray silk stockings and red, pointed slippers.

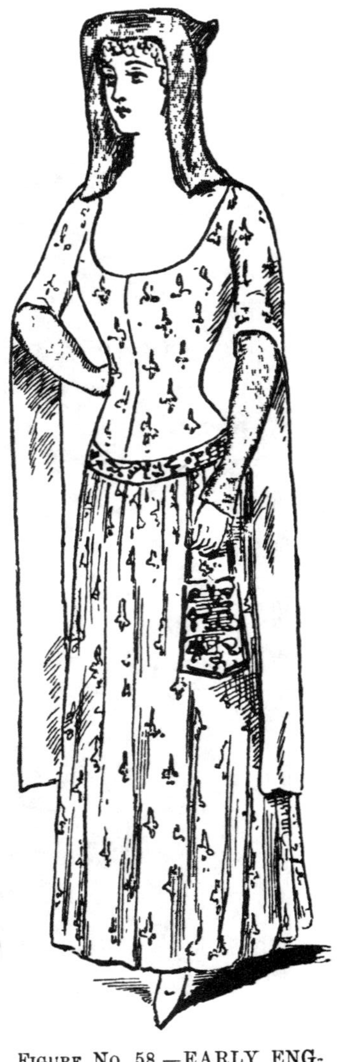

FIGURE No 58.—EARLY ENGLISH COSTUME.

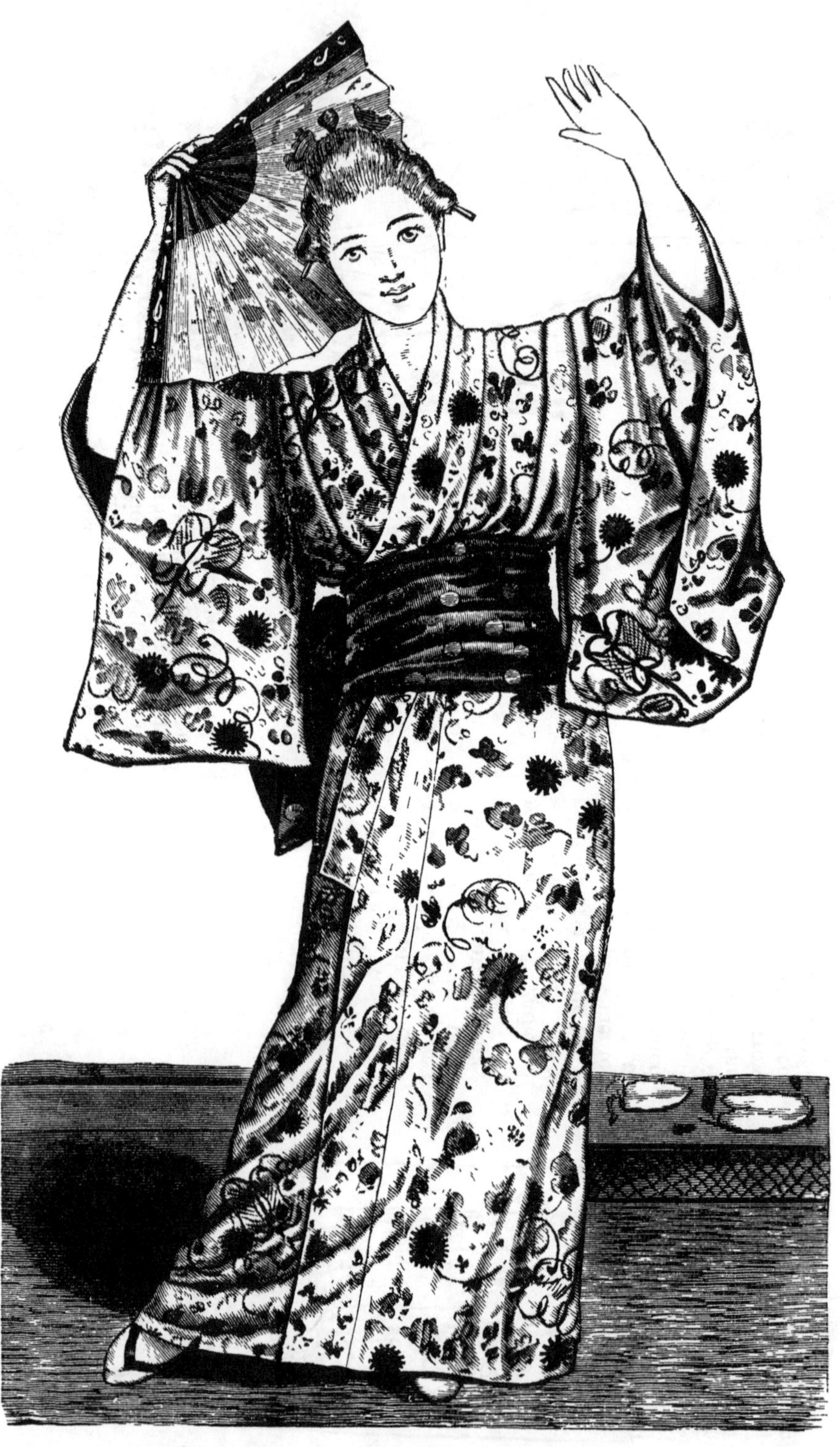

FIGURE No. 59.—JAPANESE KIMONO COSTUME.

(For description see next page.)

FIGURE No. 59.—JAPANESE KIMONO COSTUME. —This costume may be made of sateen or silk that is figured or brocaded in a Japanese design. A back view of it may be seen on page 29. The sash is of polka-dotted silk tied in a huge bow at the back. The gown should be worn over two or three soft silk petticoats or a fine cambric one.

FIGURE No. 60—JAPANESE GENTLEMAN.—The kimono and a loose blouse of China silk comprise this costume. A smooth dark face and closely cut hair render the effect of the costume much more illusive than a fair, bearded face. Japanese shoes should be worn, and white stockings. Sateen is a good substitute for silk in making this costume, and less expensive.

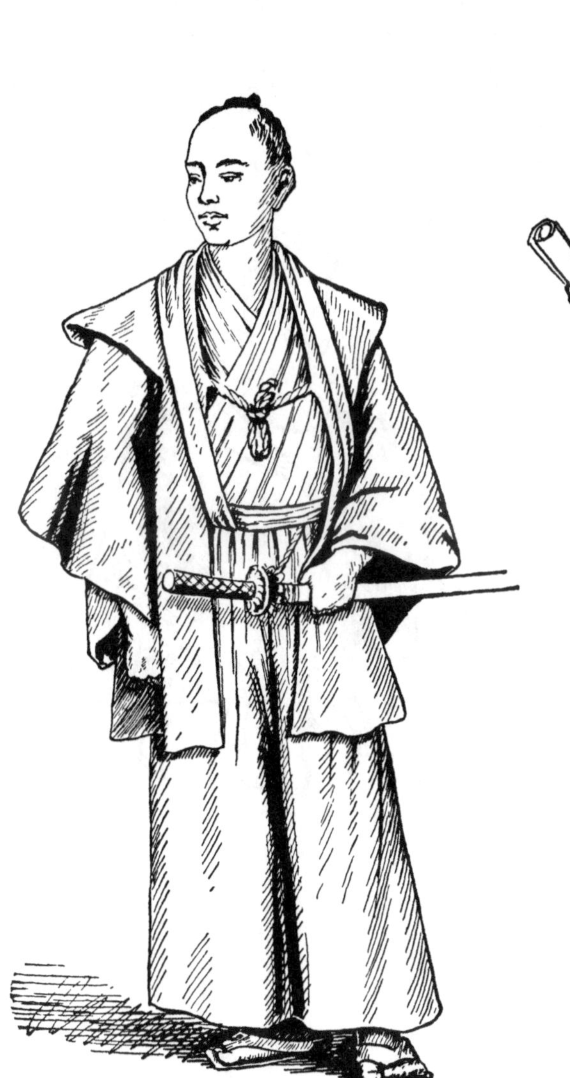

FIGURE No. 60.—JAPANESE GENTLEMAN.

FIGURE No. 61.—JAPANESE STUDENT.—This costume may be made of flowered or figured silk or sateen, or of China silk or Japanese or other Oriental stuffs. The cap may be made of silk or satin or of glazed paper, and decorated with gilt paper or braid. A Japanese fan or parasol, and Japanese shoes should complete the costume.

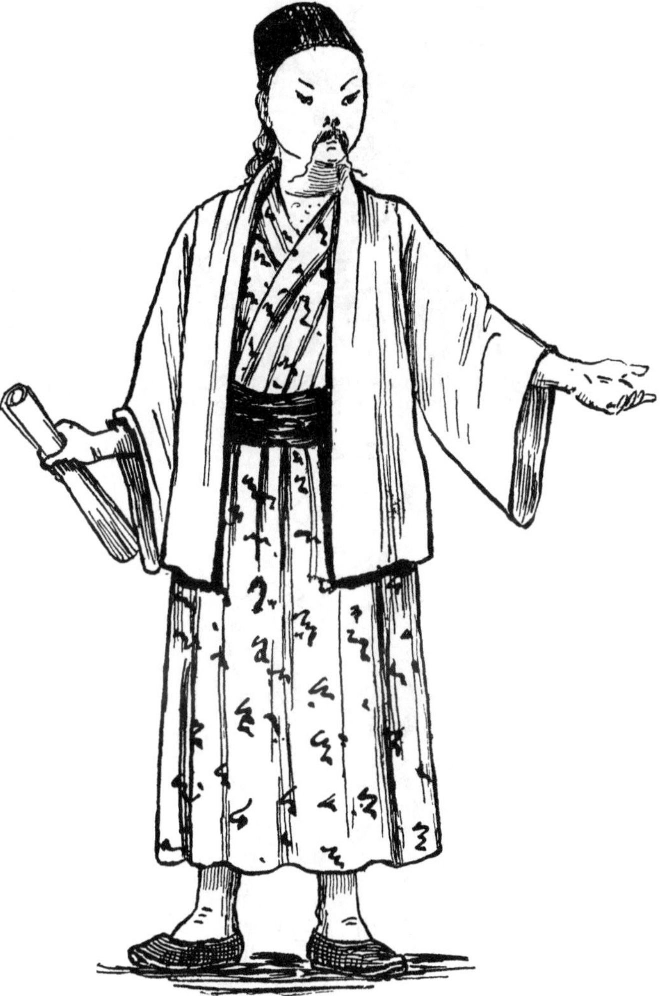

FIGURE No. 61.—JAPANESE STUDENT.

FIGURE No. 62.—ORANGE GIRL. (For illustration see next page.)—Skirt, back of waist, and puffed sleeves of red woolen goods. Bodice-front of black velvet laced over a white mull fichu. Apron of flowered cambric; head-dress formed of a red-and-white striped wool kerchief arranged in Italian style. Bracelets of gold; necklace of pearl.

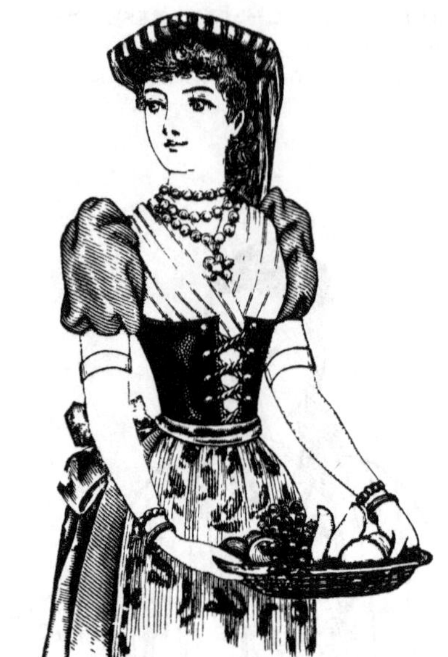

FIGURE No. 62.—ORANGE GIRL.
(For description see preceding page.)

FIGURE No. 63.—LADY OF THE XVI. CENTURY.—The skirt of this costume is of pale yellow striped with black and trimmed at the bottom with a broad band of dull purple. The apron is of dull red broidered with green. The waist and puffed sleeves are of a deep, greenish blue, and the lower sleeve is of yellow broidered with black. The girdle is also of yellow, and the cap is white. The bag is of deep-red satin trimmed with yellow, and is suspended by a red ribbon ornamented with gilt beads. A white ruff is about the neck and wrists, and the beads are of amber.

FIGURE No. 64.—XVI. CENTURY COURTIER. This costume is made entirely of black and is worn with black tights. The ruff at the neck and the finish at the wrists are both white. It is frequently used for the character of Mephistopheles, in which event the costume, cap, tights and foot-gear are of bright scarlet, two long quill feathers are fastened to the cap, and the white ruff and wrist decorations are ommitted.

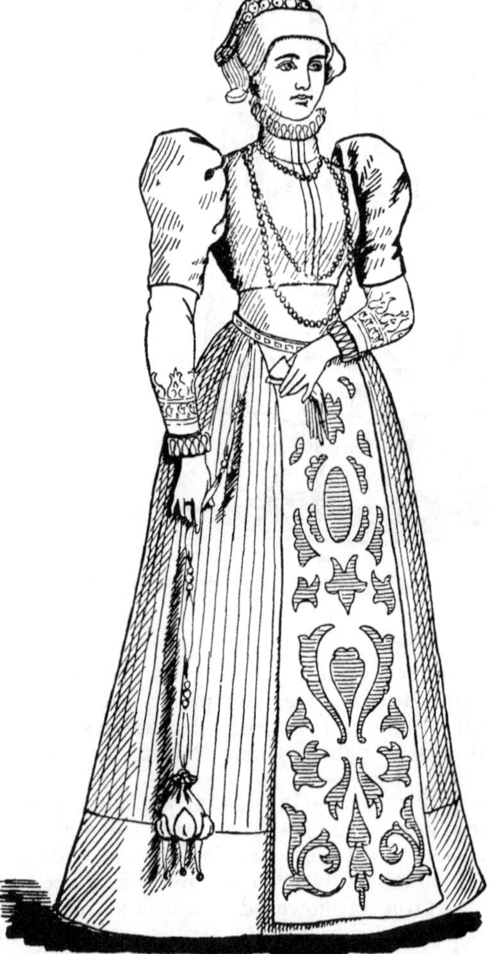

FIGURE No. 63.—LADY OF THE XVI CENTURY.

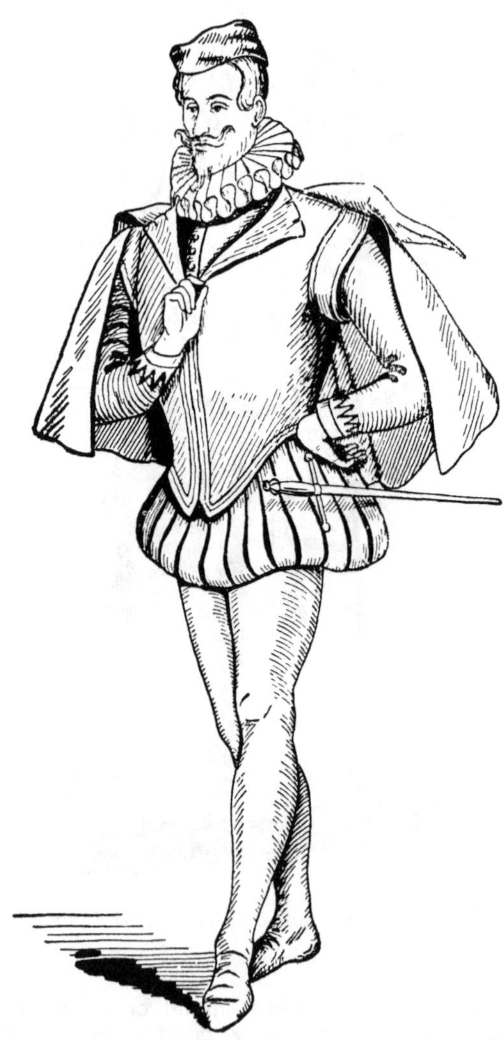

FIGURE No. 64.—XVI. CENTURY COURTIER.

FIGURE NO. 65.—EMPIRE COSTUME.—Short-waisted gown of soft cashmere or silk trimmed with a full frill of deep lace around the low neck. Full puffed sleeves completed with lace frills. Ribbon belt with a full bow at the left side. Hair dressed high and may be powdered.

FIGURE NO. 66.—ABBÉ (LOUIS XIV.)—Black satin coat and cape, with black velvet cravat. Black satin trousers, black silk stockings and black patent-leather shoes with silver buckles. Shirt of white mull or cambric, with frills at the wrists. Broad-brimmed black hat. Soft leather gloves.

FIGURE NO. 67.—POLISH CAVALIER.—The blouse to this costume is of white silk or cashmere, closely gathered at the top. Over this is worn a frock of lavender or pale-blue satin with double sleeves and a vest. The latter and the close sleeves are red satin embroidered with gold. The loose sleeves of the frock are lined with yellow silk and, like other parts of the garment, are decorated with gold embroidery and bands of white fur. The breeches are of red satin, the stockings lavender or blue, and the wrinkled boots lined with fur. The cap is made of lavender or blue satin and yellow feathers.

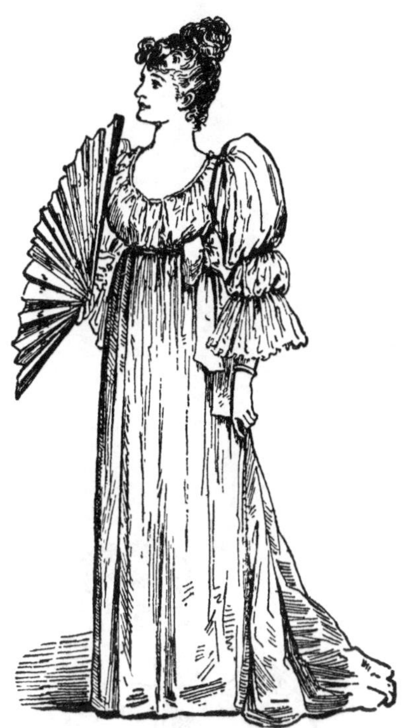

FIGURE NO. 65.—EMPIRE COSTUME.

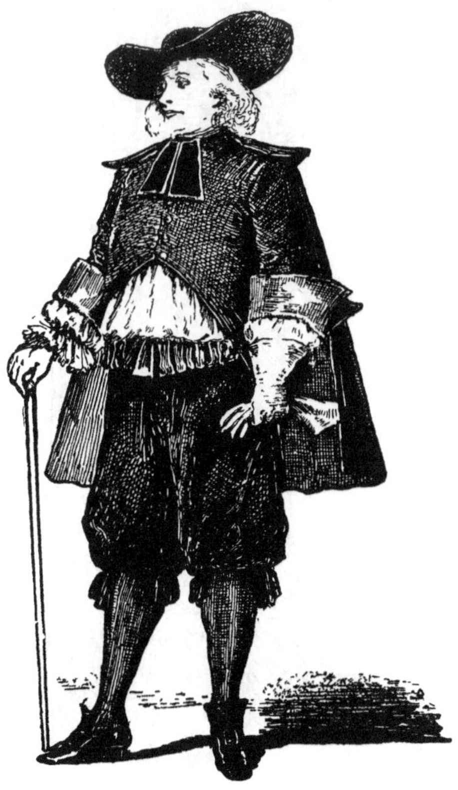

FIGURE NO. 66.—ABBÉ. (LOUIS XIV.)

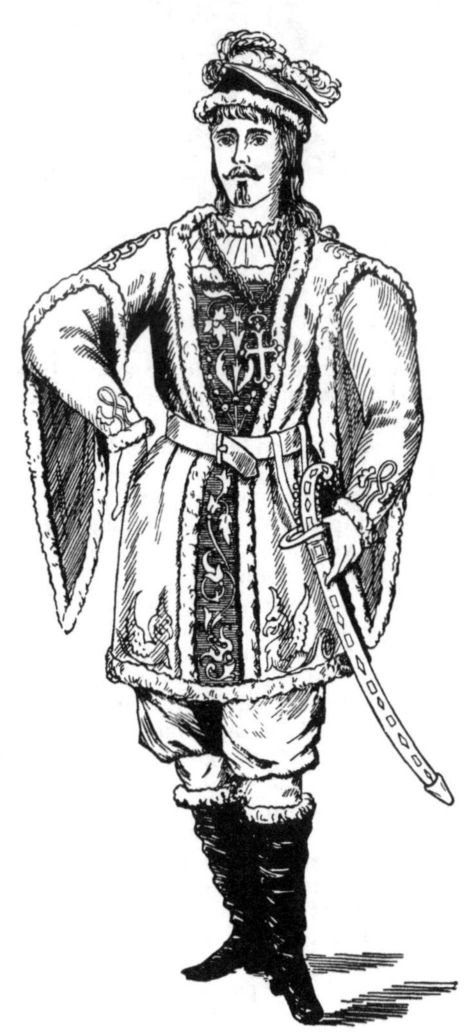

FIGURE NO. 67.—POLISH CAVALIER.

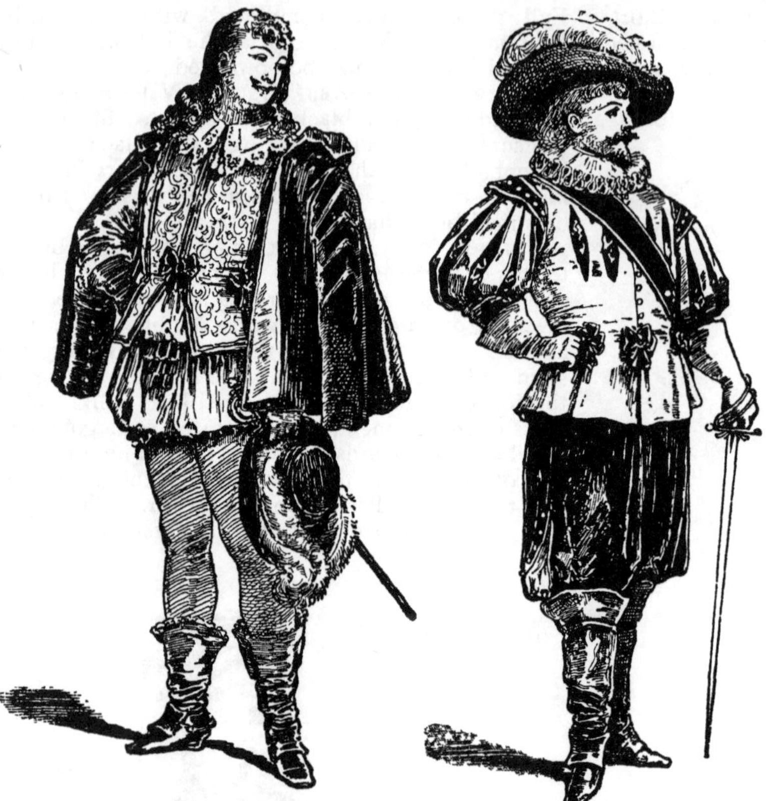

FIGURE No. 68.—DUTCH CAVALIER. FIGURE No 69—LANSQUENET. (LOUIS XIII.)

FIGURE No. 68.—DUTCH CAVALIER.—White full shirt of cambric or silk. Jacket of pale-blue satin embroidered with gold or silver, edged with gold or silver braid, and finished with ribbon bows and a linen collar edged with lace. Plain sleeves and full trunks of pale-blue satin or silk, gray hose and black top boots. Cloak of black velvet lined with yellow silk. Black velvet hat with long white plumes.

FIGURE No. 69.—LANSQUENET. (LOUIS XIII.)—Doublet of fawn-color slashed with red satin and completed with red bows, gilt braid and buttons. Sword-sash of red velvet bound with gilt braid. Full trousers of red satin, high-top boots of patent leather. Gray gauntlet-gloves; red velvet hat with gray plume. Full ruff of muslin about the neck.

FIGURE No. 70.—AMY ROBSART.—Costume of pale-pink plain and brocaded satin; the plain being used for the petticoat and tight sleeves, and the brocade for the waist and the sides and back of the skirt, and the over sleeves. Sleeve-puffs and frills of pale rose-tinted chiffon. Decorations of pearl passemnterie, fringe and embroidery, and an edging of pearl beads. Pointed cap also edged with beads.

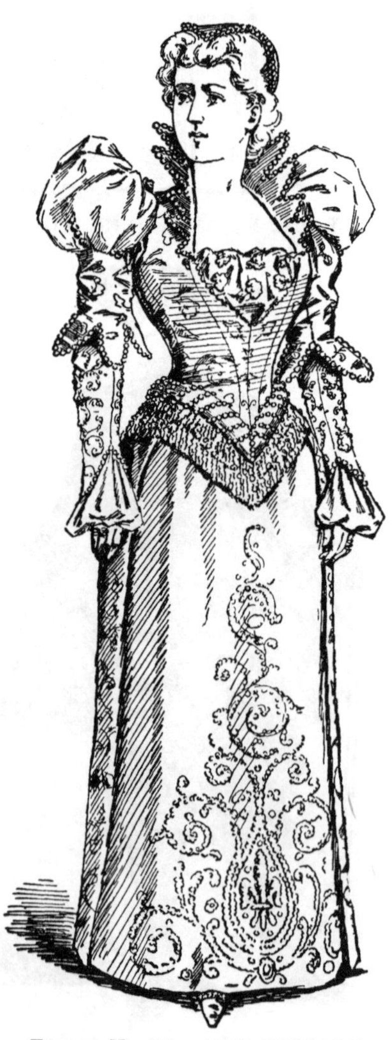

FIGURE No 70.—AMY ROBSART.

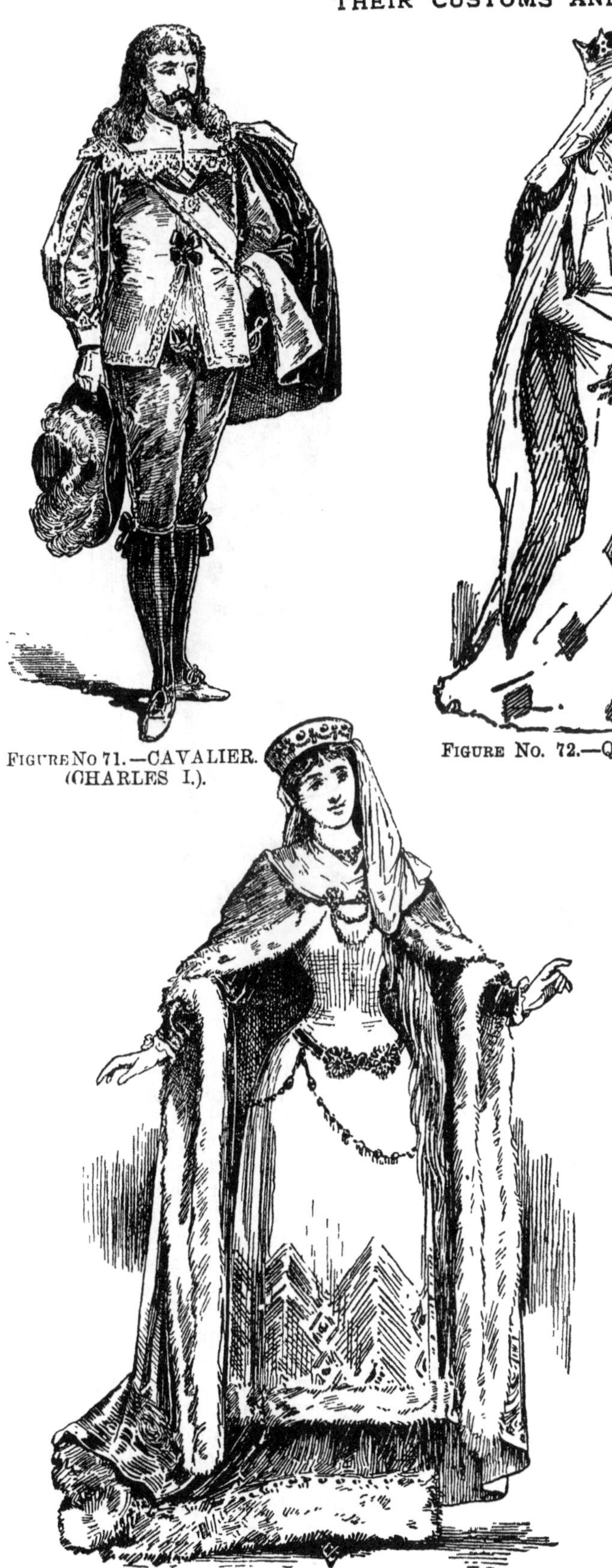

FIGURE No 71.—CAVALIER. (CHARLES I.).

FIGURE No. 72.—QUEEN OF DIAMONDS.

FIGURE No 73.—ROWENA.

FIGURE No. 71.—CAVALIER. (CHARLES I.)—Doublet and trousers of lavender satin ; shirt of white silk mull completed with a broad lace-trimmed collar. Doublet, sides of trousers, and satin sword-sash edged with silver lace. Sleeves slashed to show shirt sleeves, and completed with tiny silver buttons and lace-trimmed cuffs. Cape of Royal-purple velvet lined with silver-colored silk. Velvet hat with silver or lavender plume. Purple silk stockings and light-gray shoes with silver buckles. Silver garters fastened with ribbon bows. Blonde wig of long curly hair.

FIGURE No. 72.—QUEEN OF DIAMONDS.—Long close robe of white cotton, woolen, silk or satin material, on which are sewn or pasted large diamond-shaped sections of red or black fabric or paper. Long mantle of white Canton flannel lined with red and bordered with red or black diamonds. Crown of gilt paper cut in diamond-points and worn over a white gauze veil. Sceptre of gilt.

FIGURE No. 73.—ROWENA.—Over-gown and mantle of red satin trimmed with white, real or imitation fur to represent ermine; soft collar of white silk at neck of mantle. Under-gown of purple trimmed with the fur. Gilt crown studded with jewels and worn over a gauze veil. Golden chains, girdle and jeweled ornaments complete the *tout ensemble.*

In selecting the colors for this costume the complexion of the wearer and individual taste must govern the choice.

FIGURE NO. 74.—JOAN OF ARC.—Skirt and waist of blue satin embroidered with silver in *fleur de lys;* apparently worn over armor. Sleeves of armor may be imitated with pasteboard covered with silver, or gilt and bronze paper. Long loose gloves of soft leather. Leather belt and sword-strap; sword in silver scabbard. Bronze hose and pointed soft leather shoes.

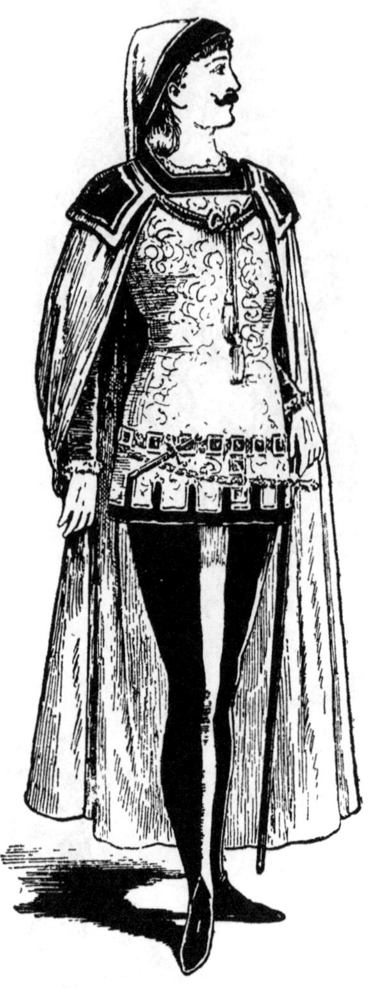

FIGURE NO. 75.—TEMPLAR.

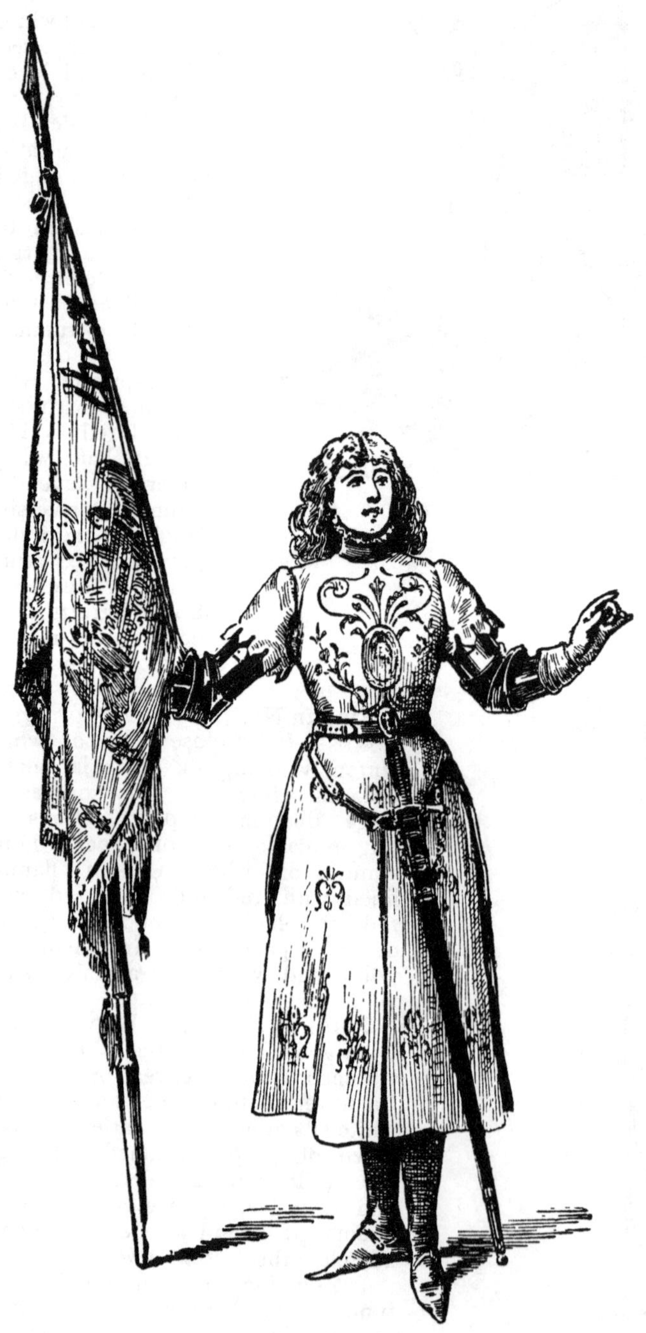

FIGURE NO. 74.—JOAN OF ARC.

FIGURE NO. 75.—TEMPLAR.—This handsome costume is composed of a close doublet closing at the side and made of yellow satin brocaded with silver. It is slashed at the bottom, bound with silver braid and underlaid with black satin. A black satin band edged with silver is about the neck, and a jeweled girdle and a silver sword-chain are about the hips. The hood and mantle are of a deeper yellow than the doublet, which has plain sleeves, and are trimmed with the black satin and silver braid. Silver cord and tassels secure the cape. Black and yellow tights and black pointed shoes complete the costume. Red and black is a favorite combination for this costume.

FIGURE NO. 76.—LADY OF THE TUDOR PERIOD.—Black and white satin, with the white satin handsomely decorated with gold braid, were used in making this costume. The engraving clearly depicts the details of the combination and the style of the costume, and no special description of its various portions is necessary. Yellow, pale-blue, pink or lavender satin may be used in place of the white, and red, blue, brown or purple satin in place of the black.

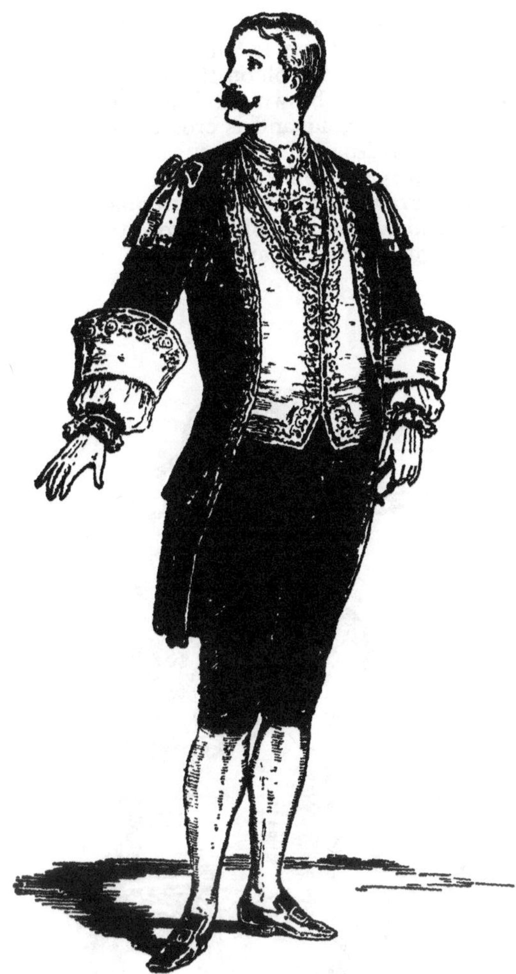

FIGURE NO. 77.—LORD CHESTERFIELD.

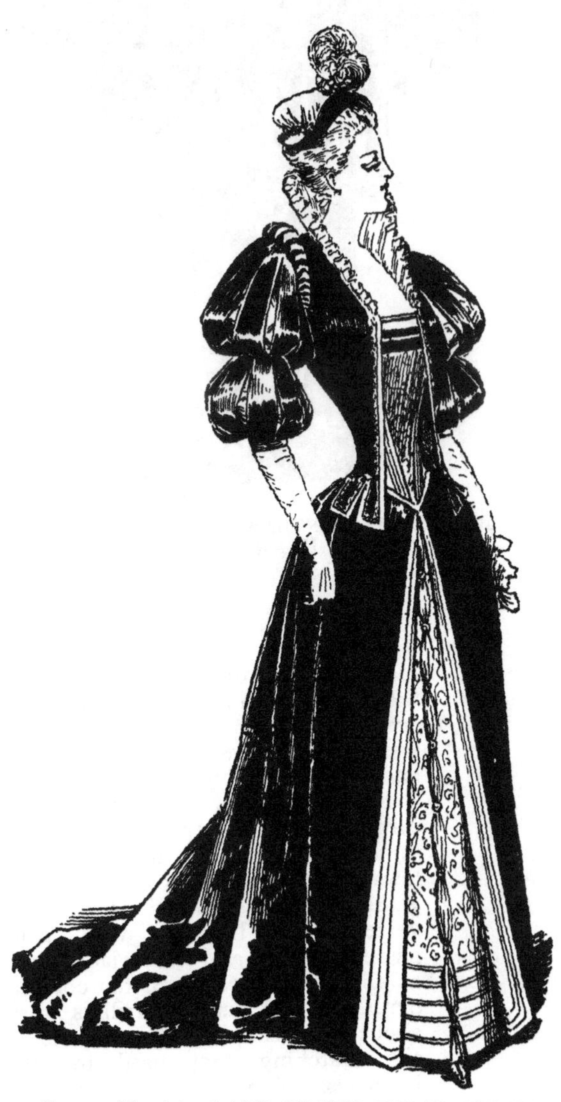

FIGURE NO. 76.—LADY OF THE TUDOR PERIOD

FIGURE NO. 77.—LORD CHESTERFIELD.—Coat and breeches of black satin; coat trimmed with gold passementerie and white bows. Sleeves faced with white and, like the white satin vest, trimmed with gold passementerie. White silk shirt with cravat and ruffles of white lace. White silk stockings, and black patent-leather shoes with gold or silver, or paste buckles. Any pale tint of satin may be used in place of the white for this costume, pale-blue, lavender, buff, drab or Nile-green being especially pretty when in combination with black or plum color

FIGURE NO. 78.—FRENCH GENERAL.—This costume is suitable for the character of Napoleon Bonaparte. The coat is of brown cloth heavily trimmed with gold, and is crossed by a gold sword-band, while a sash of red, white and blue encircles the waist. Brown hat trimmed with gold braid and a tiny tri-colored rosette. White wool breeches and gold belt; black gold-trimmed boots complete the lower portion of this military costume. A white shirt and black satin cravat are worn under the coat and a white or buff vest.

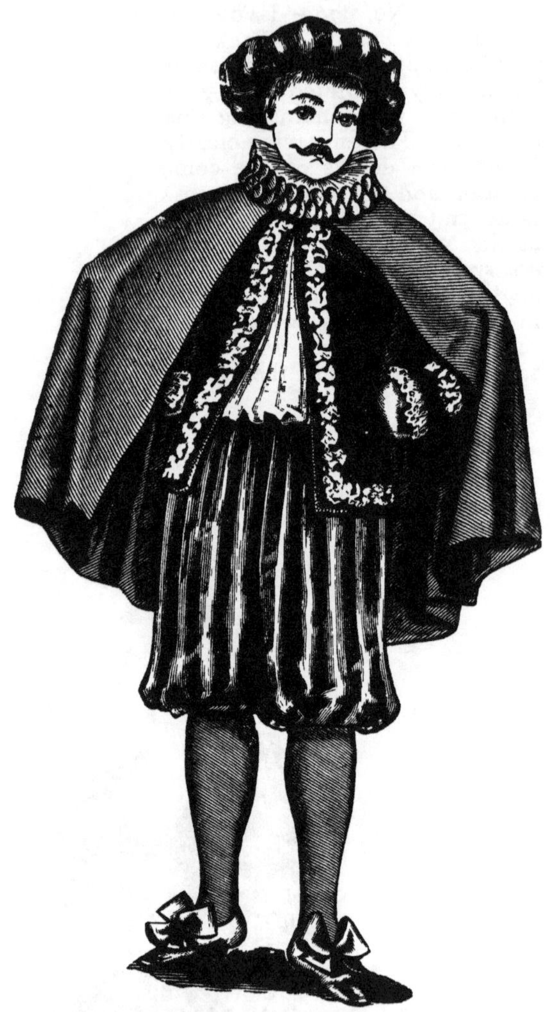

FIGURE NO. 79.—GENTLEMAN OF THE TIME OF HENRI II.

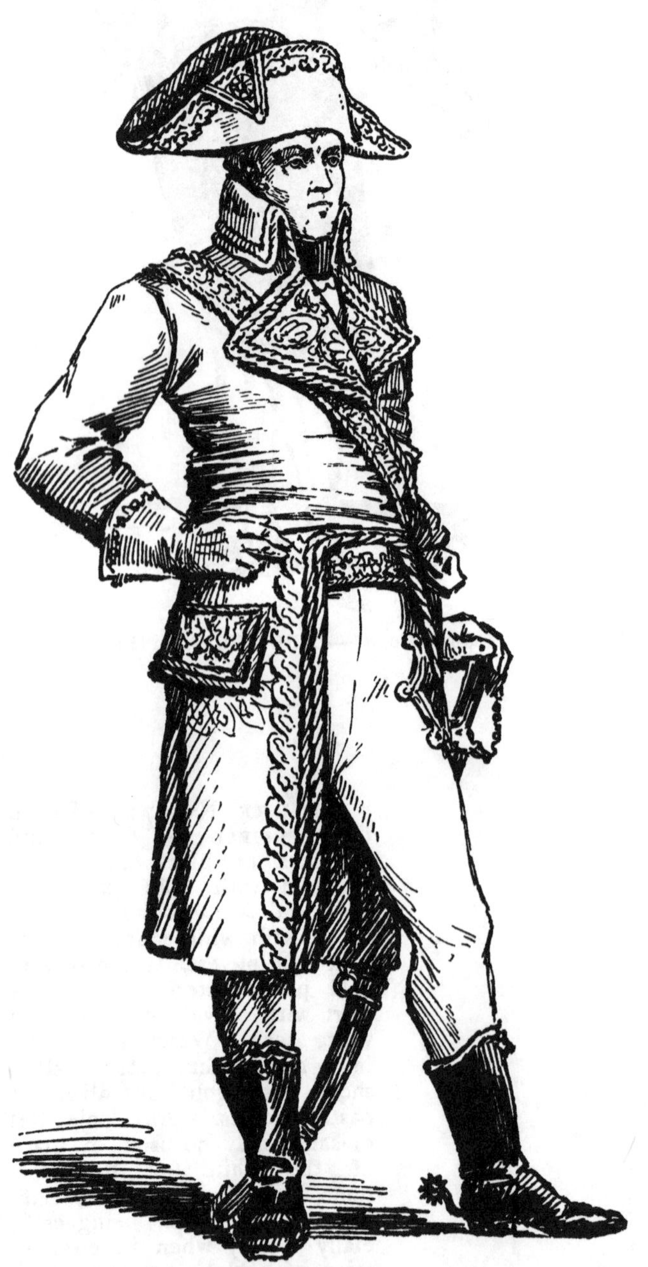

FIGURE NO. 78.—FRENCH GENERAL.

FIGURE NO. 79.—GENTLEMAN OF THE TIME OF HENRI II.—The costume represented is made as follows: knee-breeches of black silk; gathered white silk blouse; black velvet jacket trimmed with gold passementerie, and with lace frills at the wrists; cape of tan-colored cloth. A stiff cambric frill is worn about the neck, and the cap is of silk matching that used for the breeches. The hose are of tan silk; and the low-cut shoes are of tan suéde decorated with tan ribbon bows.

FIGURES NOS. 80 AND 81. —REVOLUTIONARY COSTUME.— These two engravings show a side and back view of the same costume made up in different colors. Figure No. 80 represents it with a black satin coat with a white satin vest and knee-breeches, white stockings and black buckle-shoes; lace frills and cravat. Figure No. 81 shows the coat as made of brocaded gray satin. Any pretty rich tint may be selected for the coat, either in plain or brocaded goods. Silver buttons are generally used. Sometimes the vest and breeches are made of pale-blue satin, or of any pretty pale tint preferred. The stockings may be of the tint of the vest and breeches.

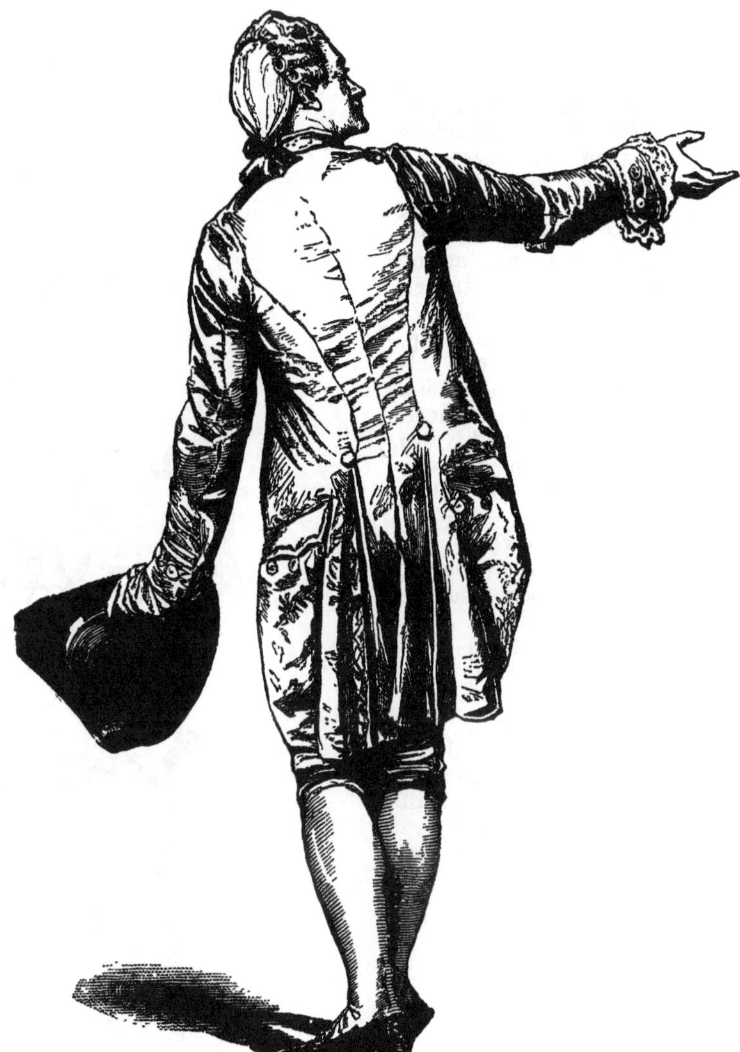

FIGURE No. 81.—REVOLUTIONARY COSTUME.

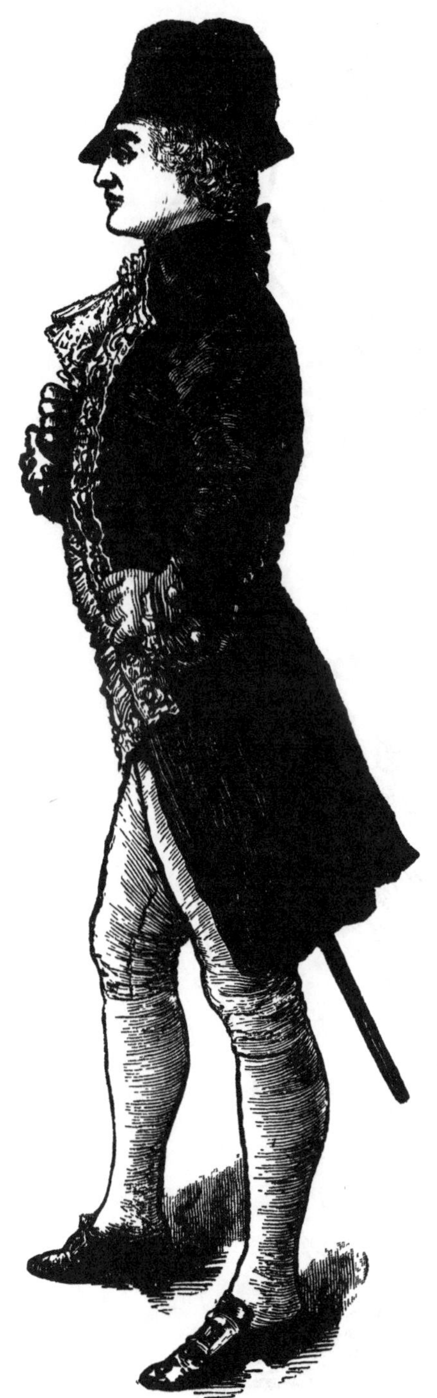

FIGURE No. 80.—REVOLUTIONARY COSTUME.

FIGURE NO. 82.—HAMLET.—Doublet of black velvet cut in pointed tabs around the bottom and edged with jet beads; opens low on the breast and is faced with silk and carelessly turned back over a white muslin shirt also open at the throat and turned back. The sleeves are full at the top, close below the elbows and turned back in cuffs that are faced with silk and also edged with beads. Sword-belt of velvet to which is also attached a velvet pouch edged with beads. Long black mantle of satin lined with silk and edged with beads, and hung from the shoulders by a heavy silk cord with tasseled ends. Black silk tights and pointed black shoes. A small round black velvet cap may be worn if desired.

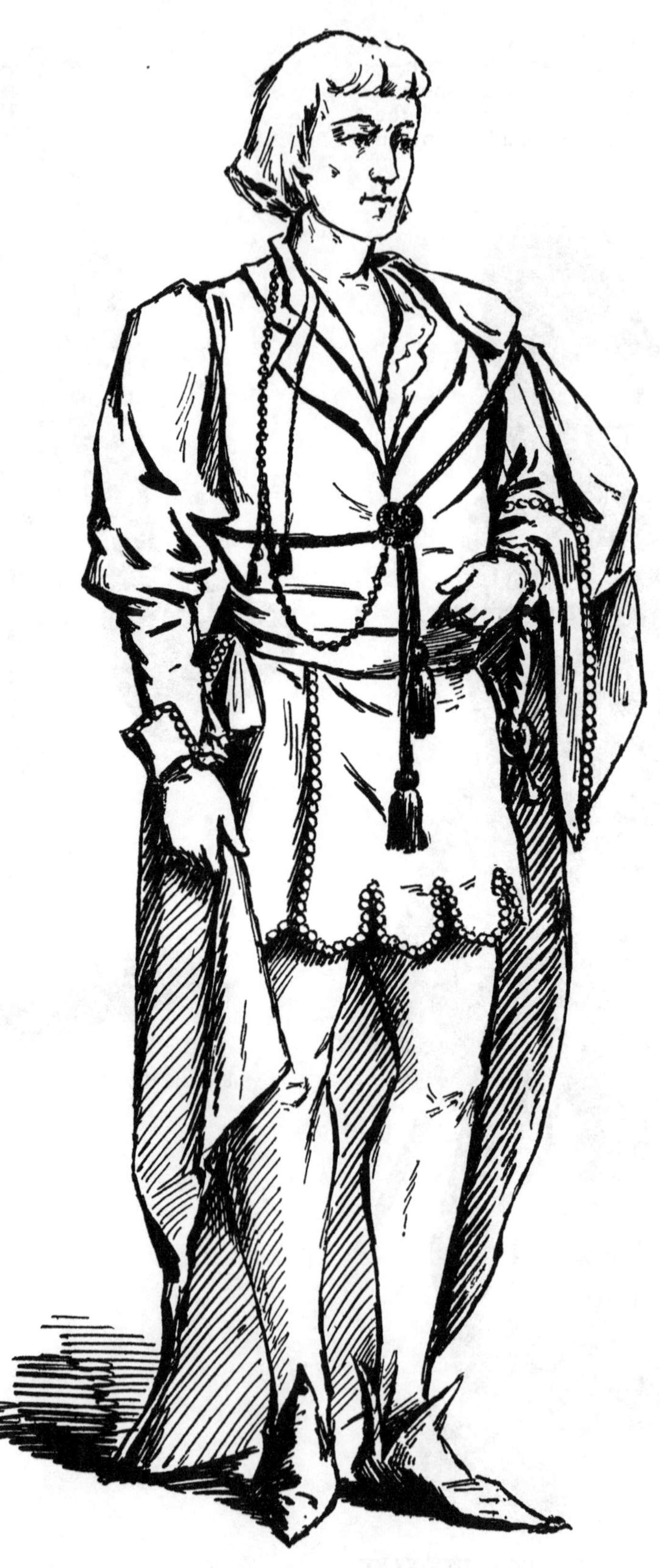

FIGURE NO. 82.—HAMLET.

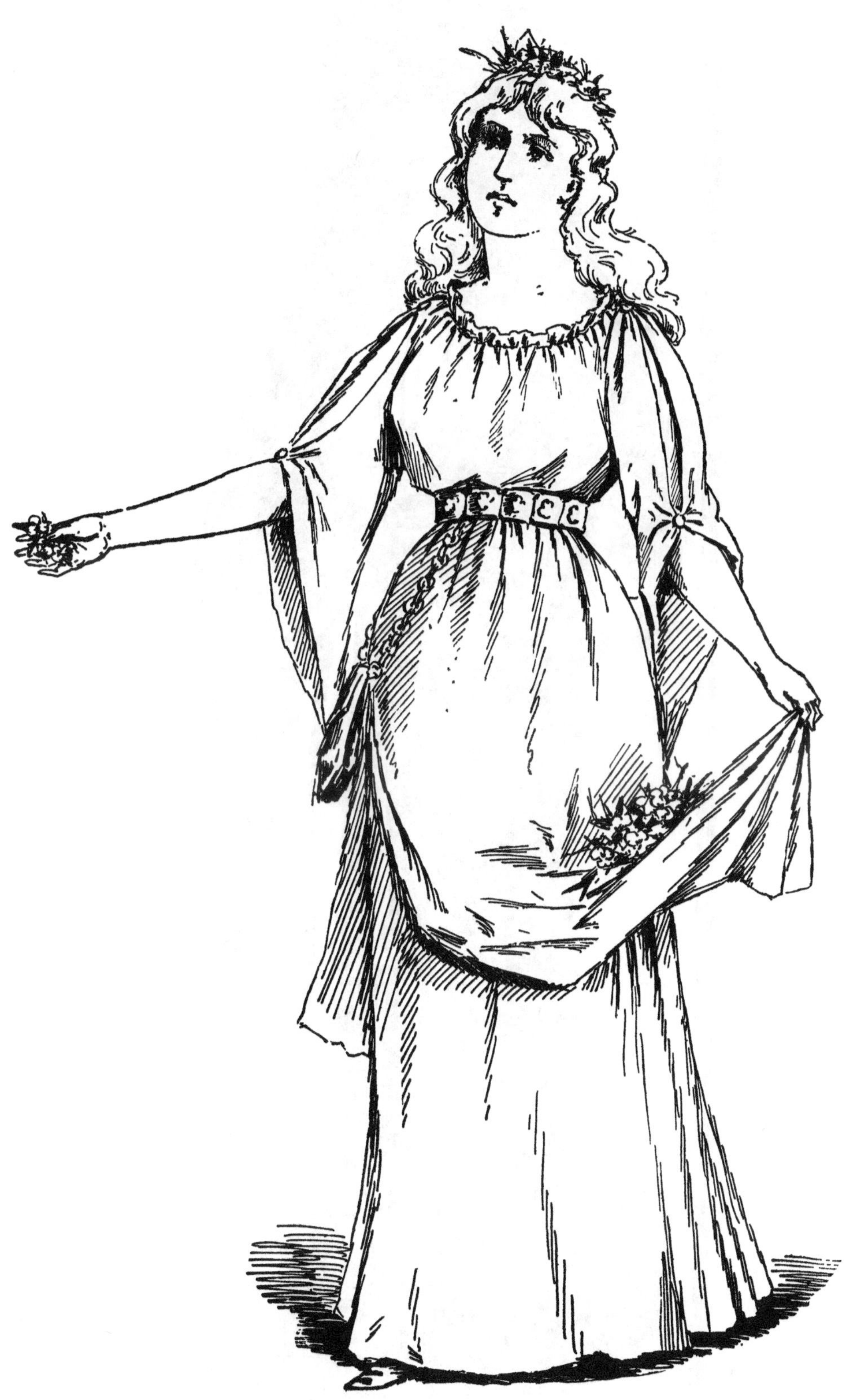

FIGURE No. 83.—OPHELIA.

FIGURE No. 83. — OPHELIA. — This is a very simple costume to arrange, as may be seen by an inspection of the engraving which fully portrays it. The gown is made of some soft white stuff, and is girdled with a jewelled gold band which also supports a pouch or bag at the right side. In her drapery Ophelia carries rosemary and pansies; while her hair, which is loose and flowing, is wreathed with field blossoms and wheat.

FIGURE No. 84.—CLEOPATRA COSTUME. (Also suitable for an Eastern Princess.)—Robe of ivory Bengaline silk, embroidered around the edges and the hem of the skirt with lotus blossoms and a band in coral-tinted silk. Long mantle of coral crépon ornamented to correspond, and with the ends caught up by a pale-blue girdle ornamented with sparkling gems. Necklace of diamonds and turquoises. Hair flowing and crowned with a wealth of red roses. Scepter imitating a reed.

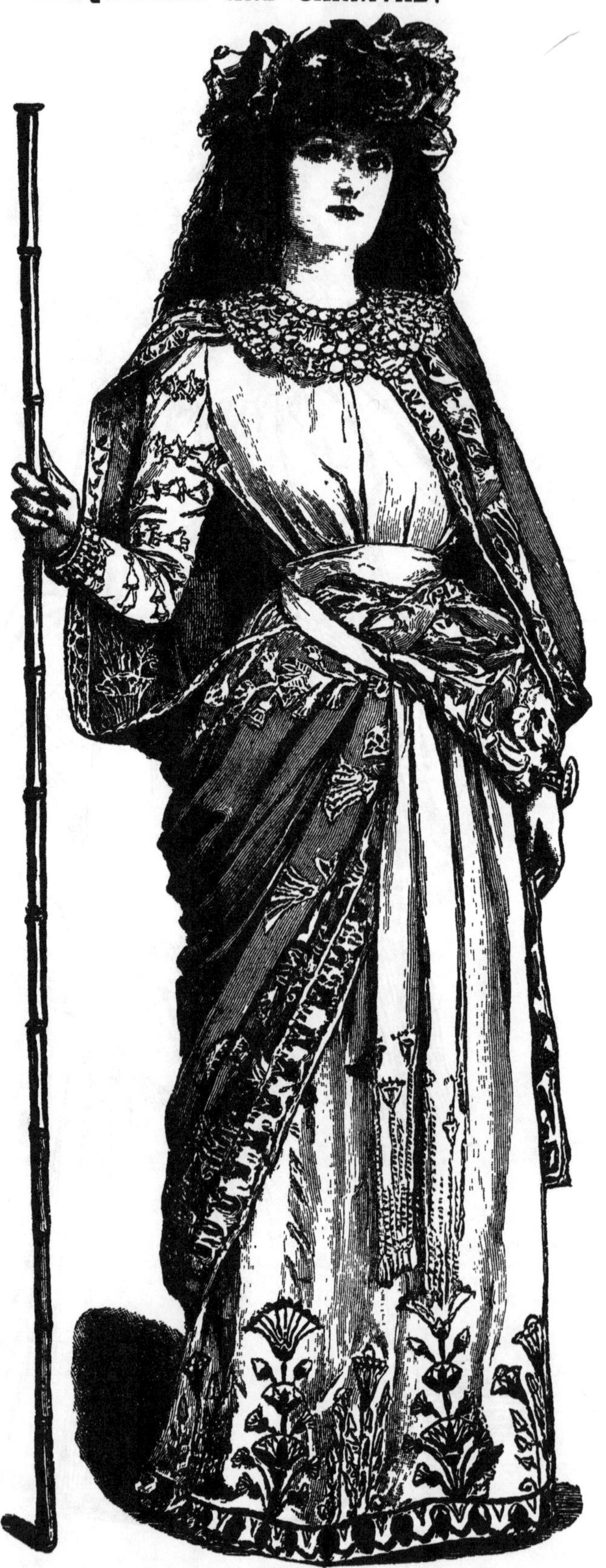

FIGURE No. 84.—CLEOPATRA COSTUME. (Worn by Mrs. Potter.)

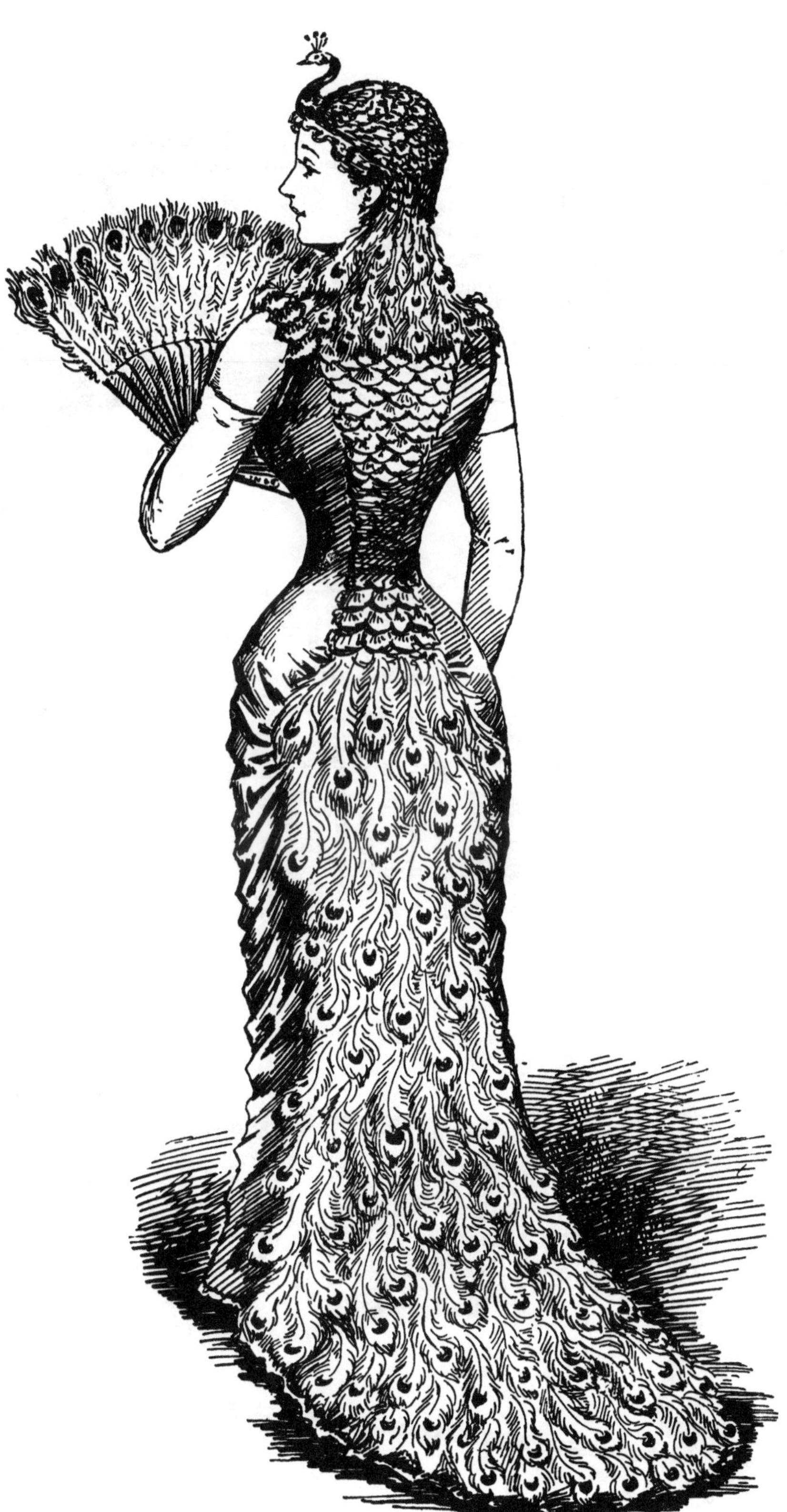

FIGURE NO. 85.—PEACOCK COSTUME.

FIGURE NO. 85.—PEACOCK COSTUME.—This gown is made in Princess style from bronze-green satin and is handsomely draped across the front. The train is covered with real peacock feathers sewed on from the hem to the hips. From the shoulders to the hips feather-tips are arranged as seen in the picture, while a similar decoration is applied in a point on the front of the waist. The neck is low, in pompadour shape, and an emerald and sapphire necklace falls over the bust. The head-dress is composed of feathers sewed to a close cap as illustrated, with a peacock's head in front. A peacock-feather fan and peacock-green gloves complete the costume.

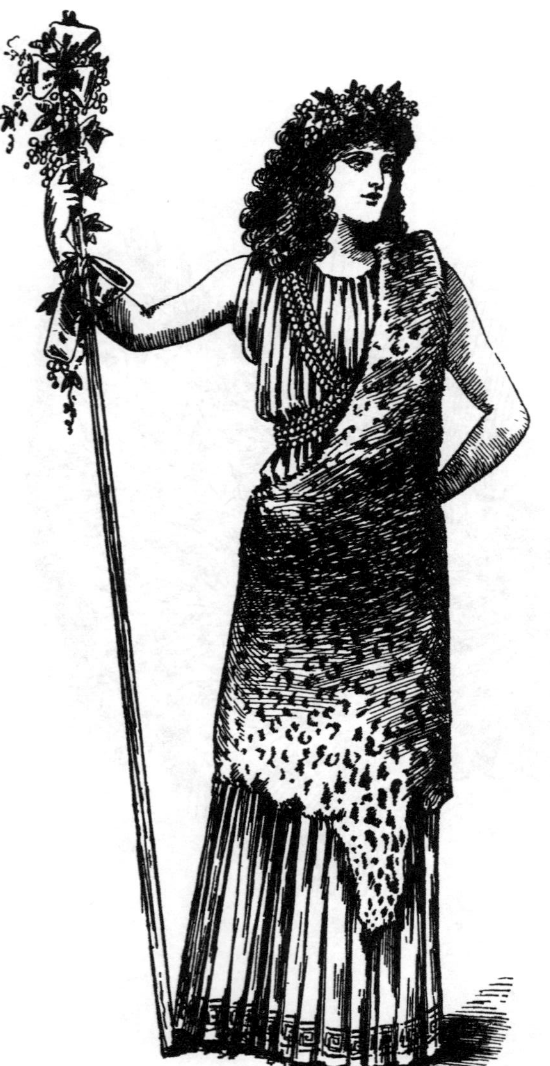

FIGURE No. 86.—BACCHANTE.

FIGURE No. 86.—BACCHANTE.—This is a very effective costume, and one not difficult to make. The dress is of yellow silk and is finished at the foot with an embroidered Grecian border. Bands of gold-beads are used to confine the upper portion of the gown to the figure, and a leopard skin is draped across the front from the left shoulder. The hair is left loose and flowing and is crowned with a wreath of grapes and vine-leaves. The long pole is also garlanded with fruit and foliage as seen in the picture. A less expensive fabric may be used for the gown, and gilt bands substituted for those of gold beads.

FIGURE No. 87.—NUN.—Gown and apron of rough gray goods plainly hemmed at the edges. Cap with deep cape of white linen, silk or fine wool goods falling in front and closed at the back. Hood of black cashmere, serge, frieze or nun's veiling lined with white. Rosary of wooden beads. Book of loose manuscripts on religious subjects. This costume may also be worn as a domino.

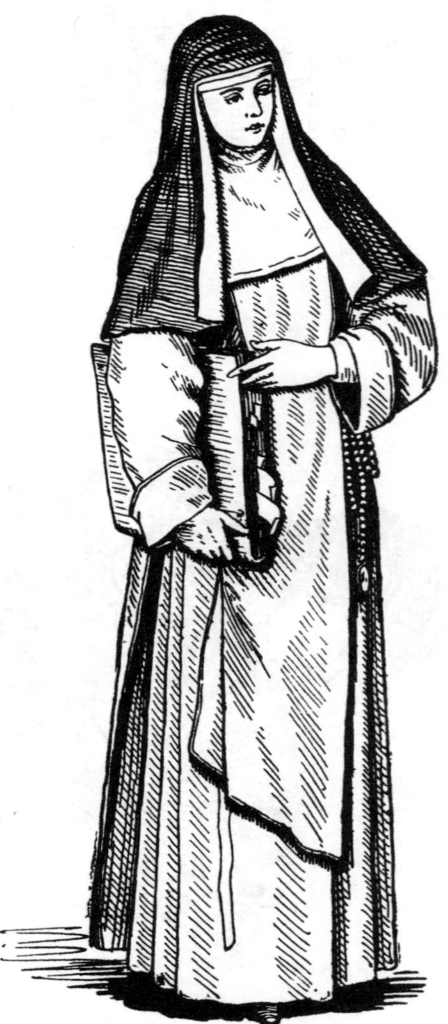

FIGURE No. 87.—NUN.

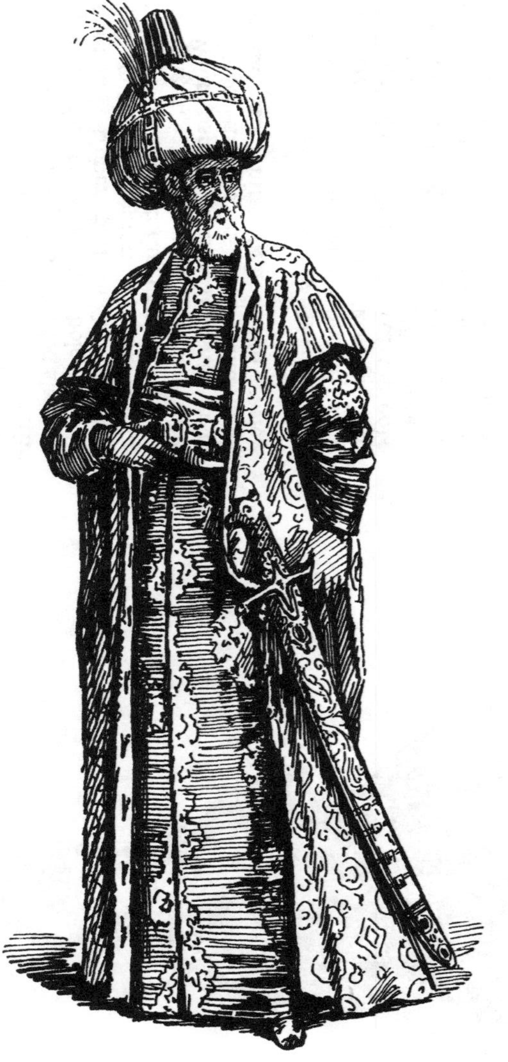

FIGURE No. 88.—TURK.

FIGURE No. 88.—TURK.—Long loose robe of brocaded green fabric held in at the waist by a pale-magenta sash and a jeweled girdle. Loose over-gown of a brocaded dull-orange color, with half sleeves; gown lined with soft white fabric resembling fur. Immense turban of white gauze mounted on a frame and completed with a red feather aigrette and a golden top and chain-ornaments. Huge Turkish sword suspended from sash by red, silken, tasselled cord.

FIGURE No. 89.—SPANISH TOREADOR.—White muslin shirt; dull-brown breeches trimmed with gold braid; yellow garters, brown stockings and black shoes. Red velvet jacket handsomely ornamented with gold; striped sash of bright colors over a vest of blue cloth. Mantle or cape of brown cloth, and hat to match in color, with a red fez or pompon. Red silk neck-tie.

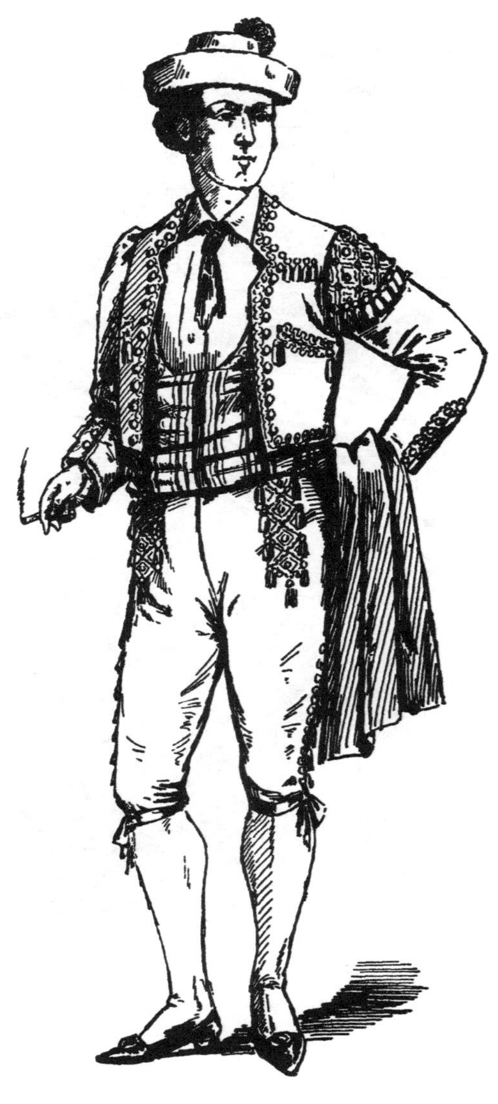

FIGURE No. 89.—SPANISH TOREADOR.

FIGURE NO. 90.—QUEEN AND PAGES.—Gown of Royal-purple silk trimmed with gold braid and imitation gems. Puffed sleeves of purple to elbow; white silk below, with lace at wrists. Upper part of bodice and collar of gilt passementerie. Long, white mantle trimmed with imitation ermine, carried by two pages. Gilt crown studded with jewels. White ostrich feather fan with gold handle. Pages dressed in scarlet and gold doublets and hats, white silk hose and scarlet slippers.

FIGURE NO. 91.—LADY IN WAITING.—Under dress of pale-blue satin trimmed with silver passementerie and white lace; girdled with a silver band. Over dress of tan-colored brocade trimmed with golden-brown velvet and bronze beads. Head-dress of the brocade and velvet and the bronze beads. The over-gown may be cut with or without a train as desired.

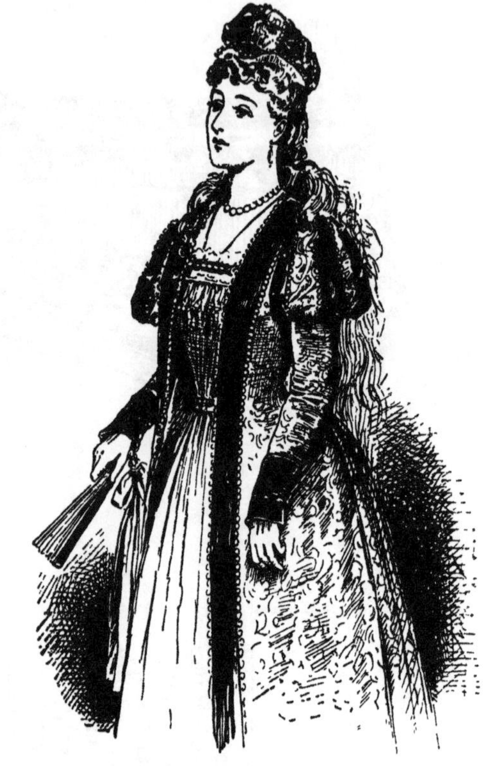

FIGURE NO. 91.—LADY IN WAITING.

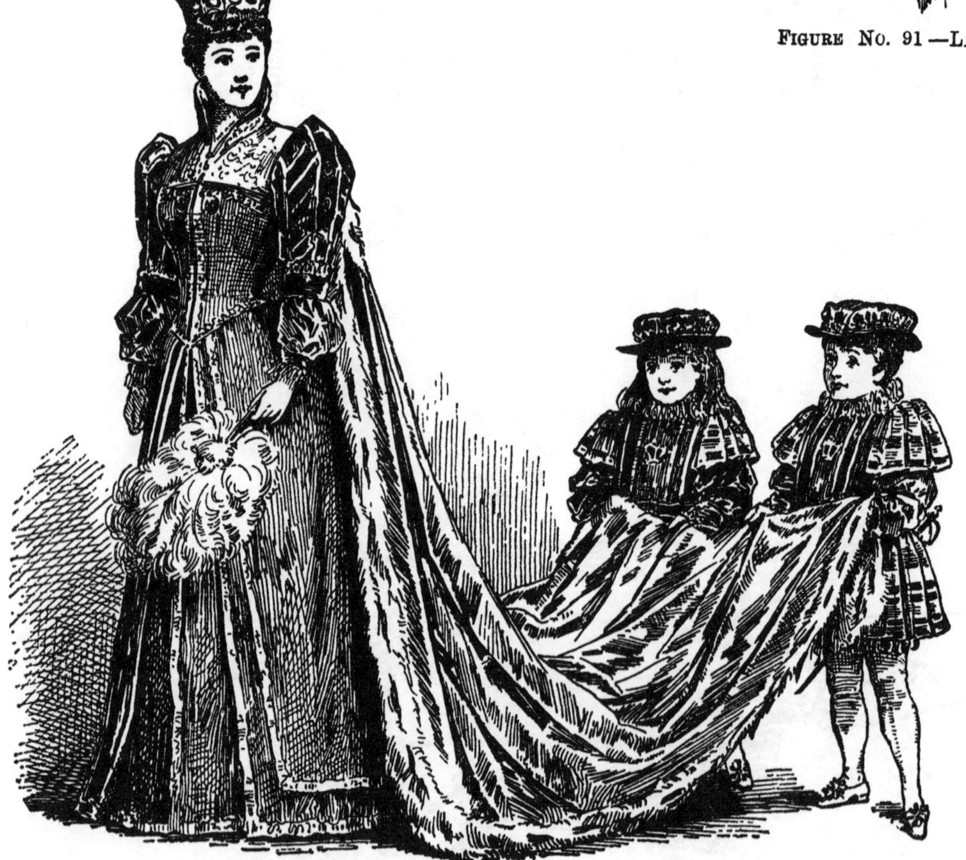

FIGURE NO. 90.—QUEEN AND PAGES.

FIGURE No. 93.—QUEEN KATHERINE.—Under-robe of silver brocade held in to the figure by a jeweled girdle or band. Sleeves of white silk mull, banded with jeweled passementerie. Trained over-robe of yellow satin decorated with jeweled passementerie; heavy jeweled band at the neck of the over-robe. Crown of gold and jewels; and hair wound with a golden cord.

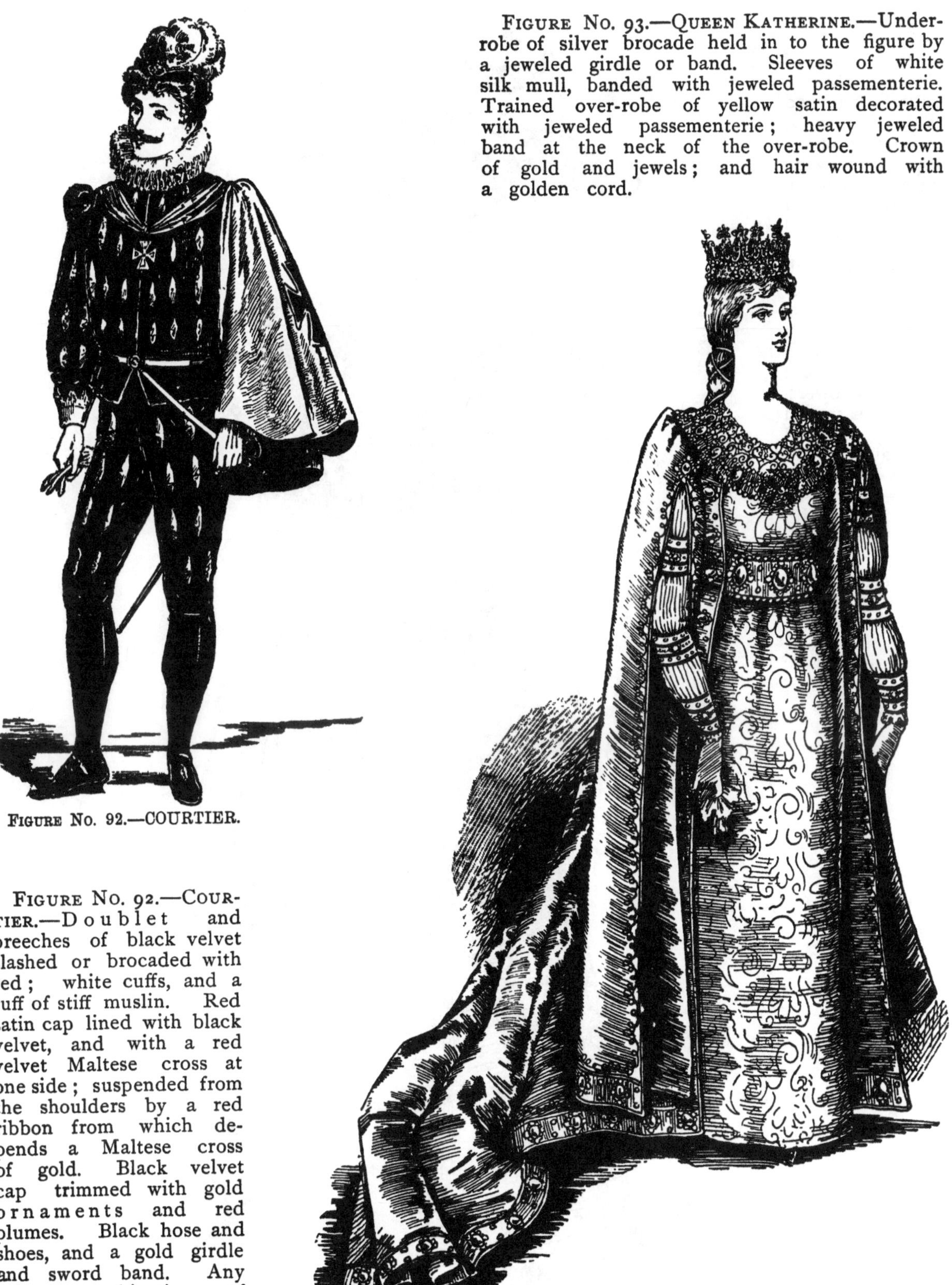

FIGURE No. 92.—COURTIER.

FIGURE No. 93.—QUEEN KATHERINE.

FIGURE No. 92.—COURTIER.—Doublet and breeches of black velvet slashed or brocaded with red; white cuffs, and a ruff of stiff muslin. Red satin cap lined with black velvet, and with a red velvet Maltese cross at one side; suspended from the shoulders by a red ribbon from which depends a Maltese cross of gold. Black velvet cap trimmed with gold ornaments and red plumes. Black hose and shoes, and a gold girdle and sword band. Any other combination of colors preferred may be used.

FIGURE No. 94.—EMPIRE COSTUME.—Dress of dove-colored satin trimmed with a row of silver cord at the top of the wide hem. Round, low-necked waist with short puffed sleeves, finished at the neck with a deep frill of pointed lace. Large gray felt hat trimmed with gray plumes and pale-pink flowers. Ribbon sash tied in long loops and ends at the right side; chatelaine pocket of gray silk lined with pink and suspended by pink ribbons. A lace shawl is carried over the arm.

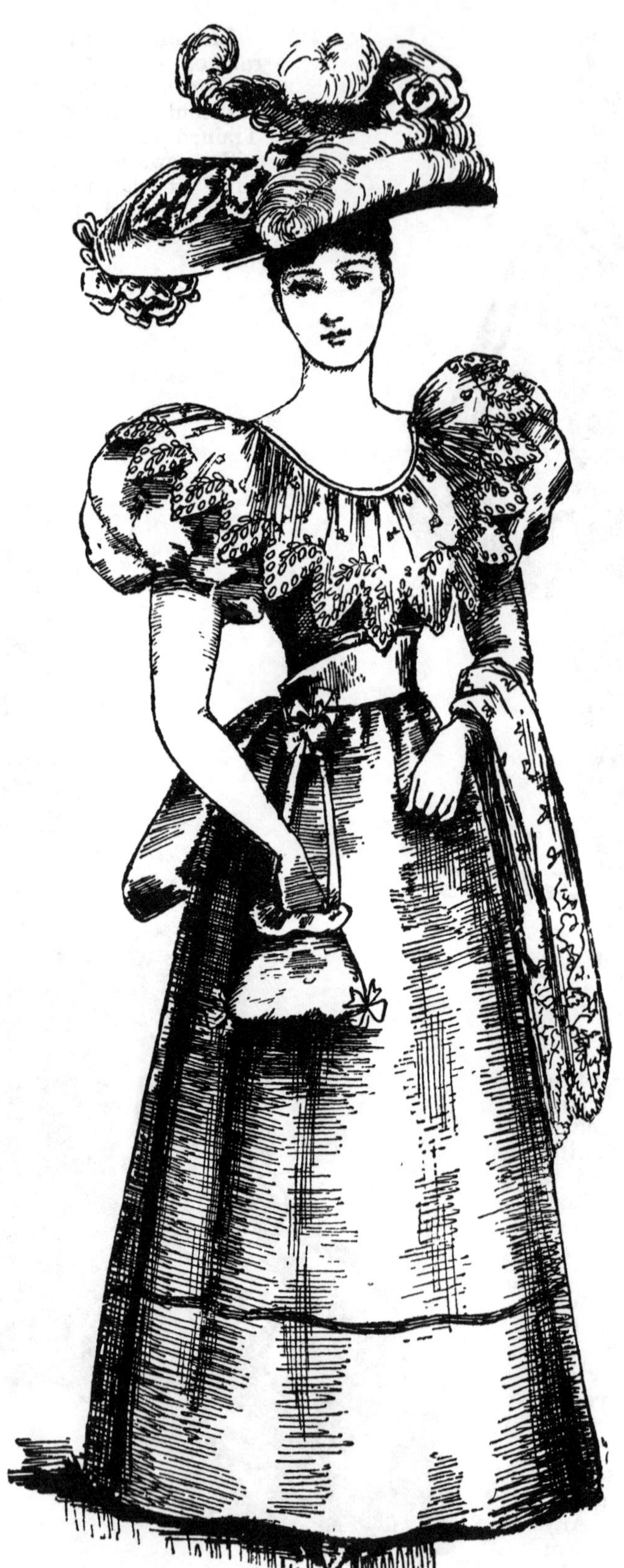

FIGURE No. 94.—EMPIRE COSTUME.

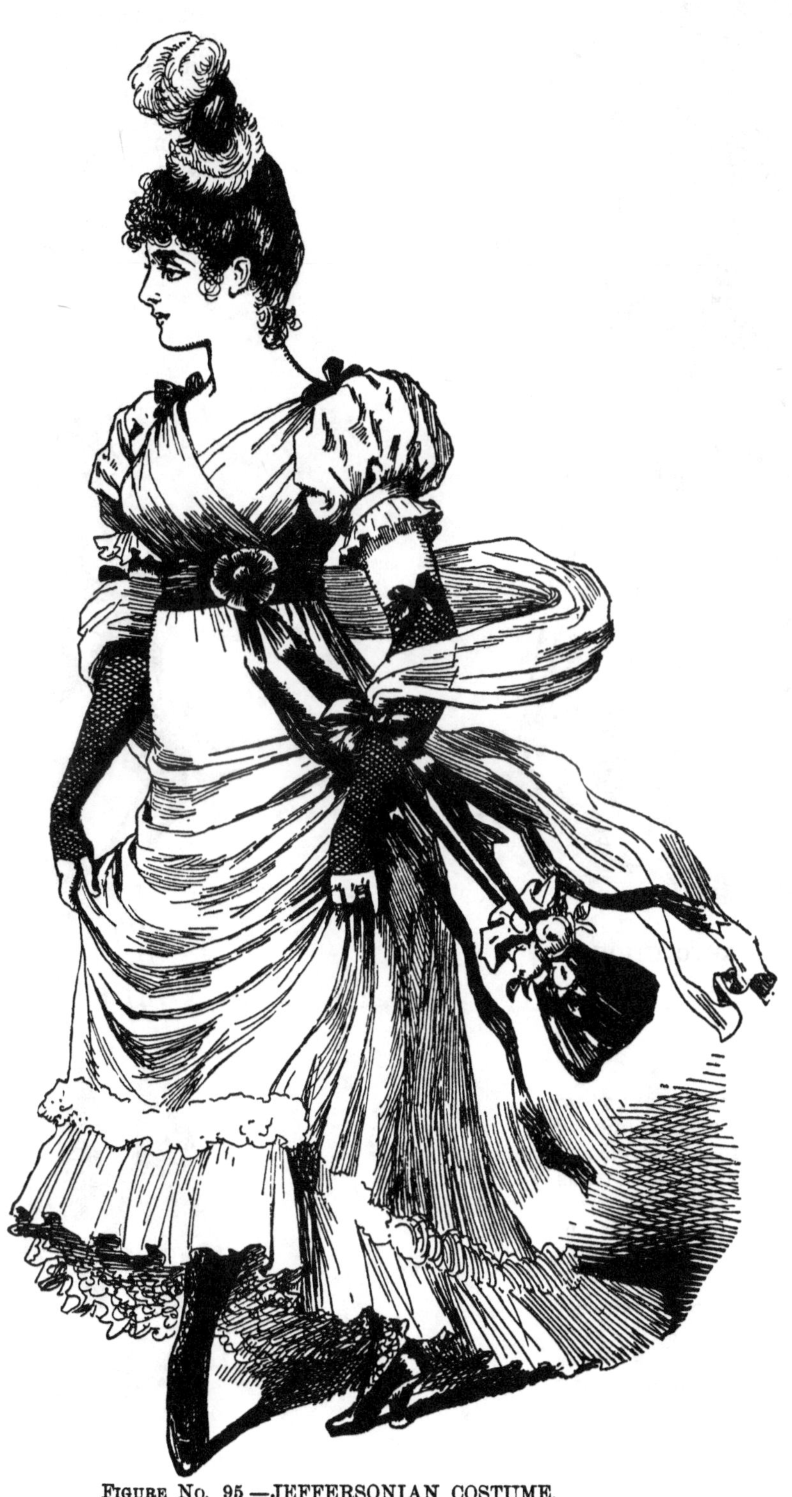

FIGURE NO. 95.—JEFFERSONIAN COSTUME.

FIGURE NO. 95.—JEFFERSONIAN COSTUME.—This pretty costume is made of pink crêpe de chine, with bows, belt, bag and streamers of marine-blue ribbon and velvet. Long mitts and fancy stockings of blue with red or black slippers. Red stockings and slippers may be worn if preferred. The scarf is of pink gauze; and pink feathers are fastened amid the puffs of the high coiffure.

FIGURE NO. 97.—BLACK DIAMOND.—White and black satin combined as illustrated compose this costume. The engraving fully explains the details of the combination. A white linen shirt and collar, with a white satin tie is worn under the waist. A white satin hat, white gloves tied with black ribbons, black stockings worn with patent-leather shoes, and a black fan complete the costume.

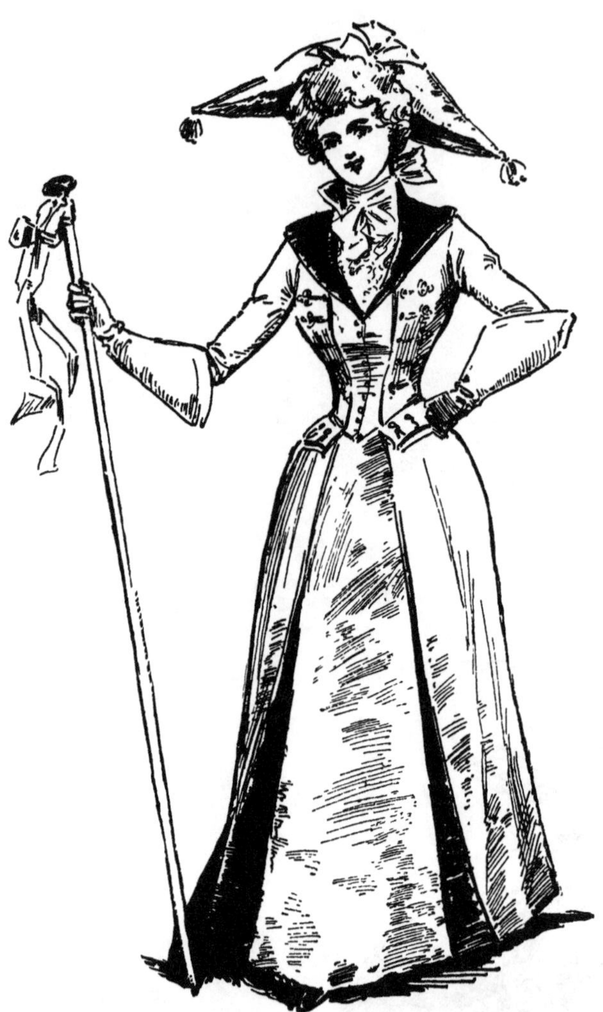

FIGURE NO. 96.—FRENCH REVOLUTIONARY COSTUME.

FIGURE NO. 96.—FRENCH REVOLUTIONARY COSTUME.—This pretty costume is made of gray satin and green velvet, and is trimmed with silver cord and buttons. The engraving fully depicts the front of the dress which, therefore, needs no description. The back of the waist is in postilion style, and that of the skirt is full and round. The front, between the revers is filled in with a lace cravat fastened at the back under a bow. The hat is of gray satin trimmed with silver tassels and ribbon bows. The hair is dressed high and powdered. Gray gauntlet gloves and a silver, ribbon-trimmed staff complete the costume

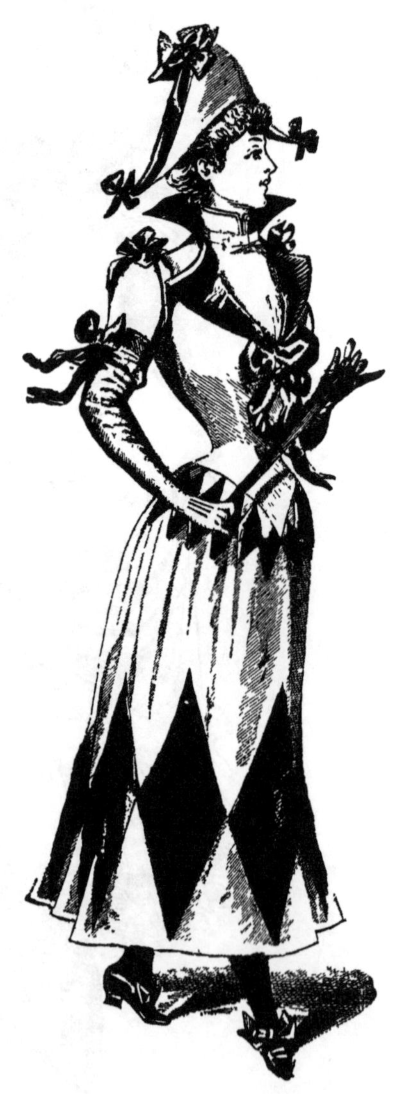

FIGURE NO. 97.—BLACK DIAMOND

FIGURE NO. 99.— ADMIRAL.—White broadcloth and navy-blue satin are combined in making this costume, together with fine white satin for the vest, and lace frills for the neck and wrists. Silver buttons are on the continental coat and a watch fob depends from the vest. A navy-blue hat trimmed with bows of silver braid, and navy-blue silk stockings with patent leather buckle-shoes complete the costume.

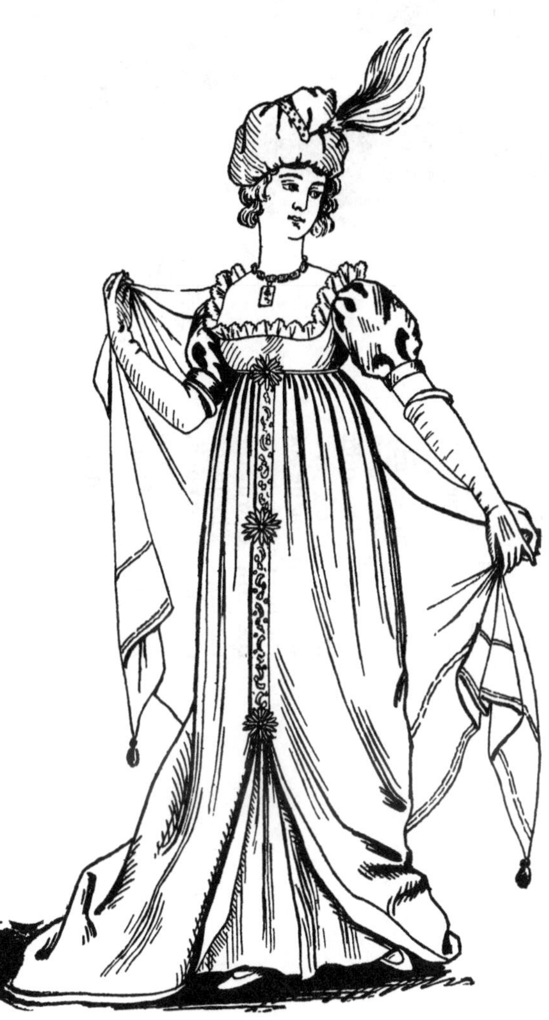

FIGURE NO. 98.—EARLY ENGLISH COSTUME.

FIGURE NO. 98.—EARLY ENGLISH COSTUME.—The dress is of red velvet or satin lined with pale yellow and worn over a white satin petticoat. A jeweled band extends down the center of the front to where the dress opens over the petticoat, and antique lace edges the neck. Turban to match the dress, trimmed with jewels and a feather aigrette. The mantle is made of white cashmere in shawl shape, and is bordered with a gilt band and tipped with gilt tassels. Long yellow gloves complete the costume.

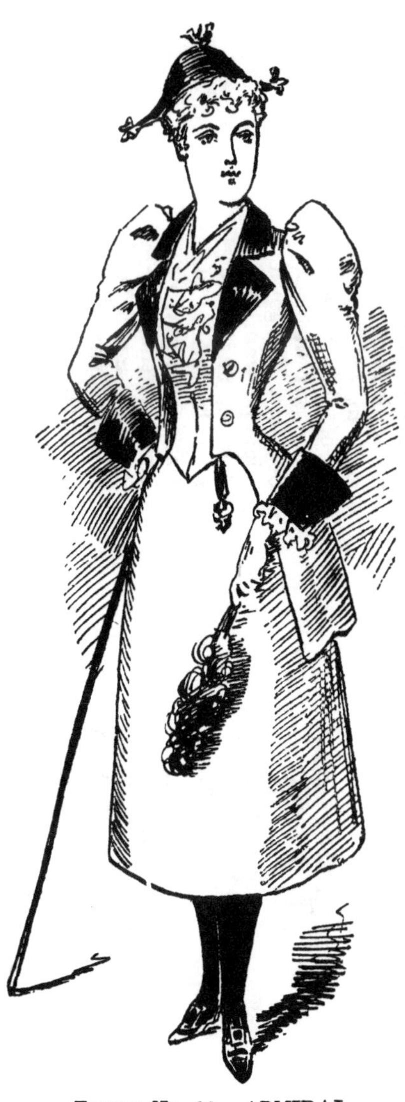

FIGURE NO. 99.—ADMIRAL

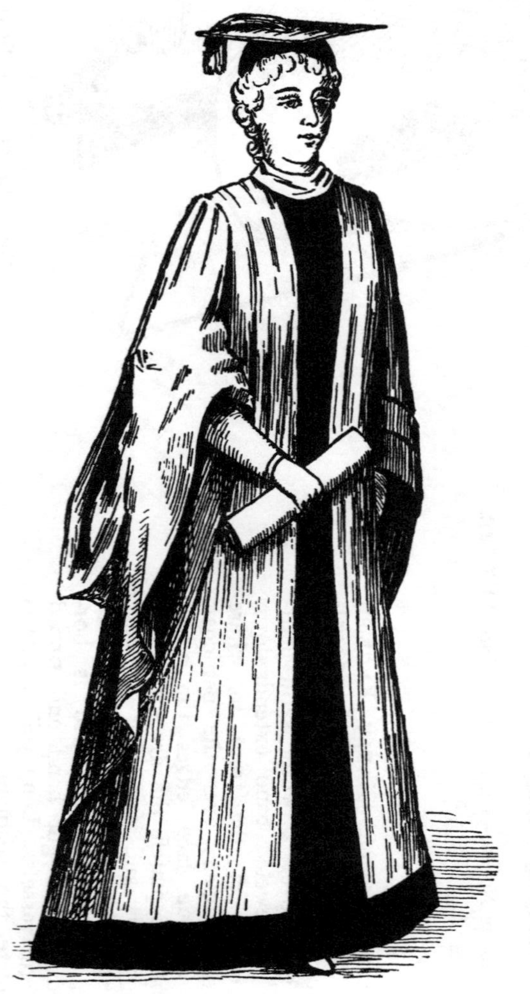

FIGURE No. 100.—GIRL GRADUATE.

FIGURE No. 100.—GIRL GRADUATE—This costume is an academical robe and cap, which may be of plain or brocaded silk in black or colors. The gown might be worn as a domino, and could then be made of black, red, gray or dark blue silk, cashmere or any light-weight material. The character of Portia is frequently dressed in this costume, and the fabric then chosen is black silk or satin, plain or brocaded.

FIGURE No. 101.—DOCTRESS.—Black and white satin are chosen for making this costume, although deep red and gray, or brown and yellow, or black and red, orange, blue or any color desired may be used. The ruffs at the neck and waist are made of the light satin, as is the frill down the closing. The black overskirt is straight around except where it is draped in front. Black gloves, hat, stockings and shoes complete the costume.

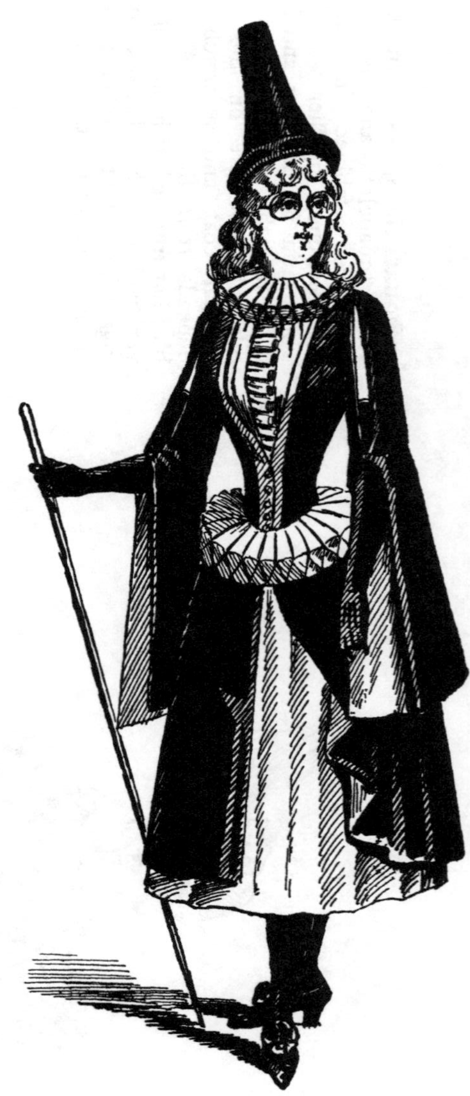

FIGURE No. 101.—DOCTRESS.

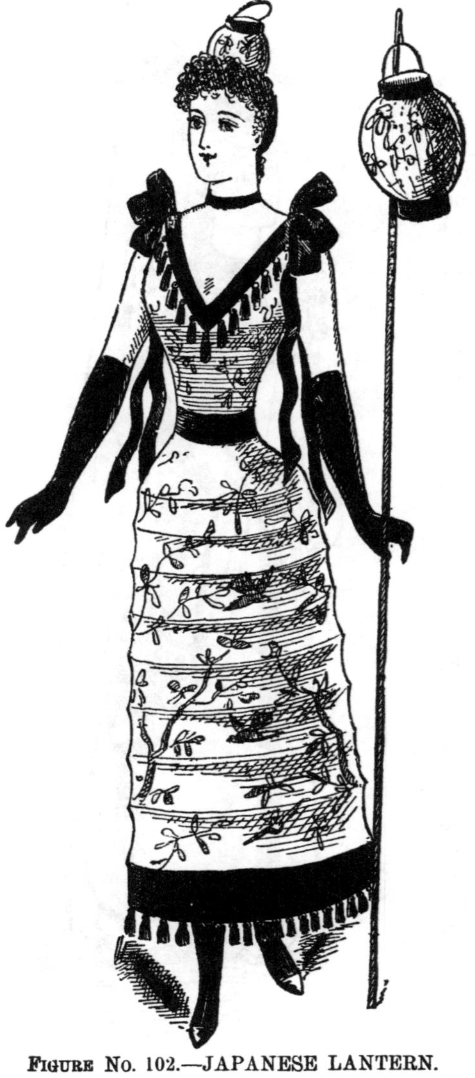

FIGURE No. 102.—JAPANESE LANTERN.

FIGURE No. 102.—JAPANESE LANTERN.—This costume is made of brocaded or printed Japanese silk, and trimmed with velvet, velvet ribbon and silk tassels. The waist is plain, smoothly fitted and cut in a V outline at the back and front. The skirt is round and very narrow, and is distended by reeds to the shape seen in the picture. Like the top of the waist it is trimmed with a band of velvet and a row of tassels. Black velvet-ribbon bows, black gloves, black stockings and slippers, and a lantern head-dress and staff complete the costume.

FIGURE No. 103.—ETRUSCAN VASE.—Brocaded silk in Oriental design and colorings was used for this costume. The engraving delineates the cut of the costume perfectly. Wires and reeds must be used in shaping it as represented. Deep-red velvet and gold braid are used for the decorations. The cap is plain silk of the color of the ground of the brocade, and is striped with the velvet, the ends of the strips being wired and sewed into the tip seen in the picture. The fan represents a vase and is made of the brocade and velvet. Gloves, slippers and stockings to match the tint of the cap are worn.

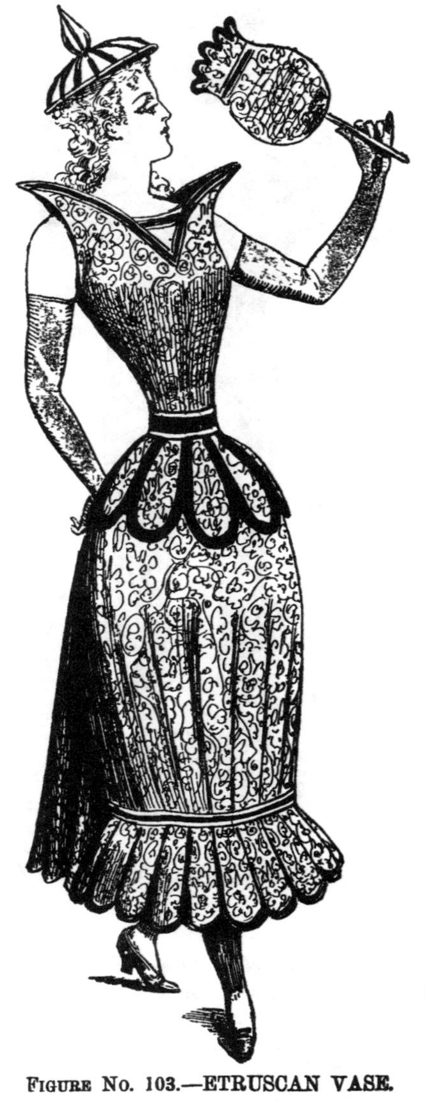

FIGURE No. 103.—ETRUSCAN VASE.

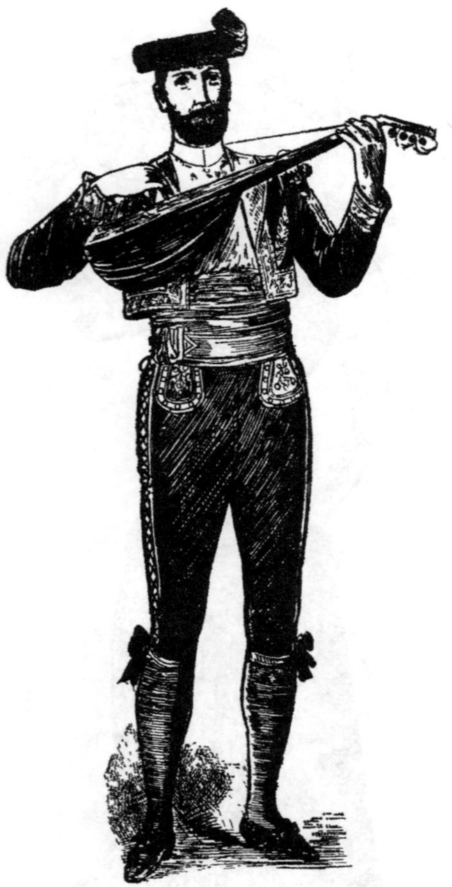

FIGURE No. 104.—MANDOLIN PLAYER.

FIGURE No. 104.—MANDOLIN PLAYER.—Shirt of soft, white muslin; red velvet jacket trimmed with gold braid; brown breeches trimmed with gold braid; blue woollen stockings and red shoes. Sash of soft tan-colored silk, and hat of brown felt with a red pompon.

FIGURE No. 105.—NORMANDY PEASANT.

FIGURE No. 105.—NORMANDY PEASANT.—Underskirt of blue and pink, (or light red) striped goods. Overskirt of plain blue (to match the stripe) lined with plain pink (or red), and turned up to show the lining and fastened back at the sides so that it falls in a sort of cascade. Blouse of white, soft-finished muslin. Bodice and bag of velveteen. The cap is of white lawn.

FIGURE No. 106.—NORMANDY BRIDE.—Gown of white cashmere trimmed with pearl and silver passementerie. Chemisette and puffed sleeves trimmed with passementerie and a network of pearl beads. Conical cap of white muslin or satin trimmed to harmonize with the costume. Long gauze or illusion veil depending from the back. Chatelaine pocket of satin trimmed with silver passementerie and pearl beads.

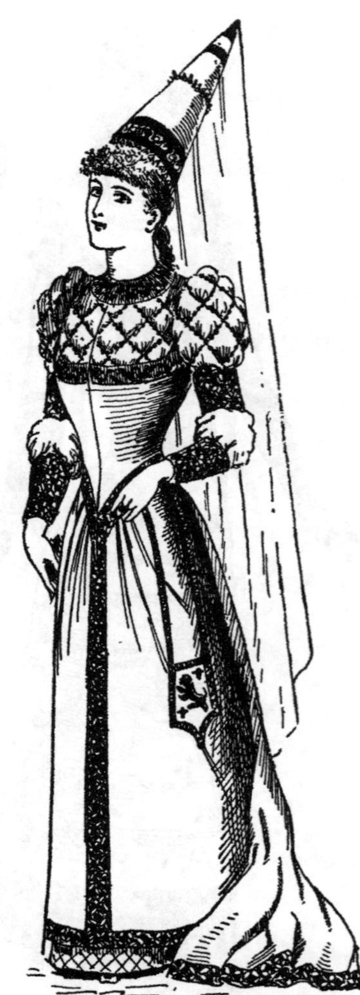

FIGURE No. 106.—NORMANDY BRIDE.

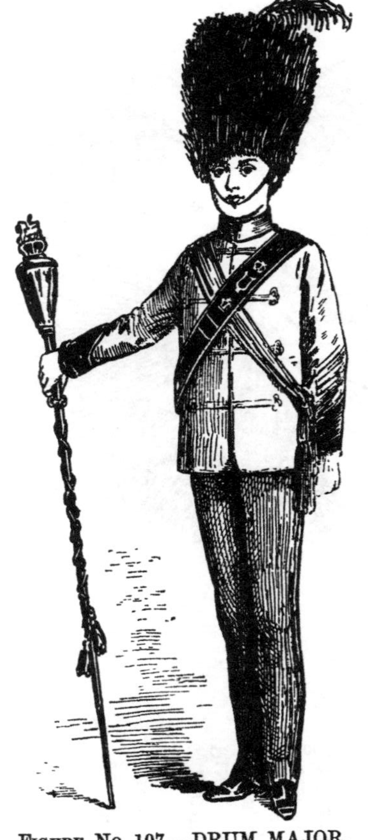

FIGURE No. 107.—DRUM MAJOR.

FIGURE No. 107.—DRUM MAJOR.—White coat; blue trousers with red side stripes; dark-blue cuffs and chest band trimmed with gold; red sash, fancy baton and a "Busby" hat.

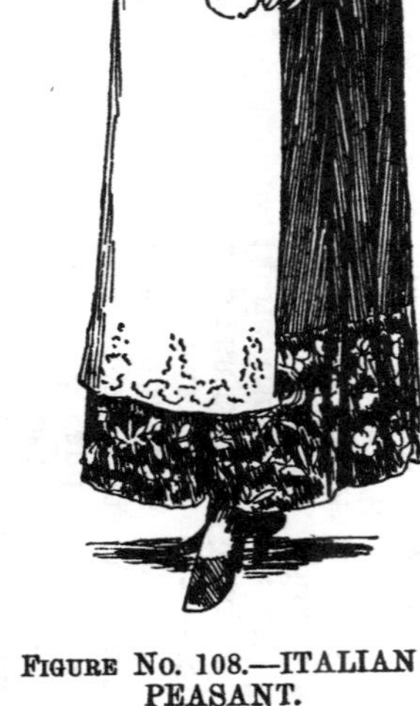

FIGURE No. 108.—ITALIAN PEASANT.

FIGURE No. 108.—ITALIAN PEASANT.—Skirt, bodice and half-sleeves of blue wool; skirt trimmed with a flounce of figured material. Chemisette, upper sleeves, apron and cuffs of white muslin; head-dress of blue wool trimmed at the sides with a strip of gay embroidery. Necklace of gold beads. White stockings and leather shoes.

FIGURE No. 109.—ITALIAN DANCING GIRL.—This is a very pretty costume for a young lady and is made as follows: The skirt is of either red or blue woolen, laid in accordion plaits, and worn over many lace petticoats. The chemisette and apron are of India muslin, or of nainsook or mull, and the bodice of black velveteen, laced with yellow.

Long earrings and a gold cross hung on velvet are usually worn; dark red or blue stockings, and either court or high buckled shoes. The head-dress is of striped material, in many colors, which is sold by the yard; and for fête days the peasant also wears an apron of similar material.

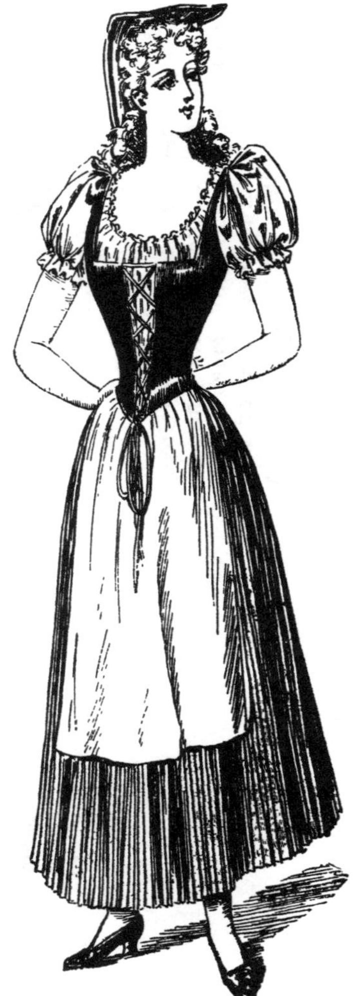

FIGURE No. 109.—ITALIAN DANCING GIRL.

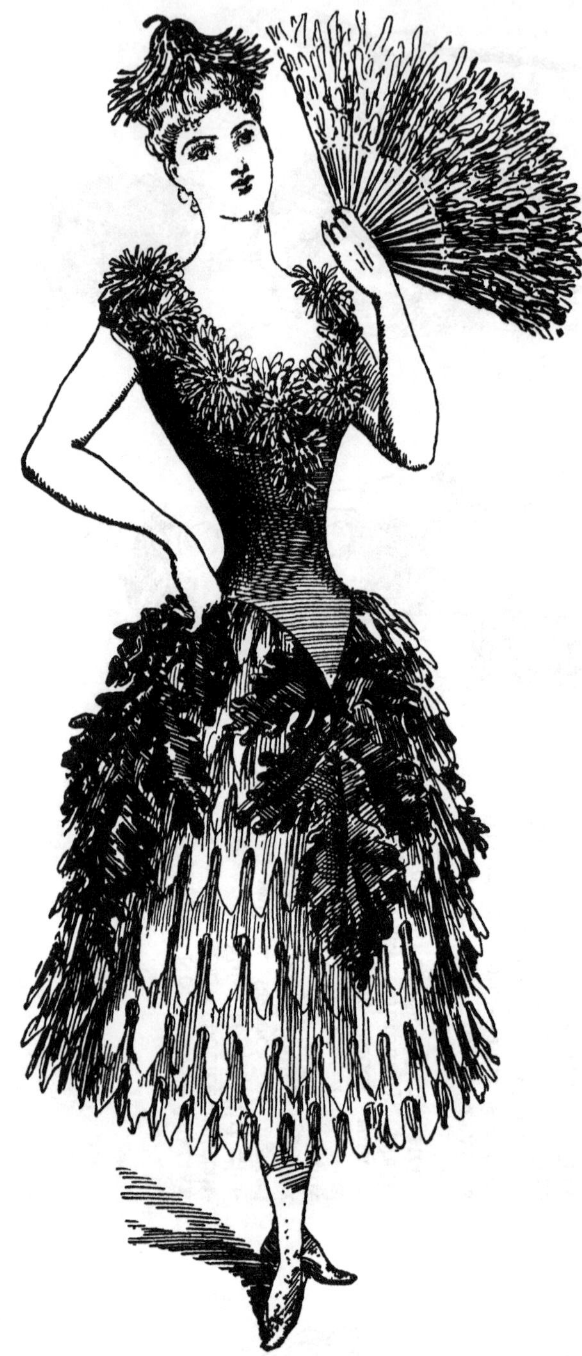

Figure No. 110.—CHRYSANTHEMUM.

Figure No. 110.—Chrysanthemum.—Green satin bodice trimmed at the top with white or yellow chrysanthemums, and with green plush leaves hanging from under its lower edge and falling over a white or yellow satin skirt cut out in petal-like tabs that are plaited or gathered on in rows. A large, artificial chrysanthemum is worn as a cap. White or yellow petal or feather fan.

(For illustrations of Nos. 111, 112 and 113, see next page.)

Figure No. 111.—Carnation Pink.—Under dress of pink silk ruffles, notched and pointed along their edges. Over dress of long green silk points. Artificial pink for head-dress. Pink gloves and stockings, and green slippers.

Figure No. 112.—June.—Dress of white mull. Bodice and band of velvet of any color preferred. Roses in the hair, about the neck and on the drapery. Stockings to match bodice, and roses on slippers.

Figure No. 113.—Roman Flower Girl.—Gown of white fabric trimmed with gay borders of printed goods. Silk sash about the waist. Roman gold necklet and armlets. Basket of artificial flowers. Hair flowing and covered at the crown with a pretty kerchief-cap.

Figure No. 114.—Garden Lily. (For illustration see page 86.)—This is a very pretty costume and is arranged as follows: The accordion-plaited underskirt is of foliage-green satin, and so are the waist and lily leaves. The lily-petals are made of white satin and wired to keep them in shape. White, yellow-tipped stamens are on the bodice and also depend from under the petals on the skirt. The top of the corsage is filled in with white chiffon, and the sleeves are of the same fabric doubled and made very full. The head-dress is made of white and green satin in the form of a lily.

Any variety of lily preferred could be used as the model for such a costume. The colorings of the various cultivated or field lilies may be easily procured.

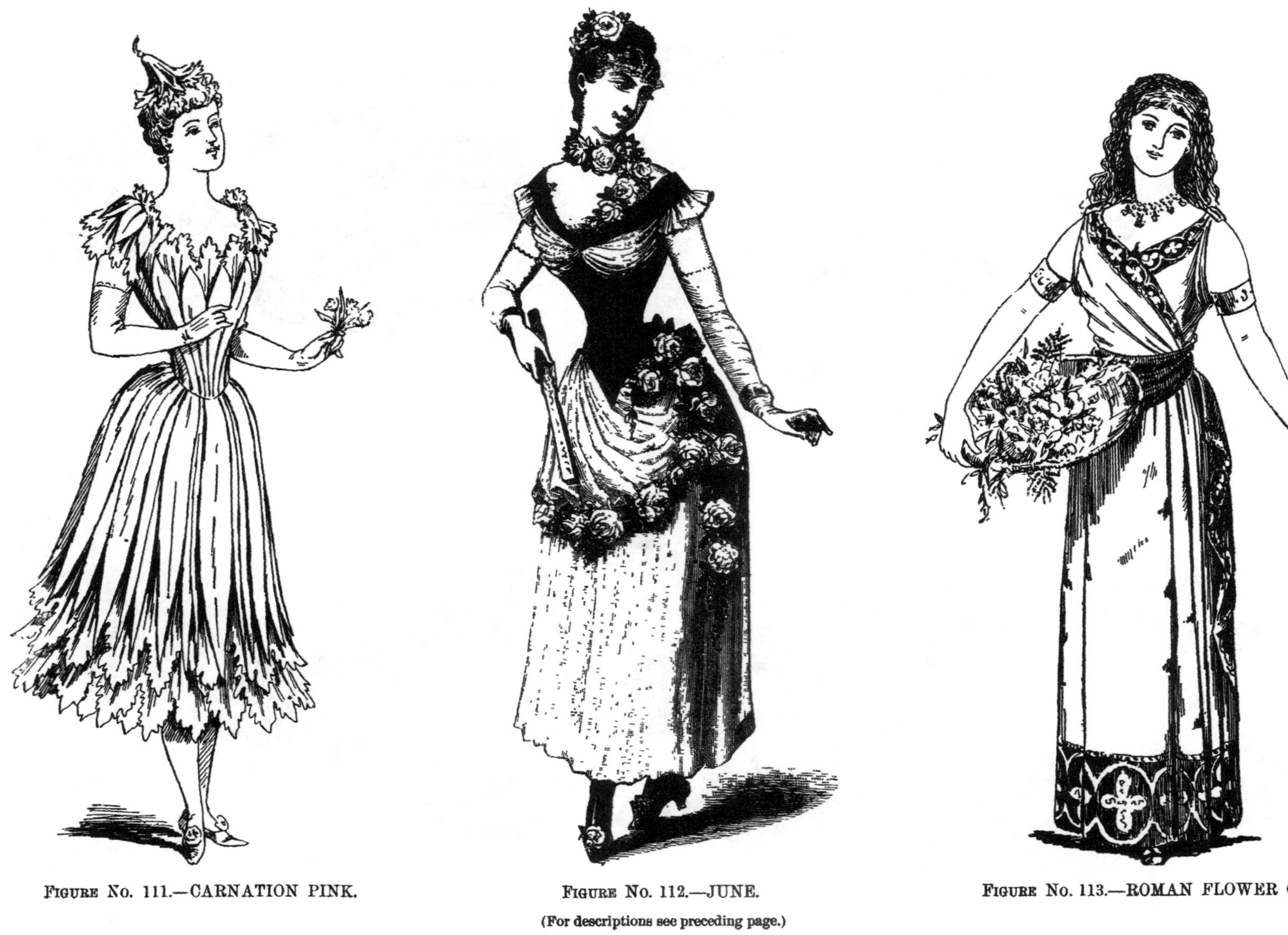

FIGURE No. 111.—CARNATION PINK.

FIGURE No. 112.—JUNE.

(For descriptions see preceding page.)

FIGURE No. 113.—ROMAN FLOWER GIRL.

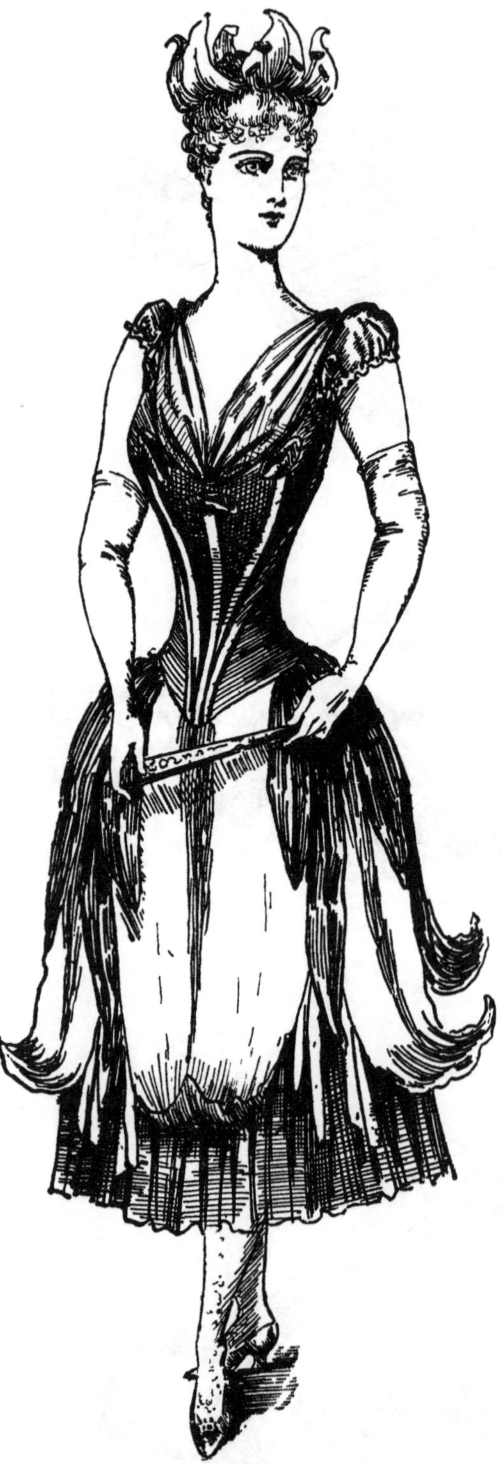

FIGURE NO. 114.—GARDEN LILY.

(For description see page 84.)

FIGURE NO. 115.—MAGPIE.—Bodice of black and white striped velvet, edged at the top with a ruche of black lace, with lace frills for the sleeves. White satin skirt draped with black lace, flounced at the edge and caught up at one side with a sash of black and white velvet. Black and white striped stockings, and black slippers and gloves. A magpie fastened to the right shoulder.

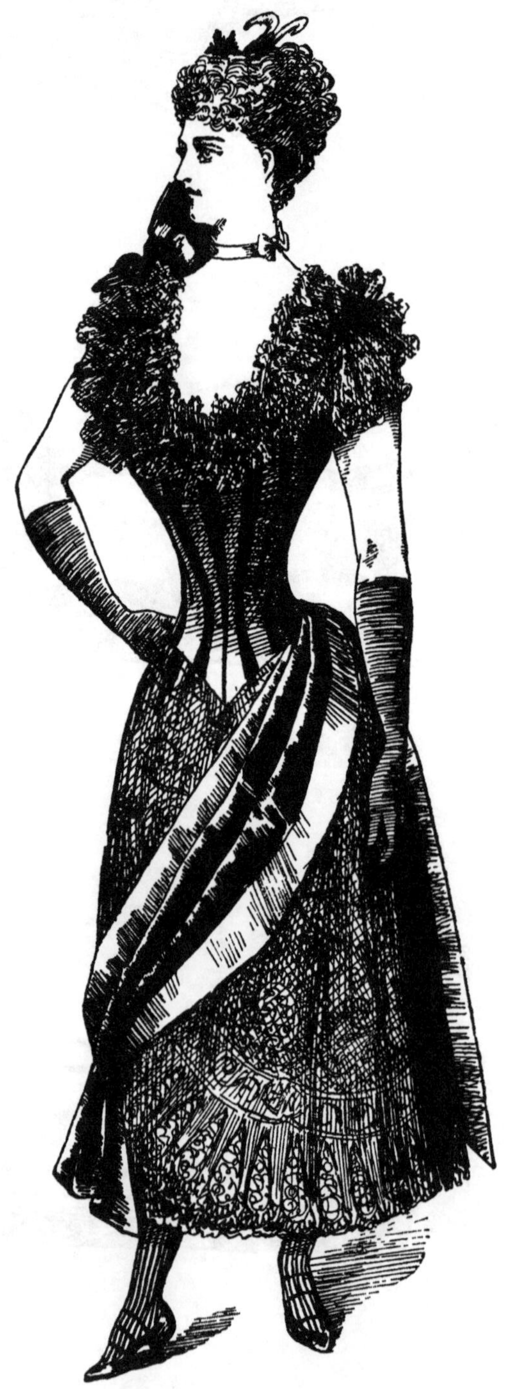

FIGURE NO. 115.—MAGPIE.

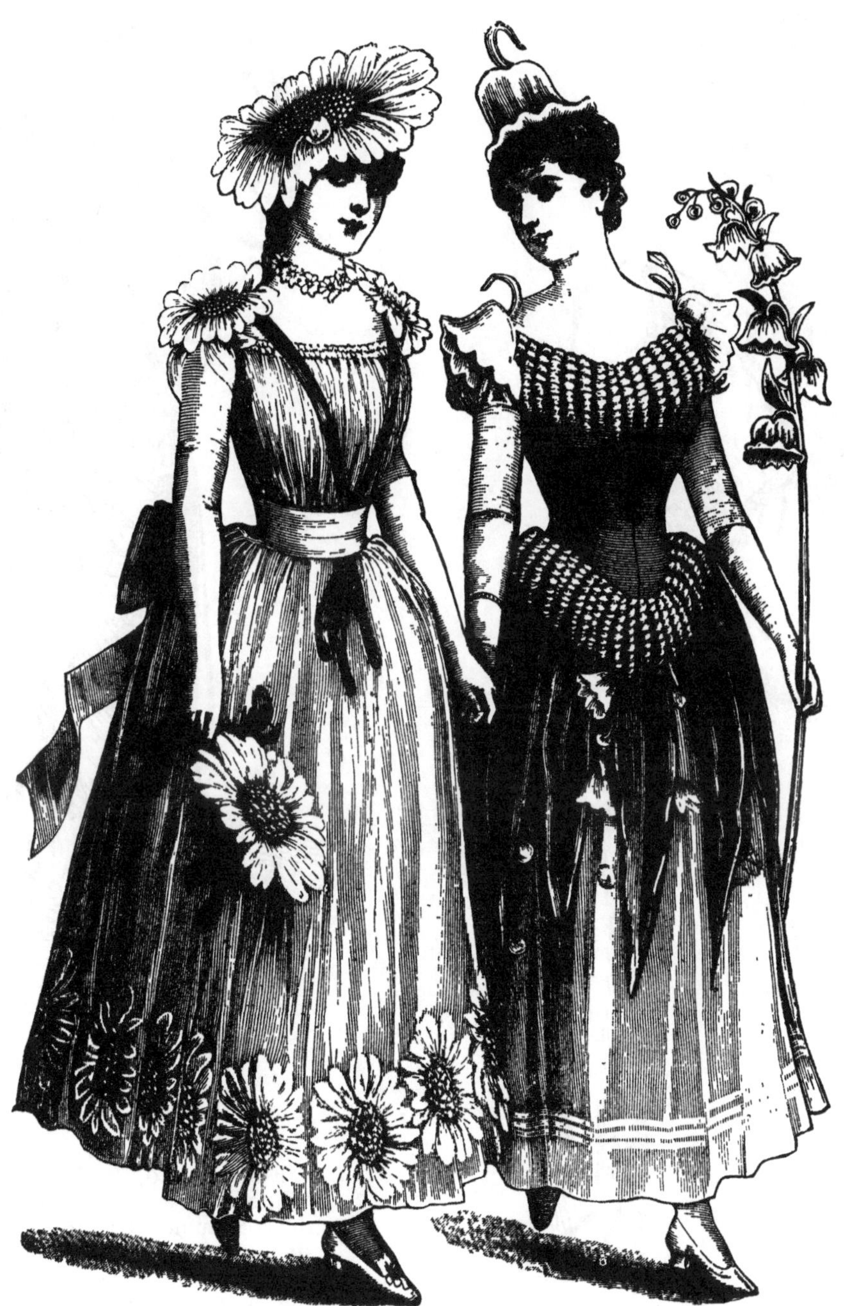

FIGURES NOS. 116 AND 117.—SUN-FLOWER AND LILY OF THE VALLEY.

FIGURES NOS. 116 AND 117. — SUN-FLOWER AND LILY OF THE VALLEY.—The sun-flower costume is made of pale yellow muslin, and completed as illustrated with artificial sun-flowers, and yellow gloves, stockings and slippers.

The other costume has a white gauze skirt and a green bodice and over-dress, the latter cut to represent lily-of-the-valley leaves. A lily-of-the-valley fringe finishes the top and bottom of the bodice, and large blossoms arranged as shown finish the costume.

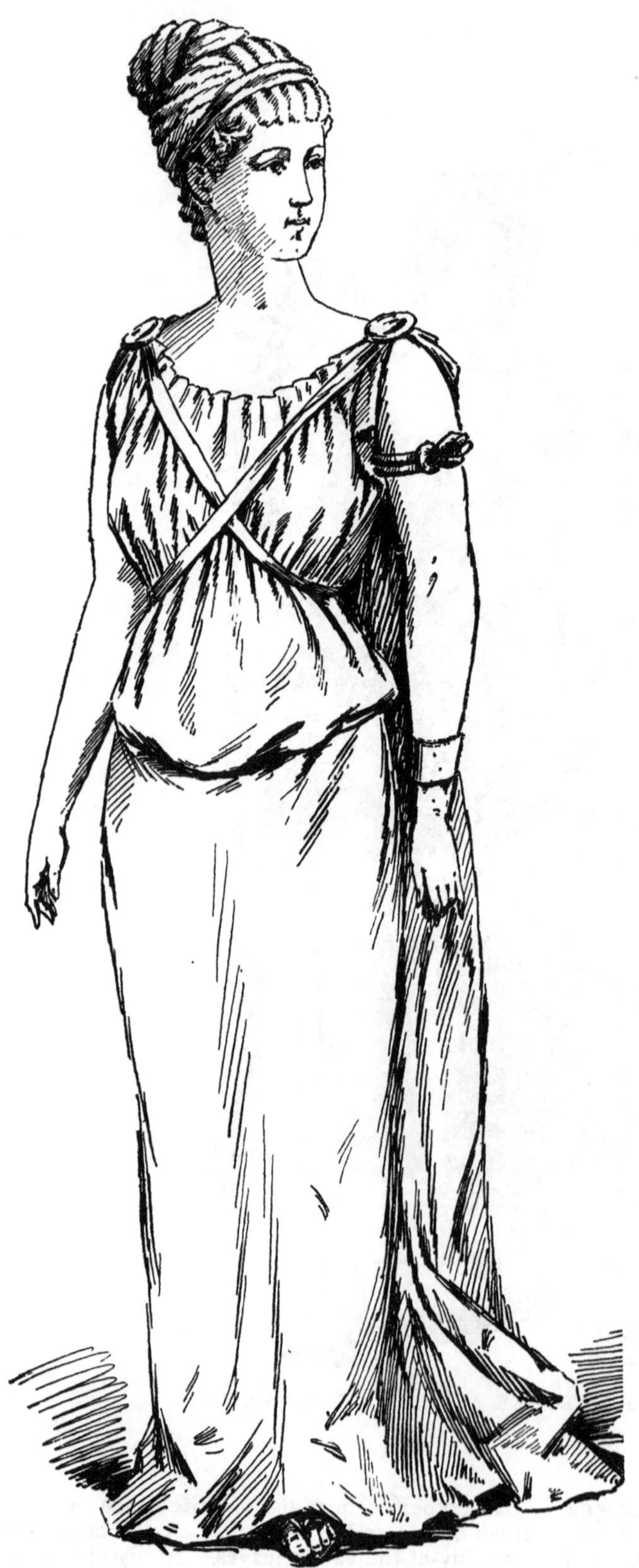

FIGURE No 118.—GALATEA.

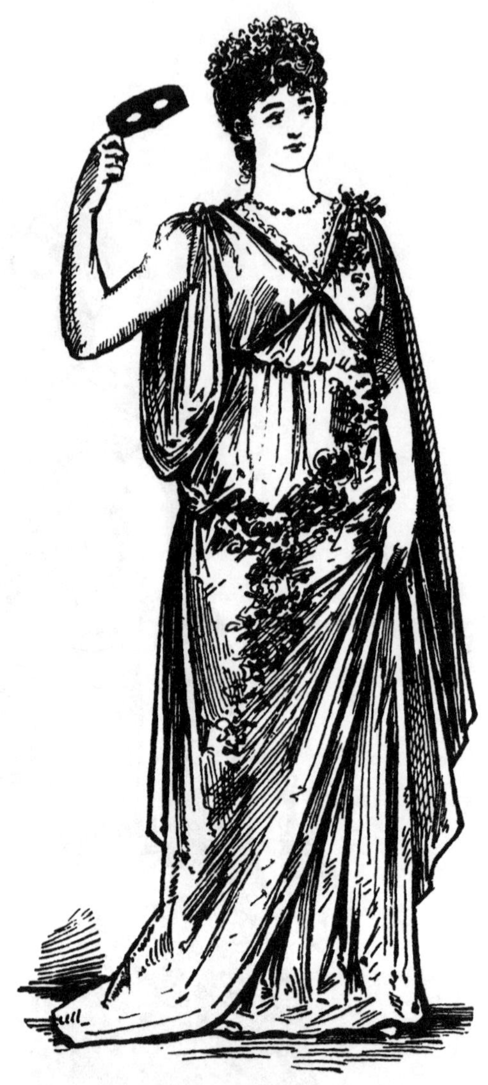

FIGURE No. 119.—ROMAN MASQUERADER.

FIGURE No. 118. — GALATEA. — White cheese cloth may be used for this costume, or any more expensive soft fabric desired. All the jewelry should be pure white, and the hair and face, neck, hands and arms should be whitened to represent marble.

FIGURE No. 119.—ROMAN MASQUERADER. — Costume of pale-yellow, soft wool fabric, garlanded with flowers, and made similarly to the one seen at figure No. 118. Wreath of blossoms on the hair, and a half-mask to be adjusted at will.

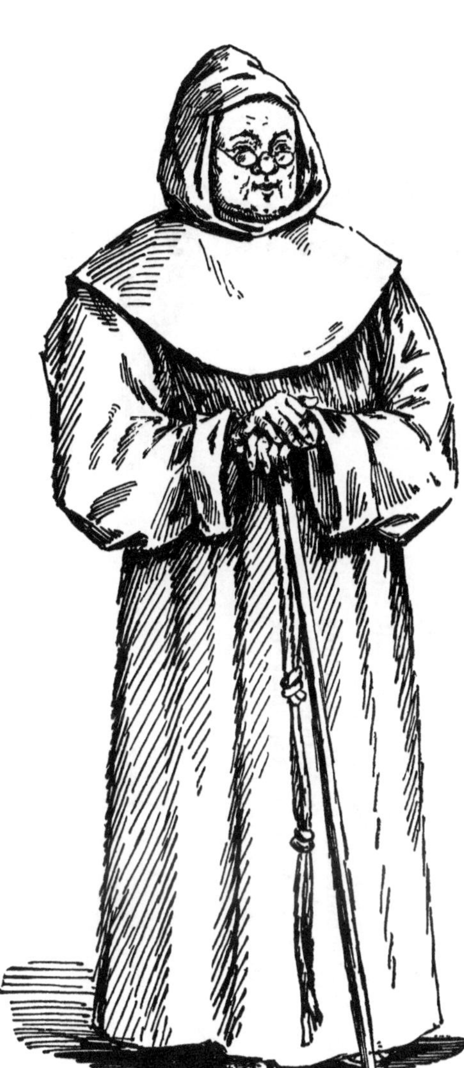

FIGURE No. 120.—FRIAR TUCK.

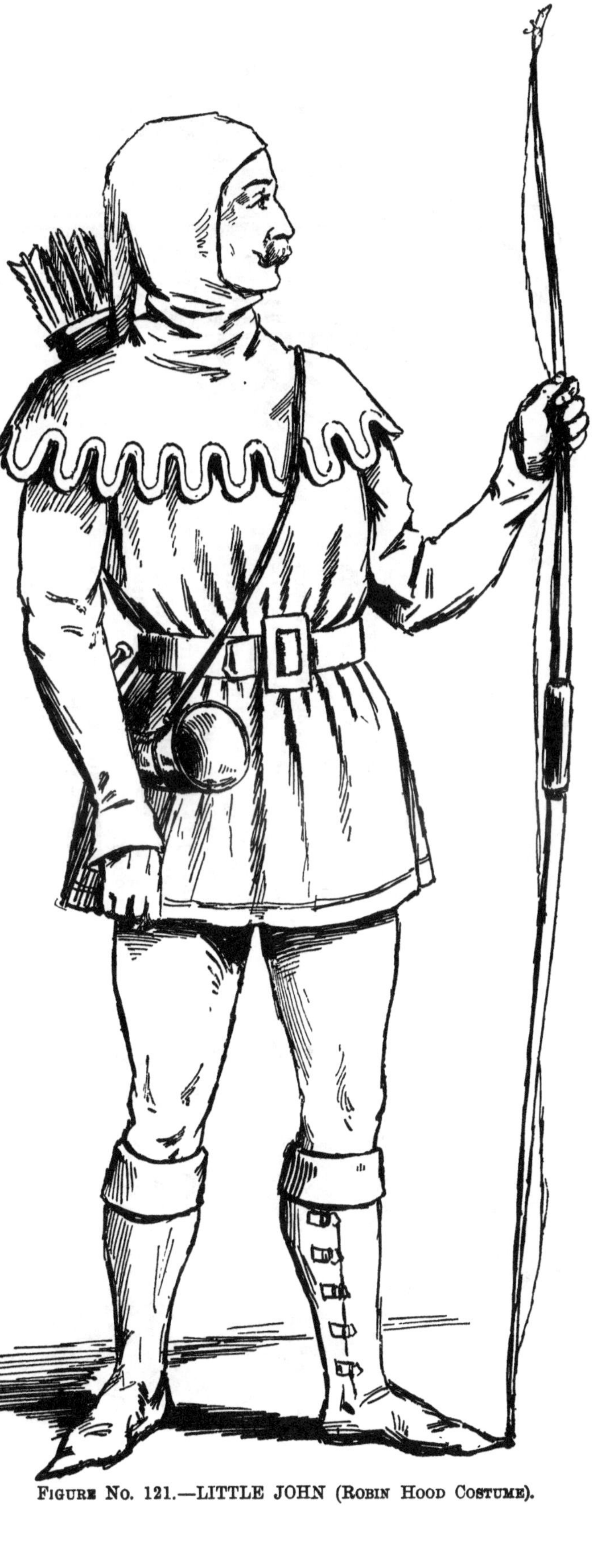

FIGURE No. 120.—FRIAR TUCK.—Robe, collar and hood of coarse brown cloth; girdled with a knotted rope. Sandals on the feet and a staff in the hands. May be worn as a domino.

FIGURE No. 121.—LITTLE JOHN. (ROBIN HOOD COSTUME.)—Tunic, hood and hose of brown cloth. Leather belt and high boots. A quiver of arrows at the back and a horn suspended from the shoulder.

FIGURE No. 121.—LITTLE JOHN (ROBIN HOOD COSTUME).

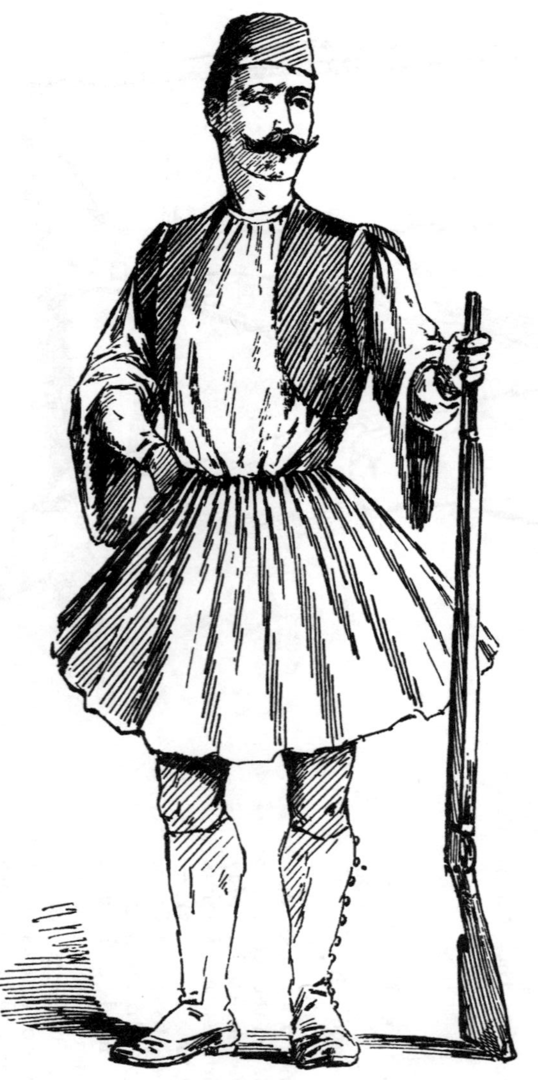

FIGURE NO. 122.—GREEK SOLDIER.

FIGURE NO. 122.—GREEK SOLDIER.—White muslin tunic, with full skirt and sleeves of the same; close under-sleeves and tights. Brown cloth zouave jacket and cap; leather shoes with long, white cloth tops, buttoned at the side. If desired, the jacket may be made of any gay-colored fabric preferred to the brown cloth mentioned.

FIGURE NO. 123.—VENETIAN COSTUME.—Silken tunic of some soft pretty tint in drab, blue or yellow, confined at the waist by a narrow leather belt. Over-garment of dull woolen fabric, with sleeves puffed to the elbows and close below them. The coat is turned over on the outside and faced with silk of the same shade. Long hose of brown or a tint matching the tunic; soft leather shoes. A close Venetian cap may be worn if desired.

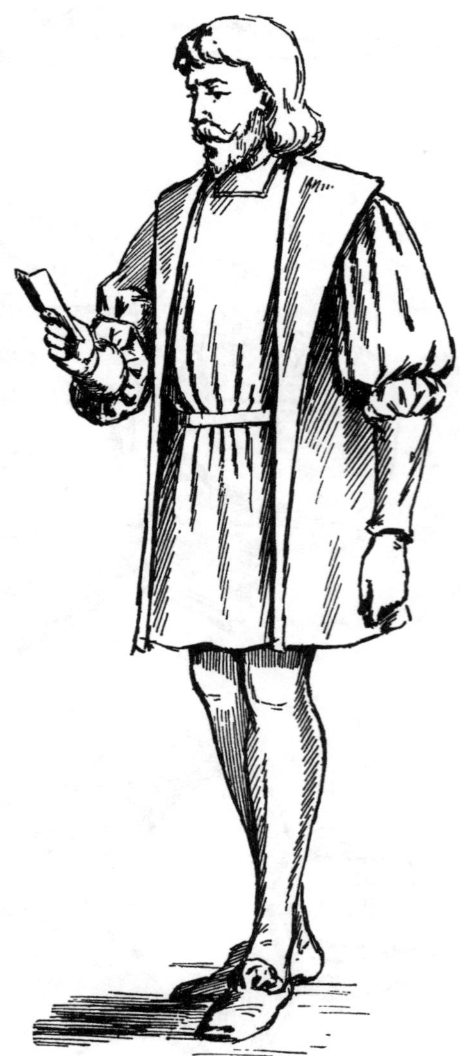

FIGURE NO. 123.—VENETIAN COSTUME.

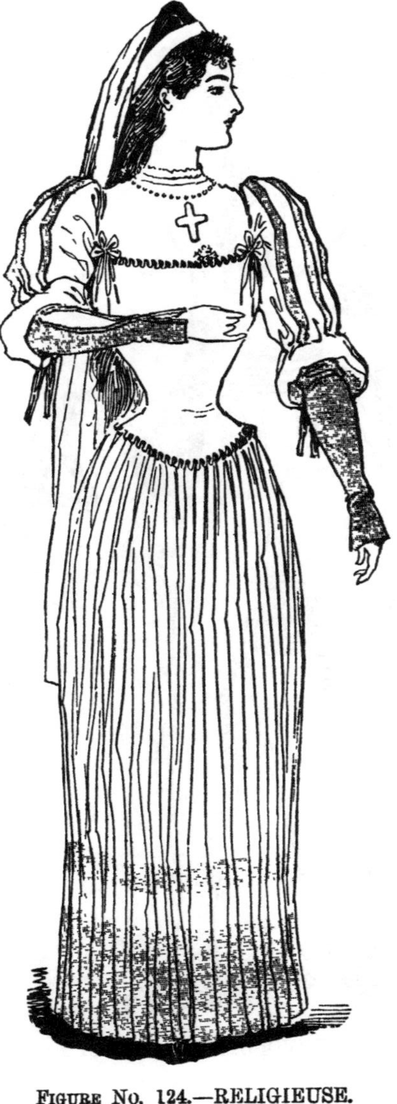

FIGURE No. 124.—RELIGIEUSE.

FIGURE No. 124.—RELIGIEUSE.—This costume is made of soft gray and white fabrics. The skirt is of white bordered in gray and is accordion-plaited. The waist is of white goods edged with rosary-bead trimming and decorated with the same to represent a bodice. The full upper sleeves are of the two fabrics intermingled, while the close undersleeves are of the gray. A gray and white pointed cap, with a long, white veil is worn, and the neck is encircled with strings of rosary beads from one of which falls a cross.

FIGURE No. 125.—DAFFODIL.—This costume is made of pale yellow crêpe or gauze and trimmed with green ribbon. The skirt and blouse are of a paler tint than the drapery which is gracefully arranged from shoulder to shoulder across the bust and back. A large artificial daffodil surmounts the hair in a picturesque manner, and a long staff completed with another large daffodil and streamers of green ribbon is carried in the hand. This costume, in appropriate colors, could be adapted for any flower preferred.

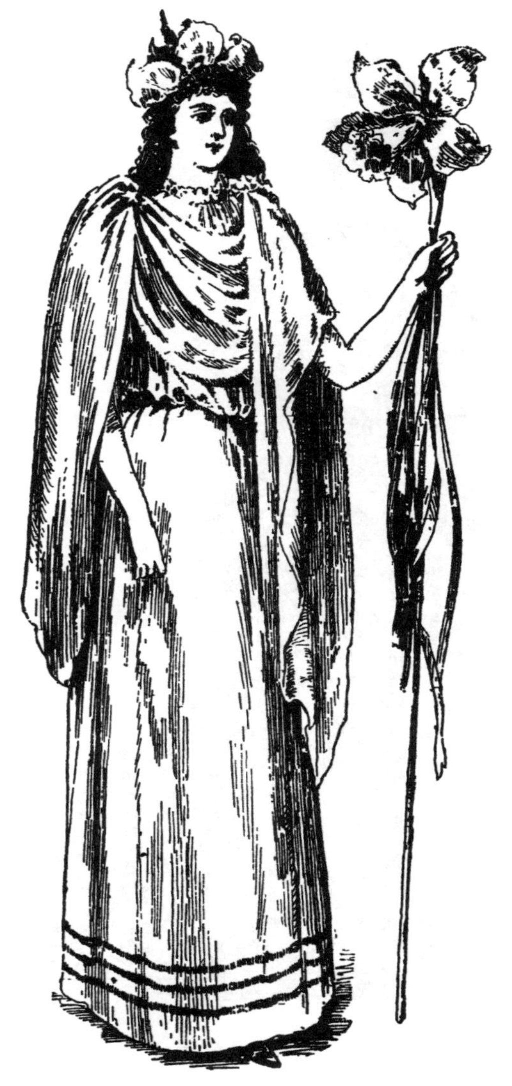

FIGURE No. 125.—DAFFODIL.

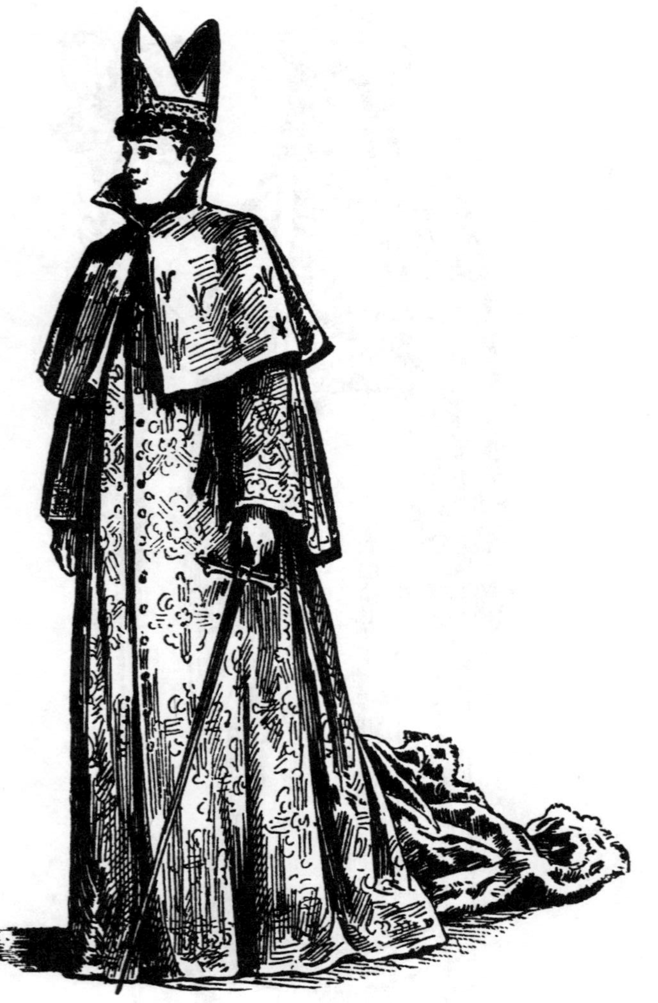

FIGURE No. 126.—BISHOP.

FIGURE No. 126.—BISHOP.—Long robe of purple silk brocaded with gold and trimmed with ermine. White cape with a high collar. Pointed hat of purple and gold. Red or white may be used for this costume either alone or in combination. Canton flannel, blackened at regular intervals, is often used to represent ermine, which is a very expensive fur.

FIGURE No. 127.—REVOLUTIONARY COSTUME.—The coat to this costume is of dark-blue satin; the vest of red-and-white striped goods; the breeches of buff colored satin; the stockings white; shoes black with silver buckles. The hat is of black satin trimmed with blue feather-trimming and satin ribbon. High collar with satin necktie, and lace ruffles. A wig should be worn.

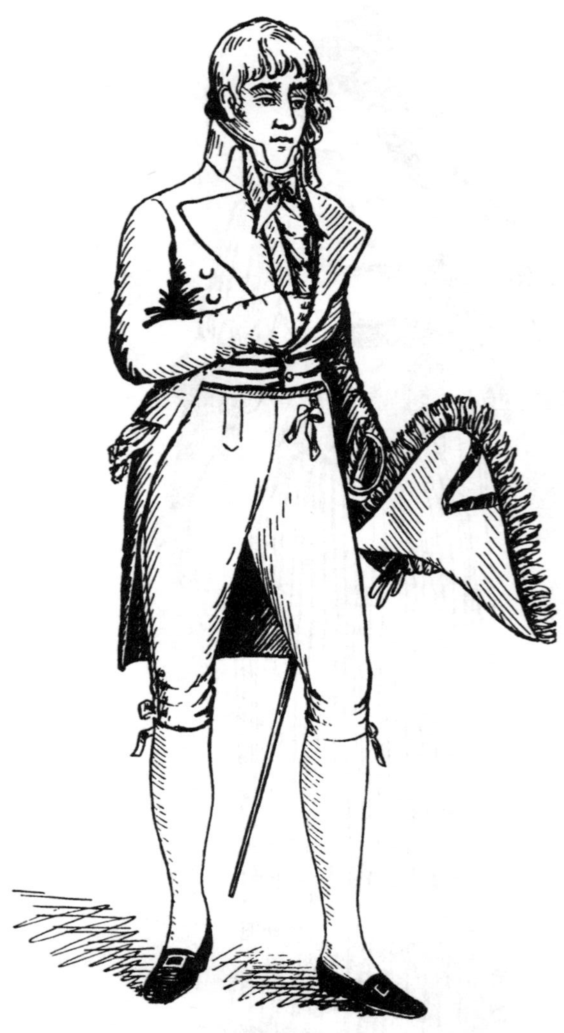

FIGURE No. 127.—REVOLUTIONARY COSTUME.

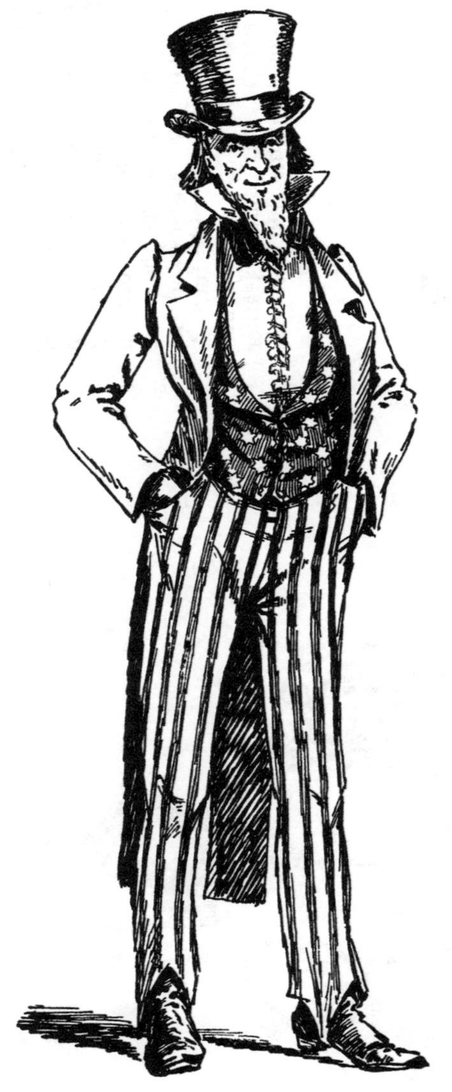

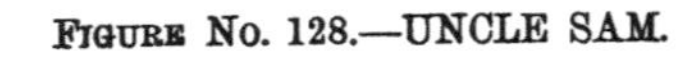

FIGURE No. 128.—UNCLE SAM.

FIGURE No. 128.—UNCLE SAM.—This is a very familiar costume and needs slight mention. The trousers are of blue or red and white striped fabric; the vest is blue dotted with white stars; and the coat may be of blue, red or white, being lined, in the latter event, with blue or red. Shirt of white with pointed collar and ruffled edges. Blue cravat and old-fashioned white beaver hat.

FIGURE No. 129. — AFRICAN DUDE.—White shirt dotted with pink; blue-and-white or pink-and-white collar and cuffs, with red neck-tie. Yellow vest, blue coat, and white trousers barred with red. Silk hat of an exaggerated bell-shape, with wide band. Eye-glass, white kid gloves, large sleeve-buttons and an ultra-fashionable cane, patent leather shoes, and white gaiter-tops complete the costume.

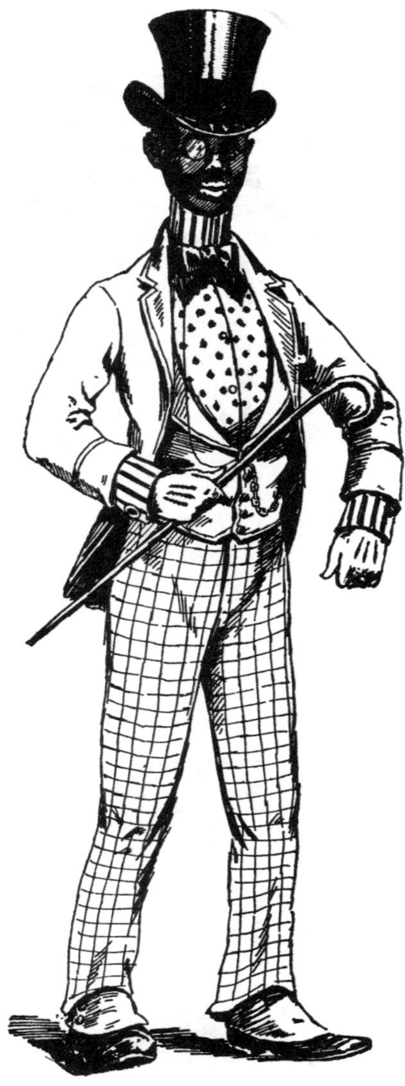

FIGURE No. 129.—AFRICAN DUDE.

FIGURE NO. 130.—SHYLOCK.—The costume of the old money-lender of Venice is very easy to make. It is composed of a frock of rough brown cloth made with a close waist and a gathered skirt and worn over a close undergarment of the same color. The loose sleeves and the skirt are trimmed with fur. A close brown cap, a leather belt and pouch, and pointed leather shoes complete the *tout ensemble.*

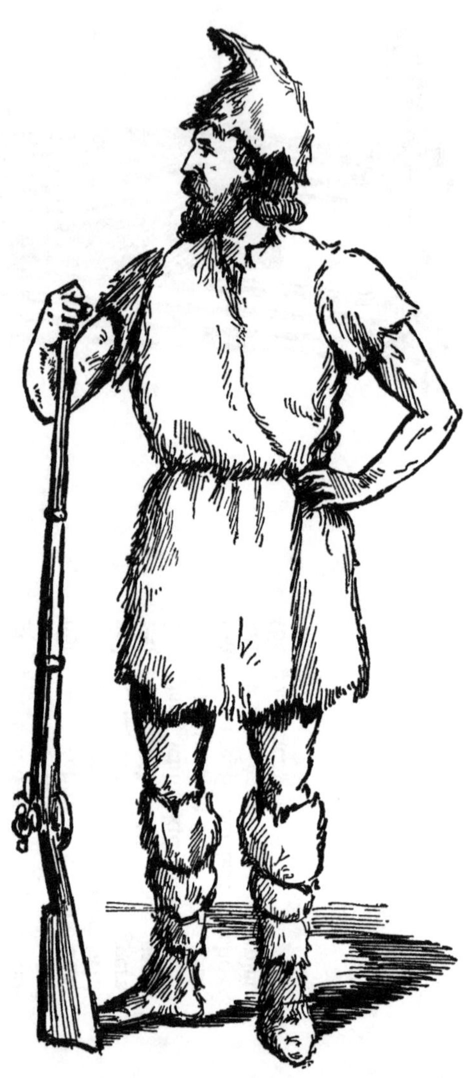

FIGURE NO. 131.—TRAPPER.

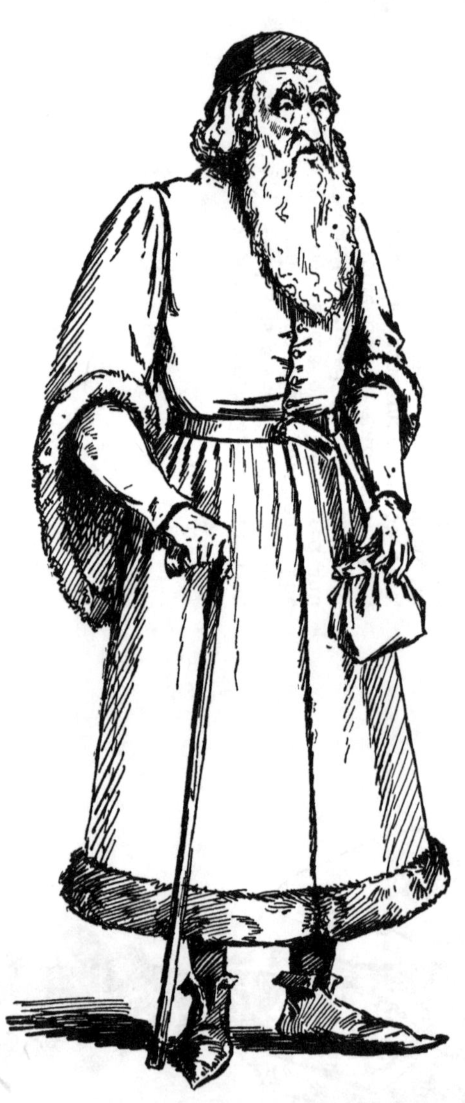

FIGURE NO. 130.—SHYLOCK.

FIGURE NO. 131.—TRAPPER.—This costume is as often chosen for the character of Robinson Crusoe as for a trapper. A close-fitting sleeveless suit of flesh-colored underwear should be worn with it. The frock, cap and boots are made of fur. Any fleecy fabric with a long nap imitative of fur may be used in place of skins in making the costume.

FIGURE No. 132.—SANTA CLAUS.—This character is here illustrated as a very old man, the impersonator wearing for the purpose a mask showing a wrinkled face and snow-white hair and beard. The long duster is of some shaggy gray material like Canton flannel, and is trimmed at all the loose edges with bands of white cotton-batting. A cord is tied about the waist, and the feet and ankles are encased in cheap fur or dyed goatskin, leather straps being adjusted about the ankles. White woolen mittens. and a round cap made of the coat material and trimmed to correspond, are worn.

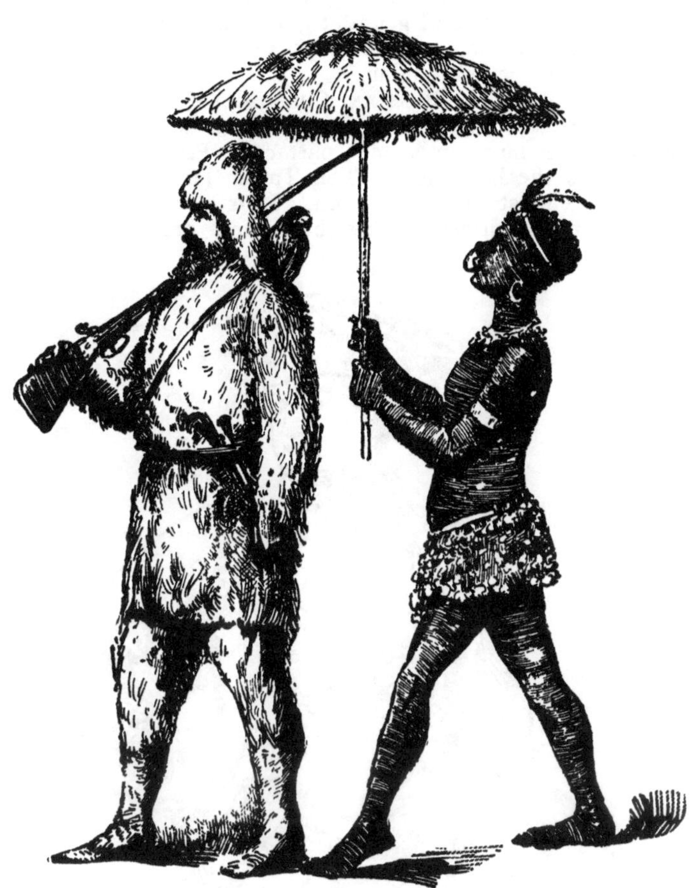

FIGURES NOS. 133 AND 134.—ROBINSON CRUSOE AND HIS MAN FRIDAY.

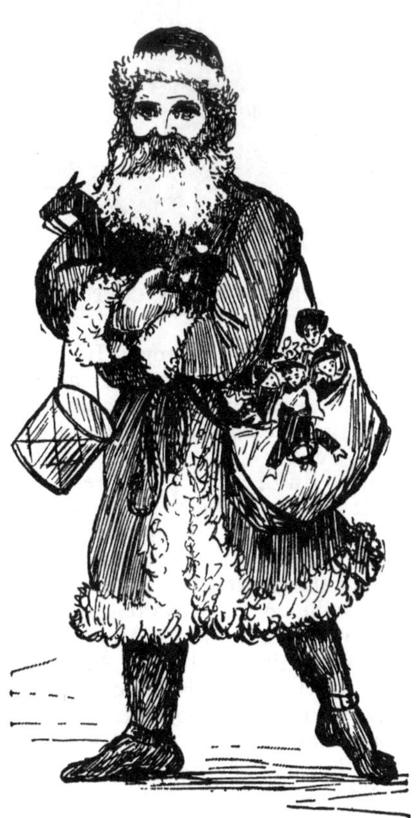

FIGURE NO. 132.—SANTA CLAUS.

FIGURES NOS. 133 AND 134.—ROBINSON CRUSOE AND HIS MAN FRIDAY.—Crusoe is dressed in a complete suit of skins, and carries a parrot on one shoulder and a gun over the other. His blouse is confined about the waist with a leather belt under which are thrust pistols, knives, etc., etc. Shaggy or furry cloth may be used in place of fur or skins, if more convenient.

Friday's costume is extremely simple to arrange and adjust. It consists of a suit of black or dark-brown woven or knitted underwear, and socks to match. A short skirt made of feathers or fringe is fastened about the hips; and a necklet of shells and beads, armlets and nose and ear-rings of gilt, a gilt head-band confining two feathers, and a feather parasol complete the costume.

FIGURE NO. 135.—CONTINENTAL COSTUME.—Blue coat trimmed with silver ornaments, red collar and cuffs. White woolen vest, buff breeches, long white over-gaiters and leather shoes. White sash, buff gauntlet-gloves, and three-cornered black hat decorated with silver lace and white fur or feather edging.

FIGURE NO. 136.—PERSIAN COSTUME.—This is a very effective costume and somewhat complicated. The most important part of a Persian's costume is the head gear. The Tartar lambskin cap is the most generally worn. It is conically shaped, about fifteen inches high, and has an

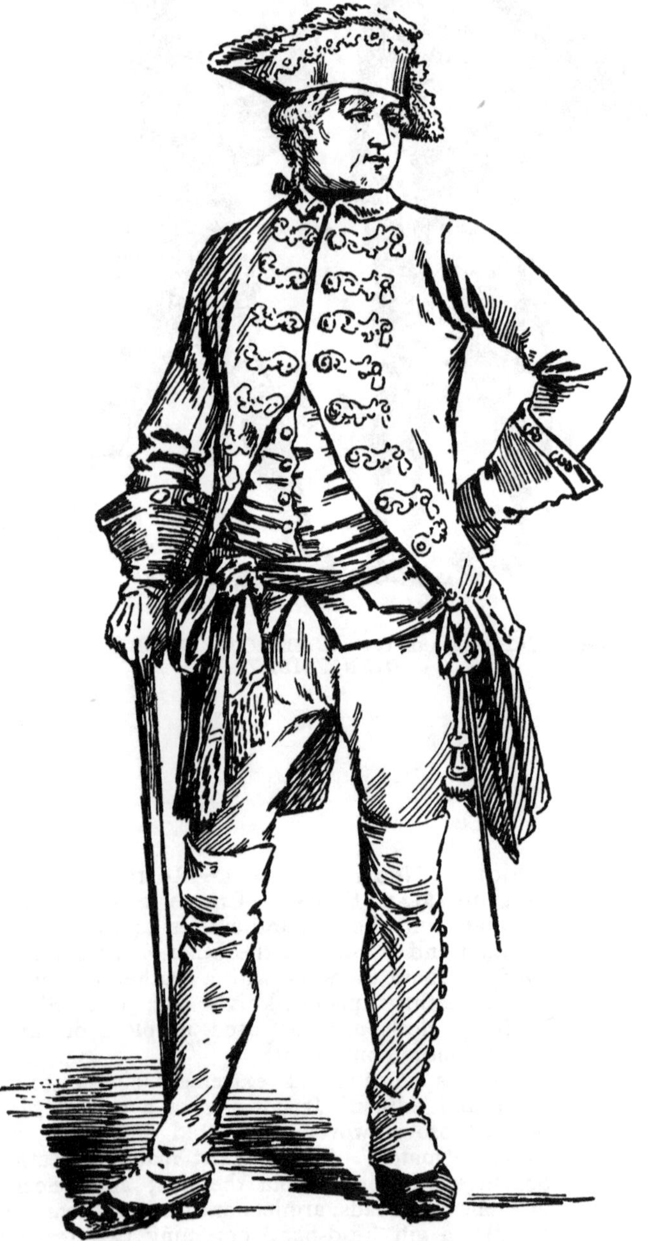

FIGURE NO. 135.—CONTINENTAL COSTUME.

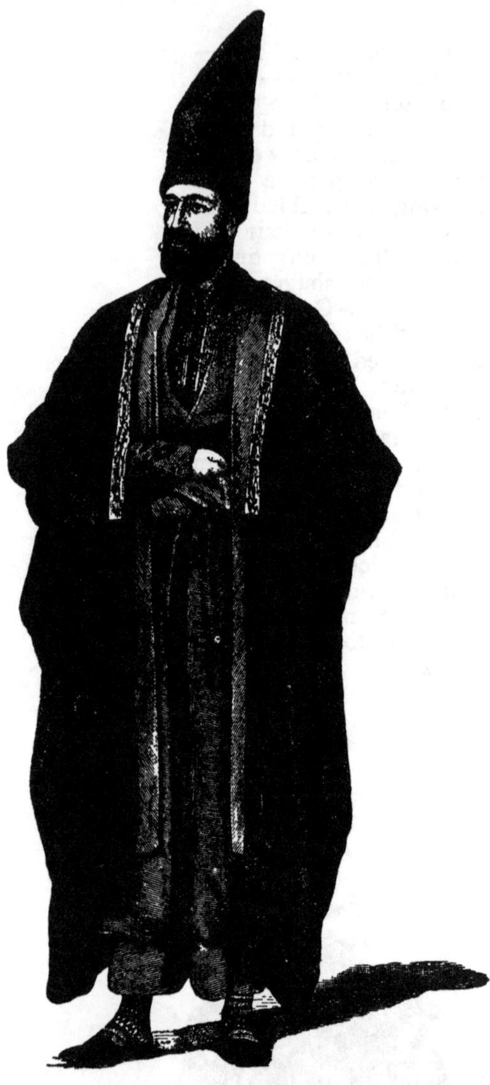

FIGURE NO. 136.—PERSIAN COSTUME.

indentation towards the top. It is the custom to wear it over the top of the ears, probably in remembrance of the time when cutting off ears was a common punishment in Persia. The shirt is made of thin woolen stuff; the poor wear blue cotton. It is very short, only reaching from neck to waist. Then comes the "Archeluk" made of Pers, a material printed with the finest Persian arabesques. Over this is the coat, always of one color, and made of nankeen or silk, and reaching almost to the ankle and wide enough to wrap over in front. It is fastened with a girdle consisting of a long strip of colored cloth wound several times round the waist. The rich often wear a cashmere shawl. In cool weather another coat made of a shawl, cloth or flannel with short sleeves and lined with fur, is sometimes worn. It is

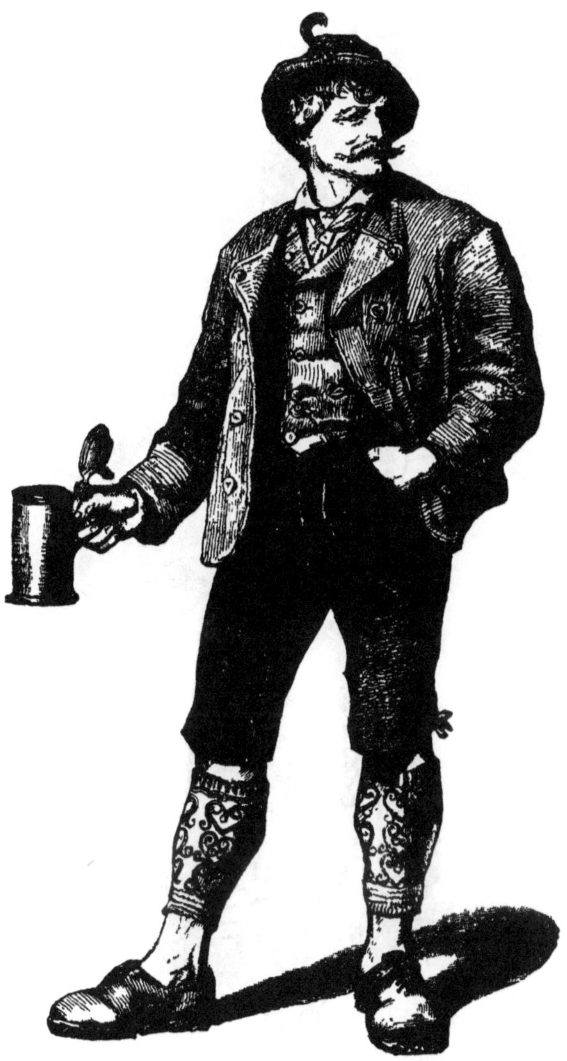

FIGURE No. 137.—BAVARIAN PEASANT.

generally gray and always of one color only. On state occasions the Persian throws a wide mantle over his whole costume which covers him from head to foot. The trousers are made very wide to allow the wearer to sit cross-legged. Short stockings and slippers cover the feet. Almost every article of Persian attire is trimmed with shawl stripes.

FIGURE No. 137.—BAVARIAN PEASANT.—Gray felt or cloth jacket with green facings and harts-horn buttons. Velvet or cloth waist-coat of any color preferred, with silver-coin buttons. Short trousers of deer or chamois skin made so as to give free play to the knees which, like the ankles are always bare. Over the calf of the leg is worn the coarse modern "Lofer" or wooden-gaiter of white or gray, decorated with woven or sewn-on ornaments. Coarse hob-nailed shoes; a soft, green felt hat decorated with a cock's-feather or a bit of eagle's plumage, and a soft, bright-colored neck-handkerchief complete the costume.

FIGURE No. 138.—AUNT DINAH.—Blue or red gingham or flannel dress which may be trimmed with gay stripes. White apron; three-cornered kerchief of white or some gay color folded over the breast. A bright bandanna handkerchief worn turban-style upon the woolly wig. Face and hands blackened, and lips reddened. A pair of iron-framed spectacles may be worn.

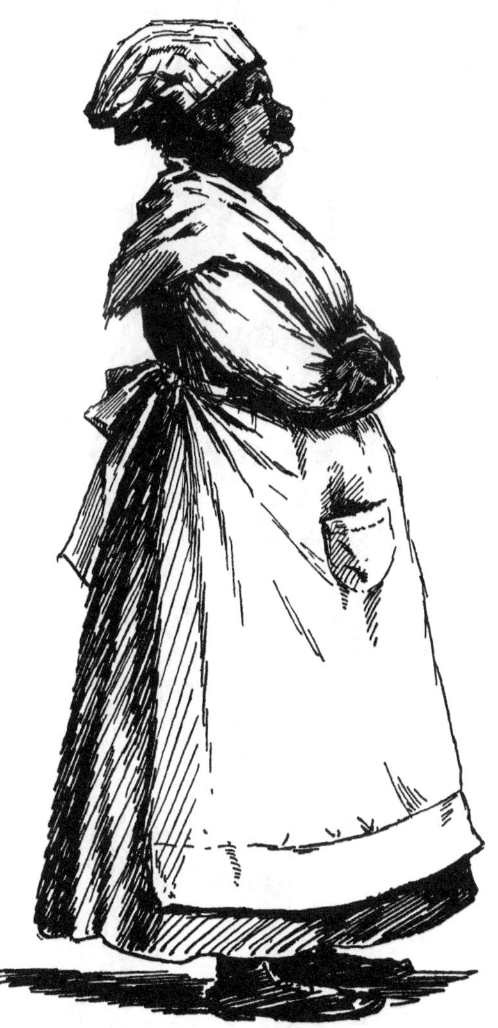

FIGURE No. 138.—AUNT DINAH.

FIGURE NO. 139.—SPRING.—This costume may be made of white or very pale-green cashmere, silk, gauze or crêpe. All of its edges are decorated with garlands of trailing arbutus or any other early spring blossom preferred. Birds are fastened upon the shoulders and one nestles in the hair; while a number of birds arranged to represent a flight cross the front of the skirt. Delicate green stockings embroidered with blossoms are worn with brown slippers. A basket of spring flowers completes the costume.

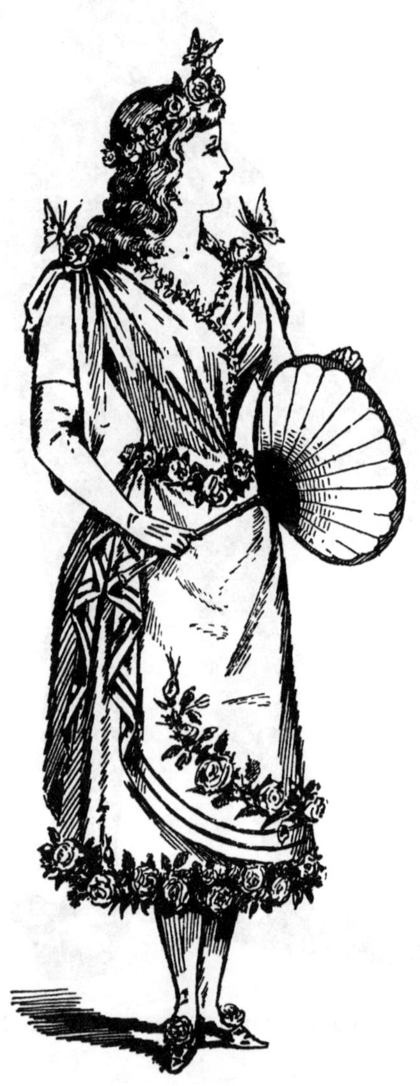

FIGURE NO. 140.—SUMMER.

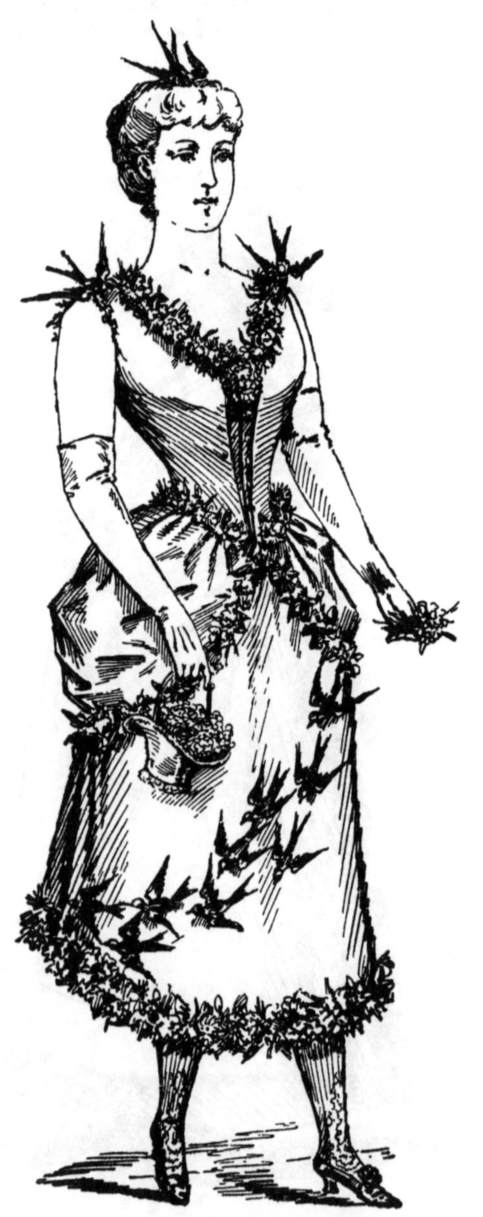

FIGURE NO. 139.—SPRING.

FIGURE NO. 140.—SUMMER.—This pretty costume is made of pale-pink tarletan, and is decorated with green ribbon and garlands of roses. The waist is in surplice style, and the Greek effect is observed in the drapery. Artificial butterflies are poised over the roses on the shoulders and head. Pink gloves and stockings, dark green slippers with pink rosettes, and a pink gauze fan complete the costume.

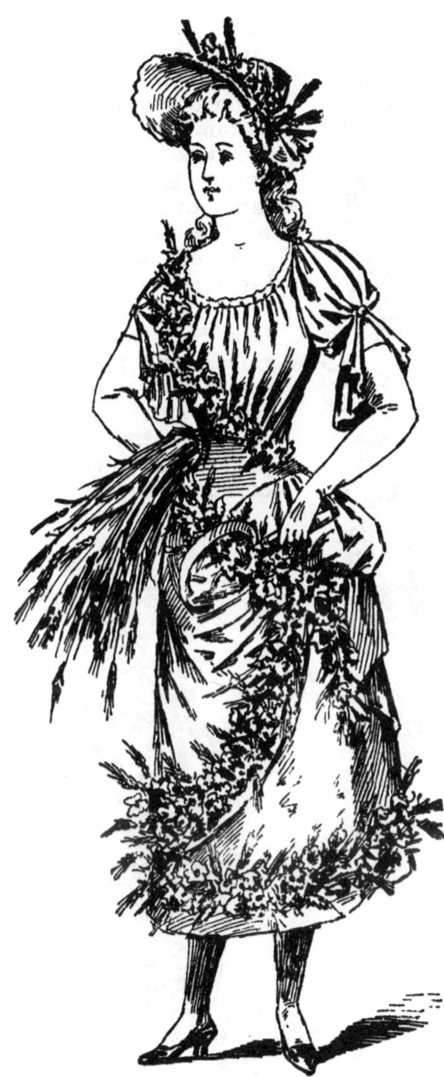

FIGURE NO. 141.—AUTUMN.

FIGURE NO. 141.—AUTUMN.—Dress of golden-brown satin and red gauze, the latter being used for the full waist and sleeves and part of the drapery. The decorations consist of garlands of grain, golden-rod and asters. Hat of brown straw trimmed with the grain and blossoms. Carries a sheaf of grain under one arm, and a sickle in the other hand. Red stockings and brown slippers complete the costume.

FIGURE NO. 142.—WINTER.—This is a unique costume, but one easily made. The foundation may be either of white or ice-green wool, and the whole surface is studded with crystal nail-heads or beads. Swan's down is used to decorate the costume as seen in the engraving, and a bit of holly, with its red berries is fastened to the muff and cap. Strings of crystal beads are fastened to the neck, wrists and lower edge of the waist to represent icicles. The shoes are also trimmed with swan's down. This is a very effective costume under the lights of a ball-room.

FIGURE NO. 143.—EGYPT (For illustration see next page).—This costume may be made of satin, silk or Oriental stuffs in the rich dull tints of the East. The dress might be of a deep-copper hue with a network of gold cord. The head-dress might be of a dull-blue-and-gold striped fabric, and the drapery, which is caught up alike at the back and front, of a fabric introducing the

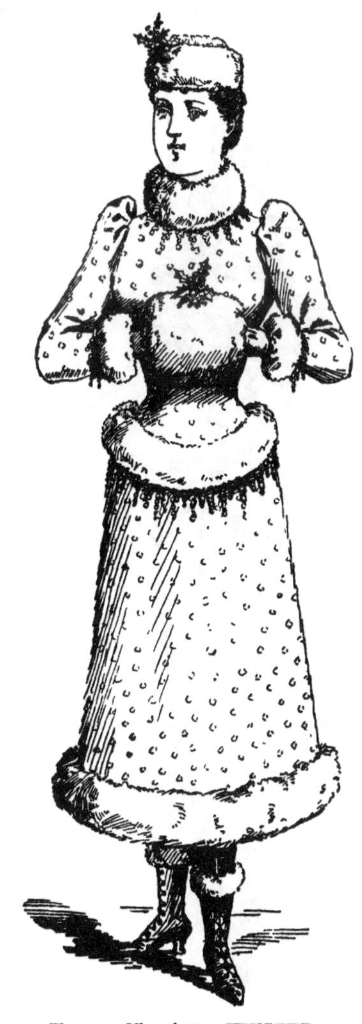

FIGURE NO. 142.—WINTER.

blue, copper and gold tints; the stomacher and pendant of gilt braid, or gilt paper with embroideries of silk or imitation gems upon them. The jewelry should be antique in style and worn plentifully. The fan is a palm with a jeweled handle. Anklets of gold, silver or imitation jewels may also be worn.

FIGURE No. 144.—JAPANESE COSTUME.—Plain and brocaded yellow satin form this costume. The brocading is black, and black braid is used to finish the plain satin sections. A yellow sash is about the waist and is tied in a huge bow at the back. A large yellow fan bordered with black, a Japanese coiffure and wooden shoes complete the costume.

FIGURE No. 145.—JOSEPHINE COSTUME.—Gray satin under-dress trimmed with silver braid. Over-dress of pink brocade embroidered with gray. Pink scarf with fringed ends. Gray hat trimmed with pink ribbon and pink and gray tips. Pink ribbon belt and bows; pink stockings and gray slippers, and a silver handled staff complete the costume.

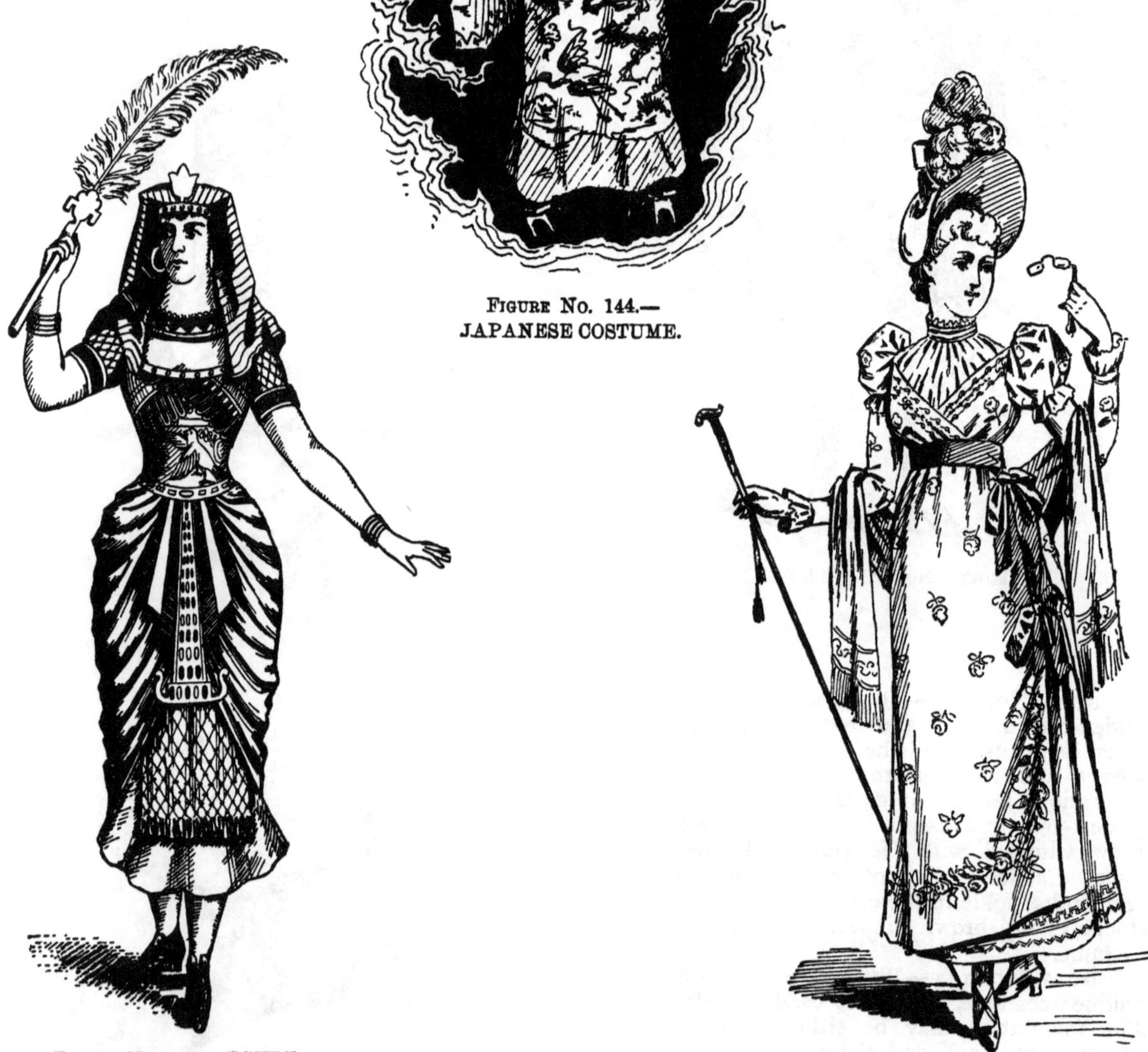

FIGURE No. 144.—JAPANESE COSTUME.

FIGURE No. 143.—EGYPT.
(For description see preceding page.)

FIGURE No. 145.—JOSEPHINE COSTUME.

FIGURE No. 146.—SONG.—White silk or cashmere is used for the skirt and the drapery above the bodice. The latter is of pink satin trimmed with gold bands. The skirt drapery is of a pale-gray gauze ornamented with laurel leaves and musical instruments made of pasteboard covered with gilt paper. Knots of gauze are on the shoulders. The ribbons decorating the lyre are pink, and the notes and bars on the skirt may be painted or made with pen and ink. The ornaments upon the neckband may be made of jet beads.

FIGURE No. 147.—EMPIRE RIDING COSTUME.—Gown or habit of dark-green cloth with silver buttons, white mull fichu and sleeve-ruffles. Green hat with silver-colored plumes; gray shoes with silver buttons; silver-mounted riding whip.

FIGURE No. 148.—CARMEN.—This is a very showy as well as graceful costume, and is arranged as follows: Skirt of pale-blue satin, trimmed with pearls. Sash of yellow and red very soft satin, fringed at the ends. Bodice and cap of black velvet trimmed with pearls. Necklet of sapphires, rubies and topazes. The gloves may be ommitted and narrow bands of gold worn upon the arms. Black stockings, and slippers with crossed ribbons of yellow. Long streamers of red, yellow and blue ribbons on the tambourine.

FIGURE No. 147.—EMPIRE RIDING COSTUME.

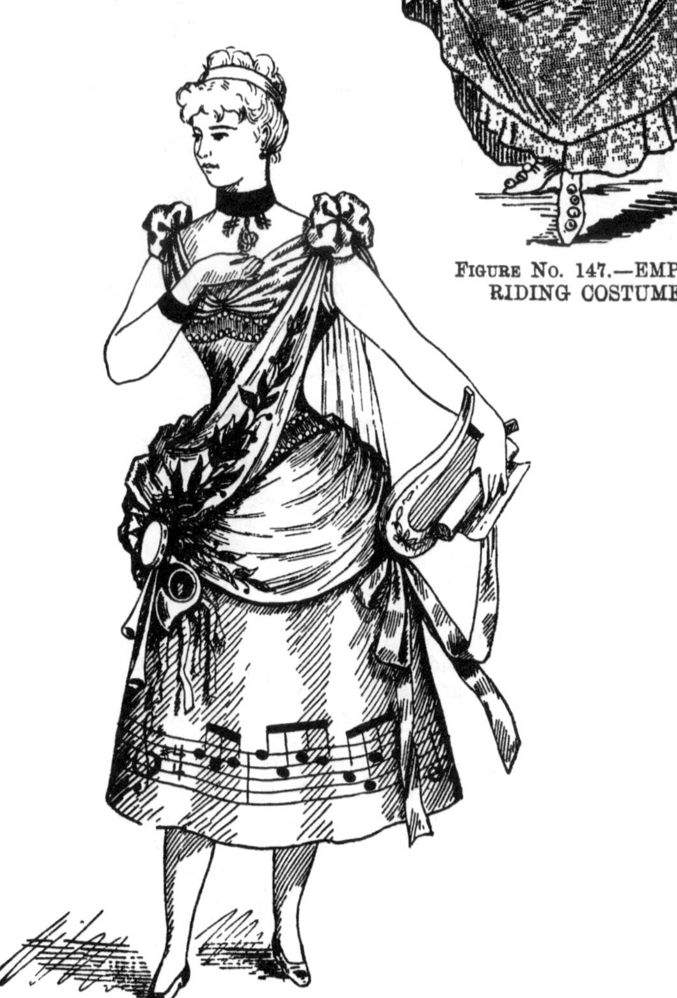

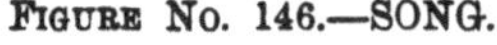

FIGURE No. 146.—SONG.

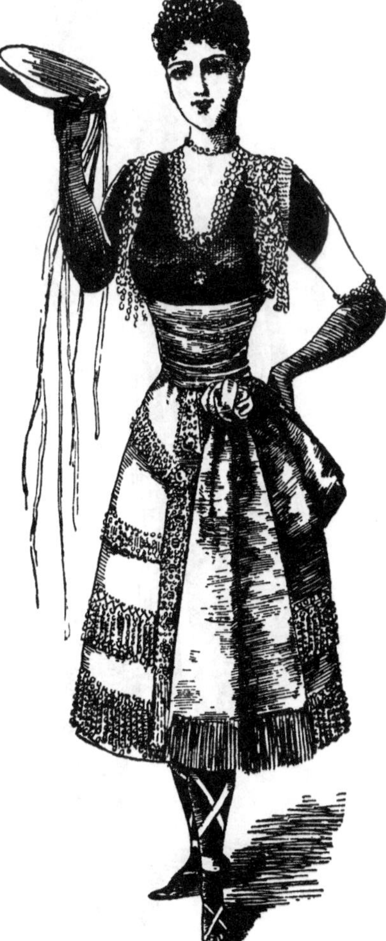

FIGURE No. 148.—CARMEN.

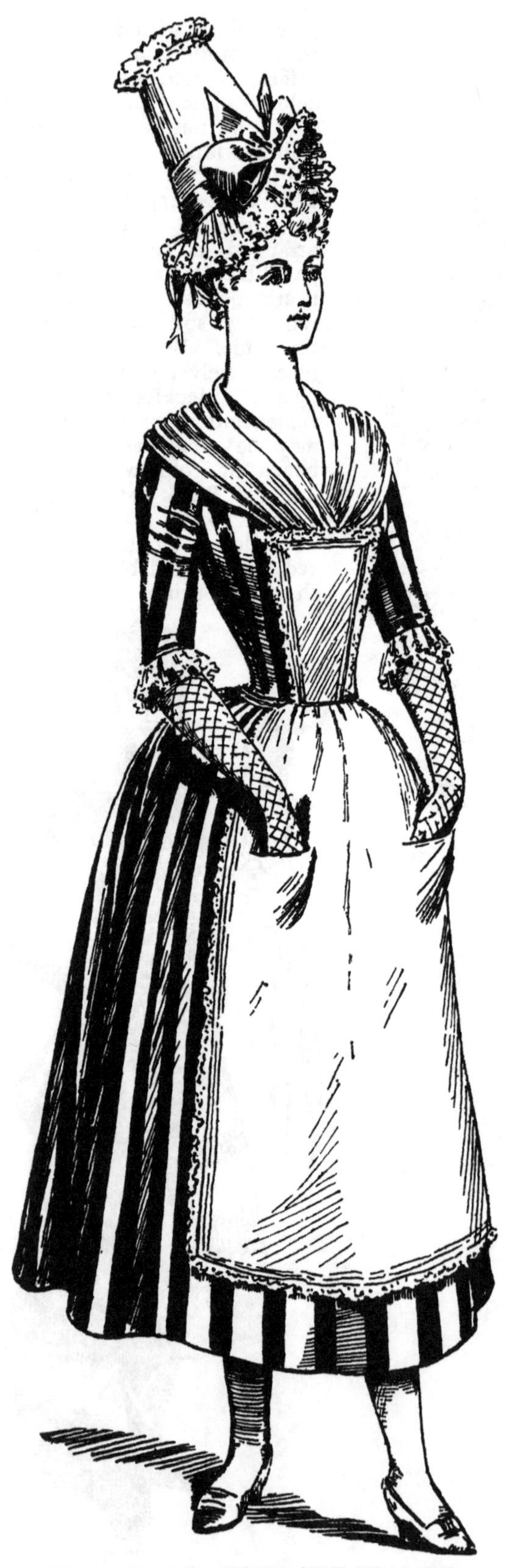

FIGURE No. 149.—NORMANDY PEASANT.

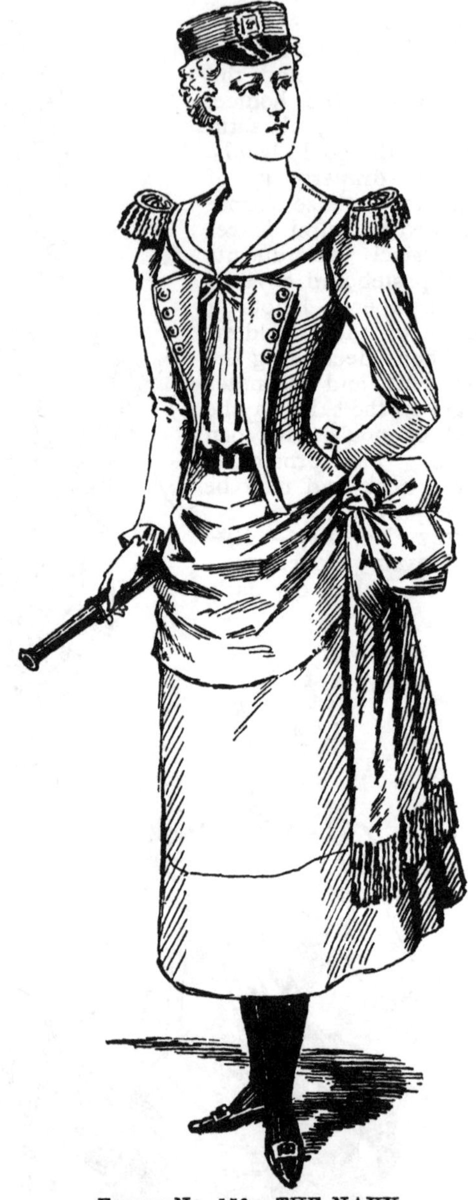

FIGURE No. 150—THE NAVY.

FIGURE NO. 149.—NORMANDY PEASANT.—Gown of blue-and-white striped goods, with half-sleeves finished at the elbows with lace ruffles. Apron of white muslin trimmed with narrow lace; fichu of white mull. Picturesque cap of starched white muslin trimmed with frills of lace and a band and bow of blue ribbon. Netted mitts of white or blue silk. White stockings and blue slippers.

FIGURE NO. 150.—THE NAVY.—Costume of white wool with facings and collar of pale-blue silk. Shirt of white silk with blue belt; silver buckles and buttons, and silver epaulets. White cap with silver ornaments, blue stockings and black slippers. The sash may combine the national colors of any country preferred. A marine telescope or glass is carried.

twined about the upper part of the arm. Smaller serpent upon the other wrist. Fan of impian or peacock feathers with a handle of gold.

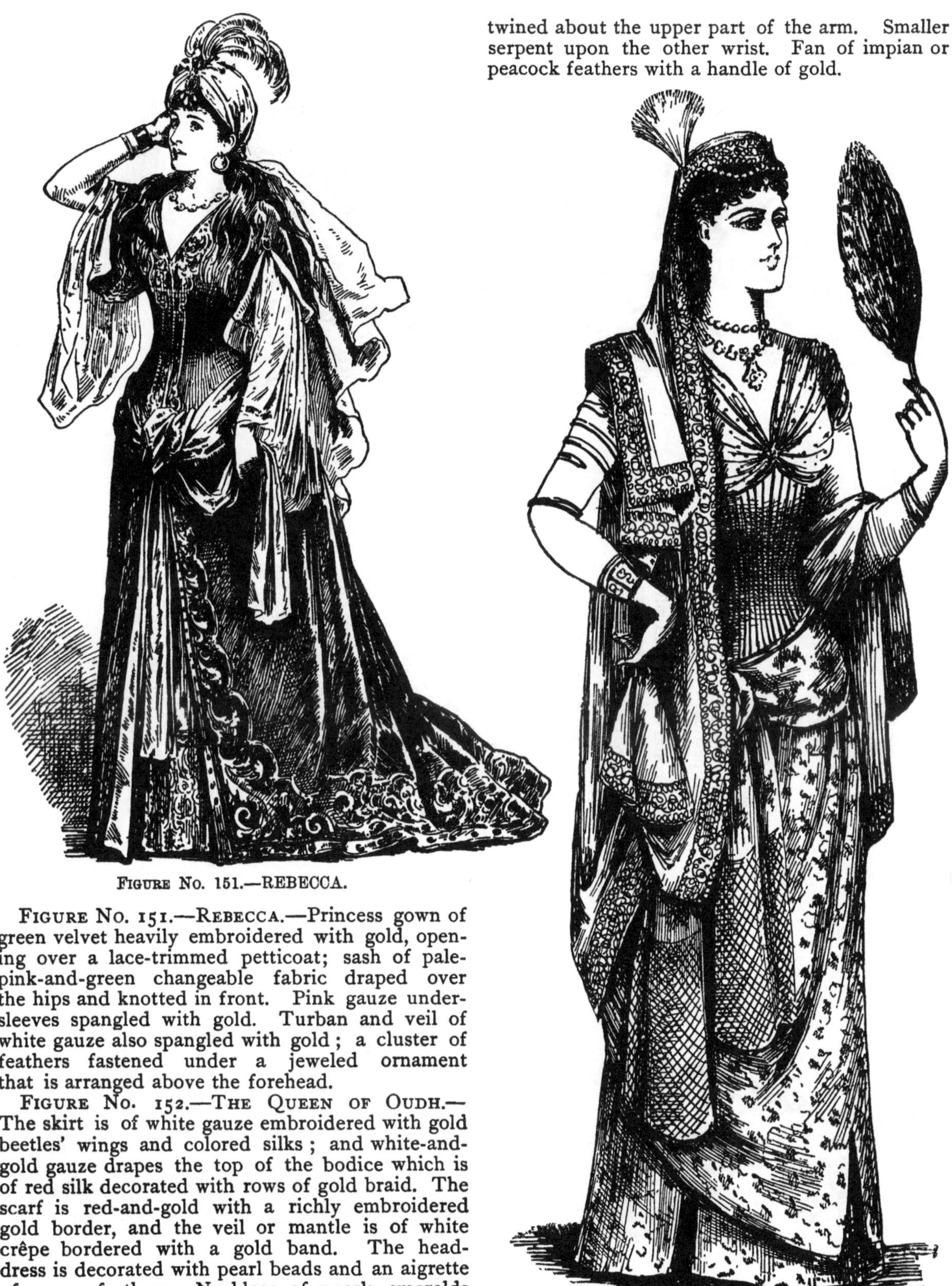

FIGURE No. 151.—REBECCA.

FIGURE No. 152.—THE QUEEN OF OUDH.

FIGURE No. 151.—REBECCA.—Princess gown of green velvet heavily embroidered with gold, opening over a lace-trimmed petticoat; sash of pale-pink-and-green changeable fabric draped over the hips and knotted in front. Pink gauze under-sleeves spangled with gold. Turban and veil of white gauze also spangled with gold; a cluster of feathers fastened under a jeweled ornament that is arranged above the forehead.

FIGURE No. 152.—THE QUEEN OF OUDH.—The skirt is of white gauze embroidered with gold beetles' wings and colored silks; and white-and-gold gauze drapes the top of the bodice which is of red silk decorated with rows of gold braid. The scarf is red-and-gold with a richly embroidered gold border, and the veil or mantle is of white crêpe bordered with a gold band. The head-dress is decorated with pearl beads and an aigrette of osprey feathers. Necklace of pearls, emeralds and rubies, with a diamond pendant. A broad jeweled band about one wrist with golden serpent

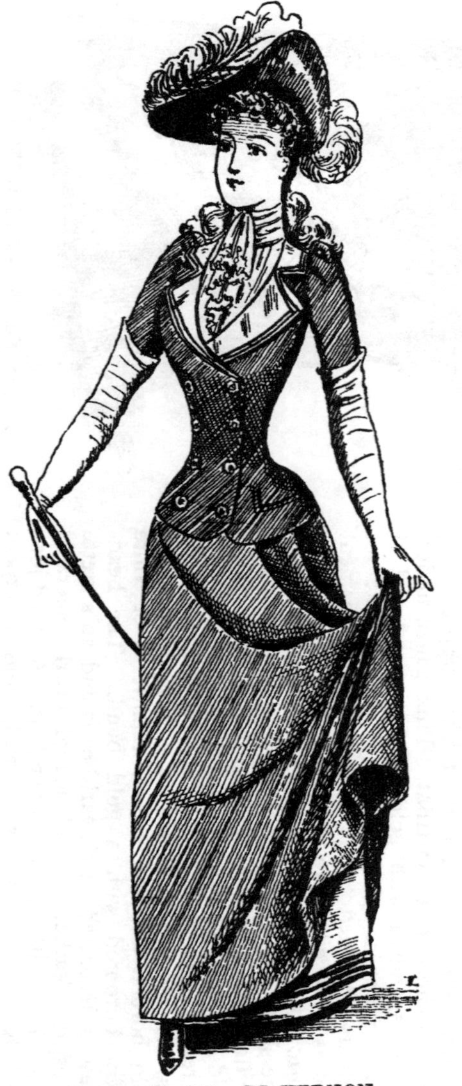

FIGURE No. 153.—DI VERNON.

FIGURE No. 153.—DI VERNON.—Coat and skirt of dark-green cloth. Skirt worn over a silver-colored satin petticoat trimmed with green ribbon. Coat lapels and collar faced with silver-colored satin and turned back to show a white silk chemisette and lace cravat; silver buttons to close the front. Large round hat of green with silver-colored plumes; long gray gloves and a riding whip complete the costume.

FIGURE No. 154.—BUTTERFLY.—Costume of pale-yellow chenille-tufted lace or gauze, made over a deeper shade of satin. Drapery caught here and there with brown and yellow butterflies. Large imitation butterfly-wings of the same tints fastened to the shoulders. Antennæ or feelers fastened in the hair above the brow. Fan opening in the form of a butterfly. Yellow stockings and brown slippers tipped with butterflies.

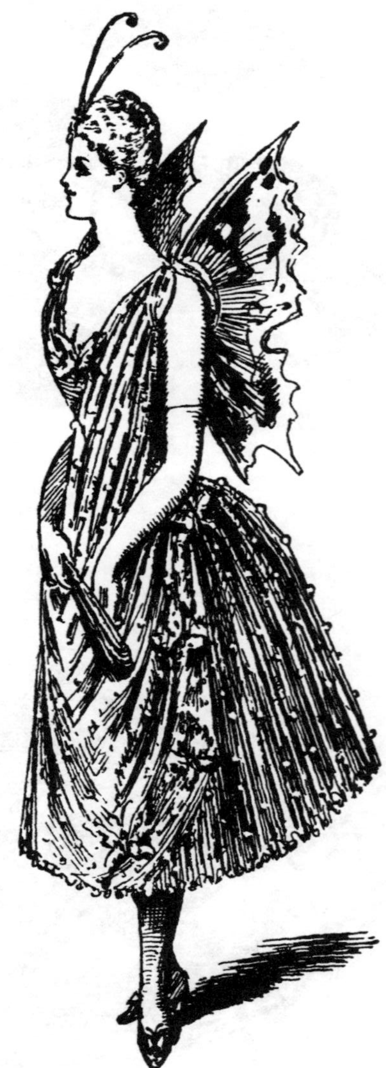

FIGURE No. 154.—BUTTERFLY.

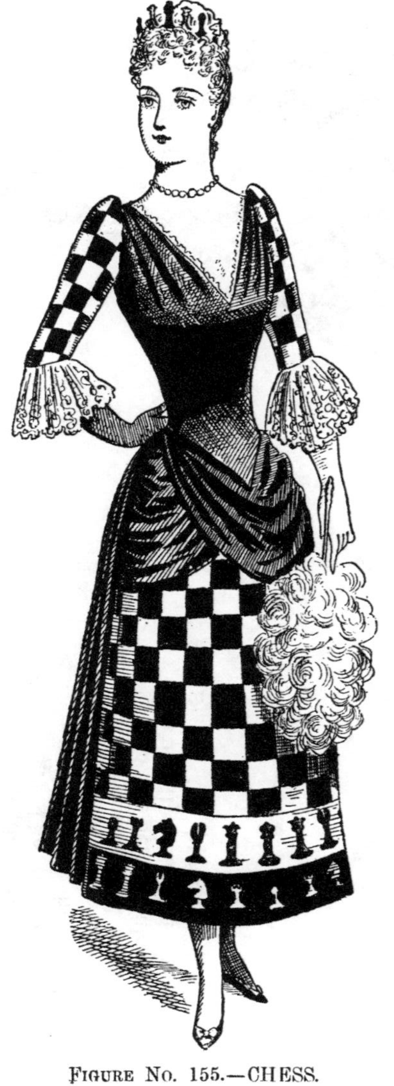

FIGURE No. 155.—CHESS.

FIGURE No. 155.—CHESS.—Red and black satin are combined in this costume. If the blocked satin cannot be found, the effect may be produced by interweaving strips of the two colors, either of satin or of ribbon. The chess figures may be painted upon the strips for the skirt, and cut from card-board and covered for the head-dress. A red fan, red stockings and black slippers complete the costume.

FIGURE No. 156.—CARDS.—This is always a popular costume and can be easily made. The skirt is made of light-colored satin laid in wide box-plaits, and upon each plait is sewed a cluster of cards. The drapery is a long, straight piece of satin gathered up at the center and ending under the plaits at the side, and is also ornamented with cards. Along its lower edge and the bottom of the skirt are sewed metal discs colored to imitate poker chips. The waist is of white Surah silk edged with lace. The girdle is of deep red velvet. The fan is made by sewing cards and ostrich tips to a palm-leaf fan that has been cut down to the size desired. A knot of feathers and a cluster of ribbon loops are upon the left shoulder.

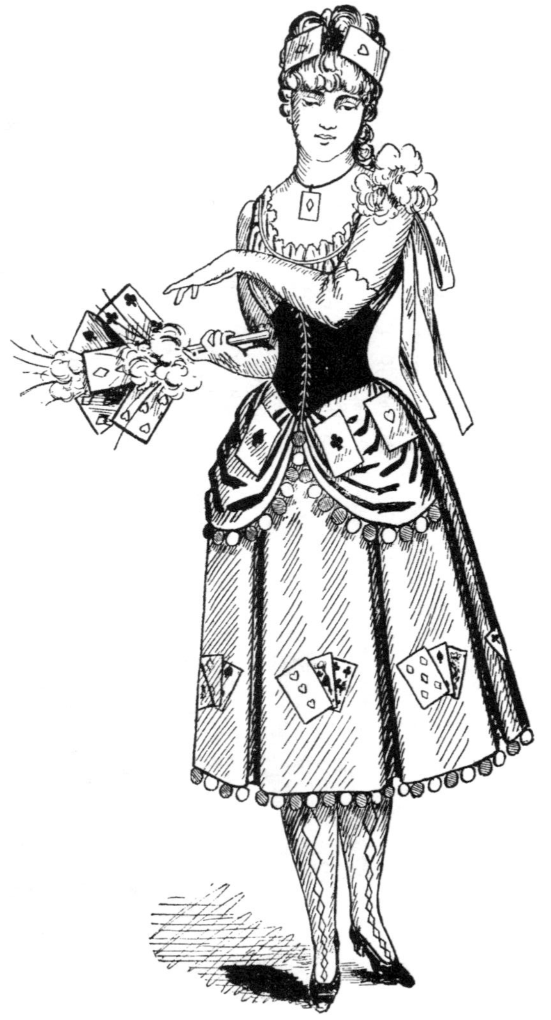

FIGURE No. 156.—CARDS.

FIGURE NO. 158.—WITCH.—Black and yellow satin are used for this costume whose details are made clear by the engraving. The pointed hat of yellow is encircled by a black snake, while a mouse is fastened to the bodice and a cat is perched on the left shoulder. An owl is usually fastened in the splints of the broom.

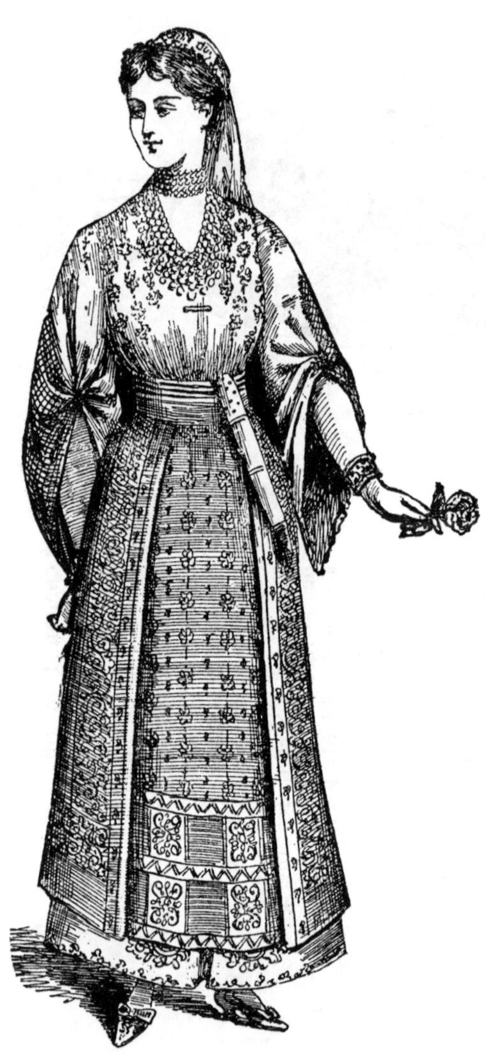

FIGURE NO. 157.—ROUMANIAN COSTUME.

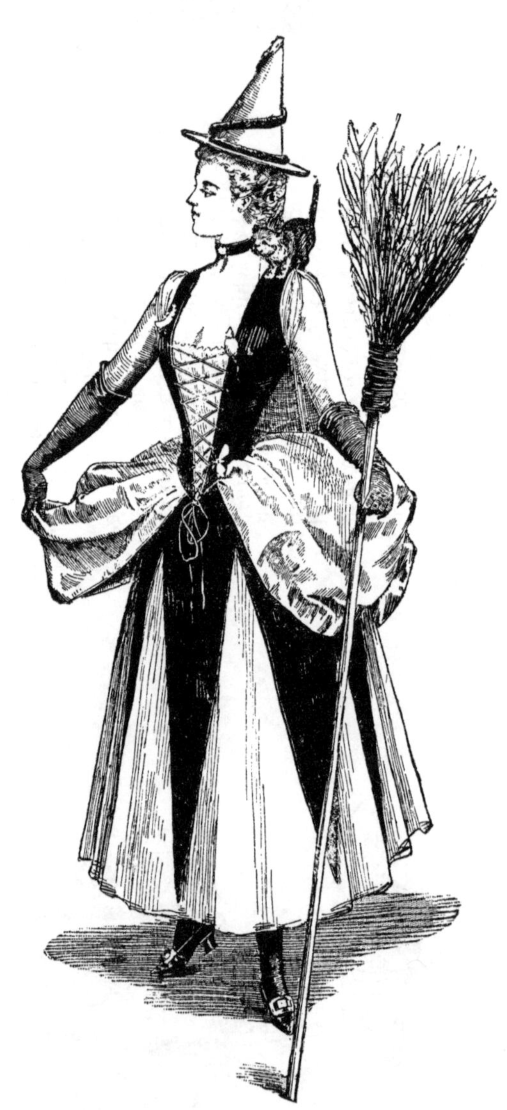

FIGURE NO. 158.—WITCH.

FIGURE NO. 157.—ROUMANIAN COSTUME.—This is a very striking costume in white, black and gold. It is arranged as follows: The bodice, under-skirt and cap are made of some white fabric, such as satin, cashmere, or muslin embroidered in black. The over-dress is of black embroidered in gold and bright colors. Veil of white tissue. Necklet of pearls and gold; and pearl trimming about the neck of the bodice. Roman gold bracelets. Black slippers with gilt bows. Stockings of dull red. Folded belt of black fabric, with sheathed dagger suspended from it.

FIGURE NO. 159.—FOOL.—This is a good costume for a masquerade or pantomime. It is made of a cheap, pure-white fabric—muslin will do—and decorated with red or blue, or red *and* blue. The face must be whitened with chalk or some theatrical whitening-preparation, and blue and red patches must be painted upon the cheeks and forehead. The hat is of soft white felt. Other colors may be chosen, but those named are conventional and almost always selected.

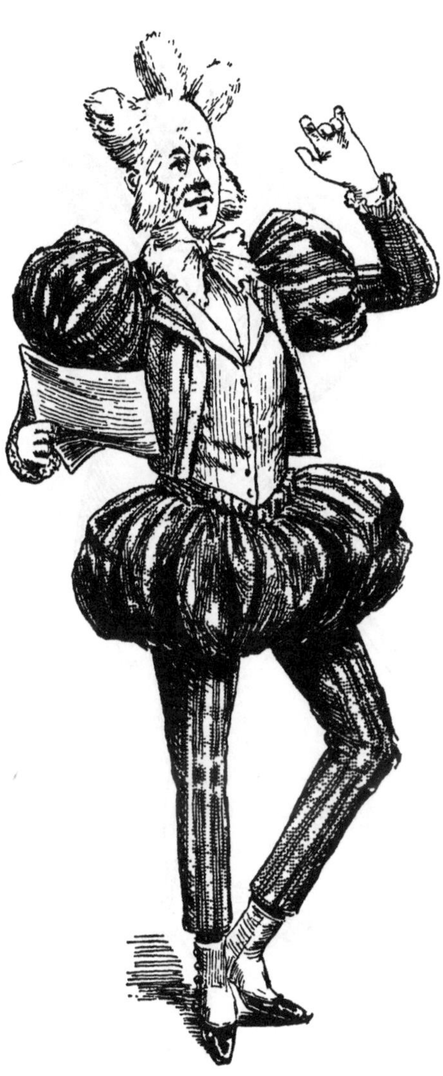

FIGURE NO. 160.—PUNCHINELLO.

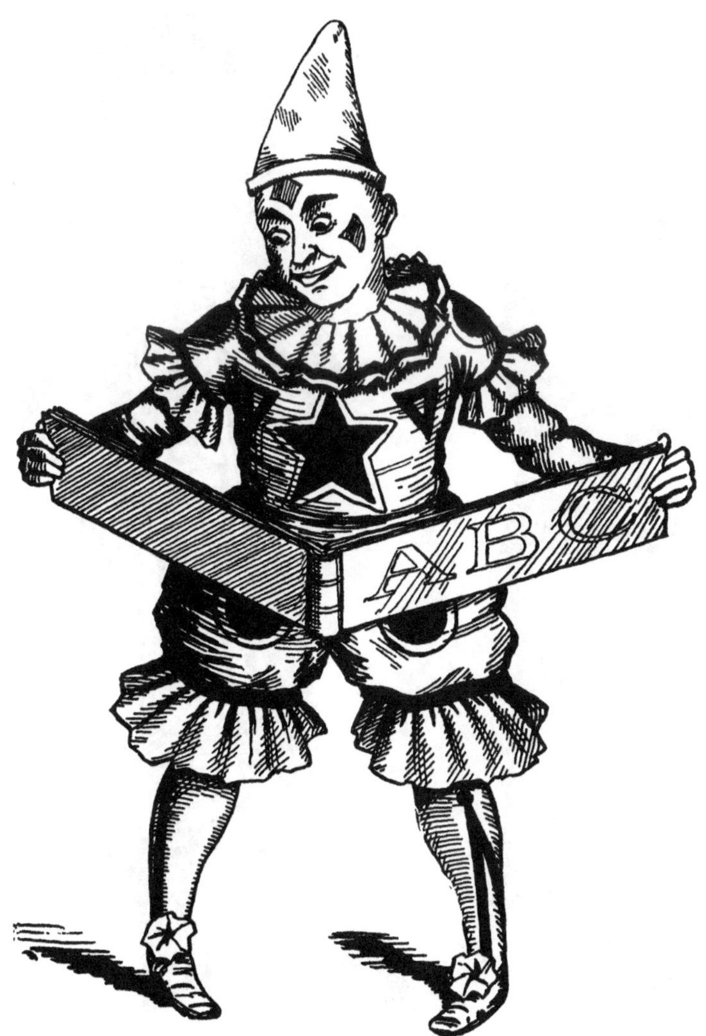

FIGURE NO. 159.—FOOL.

FIGURE NO. 160.—PUNCHINELLO.—This grotesque costume is made of gayly-striped cotton fabric, and the method of its arrangement is fully shown by the picture. The vest is white striped with red, blue or yellow, and the cravat is of white lace. A white wig of eccentric shape, and whiskers to match, are worn. Patent-leather shoes and white gaiter-tops complete the costume.

FIGURE NO. 162.—CLOWNESSE.—Black and yellow are the colors used in this costume, the arrangement of which is perfectly shown by the engraving. The ruffs of black are all edged with yellow, and the black figures are painted upon the skirt. A large yellow butterfly is upon the corsage, while antennæ and a clown's hat complete the powdered coiffure.

FIGURE NO. 163.—CROSSING SWEEPER.—Bodice and skirt of dark-blue trimmed with red. White muslin chemisette with full sleeves; gray apron and dark-gray hat trimmed with red and blue ribbon, white mull and faded pink roses. Gray stockings and red slippers. Hair in loose curls. Broom of twigs.

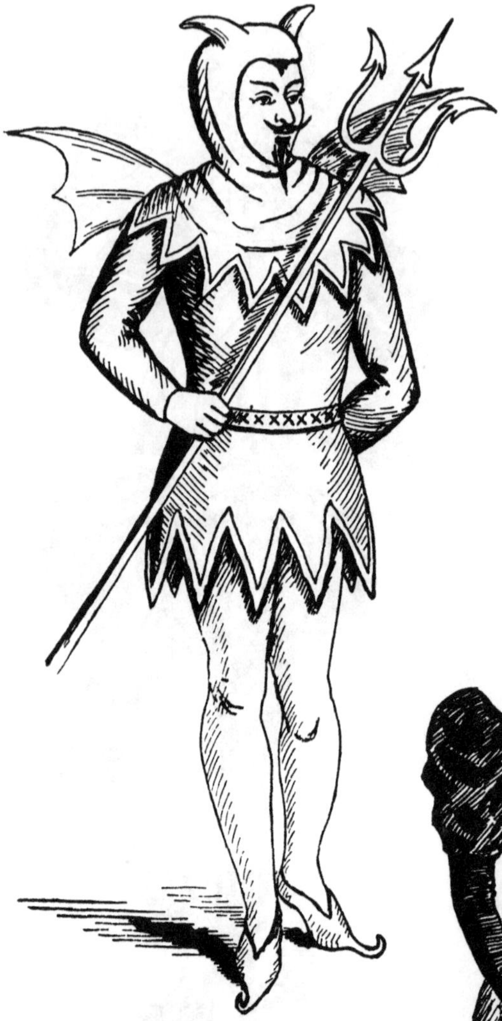

FIGURE NO. 161.—DEVIL.

FIGURE NO. 161.—DEVIL.—This costume is made entirely of scarlet cashmere or flannel, and is worn with scarlet tights and shoes. If desired the points may be bound with black. The fork may be fashioned from wood and painted to represent silver, gold or iron. This costume is also frequently worn by "Mephistopheles."

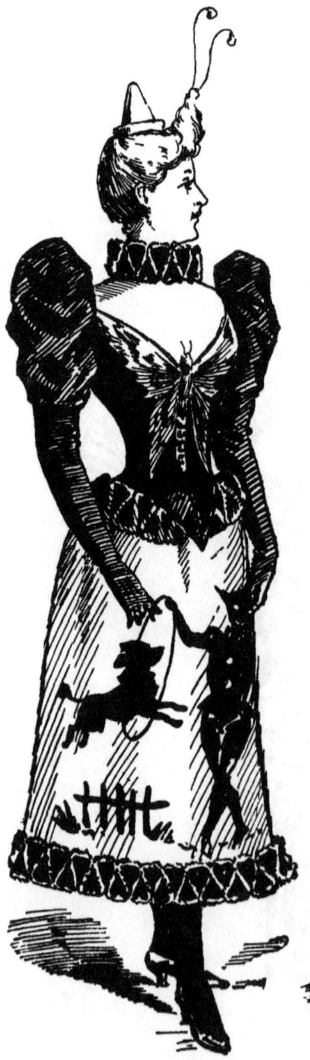

FIGURE NO. 162.—CLOWNESSE.

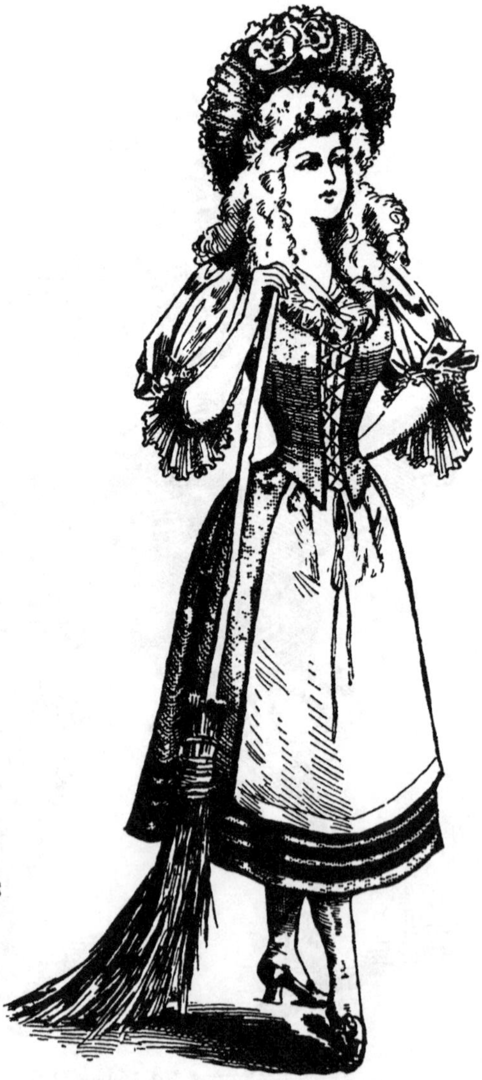

FIGURE NO. 163.—CROSSING SWEEPER.

FIGURE NO. 164.—CLOWN.—This costume is made of white muslin edged and figured with red, and the engraving fully explains its method of construction. White tights and red slippers are worn, and the hands, arms and face are whitened with chalk. Red patches are applied to the face, and a tufted red wig is worn.

FIGURES NOS. 165 AND 166.—SWISS CLOWNS.—Any coarse fabric of any color preferred may be used for these costumes, whose details are made extremely simple to follow by observing the pictures. The neck frills are of muslin, and the hats are of white felt stretched into the shapes delineated. Coarse woolen stockings and wooden shoes are worn. False noses and cosmetics are used to make up the faces.

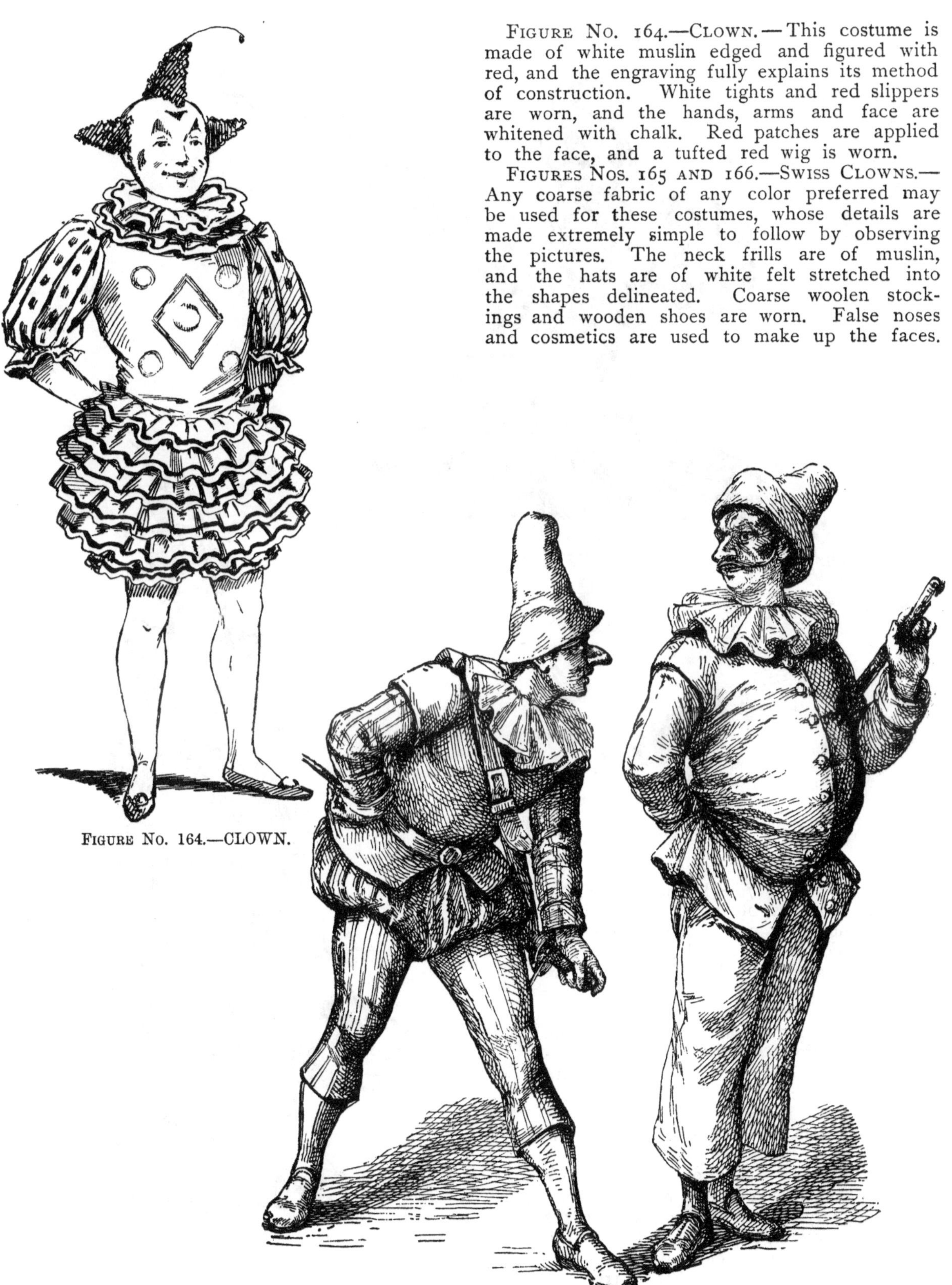

FIGURE NO. 164.—CLOWN.

FIGURES NOS. 165 AND 166.—SWISS CLOWNS.

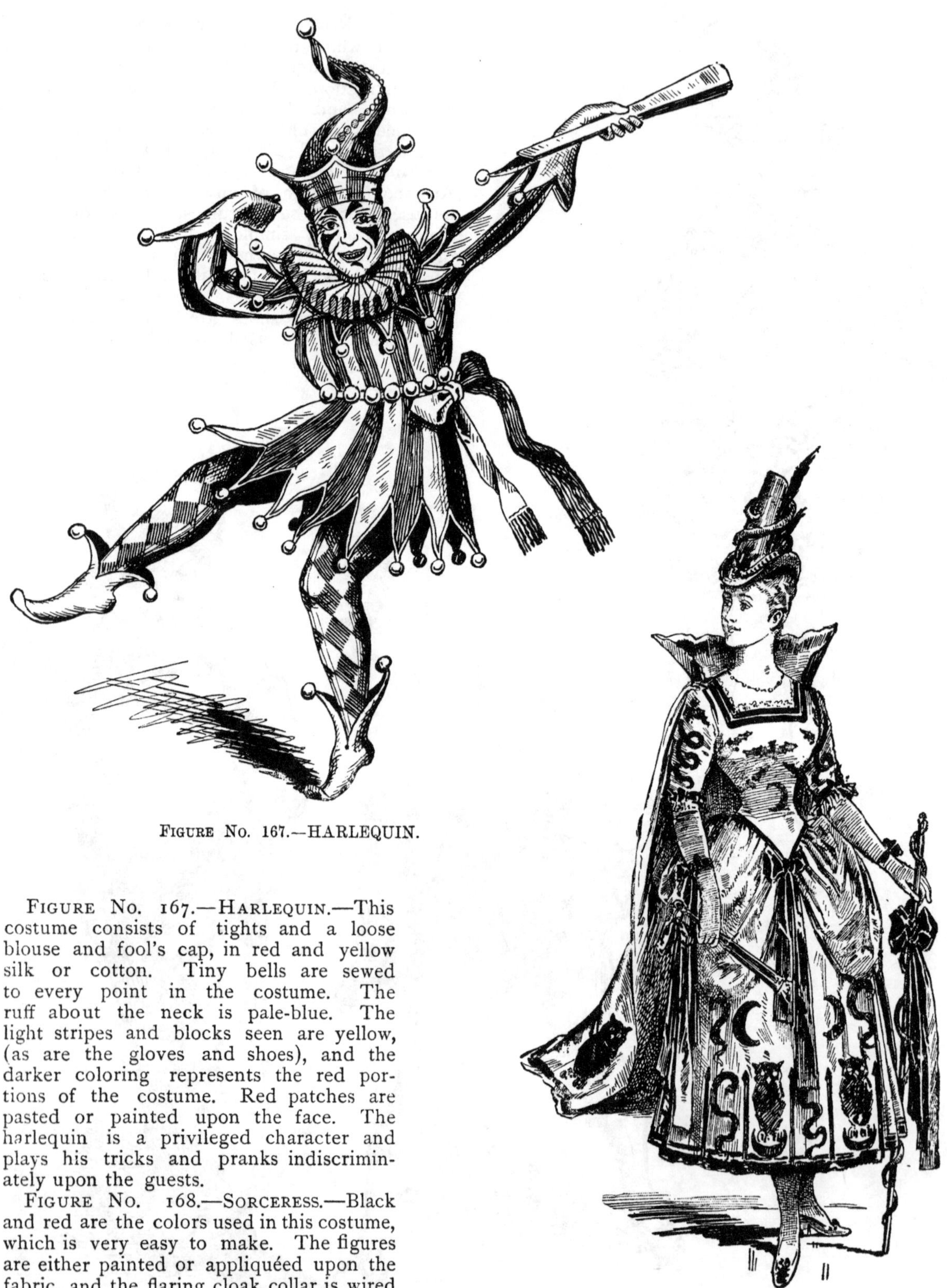

FIGURE No. 167.—HARLEQUIN.

FIGURE No. 168.—SORCERESS.

FIGURE No. 167.—HARLEQUIN.—This costume consists of tights and a loose blouse and fool's cap, in red and yellow silk or cotton. Tiny bells are sewed to every point in the costume. The ruff about the neck is pale-blue. The light stripes and blocks seen are yellow, (as are the gloves and shoes), and the darker coloring represents the red portions of the costume. Red patches are pasted or painted upon the face. The harlequin is a privileged character and plays his tricks and pranks indiscriminately upon the guests.

FIGURE No. 168.—SORCERESS.—Black and red are the colors used in this costume, which is very easy to make. The figures are either painted or appliquéed upon the fabric, and the flaring cloak collar is wired to hold it in shape. The hat is trimmed with a snake and a bird; while a serpent is twined about the ribbon-trimmed wand.

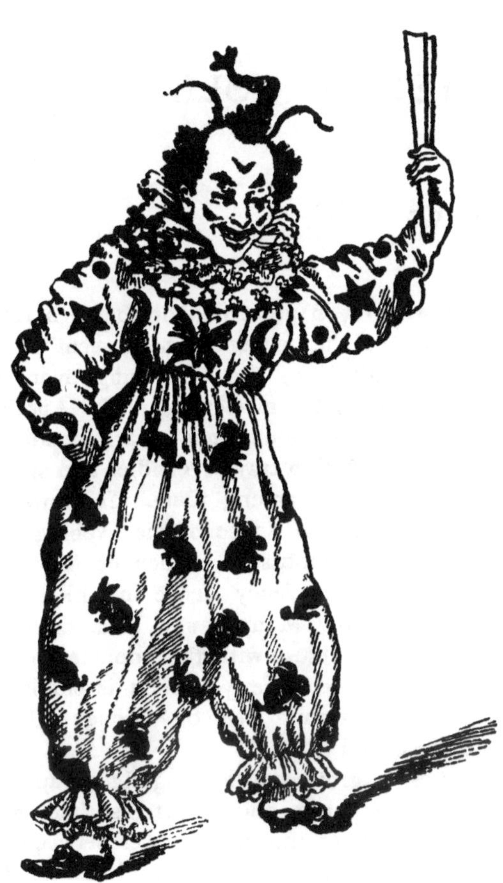

FIGURE NO. 169.—FRENCH CLOWN.

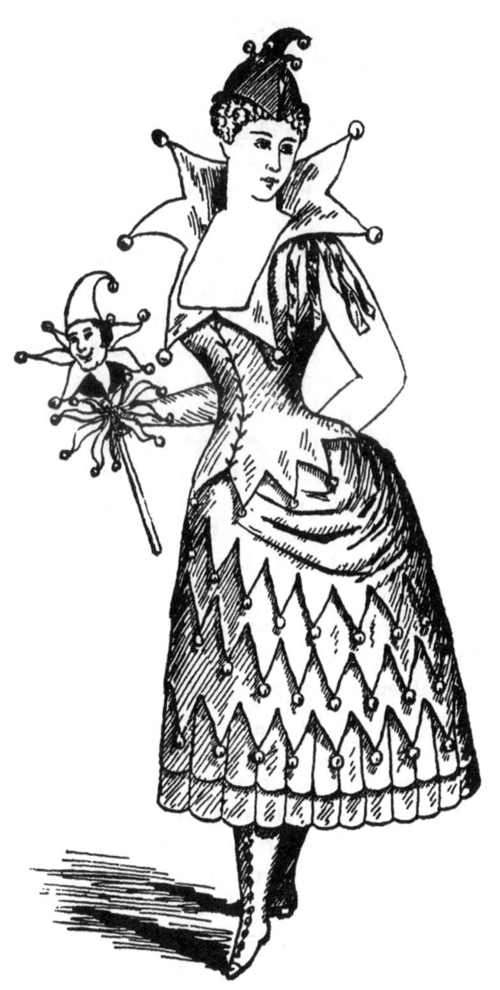

FIGURE NO. 170.—FOLLY.

FIGURE NO. 169.—FRENCH CLOWN.—White muslin is the foundation fabric of this costume, and the figures are either painted on in red, or are appliquéed on, being cut from red paper or muslin. White stockings and red shoes are worn, and the hands and face are chalked. Red patches are on the face and a fantastic wig of red or jet-black is worn.

FIGURE NO. 170.—FOLLY.—The skirt of this costume is made of white satin and trimmed with plaitings of the same. The three overskirts are of alternating colors cut in Vandyke points that are edged with gold braid and tipped with tiny bells. The engraving fully explains the shape and finish of the waist. A carnival cap is worn on the head and a "fool's bauble" is carried in the hand. High buttoned boots are worn over fancy stockings. The best colors to combine are pink and blue; red, yellow and black; blue and red; and black with yellow or red. The combination should appear throughout the entire costume.

ENTERTAINMENTS FOR YOUNG FOLK.

FANCY-DRESS BALLS AND PARTIES.

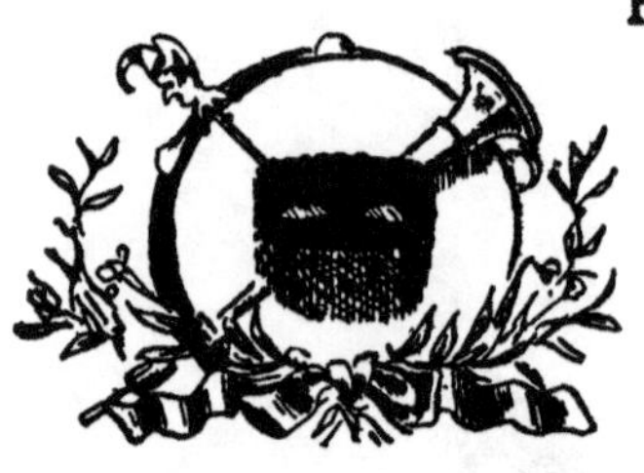

Fancy-dress parties are greatly enjoyed by young folk not yet "out" in society, but fast approaching the début period; and also by children, who seem to delight in fantastic or beautiful dresses, and very successfully assume their little characters.

It is of course understood that a ball for these coming men and women is not prolonged beyond twelve o'clock at night, and that it frequently occurs for the wee ones in the afternoon, or between the hours of five and eight or nine o'clock. Nor are the refreshments for young guests, who have not reached the honor of attending "grown up" balls, of the class set before débutantes and matrons. Delicate sandwiches, fancy cakes, confections, ices and creams, lemonade and cordials made from fruit syrups make up the menu; though sometimes the older children are served with coffee or chocolate.

A young folks' fancy-dress ball or party may begin precisely the same as one for mature guests; or the tableaux and grand march may be omitted, and when the charming little guests are assembled dancing may begin without any preliminary save the opening bars of the music. Or the comic quadrille mentioned in the description of Fancy Balls for adults may be imitated by the small guests.

At a children's party this dance is sometimes called the Singing Quadrille, as the characters are taken from some nursery book and the little masqueraders sing its rhymes. With very young folk, however, dancing often gives place to juvenile amusements, such as are afforded by conjurers, ventriloquists, Punch-and-Judy shows, magic lanterns, etc., etc. Children greatly enjoy the Horn of Plenty, or the Christmas tree in its season, from whose depths and heights endless presents pour out and down; or, in great delight they fish from a Fairy Pool for the presents which seem to tie themselves to the lines that are flung over the screens surrounding the mysterious pool. Another pleasure for them is the entrance of a fantastically dressed old man with a tray of candies and sweets which he distributes among them. If, however, they dance, the special dance of the evening is a minuet, Highland schottische, ribbon or May-pole dance or some other fancy dance in which they have been trained. Many fancy balls both for adults and children close with the popular English dance—Sir Roger de Coverly—which is similar to the American Virginia Reel or "Money Musk," as it is often called.

Sometimes a grotesque looking figure appears among the little guests and entertains them with wonderful fairy tales and ghost stories between the dances; and possibly he selects the tiniest maiden of the party for his partner for the next dance; or, seating himself in the orchestra, pretends to direct the figures of the quadrille or cotillion. Sometimes he comes as a bear tamer and leads by a small rope a brown or white bear (which is a boy dressed in a bear-skin) that does wonderful tricks and eats the candy and cake given him by the children. Perhaps a clown or a harlequin will stroll into the rooms between the dances and set the little ones wild with merriment over his queer antics; or he may present each guest with a favor which takes the form of a fancy cap, until the room seems filled with gayly crested heads. In fact, it seems almost certain that young folk may derive as much, if not more, pleasure from a fancy-dress ball or party than their adult relatives and friends.

Little folk may mask or not, as suits them or their hostess; but if they do mask, they must follow the example of their elders and unmask at a given hour—say ten o'clock if the ball is to end at twelve, or at whatever hour refreshments are served.

A pretty children's party was lately given, where the boys were dressed as mountaineers—that is, they wore knickerbockers and blouses with sashes that were tied at the left side, and their hats were decorated with gay ribbons of many colors. The girls all had white dresses and gay aprons; and each of them wore one special kind of flowers upon her head, as a garland over her shoulders or perhaps about the hem of her dress, and she was called by the name of the blossom she had chosen for herself. The flowers were not all natural—indeed, this would have been quite impossible, and, besides, if they had been cut fresh from the hot-house they would not have kept their forms and colors during the warmth of the dance. The foliage of some and the blossoms of others were arranged by a deft intermingling of nature and art, and the results were beautiful pictures and a happy time for all of the little guests.

One of the prettiest afternoon entertainments, also for small people, was arranged to occur between four and eight o'clock P. M. All the small persons (and none of them were above twelve or under five years old) were dressed just like children of a larger growth. There were tiny gentlemen in swallow-tails, high collars and white neckties; and there were gentlewomen arrayed in trains, with feathers in their coiffures, which were disposed quite *a la mode.* Some of the girls had their infantile locks thickly powdered and wore patches on their chins and cheeks, and not a little powder and rouge on their faces, after the fashion of the times which originated beauty spots and artificially whitened tresses. It was a droll and entertaining display, though not very complimentary to the elderly persons whom they imitated so perfectly. It was an answer to the Scotch petition:

"O wad some power the giftie gie us,
To see oursels as ithers see us!"

Any of the costumes illustrated or suggested on these pages will be suitable for such fancy-dress parties or balls, or for any regular masquerade entertainment.

JAPANESE PARTIES.

These parties are generally given by young girls to those of their own sex, and the time is usually in the afternoon. Each guest must dress in a kimono or Japanese dress, wear Japanese shoes or slippers, and carry a Japanese fan.

As far as possible the decorations and amusements suggested for adult Japanese parties, should be carried out; and the young guests are allowed to arrange and eat their refreshments after the Japanese style. In Japan food is served upon very low platforms or table-like elevations, and each person kneels and sits upon her heels while she eats. Our little guests may try it if they wish to, but the position is very tiresome. Japanese fruits and sweetmeats may be purchased at first-class fruit and grocery stores; but where they cannot, sweets and confections of home manufacture may take their places and be eaten from Japanese plates and dishes.

(8)

At such a party the young hostess or one of her guests may read from a volume of Japanese fairy-tales; and if she is ingenious she might study out from its pages or those of some other Japanese book games or plays that are in vogue among the children of Japan, and introduce them as pastimes for the afternoon.

A Japanese circle might be established to be held every two or three weeks, and in the meantime every member required to learn what she can of Japanese children, their customs, pleasures, studies, etc., and impart such information at the next meeting of the circle. In this way a Japanese party would add profit to pleasure.

Upon page 147 may be seen the engraving of a kimono, which is very suitable to wear at a girl's Japanese party. It should be made of silk or sateen, figured or flowered in an Oriental design.

MISSES' AND GIRLS' LADY WASHINGTON PARTIES.

These are pretty entertainments which may be given as private affairs at which games may be played, stories told, tricks performed, or exhibitions of magic or the magic lantern given. Sometimes boys are invited to these private parties, and they may come in their ordinary party attire. But, if the entertainment is given by the scholars of Sunday or other schools, either as an "exhibition" or "for sweet charity's sake," then it is imperative that the boys take part and dress in knee-breeches, cocked hats, wigs, buckled shoes and lace ruffles—veritable little gentlemen of the Revolutionary period. At such an entertainment, tableaux and plastiques representing the scenes of the Revolutionary period, would be very appropriate. Refreshments at such a gathering would be served by little Revolutionary ladies and gentlemen, and would consist of what are known as New England viands—to say nothing of tea, which, of course, will be the proper beverage of the occasion.

BREAD-AND-BUTTER PARTIES.

These are nothing more or less than little afternoon parties for young misses who are not attired in fancy dress, but arrive habited in their prettiest gowns.

At a Bread-and-Butter party the guests may chat, tell stories, play games of all kinds, or enjoy themselves in any of the many ways known to them but not understood by the average adult—who forgets that she was once a young girl, and also forgets all the things which delighted her heart in those happy days.

At a Bread-and-Butter party the refreshments consist largely of the articles named, together with an unlimited supply of jam, fruits, nuts, sweets, creams, ices and lemonade, and sometimes chocolate or fruit-syrup cordials.

LITTLE FOLKS' AFTERNOON PARTIES.

As elsewhere suggested, the wee ones from four or five years old to eight or nine usually hold their revelries in the late afternoon and early evening; for no matter how fast and furious the fun, little heads will grow heavy, little eyelids droop early over sleepy eyes, and little legs and arms gradually lose their activity by the time when little folk should be in bed. So these young lords of creation and their little sweethearts make merry between the hours of four or five o'clock or eight or nine. About six or seven supper is served and after the feast comes an hour of frolic, and then home they go full of goodies and pleasure both of which make them too sleepy to "tell mamma all about it" until next day.

The refreshments are always just what the little

ones like—cake, candy, ice-creams in dainty shapes and forms, ices in delicate tints and flavors, nuts, fruits, and lemonade or fruit-cordials; and though they should head the list we name them last because they are generally the only things left—sandwiches made with tongue, minced ham, chicken or turkey. When they are made with jelly or jam instead of meats, they are as eagerly devoured as cake; but oh! the possibilities in the way of smeared faces, stained dresses and sticky fingers.

Now these little folk may dance or play games or listen to stories, just as they choose, or as the mamma of the little hostess has arranged the programme. Sometimes older children like to play games such as you buy in a toy store. One of the games now most popular and which captivates young and old is called

TIDDLEDY-WINKS.

Just how the name was originated is not yet made public, but the game is very fascinating. There are a number of tiny bone discs about as large as a dime and of different colors, several larger discs or circular pieces of the same colors and a small cup or bowl. Each player has all the small discs of one color and a large disc of the same color, and with the large disc each little disc is pressed hard and "snapped" into the cup from the table. Each child plays in turn, and whoever gets all his discs into the cup first wins the game, which is intensely interesting and amusing to children.

Tennis Tiddledy-Winks is the same game except that a tiny tennis net is placed between the players and the cup. Both games, with full instructions, can be purchased for a small sum at almost any toy or stationery store in any large town or city.

There are many other games of a similar class that entertain children much better than dancing or romping plays; and many an afternoon party is made very enjoyable by introducing such amusements. The little hostess may provide them all, or she may ask her guests to bring any games they may have, as a part of the entertainment. Among a large collection of "Games" which cannot here be explained, but which may be purchased with full instructions were: Halma (a very popular game), Basilinda, Eckha, Parchesa, Go Bang, Base Ball, Louisa, Migration, Messenger Boy, Horse Race, Yacht Race, Fish Pond, Witches' Spell, Bulls and Bears (a Wall Street game), Lotto, Newsboy, Nellie Bly and many others. Then of course there are Dominoes, Checkers, Fox-and-Geese, Backgammon, Chess, Authors, Quotations, etc.

In "Game" parties there might be prizes given for the different games on the plan of progressive euchre prizes, unless it is found that dissatisfaction and envy creep into little hearts, heads and voices. Then it is wiser to omit the prizes.

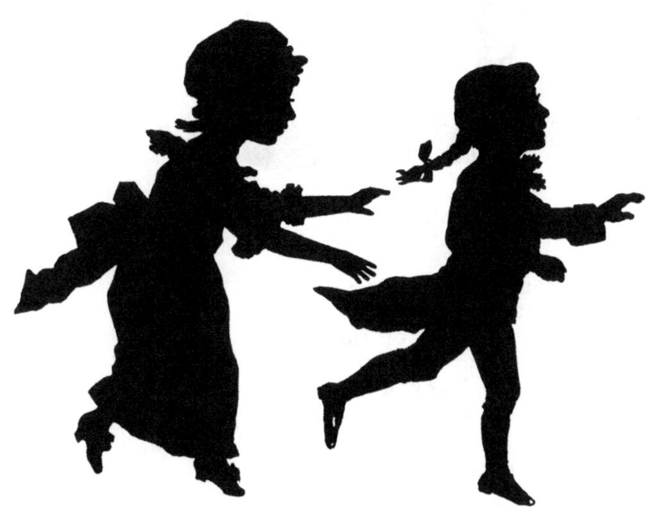

FANCY COSTUMES FOR YOUNG FOLK.

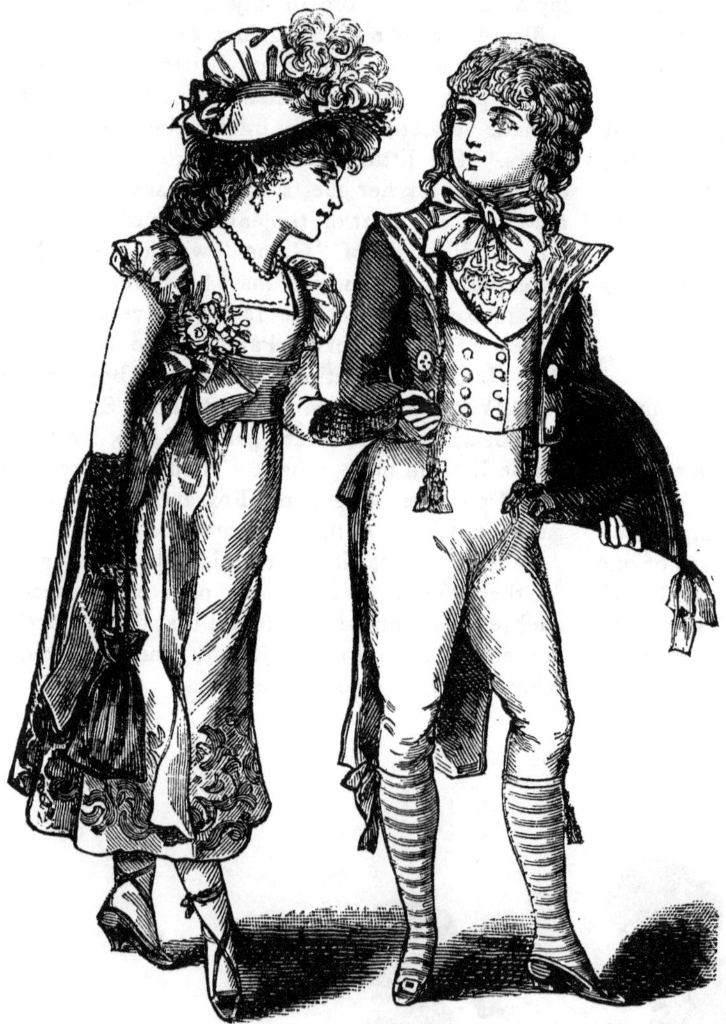

FIGURES NOS. 1 AND 2.—EMPIRE COSTUMES.

FIGURE NO. 3.—COURTIER.—Costume of pale-blue satin trimmed with silver passementerie and finished with a lace collar and ruffles. Cape of blue or tan-colored velvet lined with silver. Silver or ribbon band across the breast. Velvet hat finished with gray or tan plumes; gray stockings and gray or tan slippers with silver rosettes.

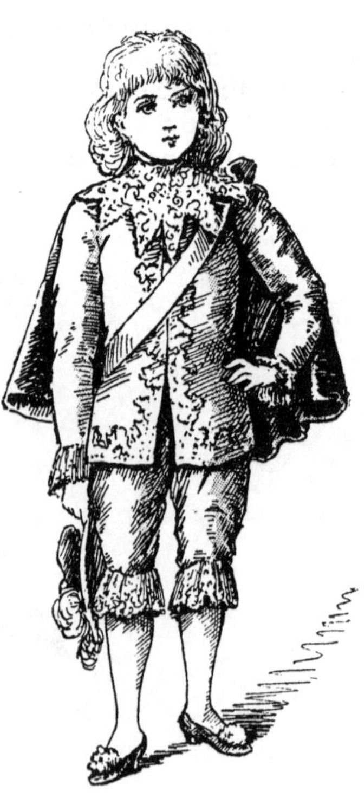

FIGURE NO. 3.—COURTIER.

FIGURES NOS. 1 AND 2.—EMPIRE COSTUMES.—The gown at figure No. 1 is made of pale-pink satin embroidered in silver, and the hat is of the same fabric trimmed with pink ribbon and tips. Pink ribbon sash about the waist; black mitts, black satin handkerchief-bag; pink stockings and black slippers. The costume at figure No. 2 is made with a white satin vest and breeches, and a dark-green coat faced with pink-and-white striped satin, and lined with pink satin. White cravat and lace ruffles, three-cornered black satin hat; pink-and-white striped stockings, and patent leather shoes or pumps.

FIGURE NO. 4.— TURKISH ZOUAVE. — White trousers and gaiter-tops, blue shirt and yellow sash; red jacket embroidered with gold; red cap with gilt tassel and crown decoration; red stockings and black shoes.

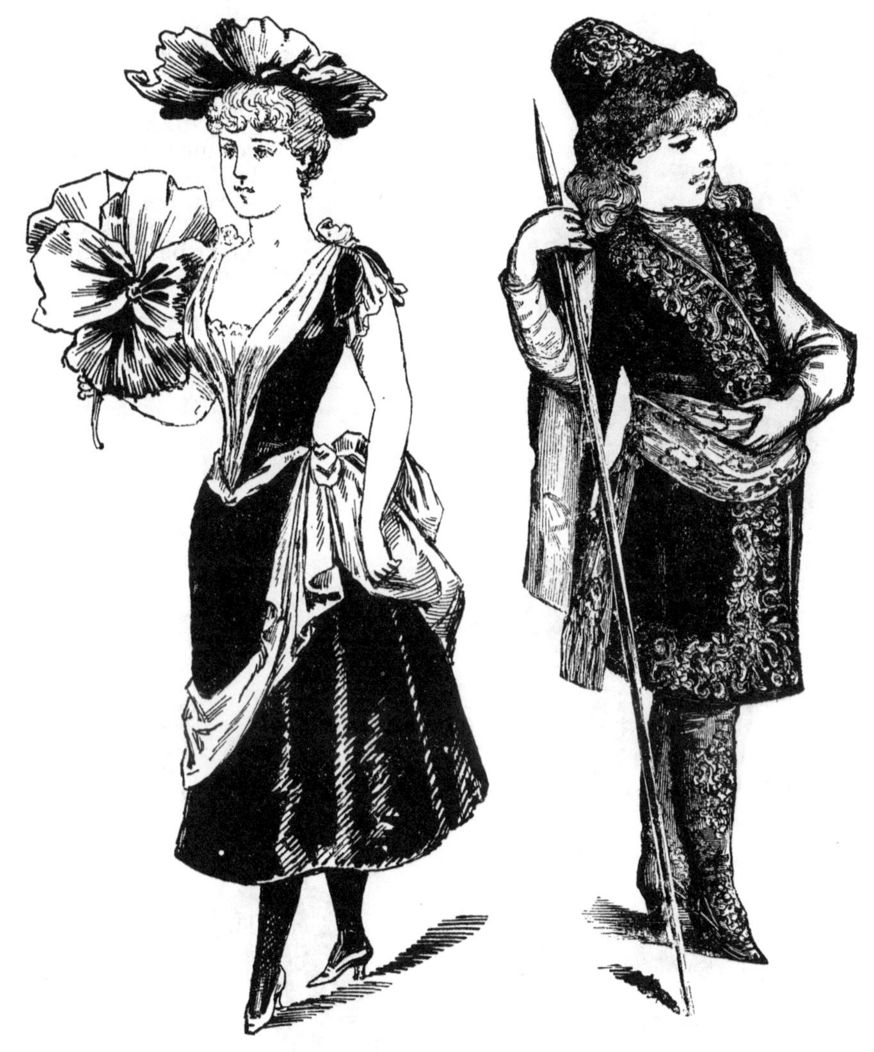

FIGURE NO. 5.—PANSY.

FIGURE NO. 6.—POLISH COSTUME.

FIGURE NO. 5.—PANSY.—Dress of pansy-purple velvet draped with lavender or pale-yellow *crêpe de chine.* Tucker of golden-brown, deep-yellow or pale-purple gauze. A large artificial pansy for hat and fan; pansies on the shoulders. Purple stockings and yellow slippers.

FIGURE NO. 6.—POLISH COSTUME.—Pale-blue shirt with long sleeves. Cap and blouse of golden-brown velvet decorated with pale-blue embroidery; fur band about the cap; pale-blue sash embroidered or brocaded with gold; blouse-sleeves lined with pale-blue. Russet-leather leggings and shoes decorated with gilt ornaments.

FIGURE NO. 4.—TURKISH ZOUAVE.

FIGURE NO. 7.—PRINCE'S COSTUME.

FIGURE NO. 7.—PRINCE'S COSTUME.—This costume is after Millais' picture of "The Princes in the Tower," and is composed of rich black velvet which is used for the blouse and cap; and black silk tights and dull-leather shoes. Two boys or girls could be dressed in such a costume and sustain the rôle of the subjects of the picture.

FIGURE NO. 8.—PEASANT COSTUME.—Dress of blue woolen goods decorated with a fancy border. Waist in bodice style and worn over a white muslin blouse with full short sleeves and a wide frill about the neck. White woolen or muslin apron prettily decorated with gay embroidery-stitches or a printed band. Fancy stockings and white shoes. Muslin cap upon the flowing hair.

FIGURE NO. 9.—FANCY COSTUME.—A striking costume is here illustrated. The blouse is of bright-red silk and the decorations are of black velvet, the same forming the hat. Red-and-black striped tights complete the costume. The latter might be used for an acrobat or gymnast.

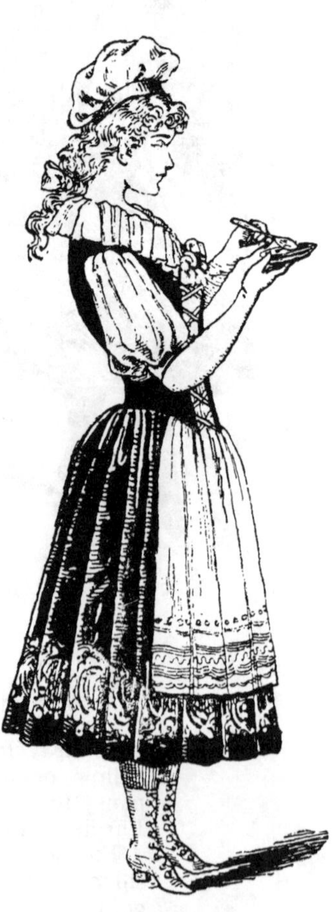

FIGURE NO. 8.—
PEASANT COSTUME.

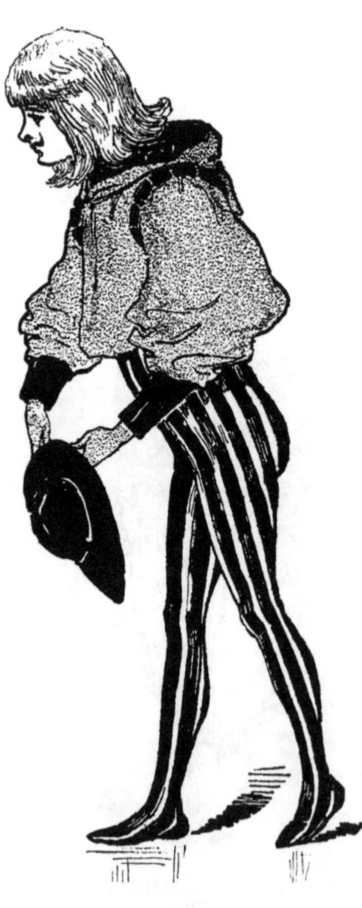

FIGURE NO. 9.—
FANCY COSTUME.

de lys in gold; similar ornament on the breast. Stockings covered with silver paper to match the bodice. Silver helmet decorated with plumes.

FIGURE No. 12.—THE ARCHER.—The dress is made of figured challis and white cambric. The full skirt is lifted at the left side over a metal belt that is adjusted diagonally from the right hip. The bodice has a square yoke of white cambric frilled at the neck and outlined with black velvet ribbon. The sleeves have puffs at the top and a wrist-trimming of black velvet. A fez of white cloth decorated with a quill feather is worn; and a bow is carried in the right hand, and a quiver of arrows is slung at the right shoulder. Leather buskins are worn.

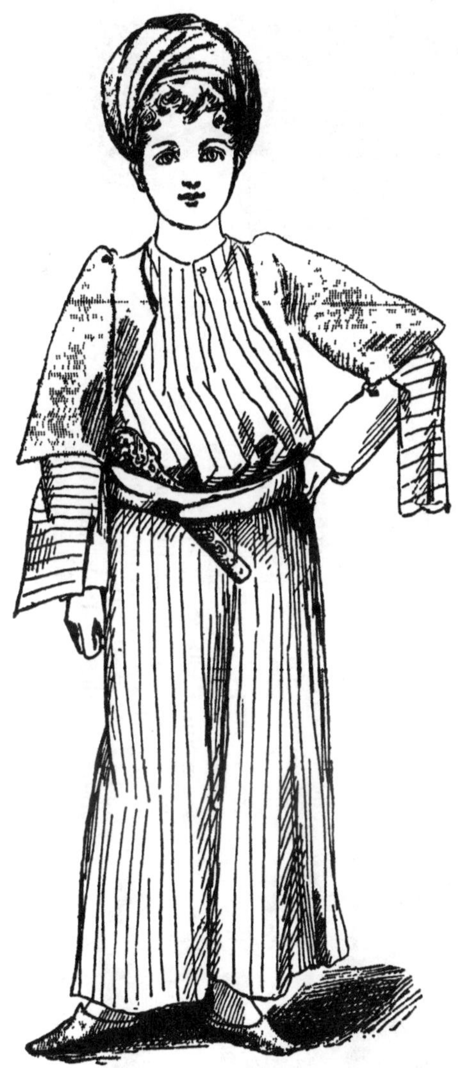

FIGURE No. 10.—SINBAD, THE SAILOR.

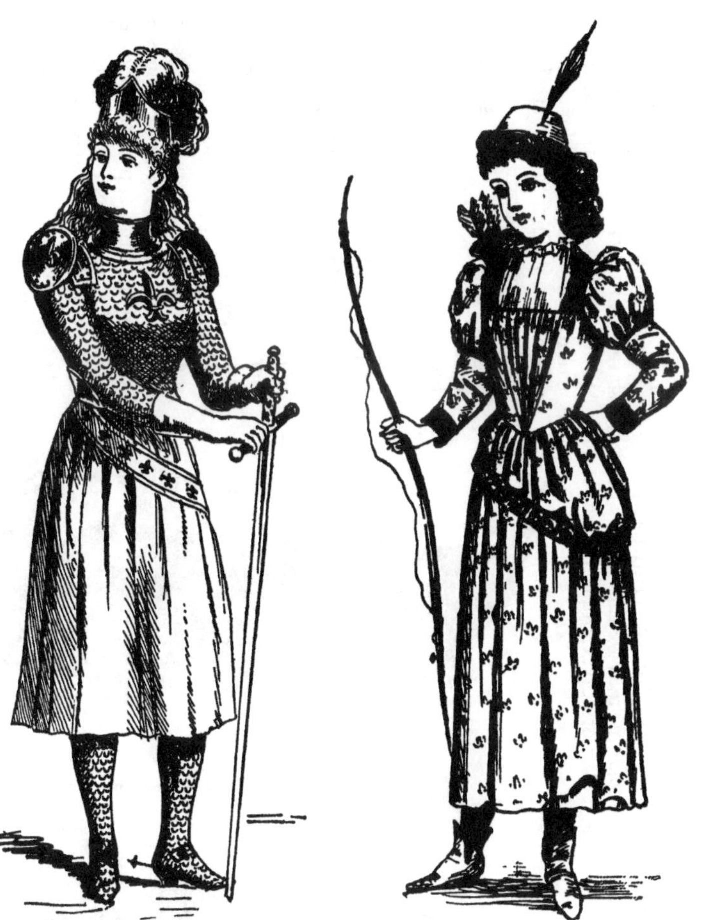

FIGURE No. 11.—JOAN OF ARC.

FIGURE No. 12.—THE ARCHER.

FIGURE No. 10.—SINBAD, THE SAILOR.—Blue and white linen, cotton or woolen fabric is used for the blouse and trousers, and plain white linen for the shirt and close sleeves. The short-sleeved jacket and turban are made of plain blue, red or yellow fabric. The belt is of white leather and holds an Arabian dagger.

FIGURE No. 11.—JOAN OF ARC.—Skirt of pale-blue cashmere. Bodice covered with silver paper arranged to represent a coat of mail. Epaulets and collar made of silver paper. Sword-band of silver decorated with *fleurs*

FIGURE NO. 13.—THE YOUNG HIGHLANDER.—The plaid for this costume may be that of any preferred clan, and the jacket of velvet, plush or velveteen.

FIGURE NO. 13.—THE YOUNG HIGHLANDER.

FIGURE NO. 14.—LITTLE SHEPHERDESS.

The sporran is decorated with a large cairngorm surrounded with Rhine stones, and the scarf is caught on the shoulder with a cairngorm pin. The Highland bonnet is decorated with an eagle's feather. The stockings match the costume, and silver buckles decorate the low shoes.

FIGURE NO. 14.—LITTLE SHEPHERDESS.—This costume is made of pink and white cashmere and green velvet. The under-skirt is of white trimmed at the edge with a silk fringe, while the upper one, which is of pink, is lifted by a simple draping at one side and edged with a deep ruffle of velvet headed by pink plush balls. A puff of muslin forms the sleeves and outlines the top of the bodice, and over the latter at one side, a strip of wide fancy straw or braid is caught with a buckle and carried over the shoulder to the back, where it is secured with a similar buckle. A scarf is draped over one shoulder and knotted on the opposite hip. Pink stockings and ribbon-strapped slippers; a green Alpine hat trimmed with white feathers and a ribbon-trimmed crook and a horn complete the costume.

FIGURE NO. 15. — JOSEPHINE COSTUME. — Dress of pink-and-green striped satin, with short waist and sleeves. Sash of plain green Surah silk. Neck cut square and finished with standing ruffles of lace. Head-dress of pink ribbon and a pearl comb. Pearl necklace, gold bracelets. Pink fan and stockings; green slippers with pink rosettes.

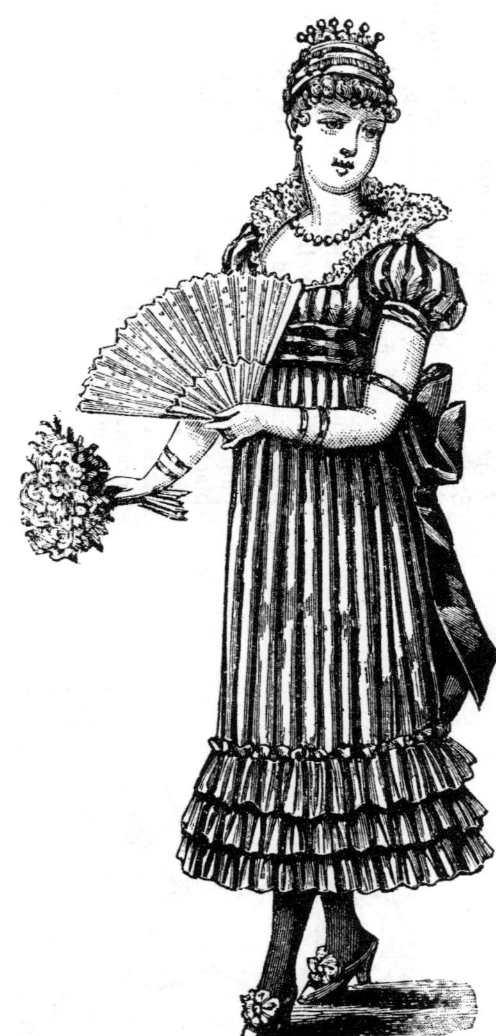

FIGURE NO. 15.—JOSEPHINE COSTUME.

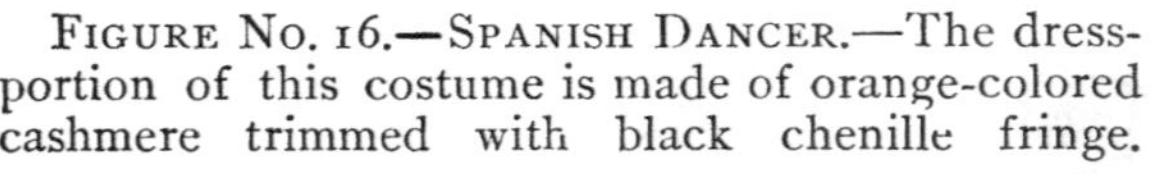

FIGURE No. 16.—SPANISH DANCER.—The dress-portion of this costume is made of orange-colored cashmere trimmed with black chenille fringe. The velvet jacket is very short and is cut with a pointed neck-edge both at the front and back, and is embroidered with gold. A lattice-work of gold and chenille is draped over the short sleeves. The hair is dressed high with a high tortoise-shell comb, from which is draped a cream-colored lace mantilla. Painted tambourine suspended from the waist and decorated with colored ribbons. Black silk mitts, and a paper fan painted to represent a bull fight. Black slippers and black stockings embroidered with gold. Jewelry may be worn if desired.

FIGURE No. 17.—EASTERN GRANDEE.—Coat and under jacket of white cloth embroidered in gold braid and many-colored beads. Gold binding on the sleeves and coat. Baggy trousers of white Surah silk, and yellow or white silk stockings, with red slippers and gold buckles. Sash of red pongee silk; round collar of red velvet and a red velvet band upon the brim of the conical white felt cap. The costume may be worn by a boy from ten to fourteen years of age.

FIGURE No. 18.—PAGE. (HENRY VIII.)—Light-gray embossed tunic; plain gray trousers, sleeves and hose. Pale-blue coat and cape lined with gray and trimmed with fur and silver lace. Blue velvet cap with gray plumes. Fancy shoes.

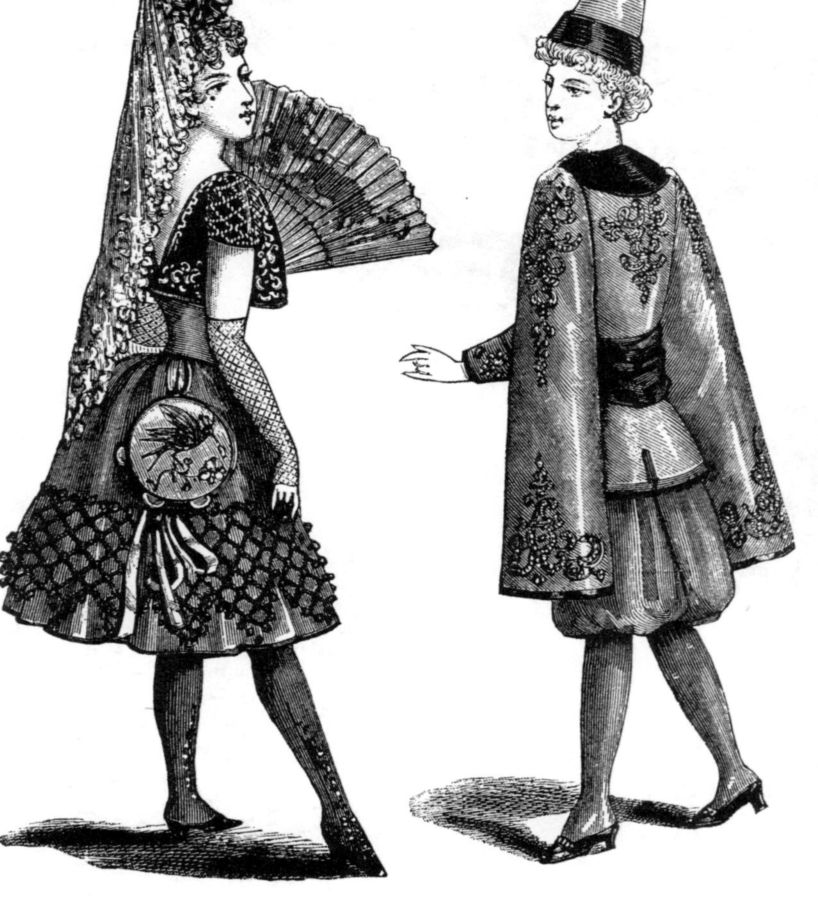

FIGURE No. 16.—SPANISH DANCER.

FIGURE No. 17.—EASTERN GRANDEE.

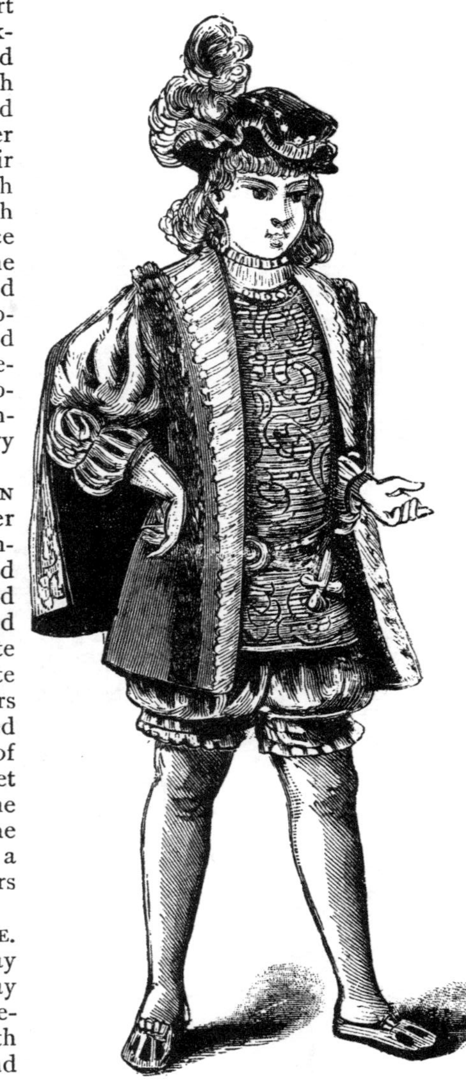

FIGURE No. 18.—PAGE. (HENRY VIII.)

FIGURE NO. 20.—TURKISH DANCING GIRL. — Dress and trousers of red satin trimmed with gold ornaments and pale-yellow bands. Pale-yellow vest; white gauze chemisette and sleeves. Head-dress of gauze, pearl beads and gold ornaments. Necklet of pearls and gold. Yellow stockings and red, gold-trimmed shoes.

FIGURE NO. 21.—MANDOLIN PLAYER —Purple tunic trimmed with silver braid. Pale-gray tucker, puffed sleeves and hose. Silver belt. Purple cap, with silver band and feather.

FIGURE NO. 19.—MOTHER GOOSE.

FIGURE NO. 19.—MOTHER GOOSE.—Dress of black satin and velvet trimmed with swan's down. Goose painted or appliquéed on skirt. White cuffs and ruff; mull tucker. Pointed hat and white cap. Black stockings and buckle-shoes. Splint broom. Colors may be used in place of black.

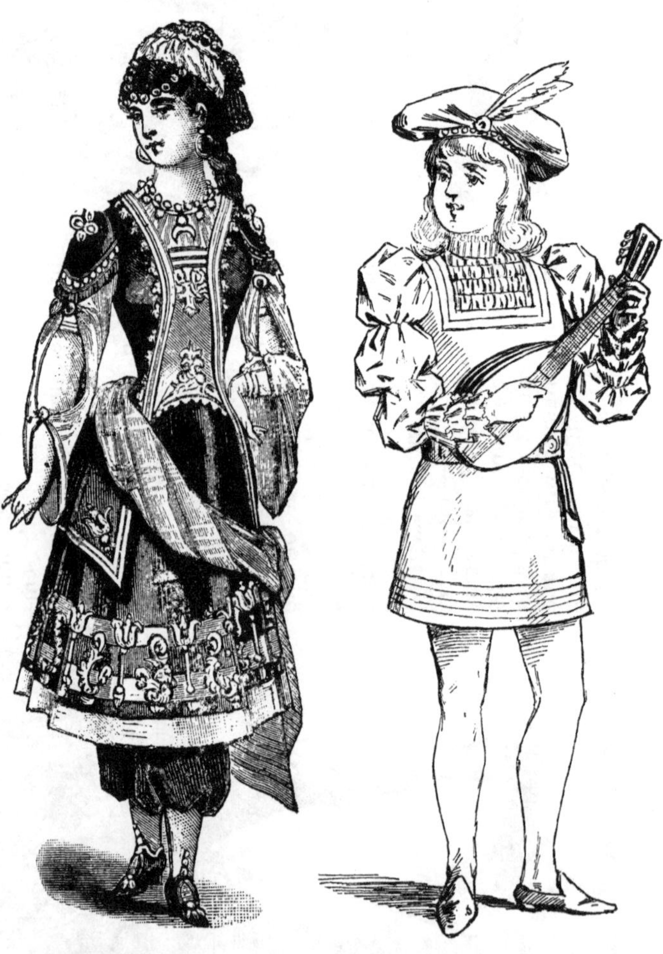

FIGURE NO. 20.—TURKISH DANCING GIRL.

FIGURE NO. 21.—MANDOLIN PLAYER.

FIGURE NO. 23.—CHINESE GENTLEMAN.—Under-robe of dark-blue China silk embroidered in gold. Light-blue blouse trimmed with silver braid and yellow embroidery. Large neck-chain of Chinese coins, and Chinese ornaments upon the breast. Yellow and blue hat, blue fan, white stockings and yellow shoes.

FIGURE NO. 24.—JAPANESE BOY.—Blouse and trousers of blue satin or silk, trimmed with yellow bands. Large yellow Japanese hat with a blue top and the brim lined with blue net. White stockings and blue sandals. The complexion may be stained a deep olive tint. The costume should be worn by a dark-haired boy or girl.

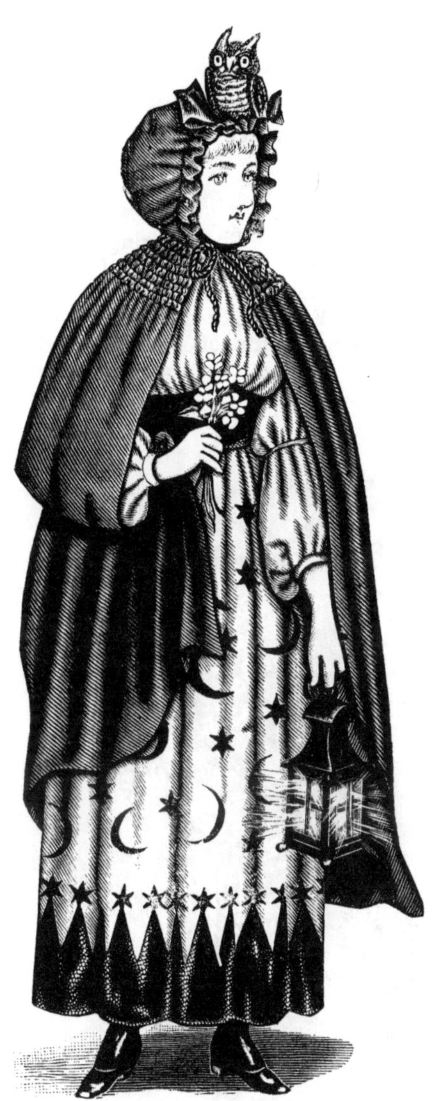

FIGURE NO. 22.—NIGHT.

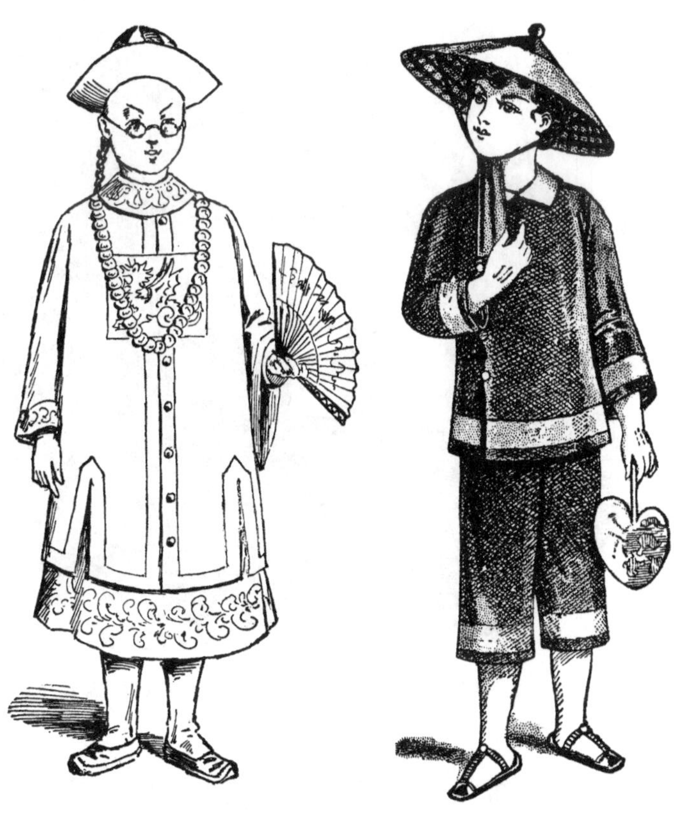

FIGURE NO. 23.—CHINESE GENTLEMAN.

FIGURE NO. 24.—JAPANESE BOY.

FIGURE NO. 22.—NIGHT.—Skirt of silver-gray wool trimmed with points and figures of black velvet. Full gray waist and velvet girdle. Black cloak with hood decorated with an owl. Carries a lighted lantern.

LITTLE LORD FAUNTLEROY COSTUMES.

FIGURE NO. 25.—FAUNTLEROY SAILOR SUIT.—This is a charming costume for a masquerade or fancy-dress party. It is made of white flannel and has collar-facings and a sash of sapphire blue Surah silk. The hat is a soft felt of dark-blue, and the costume is completed by dark-blue silk stockings and patent-leather slippers with silver buckles.

FIGURE NO. 26.—FAUNTLEROY RIDING SUIT.—This is a jaunty costume made of striped rough cloth, and is a favorite for almost any occasion requiring fancy dress. The cap may be knitted, if preferred. The leggings are of russet leather, and the gloves are of brown dog-skin with loose gauntlets.

FIGURE NO. 27.—FAUNTLEROY COURT COSTUME.—This costume is made of dark-blue velvet and is worn with a blue silk sash and lace collar and cuffs. A fine felt hat trimmed with blue plumes, and blue silk stockings and patent-leather slippers complete the costume.

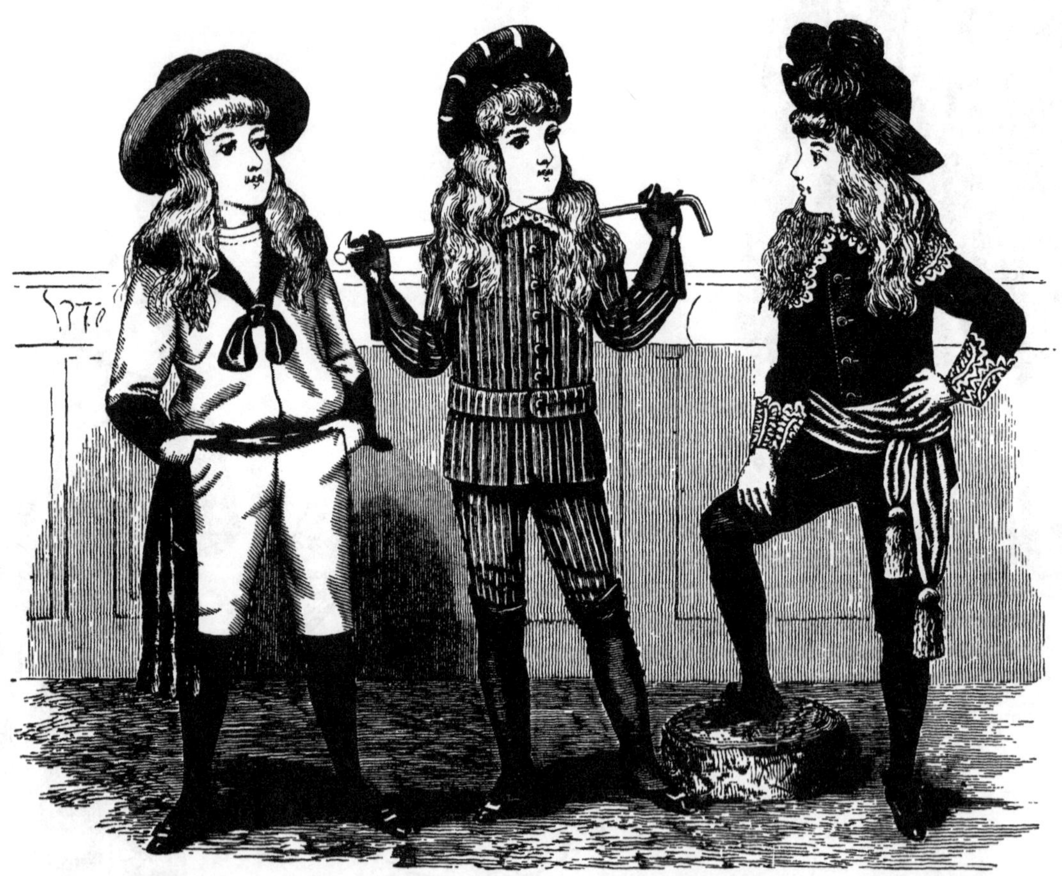

FIGURES NOS. 25, 26 AND 27.—LITTLE LORD FAUNTLEROY COSTUMES.

All of these costumes are popular with young boys, or little girls who wish to assume the character of "Little Lord Fauntleroy."

SQUIRE, CAVALIER AND COURTIER COSTUMES.

FIGURE NO. 28.—THE SQUIRE.—Vest and knee breeches of drab or buff smooth cloth, with stockings to match. Coat of dark blue or brown, with large round hat to match. White shirt with lace frill. Ribbon garters and buckle-shoes complete the costume very prettily.

FIGURE NO. 29.—THE YOUNG CAVALIER.—Black velvet, white satin and white lace are used in making these costumes. The coat of the Cavalier costume is further decorated with silver braid. Silk stockings and patent-leather low shoes complete the costume; and the Cavalier wears a garter of fancy ribbon upon his left leg.

FIGURE NO. 30.—COURTIER.—Doublet of dark red velvet opening over a full white silk or muslin shirt. Sleeves slashed at the top with pale gray. Leather belt and sword-band. Cloak of red velvet lined with gray. Gray hose and shoes. Lace ruffles at the neck and wrists. Velvet cap trimmed with gray plumes. Sword suspended at one side.

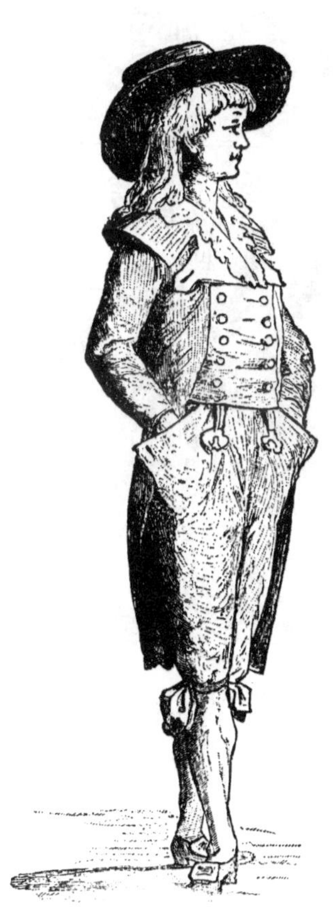

FIGURE NO. 28.—
THE SQUIRE.

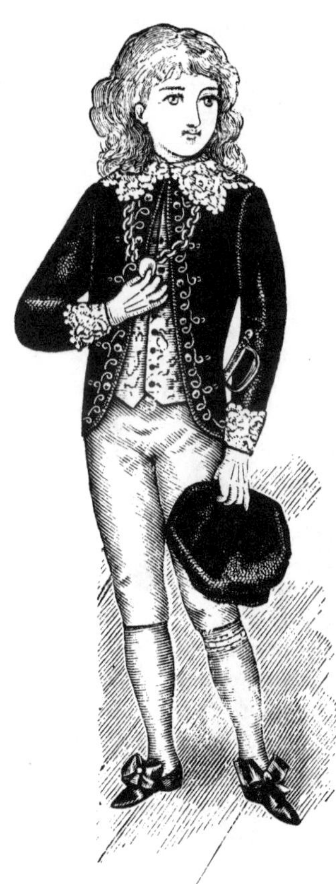

FIGURE NO. 29.—
THE YOUNG CAVALIER.

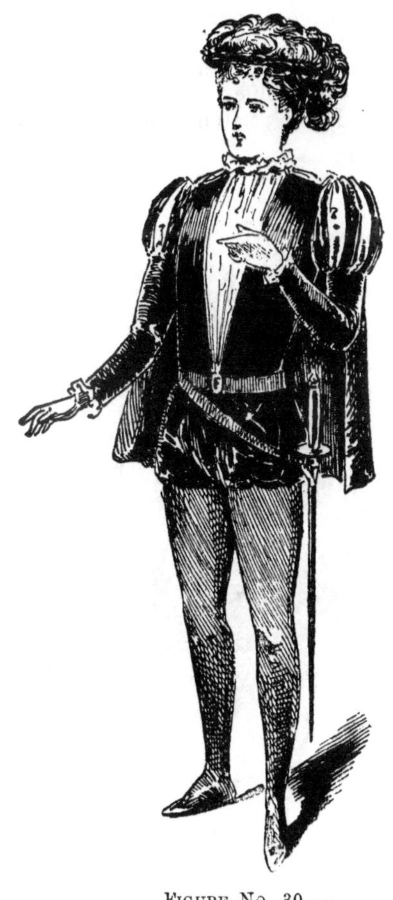

FIGURE NO. 30.—
COURTIER.

FIGURE NO. 31.—PAGE.—Doublet of black velvet with wing sleeves, worn over a yellow satin body, with left sleeve yellow and right one red. Yellow tight upon the right leg, red one upon the left; black buskins. Top of under-body and bottom of doublet trimmed with jeweled band; jeweled belt and pocket. Coat of arms upon the breast. Black velvet cap with red feather.

FIGURE NO. 32.—INCROYABLE.—Kilted skirt of pale-pink satin. Coat of green velvet with silver buttons. Vest of white satin embroidered with silver or gold or both. Large cravat of white mull. White hat with pink plume. White gauntlet-gloves; patent-leather shoes with green cloth tops. Staff mounted with silver and decorated with a ribbon bow.

FIGURE NO. 33.—GENTLEMAN OF THE XVI. CENTURY.—Vest and breeches of pale-yellow satin trimmed with silver. Light-blue coat decorated with gold passementerie; lace cravat and wrist-ruffles. Shoulder and garter knots of blue ribbon fringed with gold. Blue velvet hat trimmed with silver. Blue silk stockings clocked with silver; and black patent-leather shoes with silver buckles.

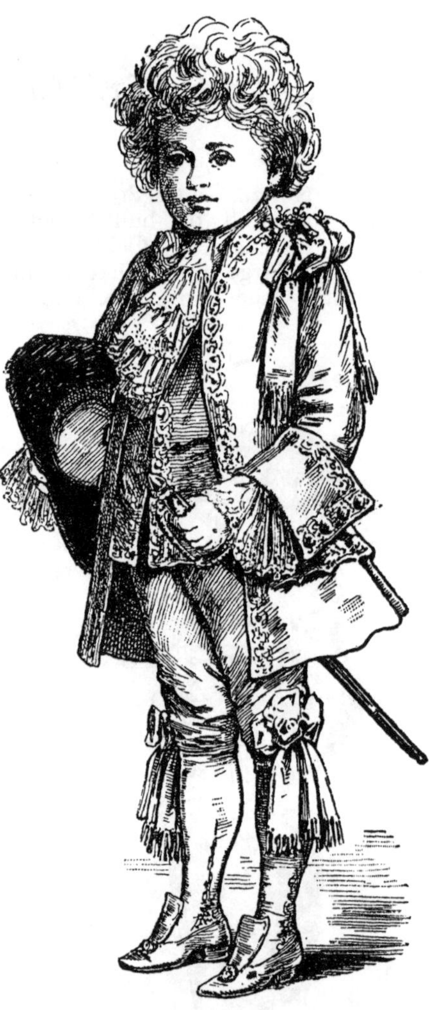

FIGURE NO. 33.—GENTLEMAN OF THE XVI. CENTURY.

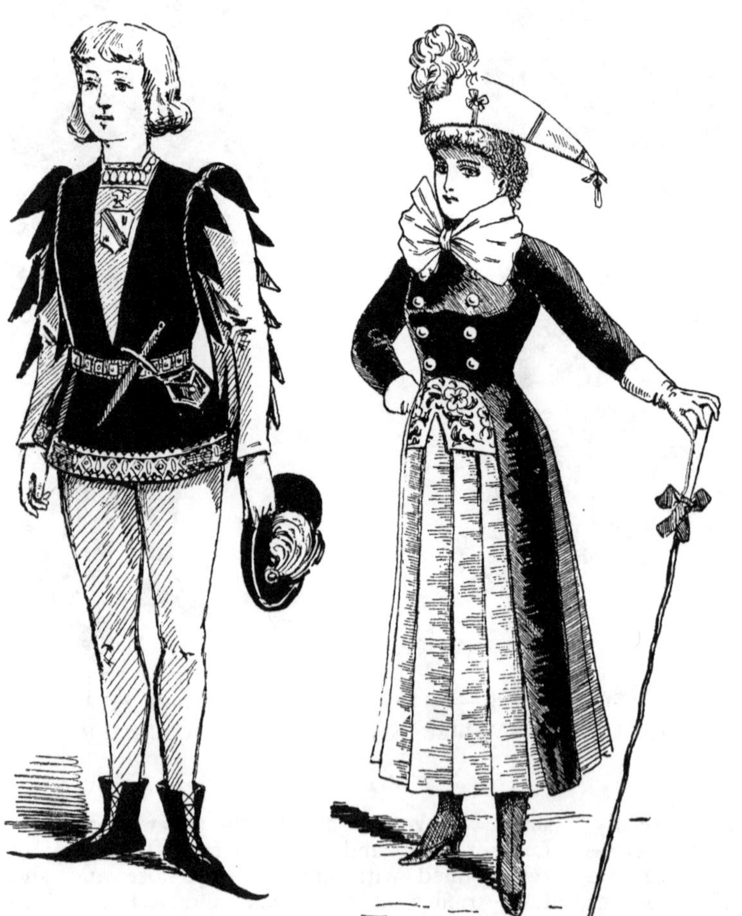

FIGURE NO. 31.—PAGE. FIGURE NO. 32.—INCROYABLE.

FIGURES NOS. 34 AND 35.—SHEPHERD AND FLORA.—Shepherd dressed in shirt and knee-breeches of blue-and-white striped cotton or woolen fabric; blue frock, white hat and stockings, and leather shoes. Garters of blue ribbon and blue ribbon bow upon crook.

Flora dressed in a white or pink gown covered with a pretty floral design, or with tiny flowers sewed upon the goods. Wreaths of flowers at the bottom of the skirt and around the short sleeves. Flowers in the hand and should be worn in the hair.

FIGURE NO. 36.—PAGE.—Hat and blouse of moss-green velvet; lighter green breeches, and silk stockings to match, with gold garters. Lace fraise at the neck and lace frills falling over the hands. Gold or silver buttons upon the blouse and breeches, and a handsome white or pale-green plume on the hat. This costume may be made in any other color preferred.

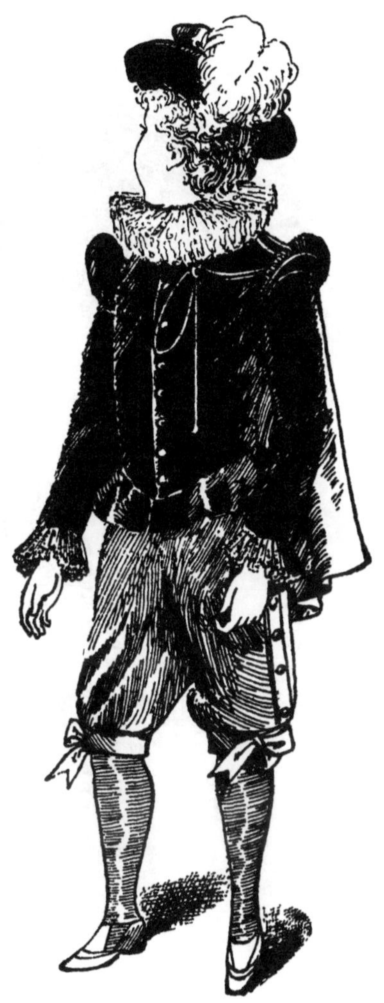

FIGURE NO. 36.—PAGE.

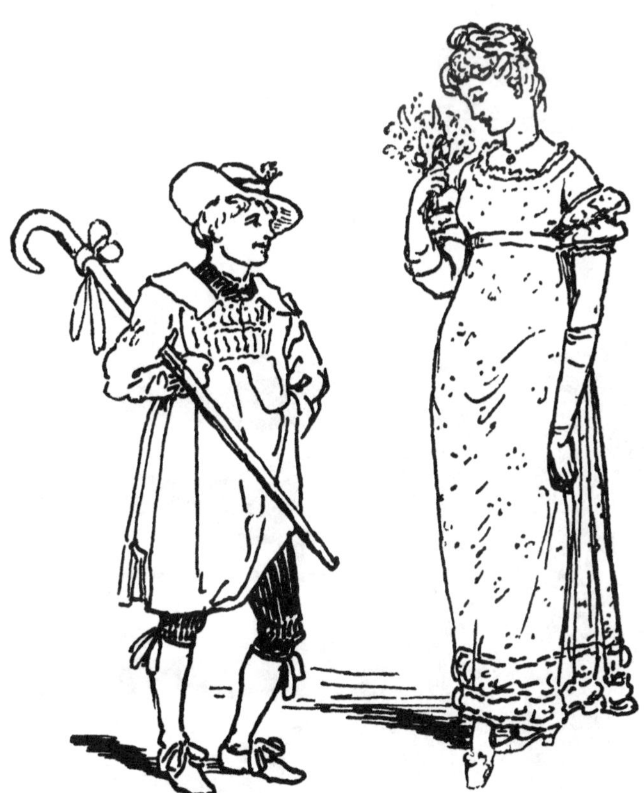

FIGURES NOS. 34 AND 35.—
SHEPHARD AND FLORA.

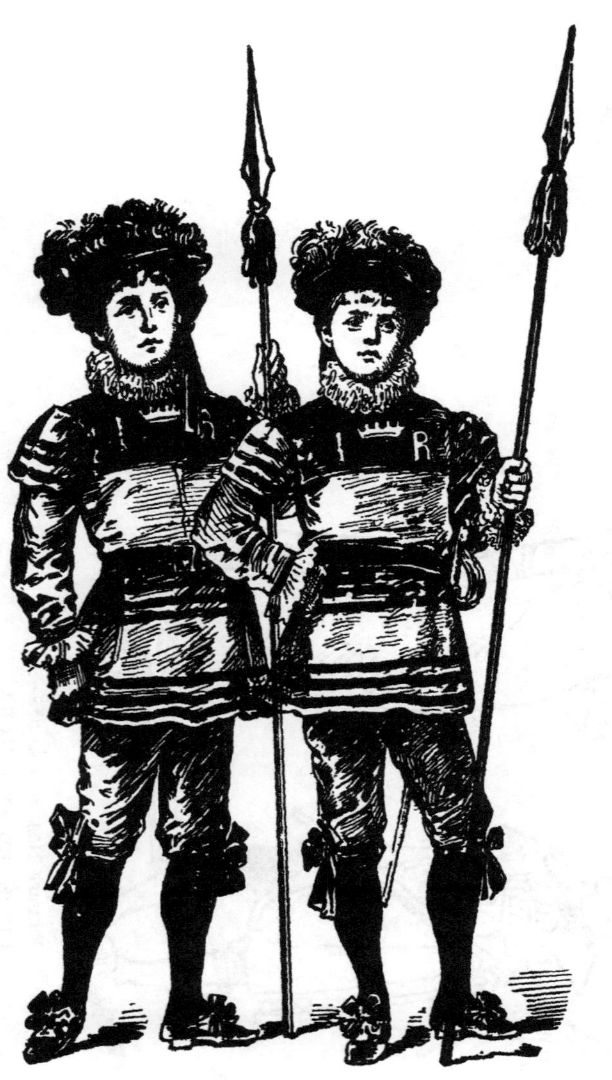

FIGURES NOS. 37 AND 38.—BEEF-EATERS. (YEOMEN OF THE GUARD.)

FIGURES NOS. 37 AND 38.—BEEF-EATERS. (YEOMEN OF THE GUARD). — These costumes are made up in red and black fabrics, which may be of silk, wool or cotton. Red satin and black velvet combine handsomely. A white muslin ruff is about the neck and lace ruffles are about the wrists. The black velvet round hats are trimmed with velvet streamers and red plumes.

FIGURE NO. 39. — TYROLESE COSTUME. — Gray woolen fabric is used for the skirt and waist of this costume, while dark-red velvet is used for the bodice and decoration, in connection with gilt braid. The hat is of the velvet and is trimmed with the braid and a lace rosette. The apron is of white woolen goods decorated with velvet and gold embroidery. Gray stockings and patent-leather shoes with gold buckles complete the costume.

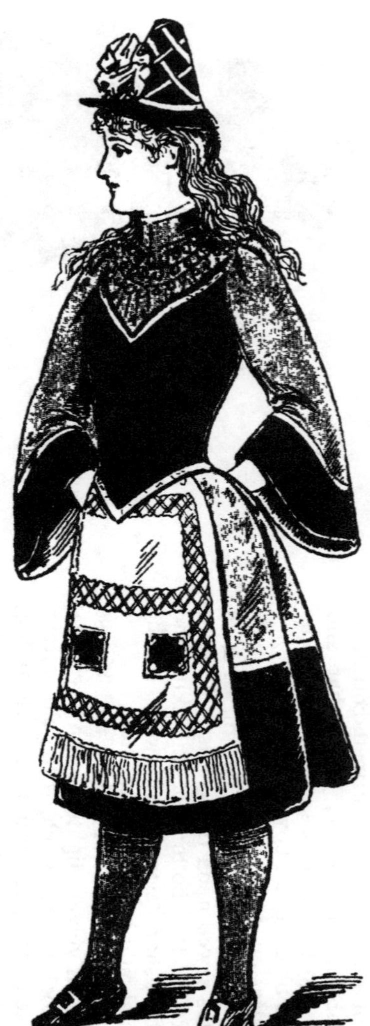

FIGURE NO. 39.—TYROLESE COSTUME.

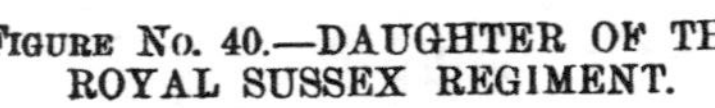

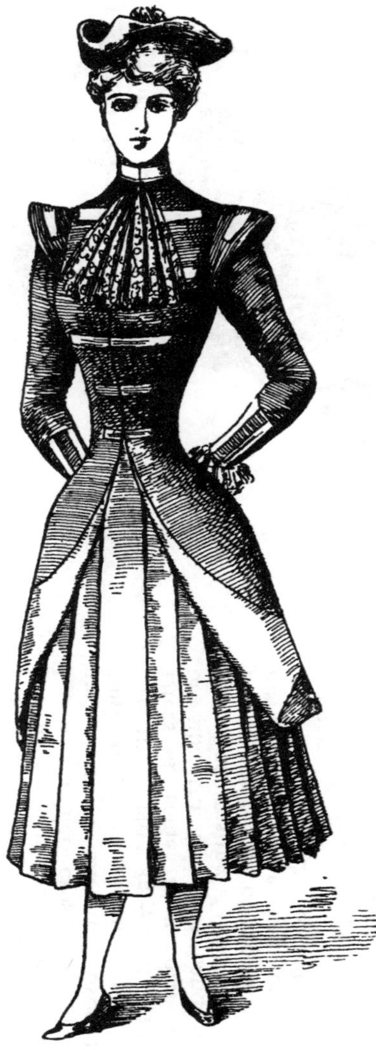

Figure No. 40.—DAUGHTER OF THE ROYAL SUSSEX REGIMENT.

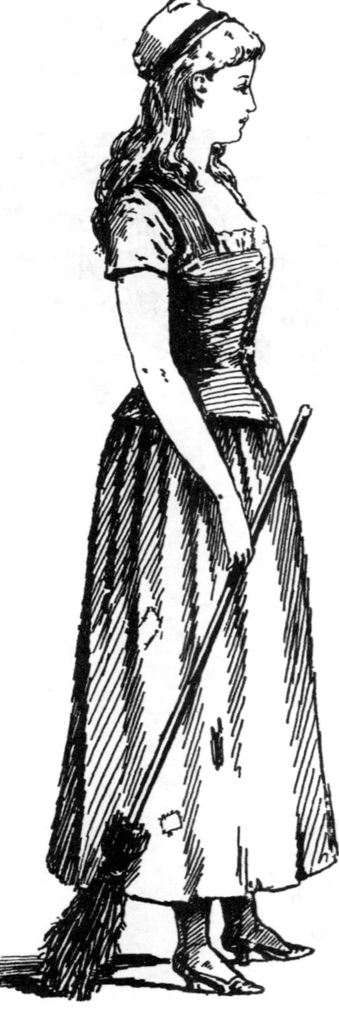

Figure No. 41.—CINDERELLA.

Figure No. 40.—Daughter of the Royal Sussex Regiment.—Red coat with yellow facings, trimmed with silver braid. White kilt skirt. Lace tie at the neck and corresponding frills at the wrists. White three-cornered hat with yellow rosette. Yellow stockings and black slippers. Powdered hair.

Figure No. 41.—Cinderella.—Brown skirt, red bodice, white chemisette and cap. Blue stockings, black slippers, splint broom.

Figure No. 42.—Paul Jones.—White shirt. Blue coat and knee-breeches. Gray stockings and black patent-leather shoes. Lace ruffles at the wrist. May be worn by a boy or girl.

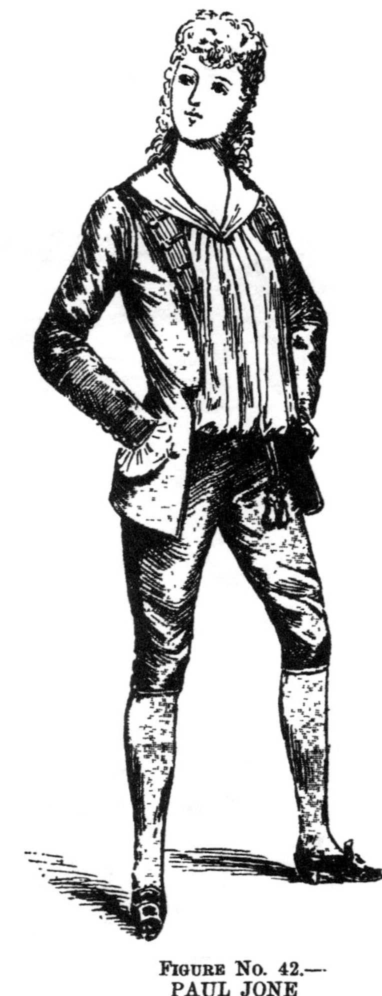

Figure No. 42.—PAUL JONE

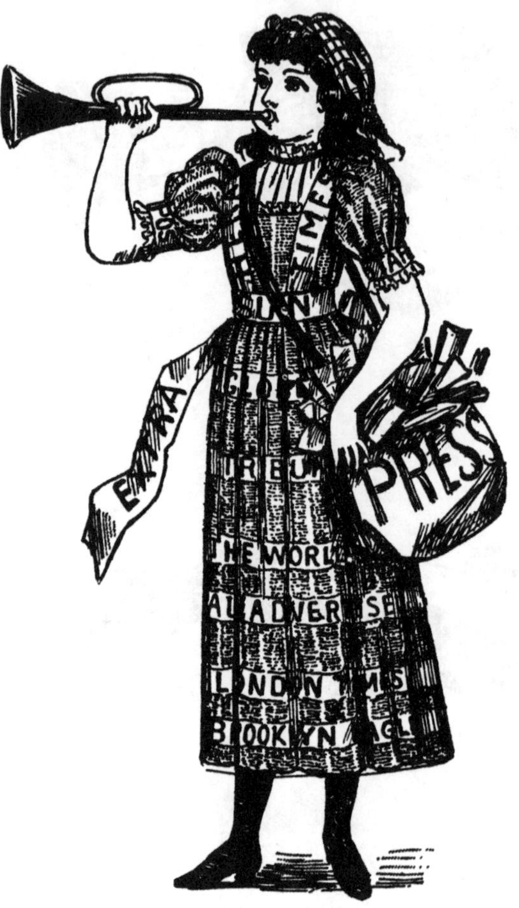

FIGURE No. 43.—THE PRESS.

FIGURE No. 44.—CROSSING SWEEPER.—Brown calico dress with tucked skirt. Fancy kerchief crossed on the breast, and a brown one tied over the hair. Blue apron and splint broom.

FIGURE No. 45.—THE ALPHABET.—Dress of some fancy color in cambric or silk, trimmed with bands of ribbon or a contrasting fabric on which are pasted the letters of the alphabet. Narrow band on the hair on which rest gilt letters. Bright colored stockings and slippers.

FIGURE No. 43.—THE PRESS.—Dress of mixed black-and-white goods trimmed with rows of white ribbon lettered in black with the names of daily papers. A red-and-white checked handkerchief is wound about the head. A bag of folded papers and a trumpet complete the costume.

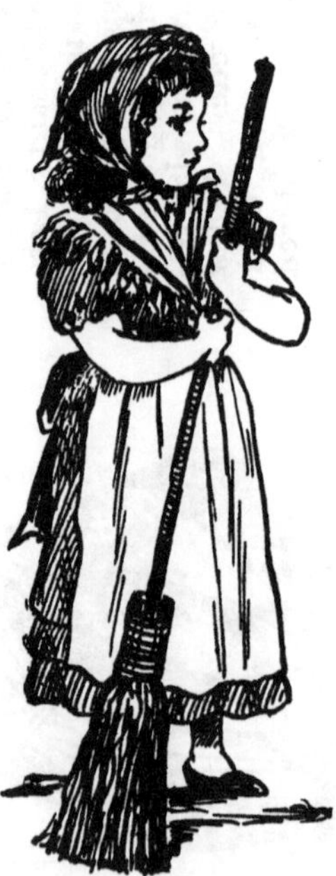

FIGURE No. 44.—CROSSING SWEEPER

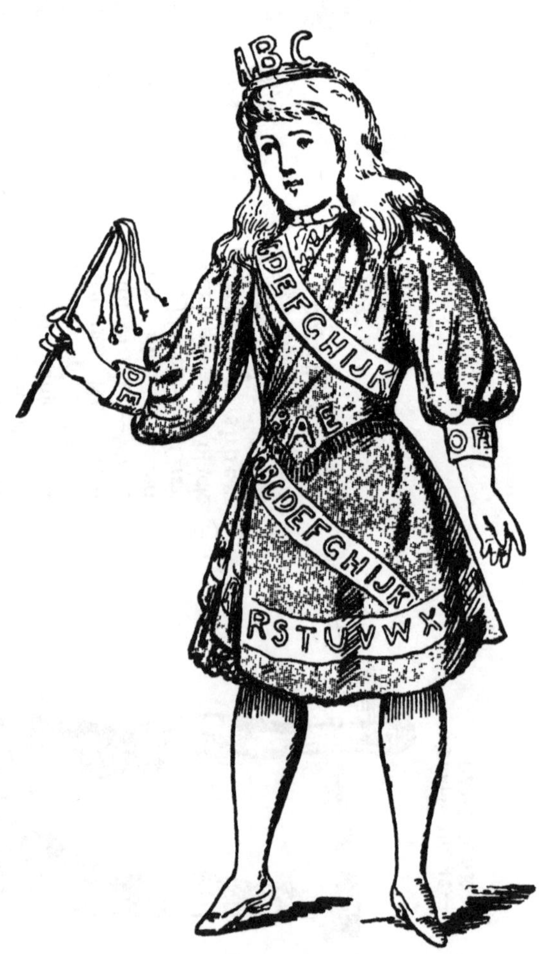

FIGURE No. 45.—THE ALPHABET.

FIGURE NO. 46.—LITTLE ITALIAN MAIDEN. --Red flannel dress worn over a shirt of white cambric; a light-blue apron trimmed with yellow ribbon, and a head-drapery of blue, yellow and red and white striped silk or wool goods. Knitted blue stockings and low cloth shoes Carries fruit in each hand.

FIGURE NO. 47.—MERCURY.—Skirt of blue satin or cashmere. Tunic and drapery of white trimmed with two shades of blue; wings fastened on the shoulders. White cap trimmed with wings. White stockings banded with blue: white sandals trimmed with blue bands and white wings. Bag of letters to be delivered to guests.

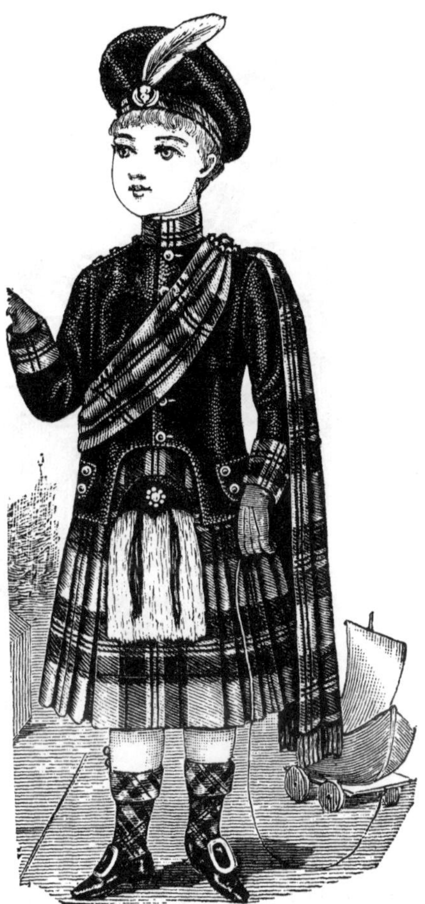

FIGURE NO. 48.—HIGHLAND LADDIE.

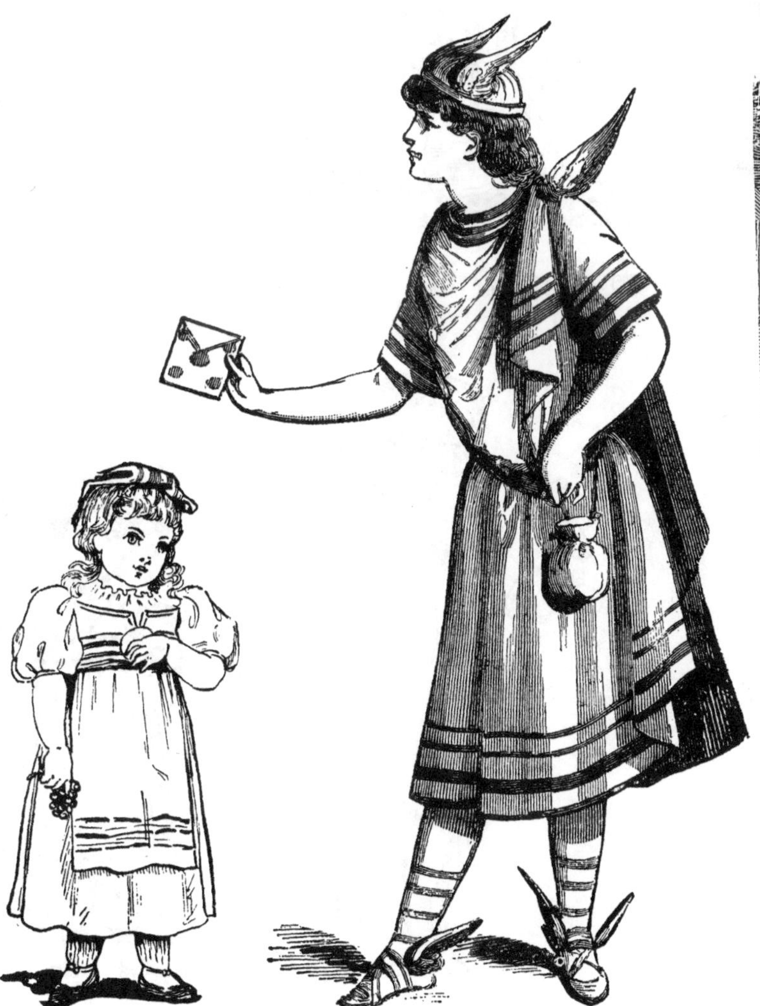

FIGURE NO. 46.—
LITTLE ITALIAN MAIDEN.

FIGURE NO. 47.—
MERCURY.

FIGURE NO. 48.—HIGHLAND LADDIE.—The little Highlander costume comprises a kilted skirt or fillibeg of plaid wool goods, with a scarf of tartan plaid fastened at the top of the left shoulder under a brooch; a plaid Scotch bonnet and a gay-checked pocket, which the Scotchman calls a sporran, are worn. A brooch fastens the stem of a quill feather to the bonnet and imparts to the lad the air of a little chieftain.

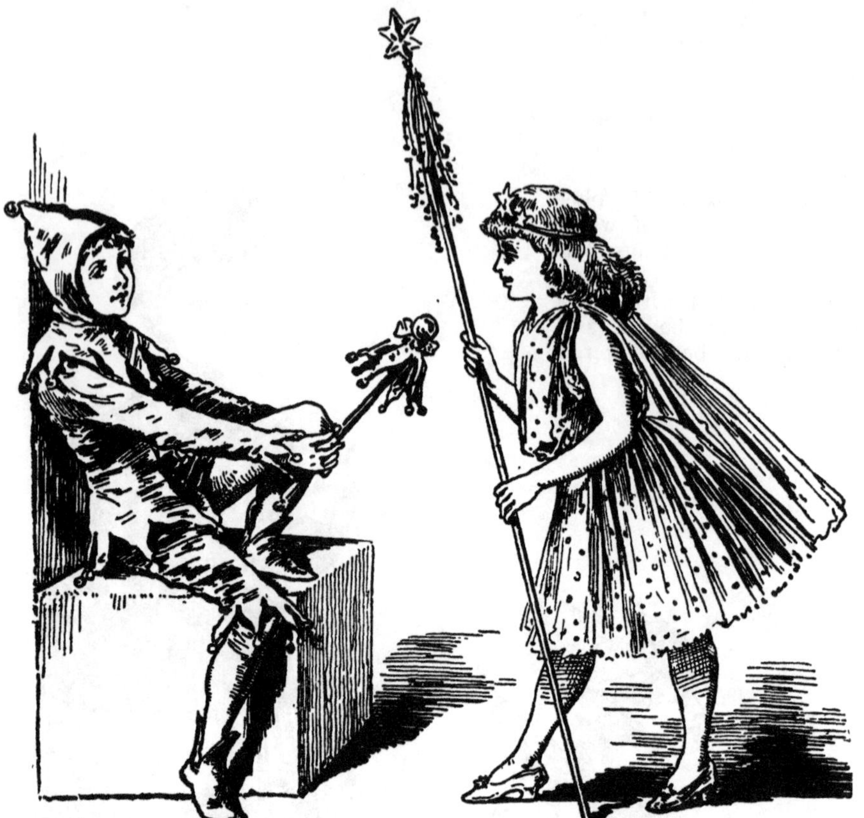

FIGURES NOS. 49 AND 50.—JESTER AND FAIRY.

FIGURE NO. 52. —SPANISH GIRL. —Full skirt of dull-blue flannel with a sleeveless waist of the same worn over a white blouse. Gay plaid snoulder-shawl and afancyapron. About the neck is a string of bright glass beads; and red stockings and low shoes, and a tambourine, complete the costume.

FIGURES NOS. 49 AND 50.—JESTER AND FAIRY.—The jester is dressed in a blue hood, breeches and shoes, and a yellow blouse and stockings. A bell is fastened to every point in the costume, and a jester's wand trimmed with ribbon and bells is carried.

The fairy is dressed in white gauze spangled with silver, has a star head-dress and a star-tipped wand, white stockings and silver shoes.

FIGURE NO. 51.—CAVALIER.—The jacket is of deep-red velveteen trimmed with gilt cord and buttons, and with lace frills at the neck and wrists. The shirt is of white silk, and the trousers of pale-blue satin trimmed with brass buttons. The stockings are white and the shoes red, and blue ribbon bows are at the knees and insteps. The hat is of pale-blue felt trimmed with red feathers.

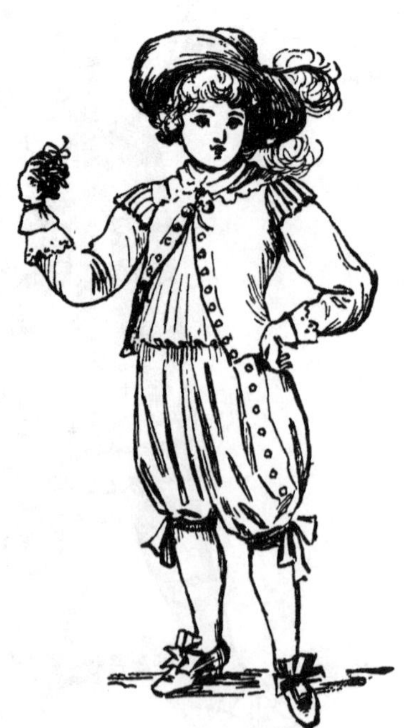

FIGURE NO. 51.—CAVALIER.

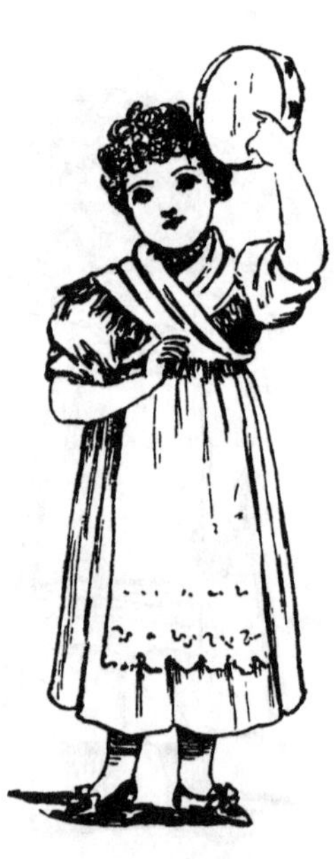

FIGURE NO. 52—SPANISH GIRL.

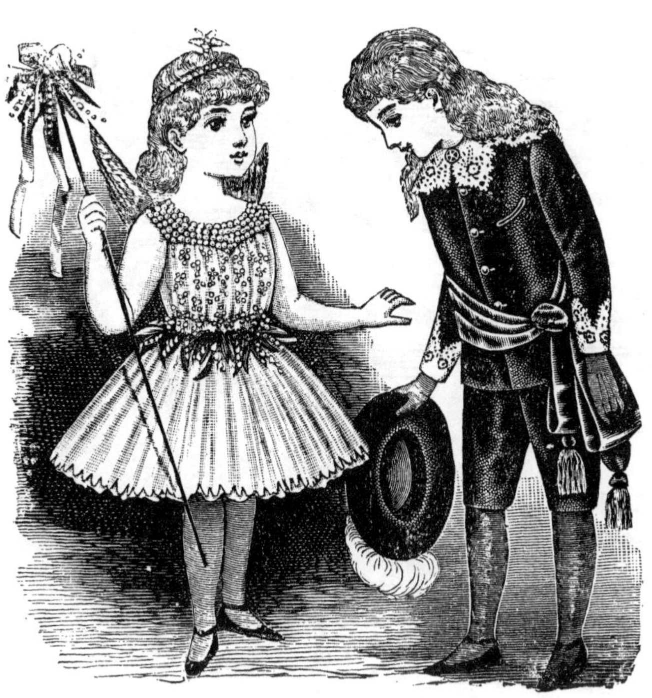

FIGURES NOS. 53 AND 54.—FAIRY AND CAVALIER.

FIGURE NO. 55.—THE LITTLE SCHOOL-MARM.—Dress of plain gray silk, serge, flannel, sateen or any suitable material, short in the waist, long in the skirt and with full sleeves. High cap of white Swiss muslin. An A B C book in one hand and a birch "switch" in the other.

FIGURE NO. 56. — PUCK. — Black evening coat worn over a suit of tights and a blue silk sash. A suit of knitted underclothing may be used in place of the tights if more convenient; but in this event the sash will have to be arranged so as to conceal the closing. A beaver hat, buckled shoes and a fancy staff complete the costume.

FIGURES NOS. 53 AND 54.—FAIRY AND CAVALIER. — The fairy is dressed as follows: The skirt is made of several layers of tarletan, all gathered up together so as to give an extended and airy effect. The yoke is thickly covered with spangles, and spangles are also sewed all over the waist. A girdle of lily leaves and spangles is worn. A band of spangles with a star in front binds the hair. Wings are fastened at the back. A cane trimmed with ribbon and spangles is carried for a wand. The stockings match the dress in color, and strapped slippers are worn.

The material of the cavalier's costume may be crimson or black velvet or velveteen. The collar and cuffs are of Vandyke lace, and the sash is of crimson Surah, with tassel-trimmed ends. The stockings and slippers are black, and the large velvet hat is trimmed with ostrich feathers.

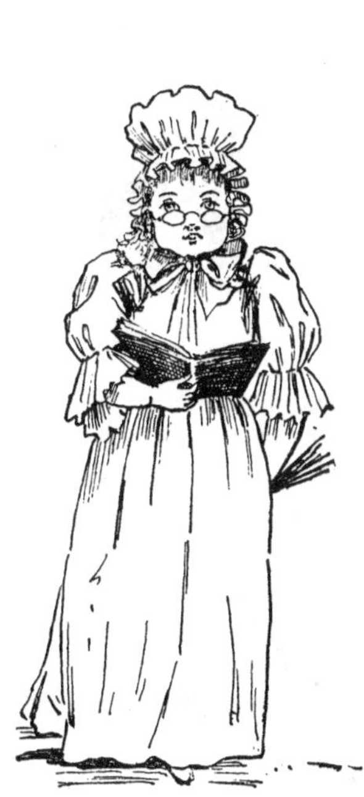

FIGURE NO. 55.—THE LITTLE SCHOOL-MARM.

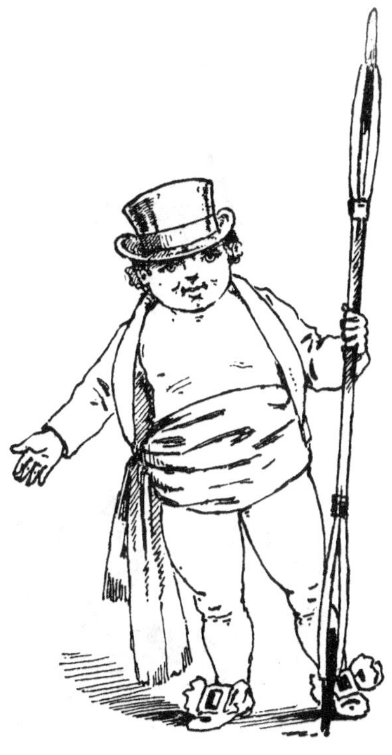

FIGURE NO. 56.—PUCK.

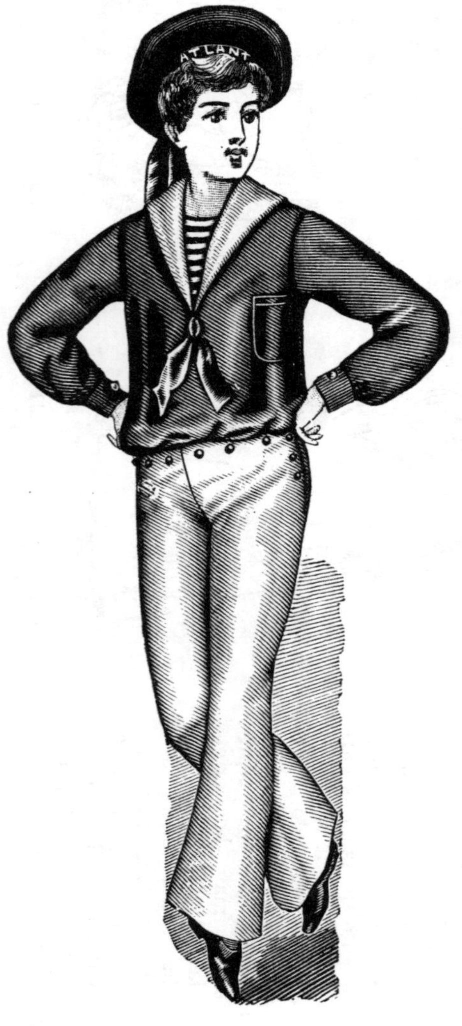

FIGURE No. 57.—JACK TAR.

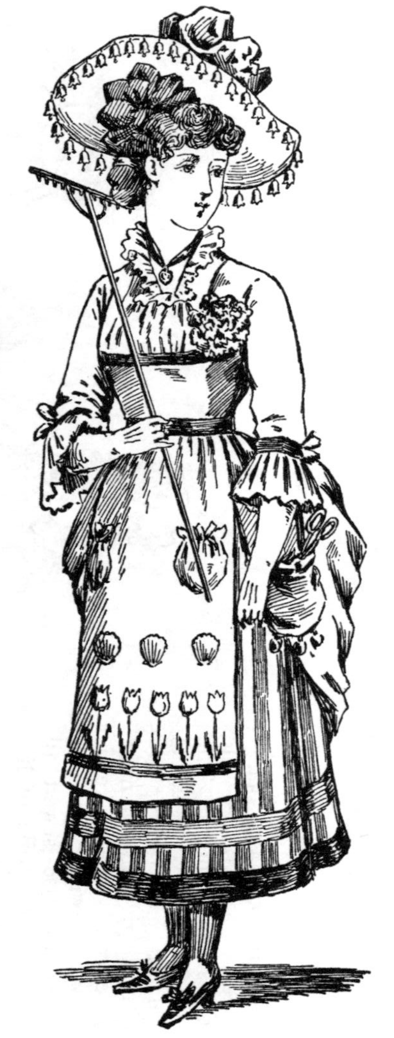

FIGURE No. 58.—MARY, QUITE CONTRARY.

FIGURE No. 57.—JACK TAR.—Blue and white blouse over blue-and-white striped jersey. White trousers and blue cap.

FIGURE No. 58.—MARY, QUITE CONTRARY.—Red-and-white striped skirt trimmed with brown and blue. Bodice and drapery of blue. Yellow apron; white tucker and elbow flounces. Yellow hat, red stockings, brown slippers.

FIGURE No. 59.—VENUS.—Dress and mantle white. Decorations and wand of silver. Sandal-slippers.

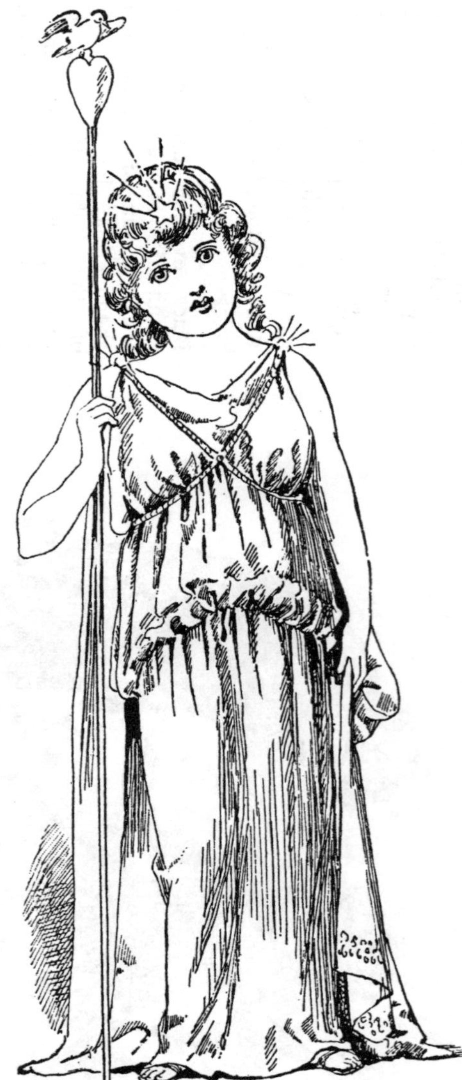

FIGURE No. 59.—VENUS.

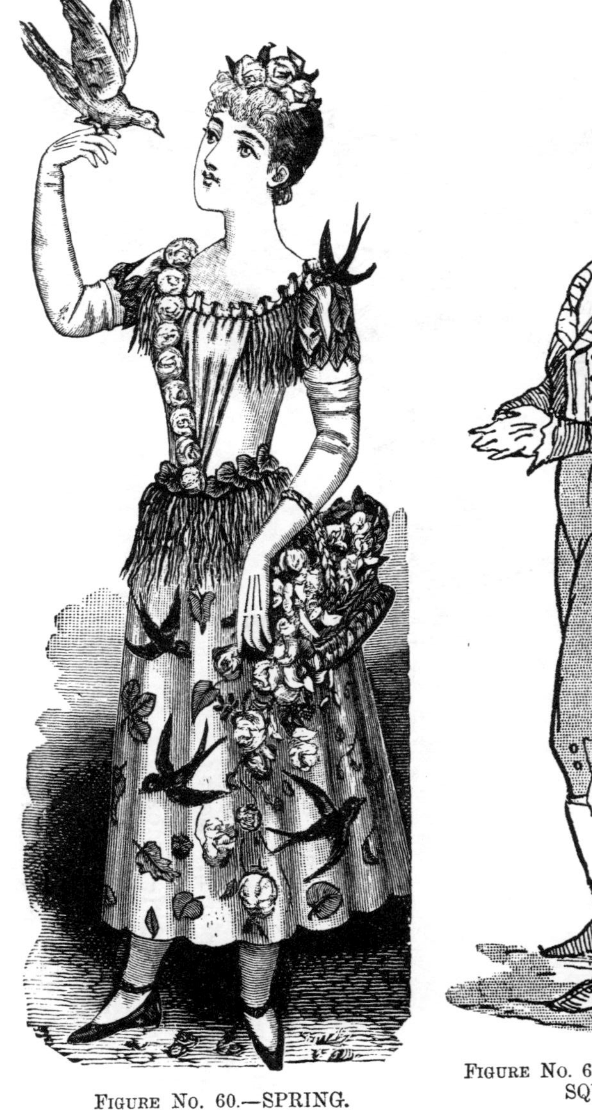

FIGURE No. 60.—SPRING.

FIGURE No. 61.—COUNTRY SQUIRE.

FIGURE No. 60.—SPRING.—Dress of white fabric decorated with birds, blossoms, foliage and grasses. Carries a basket of flowers.

FIGURE No. 61.—COUNTRY SQUIRE.—Costume of blue-and-white linen or silk, and drab cloth. Drab hat; boots with yellow or red tops.

FIGURE No. 62.—PRINCE CHARMING.—Costume of violet satin with pearl-gray stockings and violet shoes. Lace frills at the wrists and a muslin ruff at the neck.

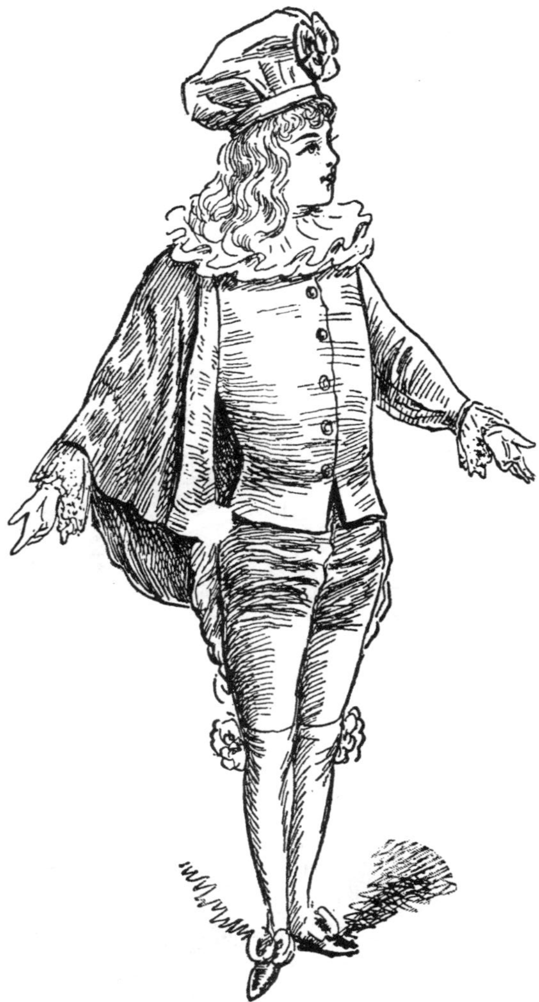

FIGURE No. 62.—PRINCE CHARMING.

Figure No. 64.—Fairy.—Dress of white gauze. Girdle, slippers, wand and head-dress of gold. Wings at the back.

Figure No. 65.—Spanish Marquis.—Jacket and breeches of red velvet trimmed with gold lace. Yellow satin body, sash and sides of trousers. Jewel-decorations upon the breast. Yellow stockings and black slippers. Turn-down collar and lace cravat.

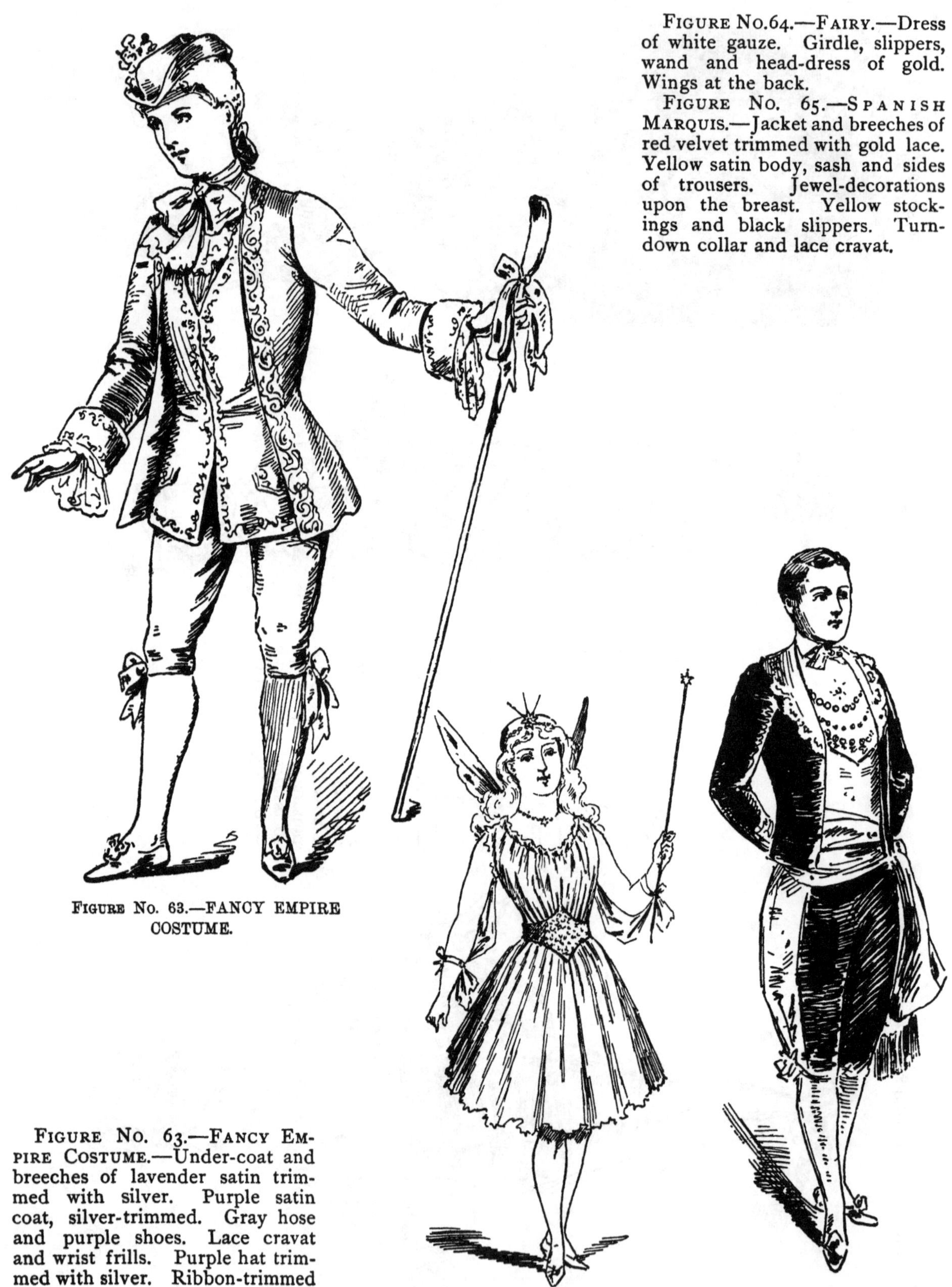

Figure No. 63.—FANCY EMPIRE COSTUME.

Figure No. 64.—FAIRY.

Figure No. 65.—SPANISH MARQUIS.

Figure No. 63.—Fancy Empire Costume.—Under-coat and breeches of lavender satin trimmed with silver. Purple satin coat, silver-trimmed. Gray hose and purple shoes. Lace cravat and wrist frills. Purple hat trimmed with silver. Ribbon-trimmed staff.

FIGURE NO. 66.—DUCHESS OF DEVONSHIRE.

FIGURE NO. 66. — DUCHESS OF DEVONSHIRE.—Gown of pink satin, short waist, narrow skirt. Full sash of pink ribbon or silk. Ruche of satin at foot of skirt. Large gray or white hat with pink plumes. Black mitts and low, buckle-shoes.

FIGURE NO. 67.—SCHOOL-BOY.—Suit of dull old-blue with silver buttons and white frills. White stockings and black shoes. Carries a whip.

FIGURE NO. 68. — CAVALIER COSTUME.—White shirt and ruff. Gray puffed under-sleeves and gray tights. Jacket and trunks of pale old-rose satin. Cloak of deep old-rose velvet lined with gray. Old-rose hat with gray plumes. Deep old-rose slippers. Red, blue, purple or brown combined with gray will make up prettily in this costume.

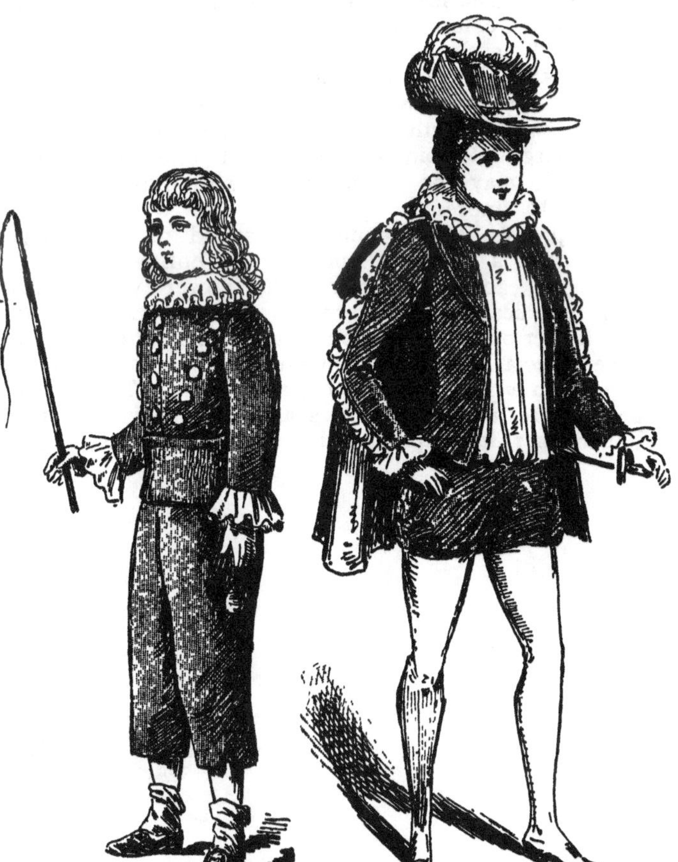

FIGURE NO. 67.—SCHOOL-BOY.

FIGURE NO. 68.—CAVALIER COSTUME.

FLORAL PROCESSION.

FIGURE No. 69.—A floral procession at a school or church entertainment is a pretty spectacle, and is easily arranged. Flora, the goddess of the kingdom of blossoms leads the procession, and must have a distinctive dress, and a scepter, in order to readily distinguish her from her subjects. She may costume herself in white or any pale color she prefers, and decorate herself with garlands composed of specimens of all of the blossoms her subjects represent, together with foliage and grasses. Her scepter may be twined with flowers and surmounted with a large blossom or branch of blossoms. Her head may be surmounted with flowers arranged to represent a crown; and a still further queenly effect could be carried out by her wearing a flower-trimmed train borne by two pages, each representing the flower with which her scepter is crowned. The costume of the leader of the procession seen in the picture is of the Grecian style, and is made of white gauze draped with a green sash of the same fabric. The other pictures represent Flora's subjects gracefully following her in couples, each couple representing two flowers that harmonize prettily in color.

Throughout this pamphlet are scattered engravings of floral costumes which may be used in floral processions, and which will also convey an exact idea of how to develop a floral costume. Original ideas may be carried out in a most effective manner, if the person in charge of the preparations is quick to perceive and originate, and is able to execute the suggestions of others' brains as well as those of her own. Green should form a portion of every costume. Great care in grouping flowers and colorings should be observed in order to produce as kaleidoscopic an effect as possible during the procession; but when the ranks are posed upon the stage, the colorings may be grouped as in a bouquet. The favorite flowers for a procession of this kind are: Lilies of various kinds; roses, tulips, daffodils, sunflowers, chrysanthemums, asters, blue-bells, pansies, daisies, marigolds, butter-cups, cowslips, violets, pinks, dahlias, hollyhocks, gladioluses, etc., etc. Single large flowers are used for head-dresses; but the finer blossoms must be arranged in wreaths or garlands.

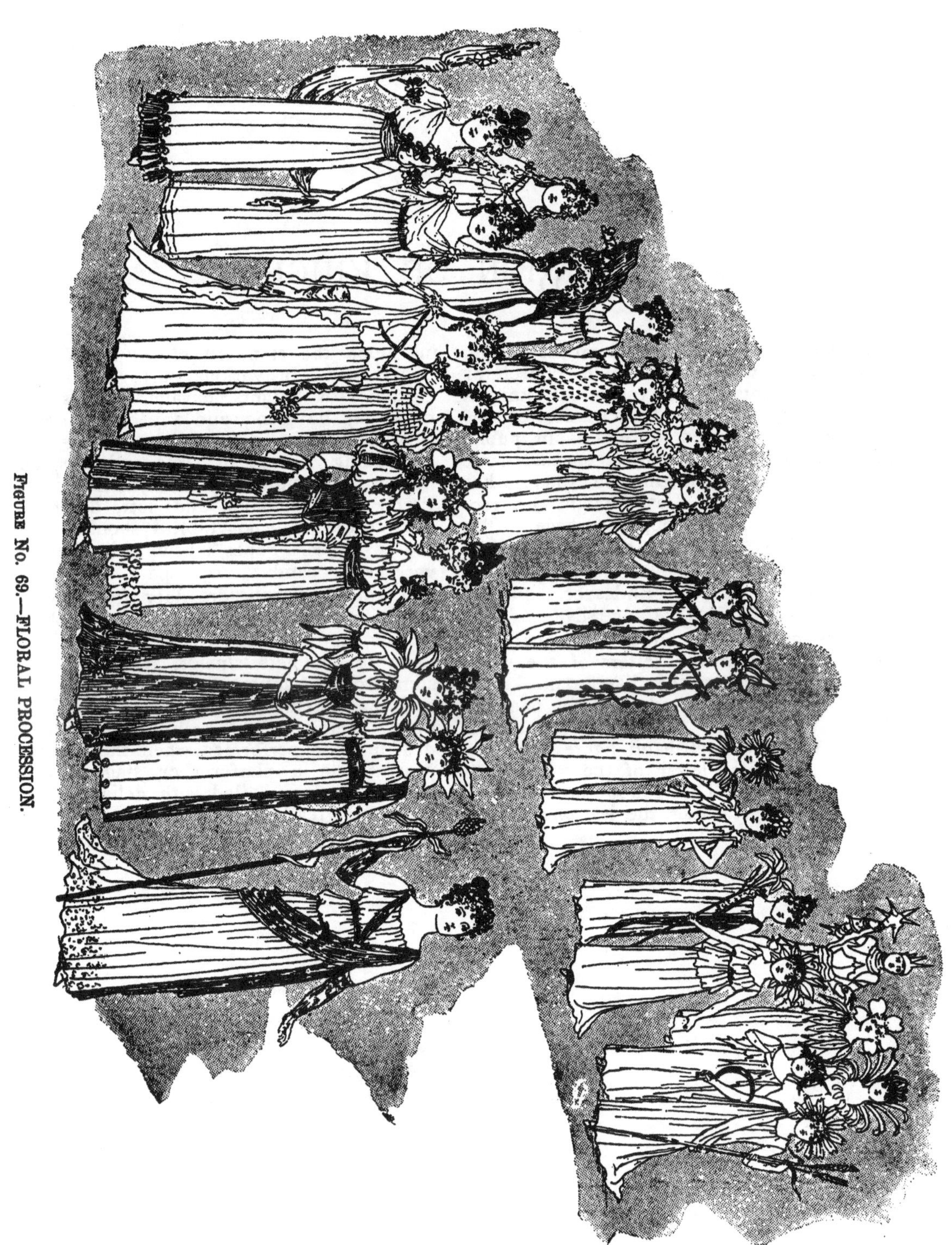

FIGURE No. 69.—FLORAL PROCESSION.

PROCESSION OF KNIGHTS.

FIGURE NO. 70.—Following a floral procession, or forming a feature by itself in church or school entertainments, a procession of knights is a very pleasing picture. A procession of this kind is especially adapted to classes in public or Sunday schools having some special name or motto by which to distinguish them. For instance, an "Endeavor Class" might be represented as seen on the opposite page. The captain, dressed as a knight of some ancient order should lead his retainers bearing a standard with the word "Endeavor" printed upon it in black, red, gold or silver. Then should follow as many retainers as would be necessary to represent the letters of the word, each retainer being dressed like some knight of old and carrying a standard with one letter of the word upon it. Referring to the standard of the lower left-hand figure upon the opposite page, the first letter of the word "Endeavor" will be seen. Then follow the remaining letters in their proper order, the last one appearing upon the standard of the last figure in the upper row. In various parts of this pamphlet costumes of knights, cavaliers, pages and courtiers may be seen; and any of them will answer very nicely for a knight in such a procession by adding a coat of arms and a standard or banner, and omitting swords, daggers, etc., etc. Pretty bright colors, and soft, dainty tints in silk, cotton or wool fabrics should be used for the costumes. Paper muslin will represent satin very well, cambric will pass muster for silk and velveteen will do duty for velvet. Gold and silver paper will make fine looking decorations, and pasteboard will form the foundations for helmets, shields, armor etc., etc. The standards or banners should all be of one color, and the letters plainly marked, sewed or pasted upon them. With a little practice a fancy drill may be performed when the procession appears upon a platform or stage. A pageant of this kind is hailed with delight by the little ones and greatly enjoyed by the adult observers.

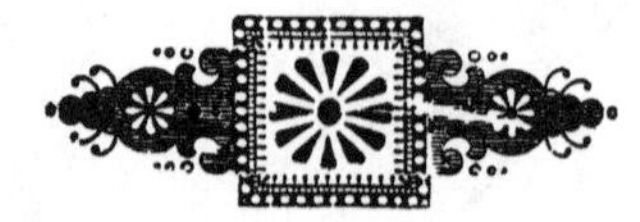

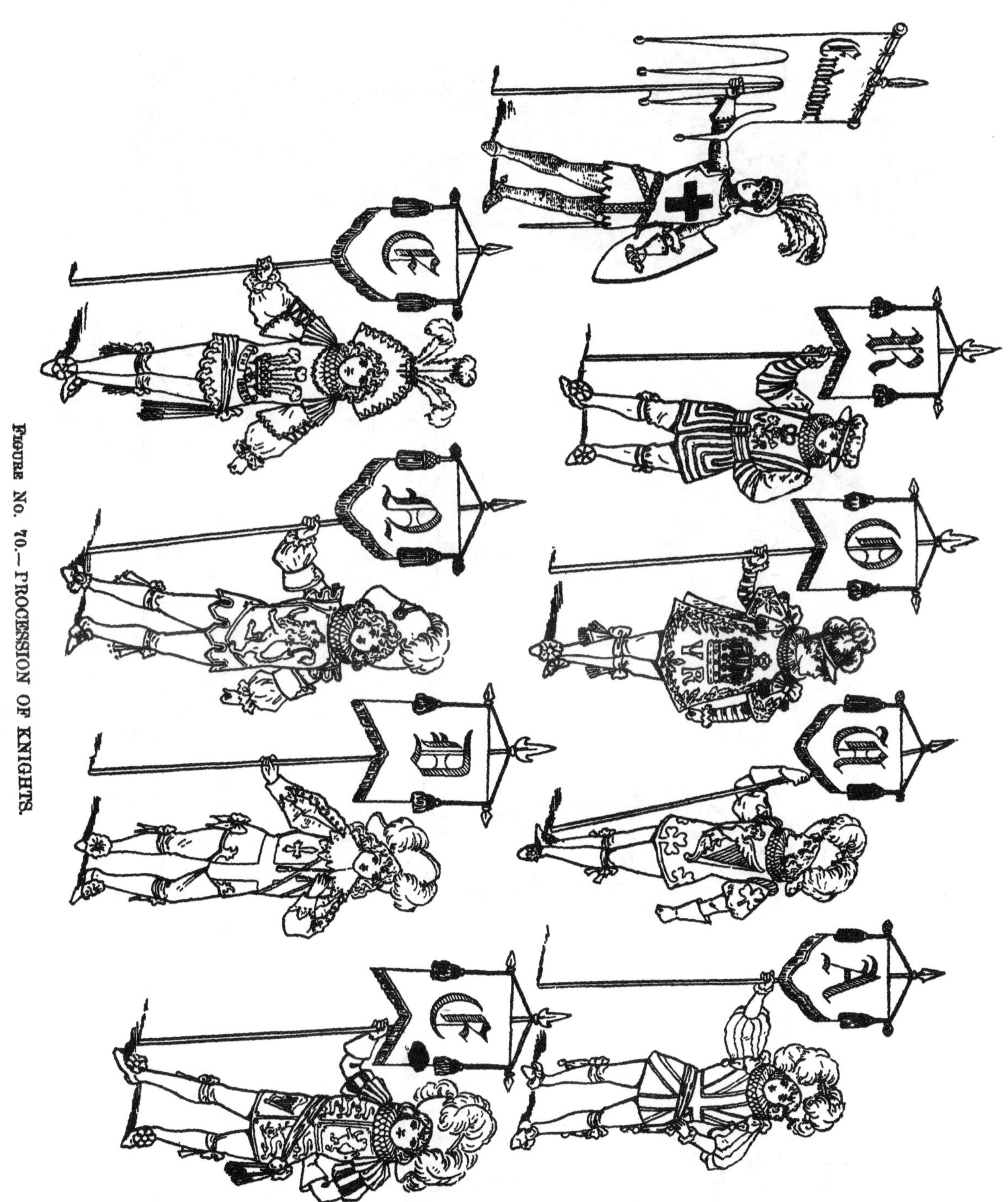

FIGURE NO. 70.—PROCESSION OF KNIGHTS.

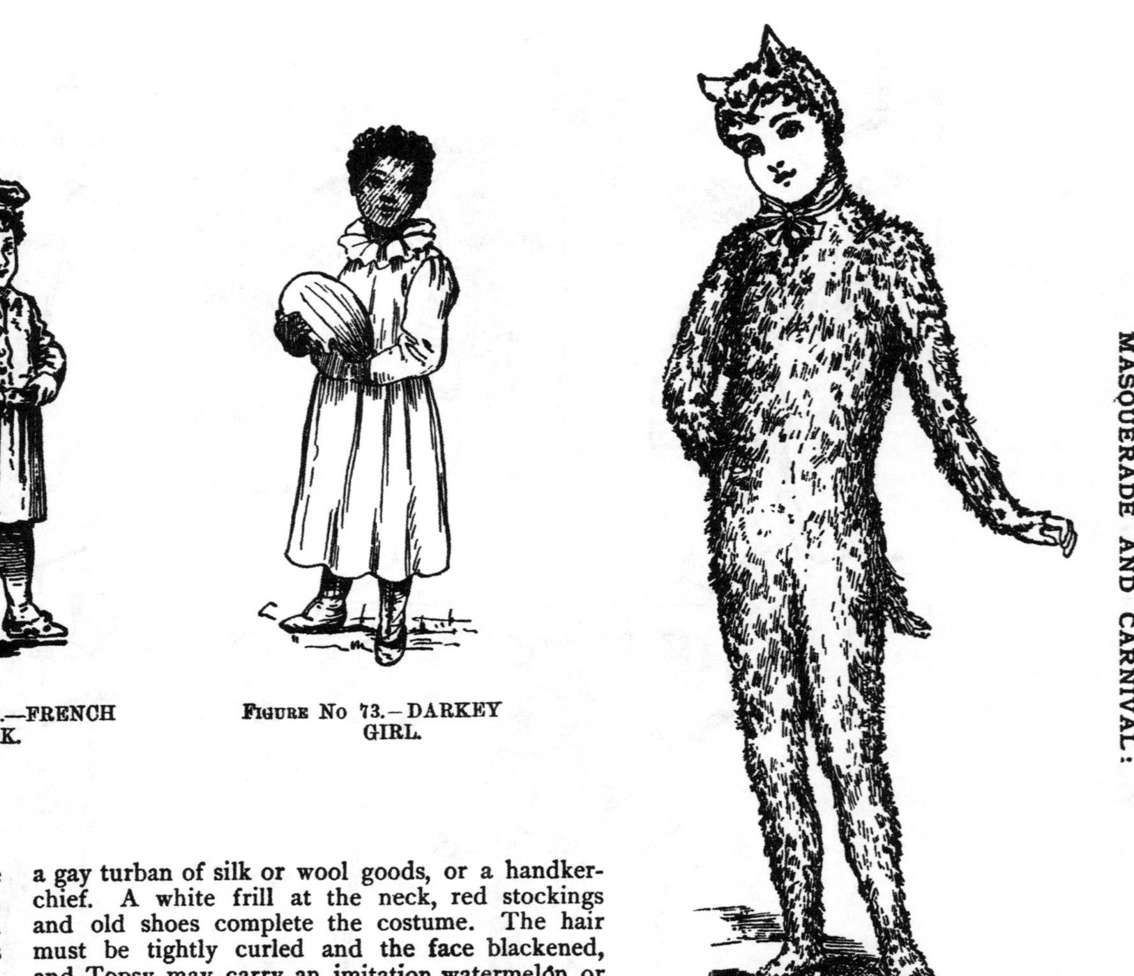

FIGURE No. 71.—SHEPHERD BOY.

FIGURE No. 72.—FRENCH COOK.

FIGURE No 73.—DARKEY GIRL.

FIGURE No. 74.—WHITE CAT.

FIGURE No. 71.—SHEPHERD BOY.—This costume is composed of a blue flannel shirt and trousers. Red suspenders, stockings and hat, and buckskin shoes. The hat is ornamented by a single heron's plume. A horn and whip are carried.

FIGURE No. 72.—FRENCH COOK.—White blouse, and a white paper cap; leather belt with a large spoon at one side. White stockings and shoes.

FIGURE No. 73.—DARKEY GIRL.—This costume is very simple. It consists of a plain dress which may be of bright plain, plaid, or figured goods, and a gay turban of silk or wool goods, or a handkerchief. A white frill at the neck, red stockings and old shoes complete the costume. The hair must be tightly curled and the face blackened, and Topsy may carry an imitation watermelon or an A B C book.

FIGURE No. 74.—WHITE CAT.—This costume may be made of long-fleeced Canton flannel; or of a suit of woven underwear covered with cotton-wool. A ribbon of any bright color preferred is tied about the neck.

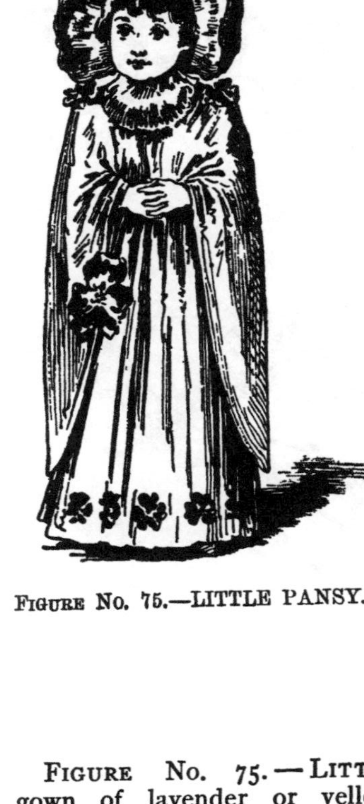
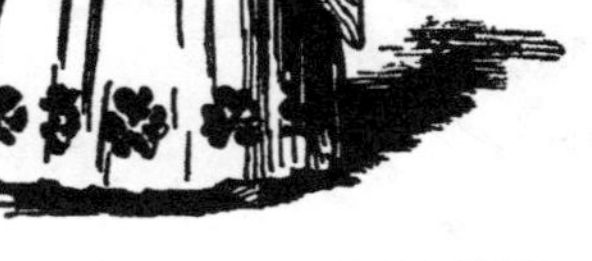

FIGURE No. 75.—LITTLE PANSY.

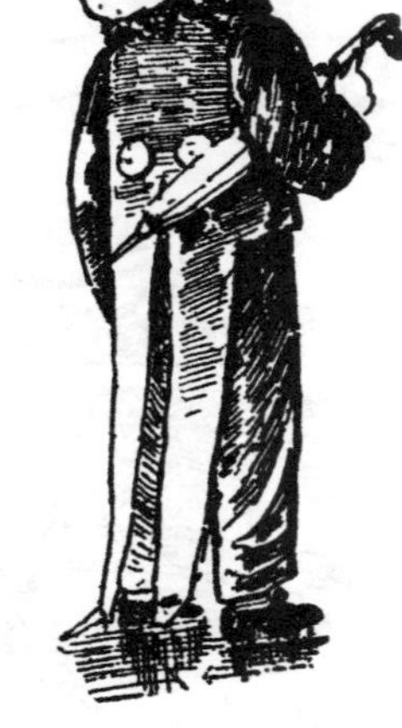

FIGURE No. 76.—THE DOCTOR.

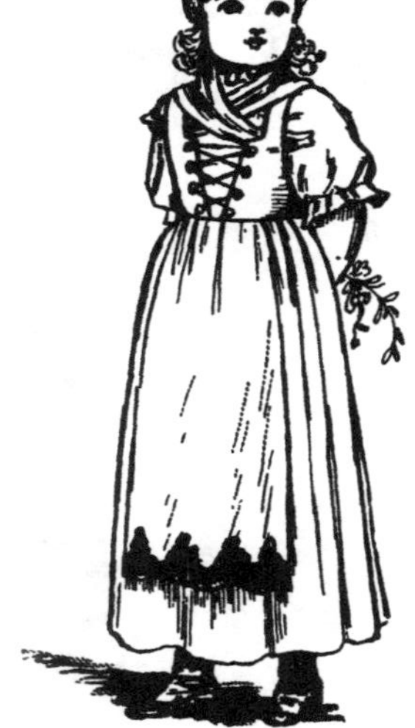

FIGURE No. 77.—DUTCH GIRL.

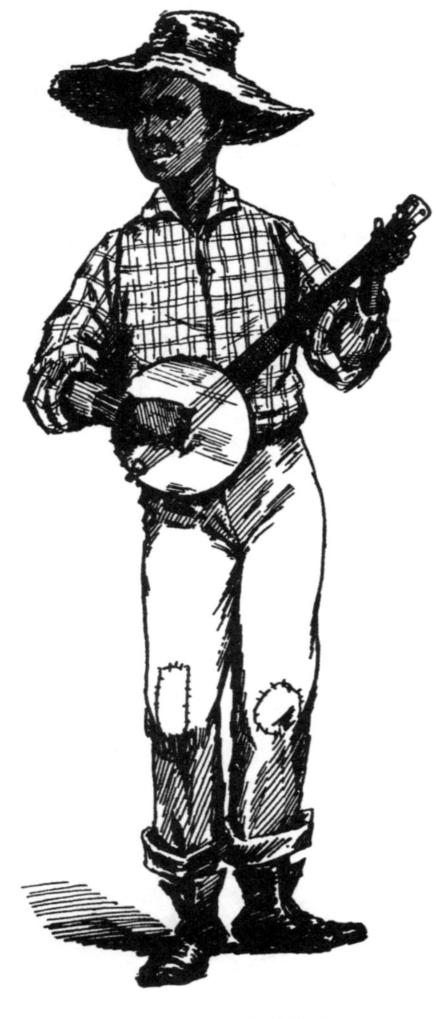

FIGURE No. 78.—SAMBO

FIGURE No. 75.—LITTLE PANSY.—Loose gown of lavender or yellow silk with angel sleeves; trimmed at the bottom with a row of pansies. Large artificial pansy-petals are so arranged as to frame the face. A smaller pansy is on each shoulder and a large one is suspended from the arm by a ribbon.

FIGURE No. 76.—THE DOCTOR.—Brown coat and vest; blue swallow-tail coat; ruffled shirt and large black cravat. Pair of iron-bowed spectacles; large white beaver hat, blue stockings and leather shoes.

FIGURE No. 77.—DUTCH GIRL.—Dress of China-blue flannel or cashmere. Waist laced over a white shirt with short full sleeves. Gay kerchief crossed over the breast, and a peasant's cap of white muslin or gay silk upon the head. Fancy white apron trimmed with color—red or blue. Red stockings and wooden shoes.

FIGURE No. 78.—Blue jean overalls, red-and-yellow checked flannel shirt; broad-brimmed soft felt or old straw hat, and old leather shoes without strings. Skin darkened, and hair closely curled or worn under a woolly wig.

FIGURE NO. 81.—LAMP-SHADE.—Dress made of some stiff fabric cut in points and folded back and forth like a fan, or finely plaited or crimped. Hat made to match and finished with ribbon rosette. Ribbon sash at waist; flesh-colored stockings and slippers to match the dress fabric.

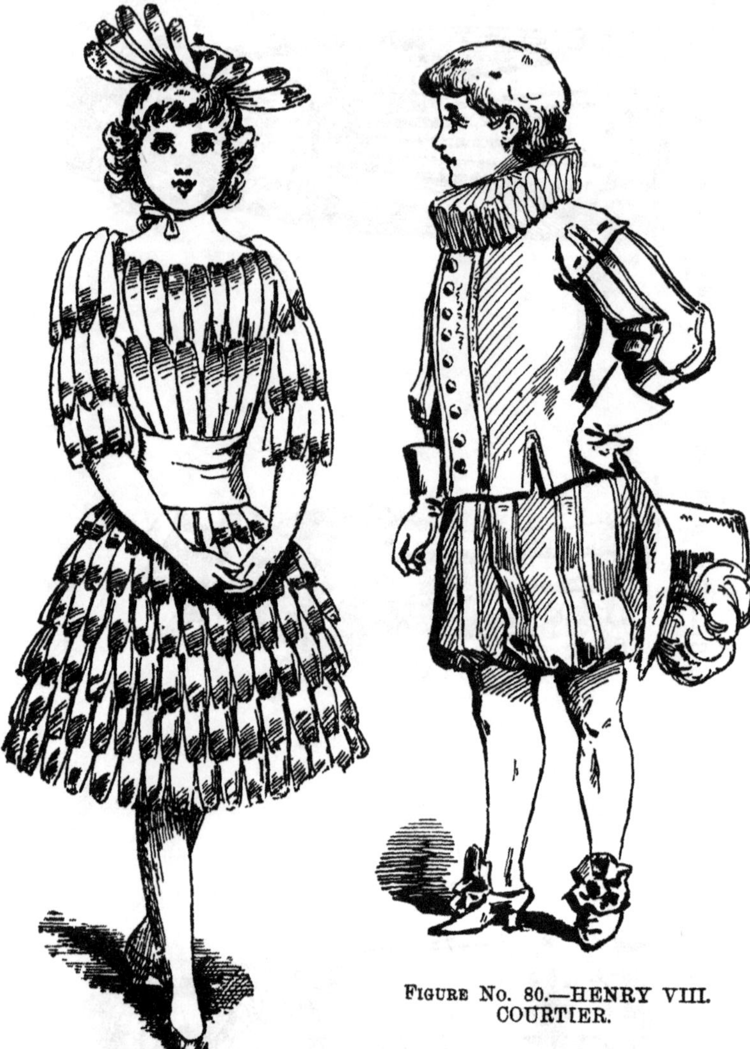

FIGURE NO. 80.—HENRY VIII. COURTIER.

FIGURE NO. 79.—FIELD DAISY.

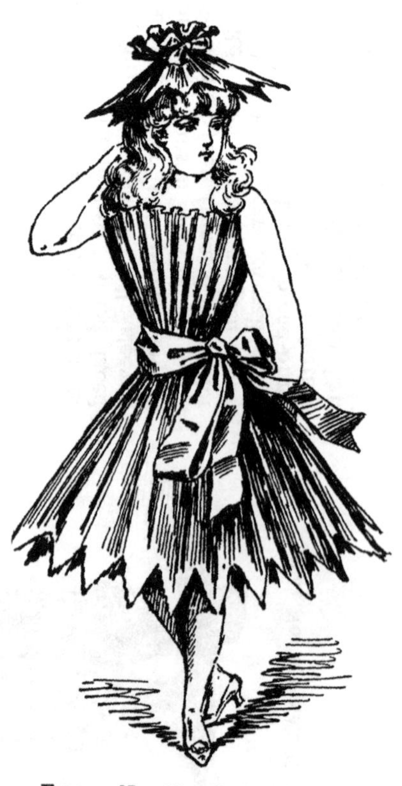

FIGURE NO. 81.—LAMP-SHADE

FIGURE NO. 79.—FIELD DAISY.—Dress foundation of white, coarse lawn or tarletan covered with daisy-petals cut from bleached muslin or white paper. Large daisy with yellow center tied on the head with yellow ribbons; yellow sash, white stockings and yellow slippers.

FIGURE NO. 80.—HENRY VIII. COURTIER.—Doublet of pale-blue satin, slashed and trimmed with silver braid. Full sleeves and trunks of pale-blue-and-scarlet striped silk; pale blue hose and scarlet shoes with silver and blue rosettes. White hat with blue plumes; and white neck-ruff and gauntlet gloves.

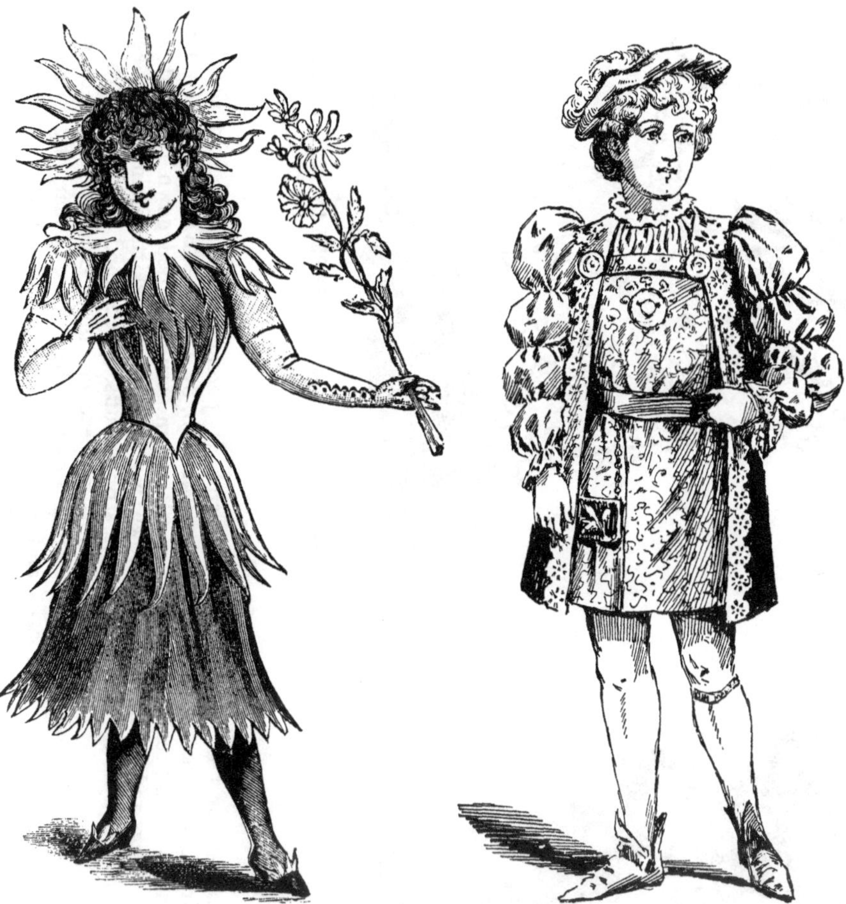

Figure No. 82.—SUNFLOWER.

Figure No. 83.—COURT DRESS.

Figure No. 84.—Buttercup.—Dress of buttercup-yellow tarletan, trimmed at the bottom with a wreath of buttercup foliage. Fancy bodice and sleeve caps of green. Yellow sash trimmed with foliage. Buttercup head-dress and fan. Yellow stockings and green slippers.

Figure No. 82.—Sunflower.—Dress of green fabric; bodice, drapery, sleeves and neck-decoration of sunflower yellow. Large artificial sunflower for head-decoration; yellow gloves and stockings, and green slippers. Carries a branch of sunflower blossoms.

Figure No. 83.—Court Dress.—Tunic of pale-green brocaded with silver; pale-green sleeves and hose, white silk shirt with lace neck and sleeve ruffles. Dark-green velvet doublet trimmed with silver lace. Pale-green hat with silver-white plume. Pouch of green leather with silver chain. Silver garter on left leg; gray suéde shoes.

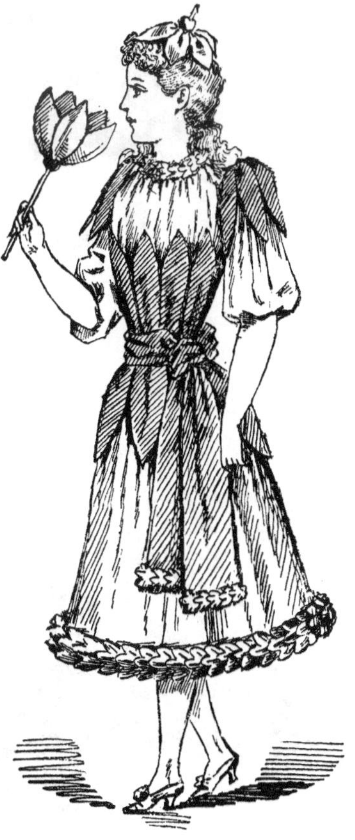

Figure No. 84.—BUTTERCUP.

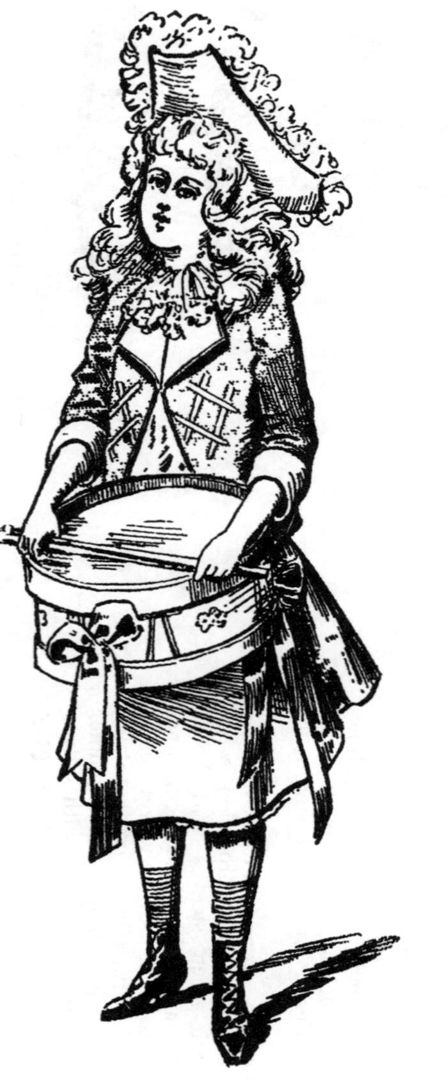

FIGURE No. 85.—DAUGHTER OF THE REGIMENT.

FIGURE No. 86.—ROBINSON CRUSOE.

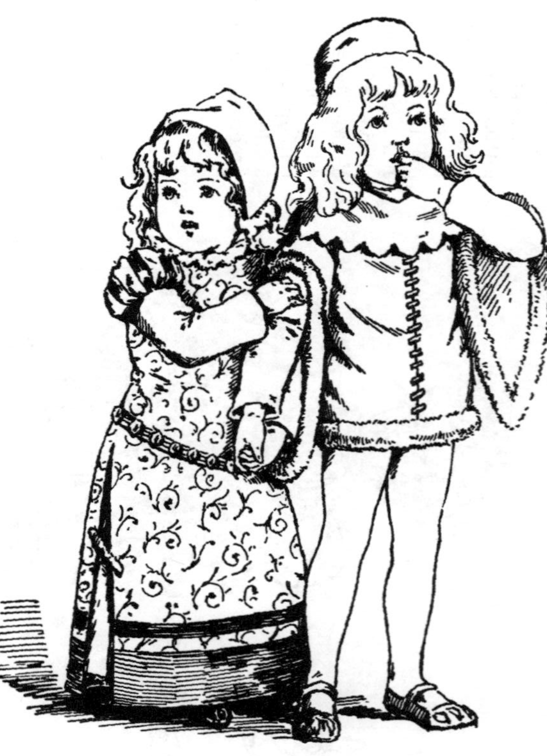

FIGURES NOS. 87 AND 88.—BABES IN THE WOODS.

FIGURE No. 85.—DAUGHTER OF THE REGIMENT.—White blouse and skirt; blue jacket faced and trimmed with white. White hat and feathers; lace cravat, blue and white stockings and patent-leather shoes. Yellow and white drum trimmed with blue and white ribbon.

FIGURE No. 86.—ROBINSON CRUSOE.—Brown waist, cap, trousers, stockings and shoes; goat-skin cape and skirt portion, and fur on cap. A parrot is perched upon the right shoulder.

FIGURES No. 87 AND 88.—BABES IN THE WOODS.—Little girl in écru brocaded gown trimmed with brown; worn over a white skirt. Plain brown sleeves with striped puffs. Red hood and fancy girdle.

Boy in peacock-blue doublet trimmed with swan's down. Red cap, collar, tight sleeves and tights; collar cut double and in scollops. Brown shoes or slippers slashed with red.

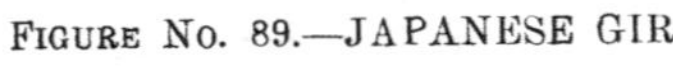

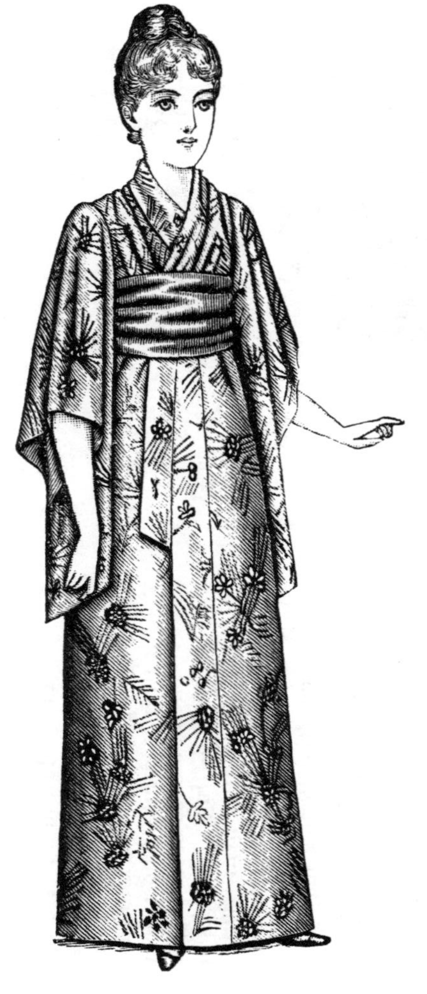

FIGURE No. 89.—JAPANESE GIRL.

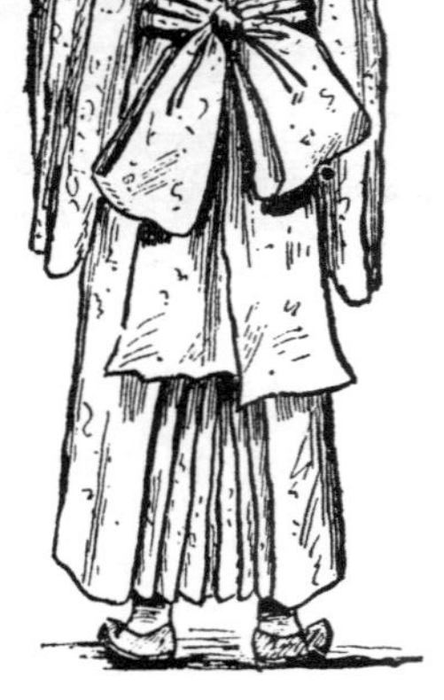

FIGURE No. 90.—
PITTI SING.

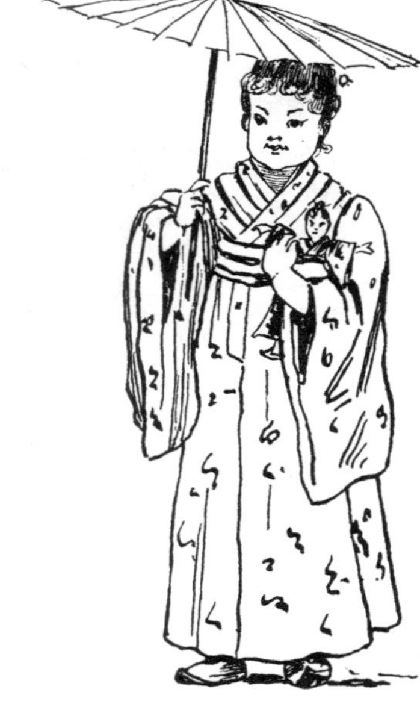

FIGURE No. 91.—
PITTI SING'S NURSE.

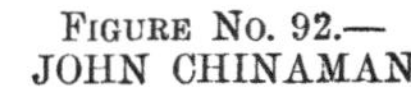

FIGURE No. 92.—
JOHN CHINAMAN.

FIGURE No. 89.—JAPANESE GIRL.—This costume may be made of flowered or figured silk, foulard or sateen. It is bound in at the waist by a broad sash of Japanese silk tied in a bow at the back. A Japanese fan or parasol, and sandals, or wooden shoes may complete the costume.

FIGURES NOS. 90 AND 91.—PITTI SING AND NURSE.—Pitti Sing is one of Three Little Maids from School in the opera of "The Mikado." Both she and the nurse are dressed in China silk or sateen kimonos. The little maid carries a fan and wears wooden shoes. The nurse has a Japanese parasol and holds the little maid's doll.

FIGURE No. 92.—JOHN CHINAMAN.—This costume may be made of blue or gray silk, sateen or flannel. Wooden shoes, white stockings and a braided pig-tail or queue complete the costume. John Chinaman may take the part of a waiter and serve tea from a tray in Chinese cups and saucers.

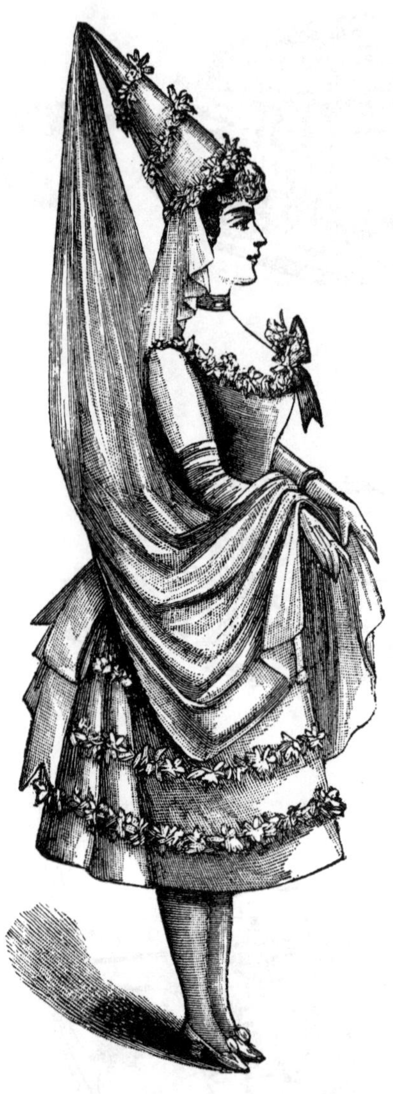

FIGURE NO. 93.—NORMANDY BRIDE.

FIGURE NO. 95. — DANCING GIRL. (For illustration see next page.)—The skirt of this costume is of scarlet wool trimmed with black bands and red ball-fringe. The black low-cut bodice is worn over a white, short-sleeved under-waist. The bodice is of velvet, and by removing the ball-fringe from its edge it is made suitable for wear with other costumes. If the skirt be red with black bands upon it and red and black balls about its hem, the bodice may be black with black or red balls, and the lacing may be of either color. The head-dress is usually of cashmere or veiling and is decorated with balls. A peasant girl does not wear gloves. Her sash may be a width of plain, plaid or striped Surah silk or of soft wool goods. A Roman silk scarf or sash is also in good taste upon any South-of-Europe peasant dress.

FIGURE NO. 93.—NORMANDY BRIDE.—Dress of white *faille francaise* or cashmere, trimmed with rows of silk chicorée ruching, or wreaths of orange blossoms or jessamine. Breast-knot and sash-bow of moiré ribbon. Sugar-loaf cap in silver-cloth or satin, flowered and finished off with a long drooping net veil; a plaited frilling of the transparent material hangs from the edge of the cap down to the shoulder.

FIGURE NO. 94.—"NIGGER" BABY.—Dress of yellow flannel; blue gingham apron, white, stiffly-starched muslin bonnet. Red stockings, and leather shoes. Carries a cotton-ball in her hand.

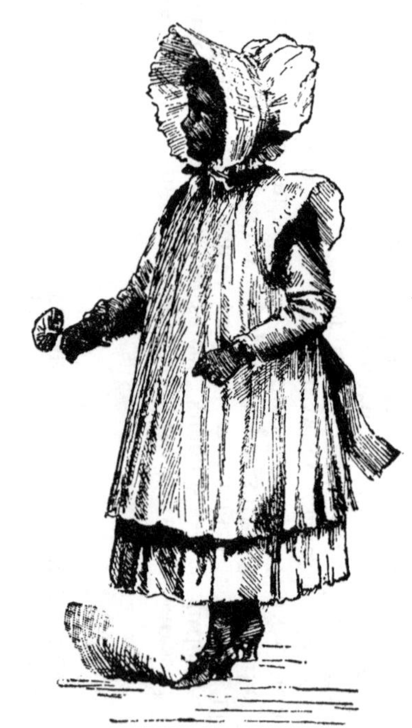

FIGURE NO. 94.— "NIGGER" BABY.

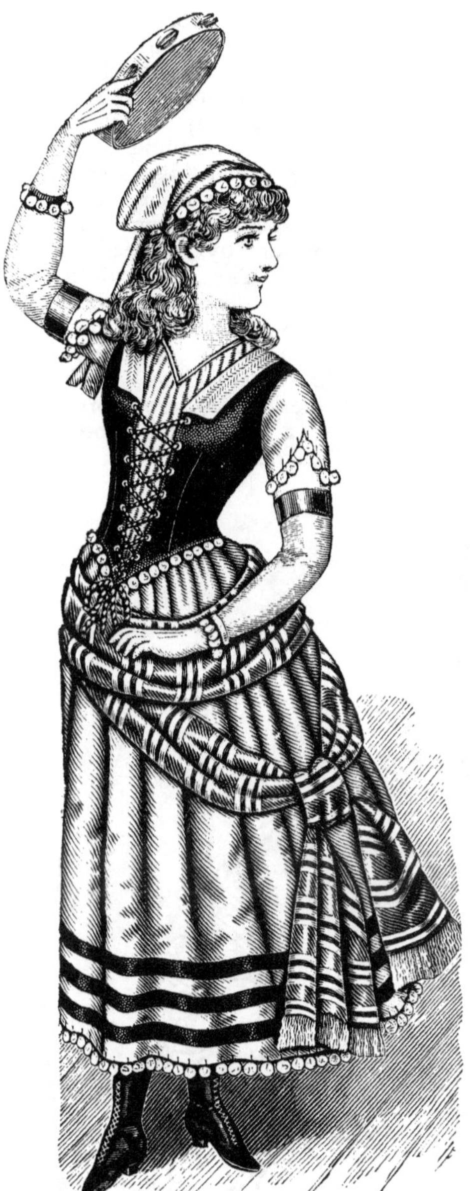

FIGURE No. 95.—DANCING GIRL.

(For description see preceding page.)

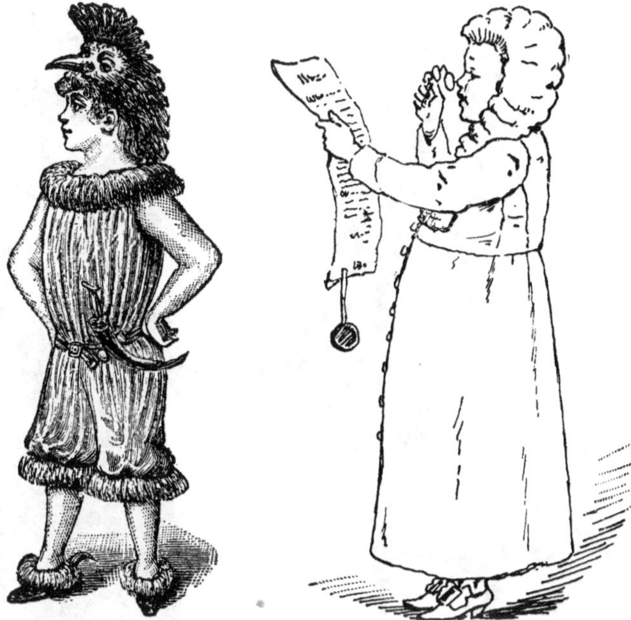

FIGURE No. 96.—FIGHTING COCK.

FIGURE No. 97.—THE CHANCELLOR.

FIGURE No. 96.—FIGHTING COCK.—Blouse and trousers of orange-red satin or cambric, trimmed with cock-feather bands. Dark shoes trimmed with cock-feathers and spurs. Leather belt, cock-spur dagger. Cock's head for head-dress.

FIGURE No. 97.—THE CHANCELLOR.—A white wig and black gown, spectacles, a legal paper with seal attached, buckled shoes and scarlet stockings complete this costume. If desired, the gown may be of blue, red, purple or drab. Large brass buttons are used to close it at the front.

FIGURE No. 98.—BABY BUNTING.—This costume consists of a dainty white dress and stockings and soft white fur shoes. Over this is fastened a white-fur skin with the head arranged as a hood. This is the veritable skin used to "wrap by-low baby bunting in," except that the artist has added a long tail and short ears to the traditional "rabbit skin."

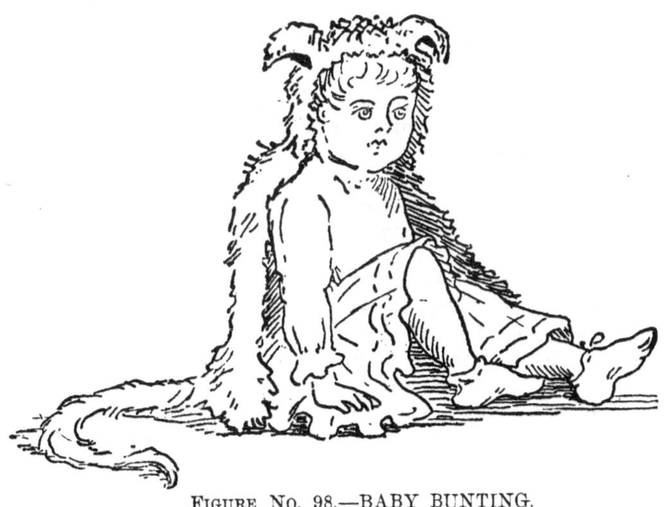

FIGURE No. 98.—BABY BUNTING.

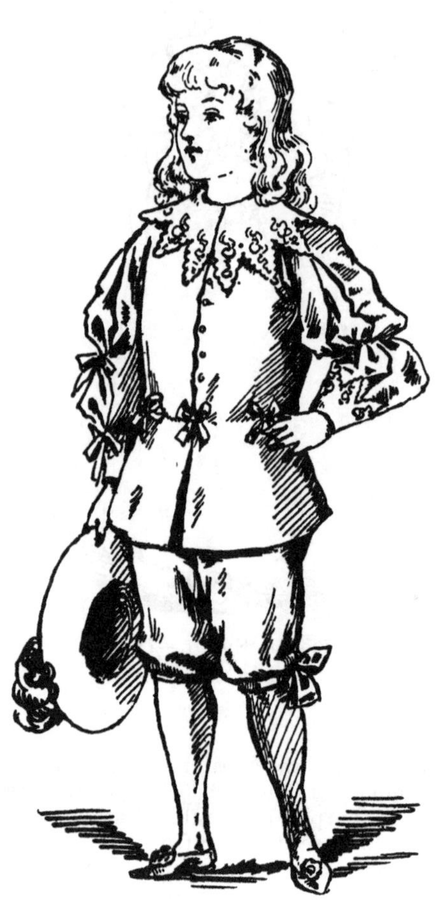

FIGURE NO. 99.—LITTLE BOY BLUE.

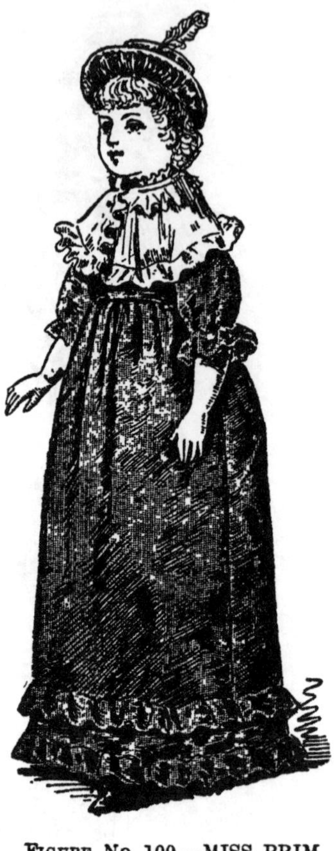

FIGURE NO. 100.—MISS PRIM.

FIGURE NO. 102. ALPINE SHEPHERD. Blue jean, drilling, flannel or any other fabric preferred may be used for this costume. A leather belt is about the waist and a horn is suspended from the shoulder by a leather strap. The tall white hat is decorated with narrow iibbon bands and a peacock's feather. White stockings and leather shoes are worn, and a shepherd's crook is carried.

FIGURE NO. 99. — LITTLE BOY BLUE.—Costume made entirely of blue from hat to slippers. Should carry a French horn or trumpet and a shepherd's crook.

FIGURE NO. 100.—MISS PRIM.—Gown and hat of Quaker-gray satin trimmed with the same. White mull cape. May carry a satin bag on the left arm and wear long, netted gray mitts.

FIGURE NO. 101.—THE TRUANT.—Blue waist, sash and trousers; white hat, collar, tie and gaiter-tops. Carries a hoop and stick.

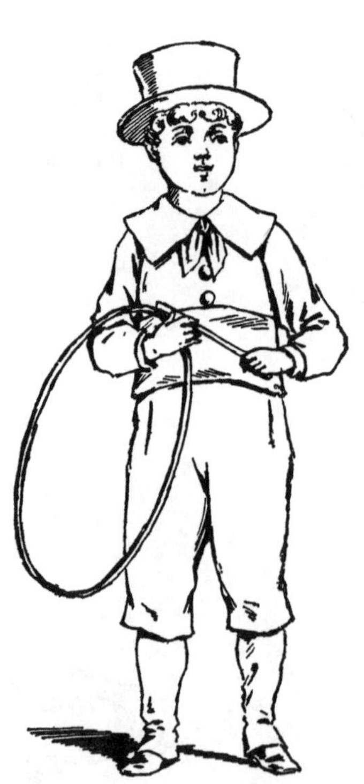

FIGURE NO. 101.—THE TRUANT.

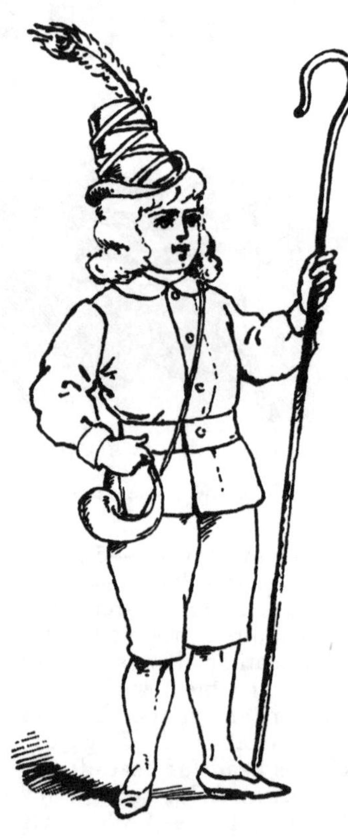

FIGURE NO. 102.—ALPINE SHEPHERD.

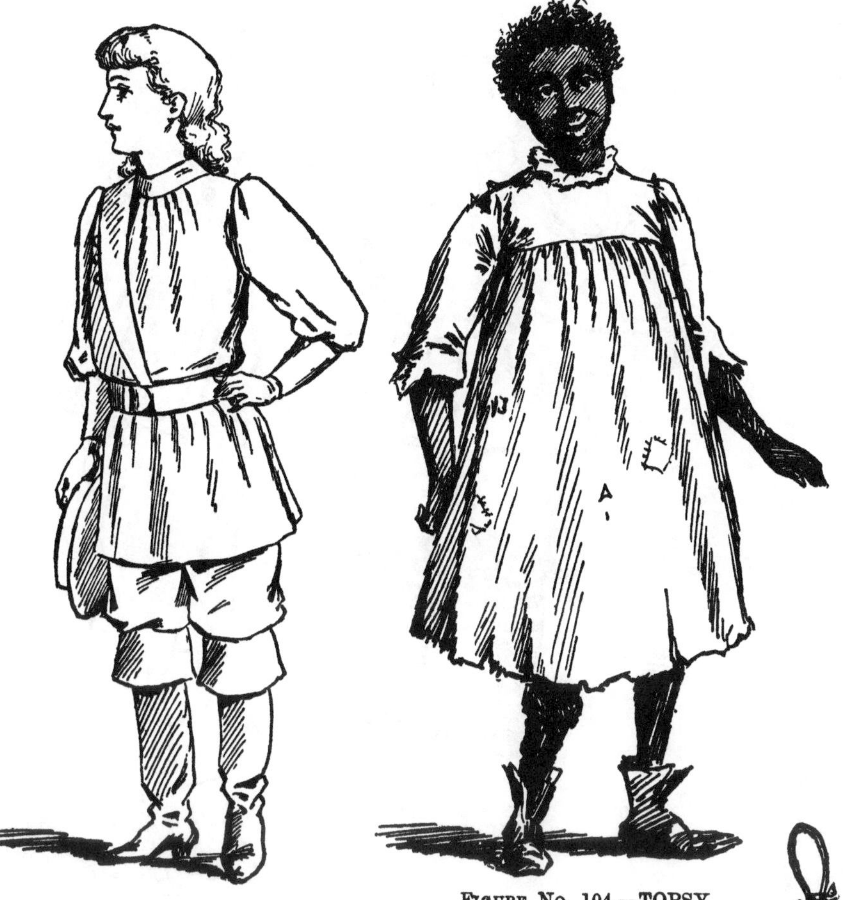

FIGURE NO. 103.—RUSSIAN COSTUME.

FIGURE NO. 104.—TOPSY.

FIGURE NO. 105.—LITTLE FARMER.—Checked gingham shirt, and overalls of blue or brown jean. An old hat of felt or straw; old boots, a hoe and a basket of potatoes complete the details of this sturdy character.

FIGURE NO. 106.—LITTLE BO-PEEP.—Skirt of pink, quilted satin; drapery of pale-blue brocade, bodice of plain blue satin. White chemisette and sleeves, with blue cuffs. Straw hat trimmed with pink and blue. Pink stockings and blue shoes. Carries a shepherd's crook.

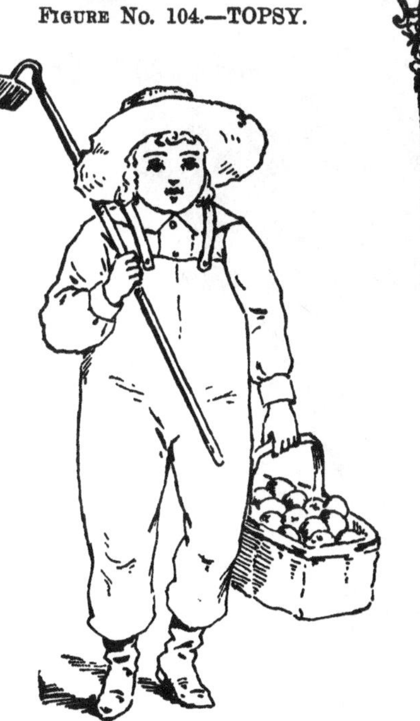

FIGURE NO. 105.—LITTLE FARMER.

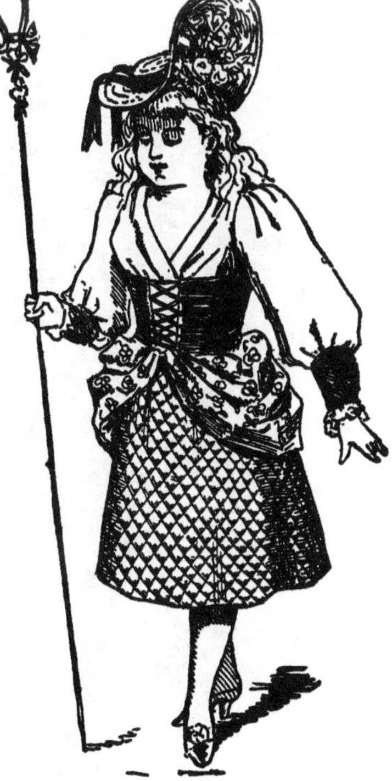

FIGURE NO. 106.—LITTLE BO-PEEP.

FIGURE NO. 103.—RUSSIAN COSTUME.—Green blouse with red collar, cuffs and sash; leather belt. Red trousers and cap; leather high-top boots, and leather cap band.

FIGURE NO. 104.—TOPSY.—Tattered Mother-Hubbard gown of blue, red, yellow or brown woolen goods. Brown woolen stockings and old leather shoes. May carry an A B C book.

FIGURE NO. 107.—LITTLE DEMON.—This costume may be used for the characters of a bat, sprite, fairy, faun or demon. It is made of black and white sateen, and decorated and girdled with strings of jet beads. The wings may be of black cambric or thin crinoline made double and stiffened by long whalebonés. They are sewed to the gloves and to the back of the waist and skirt of the dress. Black gloves and stockings, and short silvered horns fastened in the hair complete the costume.

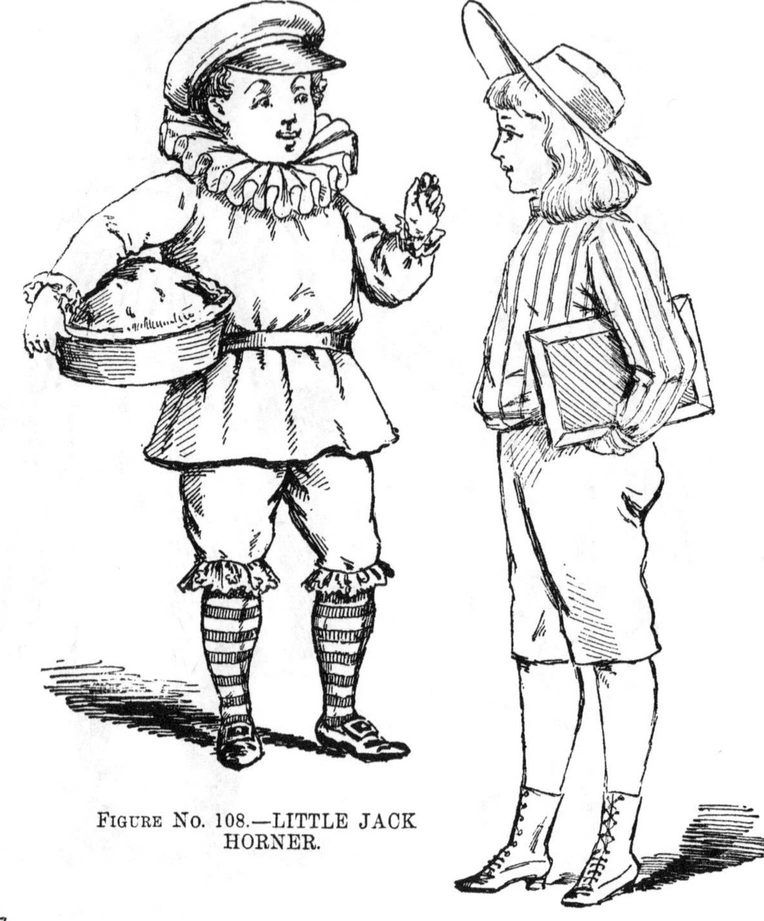

FIGURE NO. 108.—LITTLE JACK HORNER.

FIGURE NO. 109.—THE STUDENT.

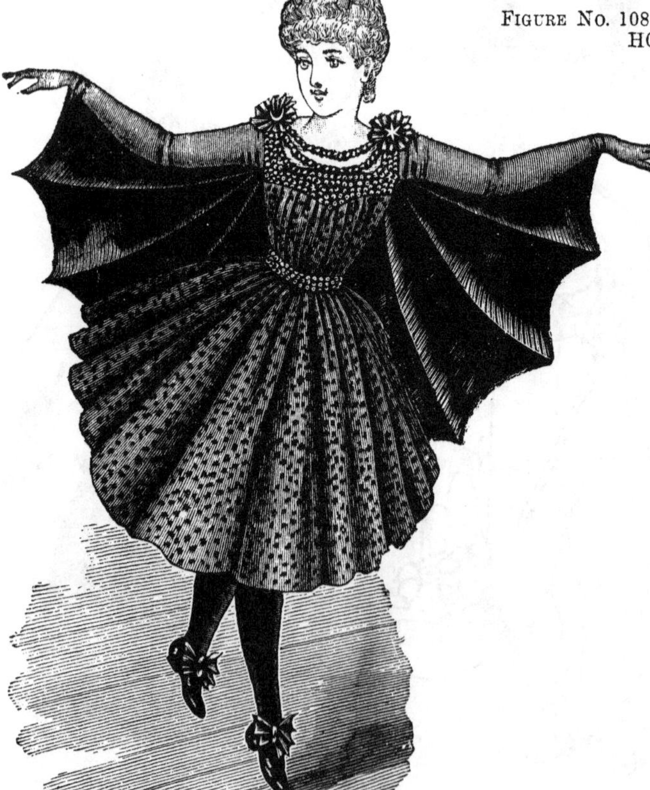

FIGURE NO. 107.—LITTLE DEMON.

FIGURE NO. 108.—LITTLE JACK HORNER.—Purple blouse, brown trousers, red-and-brown striped stockings, brown buckle-shoes; red cap with brown peak and green band. White ruff at the neck and white ruffles at the wrists and knees. Leather belt. Carries an imitation pie in which are candied plums or large raisins.

FIGURE NO. 109.—THE STUDENT.—Straw hat; blue-and-white or red-and-white striped blouse; white or blue flannel trousers with stockings to match; laced shoes. Carries a slate under one arm.

FIGURE NO. 110.—CHIMNEY SWEEP. — Entire suit made of black jersey-cloth or composed of a set of black underwear. Carries a rope, chimney-broom and ladder, and wears a belt and black shoes.

FIGURE NO. 111.—KNIGHT OF THE MALTESE CROSS.—Blouse and breeches of scarlet satin; sleeves and trunks of yellow satin; red stockings; yellow shoes with silver buckles. Leather belt, silver clasp; coat of arms suspended upon the breast.

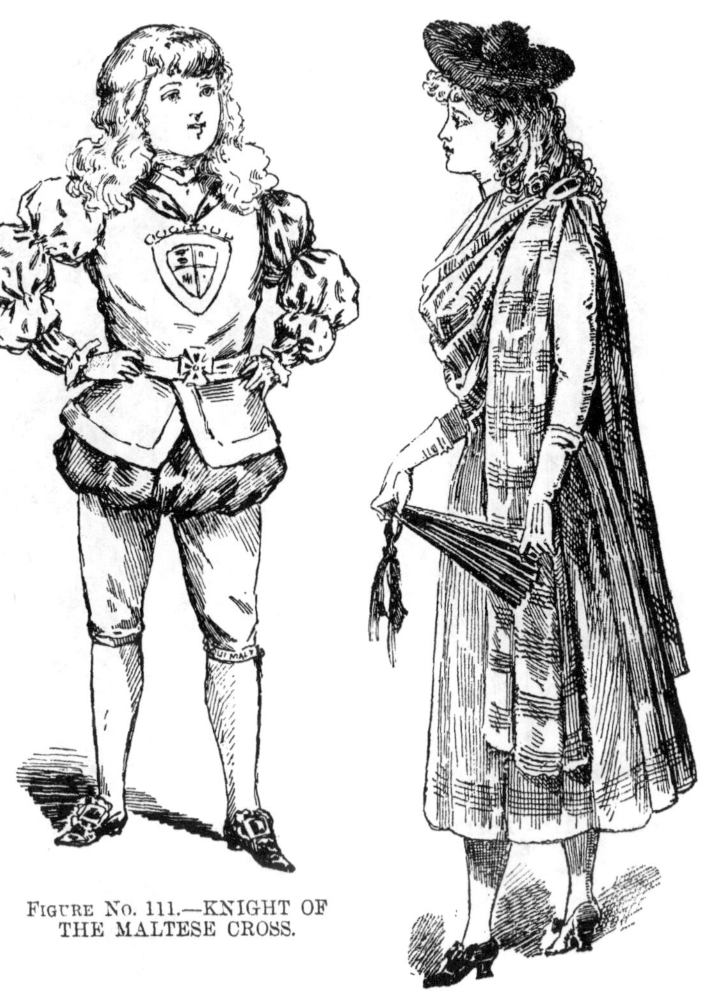

FIGURE NO. 111.—KNIGHT OF THE MALTESE CROSS.

FIGURE NO. 112.—HIGHLAND LASSIE.

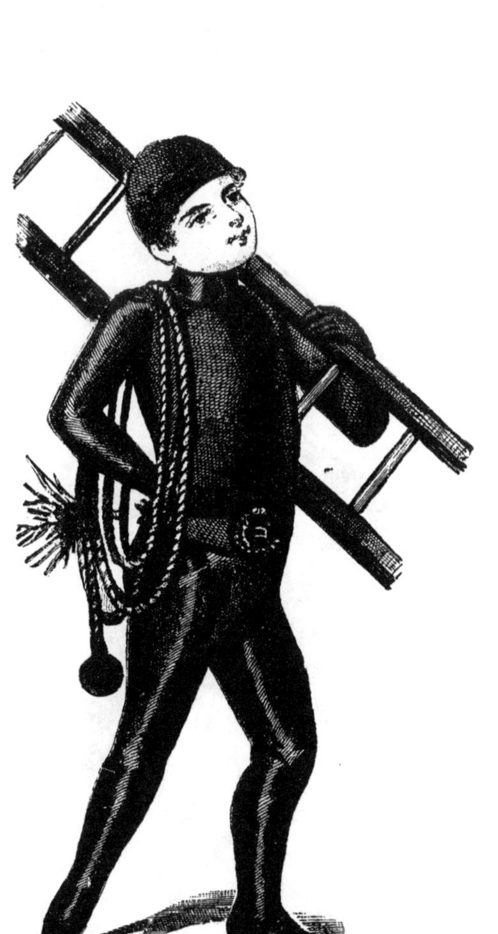

FIGURE NO. 110.—CHIMNEY SWEEP.

FIGURE NO. 112.—HIGHLAND LASSIE. — Costume of Scotch plaid or any of the clan-colors preferred. Skirt kilted, waist plain; scarf of the goods draped as shown. Cap of one of the plaid-colors. It may be composed of woven fabric, or closely crocheted, as preferred. Stockings of red, yellow, green or blue, and low red shoes. Gaiter-tops may be worn, if desired.

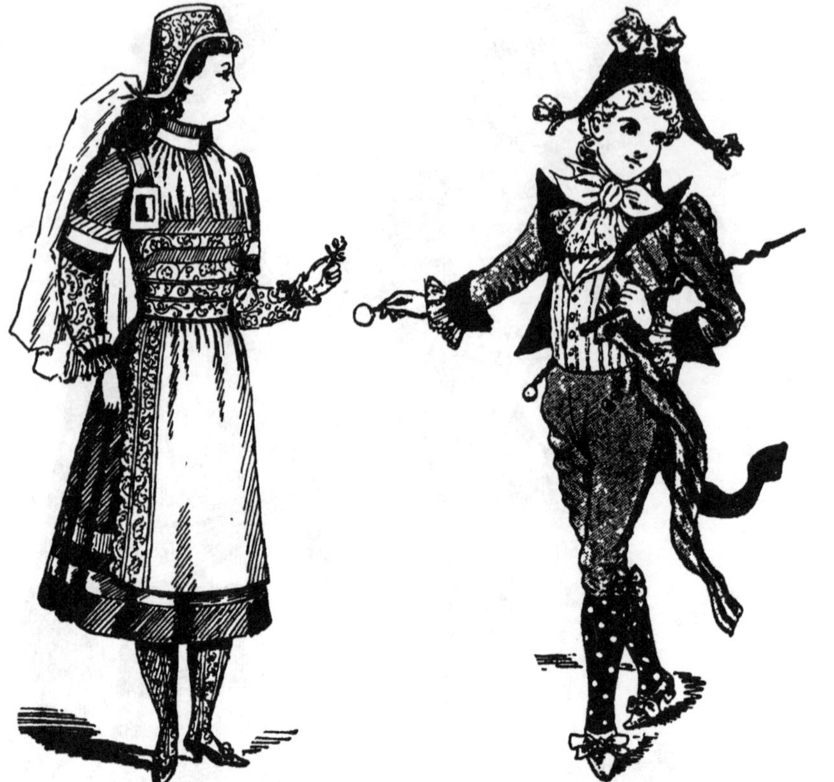

FIGURE No. 113.—BRITTANY BRIDE.

FIGURE No. 114.—ADMIRAL.

FIGURE No. 113.—BRITTANY BRIDE.—Red dress trimmed with bands of blue and yellow. Chemisette of plain white muslin; bodice and under-sleeves of embroidered muslin trimmed with blue bands; white apron trimmed with embroidery. Yellow and blue neck-bands; yellow shoulder straps with yellow buckles. White embroidered cap; plain white veil. Fancy white stockings and shoes.

FIGURE No. 114.—ADMIRAL.—Red-and-blue striped coat faced with black; blue-and-white striped vest, red breeches. Black hat trimmed with white ribbon; black stockings spotted with white and red; white shoes. Lace cravat and ruffles.

FIGURE No. 115.—BIRD COSTUME.—Blue-and-white real or paper feathers sewed upon a plain princess dress; bird in hair; stockings to match blue feathers; brown slippers, yellow gloves.

FIGURE No. 116.—WATTEAU COSTUME.—Skirt of pale-pink mull. Bodice, cloak and drapery of deep-green trimmed with pink roses and narrow pink ribbon; yellow straw hat trimmed with pink and green. Green or pink stockings with pink slippers.

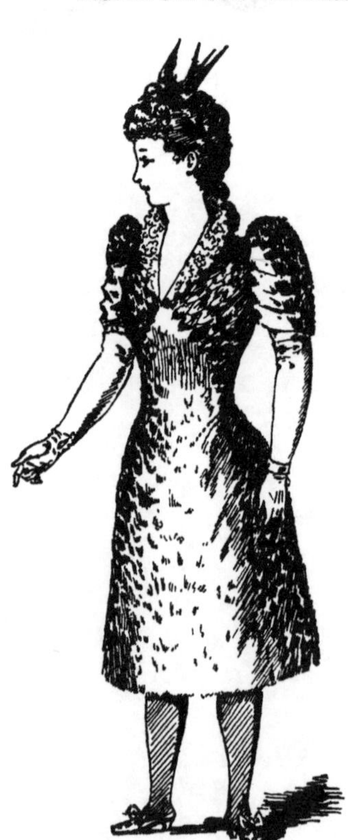

FIGURE No. 115.—BIRD COSTUME.

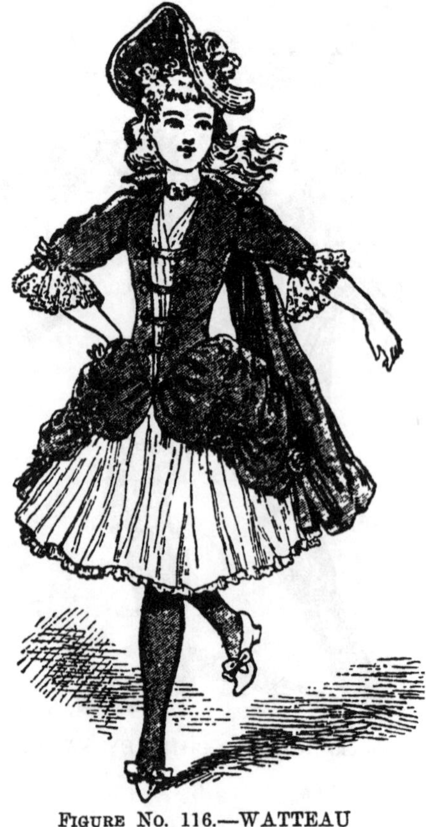

FIGURE No. 116.—WATTEAU COSTUME.

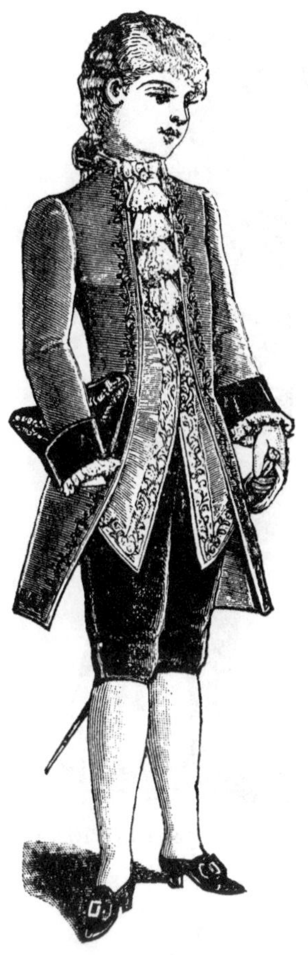

Figure No. 117.—GENTLEMAN OF OLDEN DAYS.

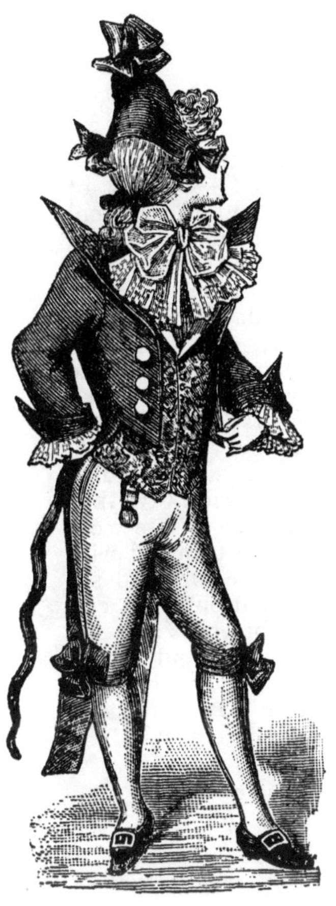

Figure No. 118.—INCROYABLE.

Figure No. 119—Fashion.—Costume of pink and blue satin—pink for the vest and petticoat and tight sleeves, and blue for the dress and flowing sleeves. White hat trimmed with blue and pink. Standing lace ruff about the neck. Hand-glass suspended from the waist by a strap; mandolin in one hand and a bouquet of flowers in the other.

Figure No. 120.—The Swell.—White dress coat and vest and white tie; black knee-breeches, silk stockings and patent-leather shoes. Black opera hat. The hair should be combed in a smooth bang over the forehead.

Figure No. 117.—Gentleman of Olden Days.—Coat of dark-gray satin trimmed with silver braid and red velvet cuffs. Vest of a lighter gray, also silver trimmed. Lace cravat and ruffles. Red velvet breeches, white silk stockings, red shoes and red velvet three-cornered hat.

Figure No. 118.—Incroyable.—Dark-green satin coat; gold-and-green brocaded vest; white satin breeches and silk stockings, patent-leather shoes and silver buckles. Lace cravat and ruffles; dark-green hat; white queue-wig.

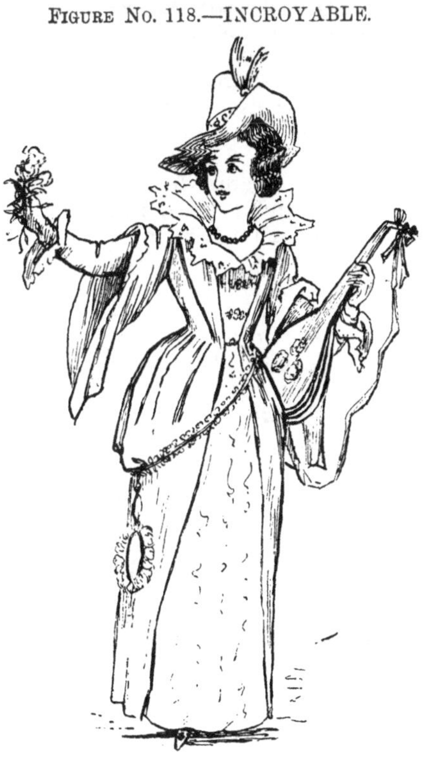

Figure No. 119.—FASHION.

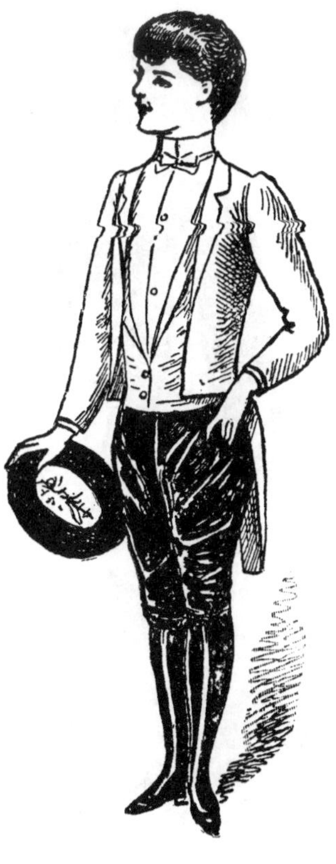

Figure No. 120.—THE SWELL.

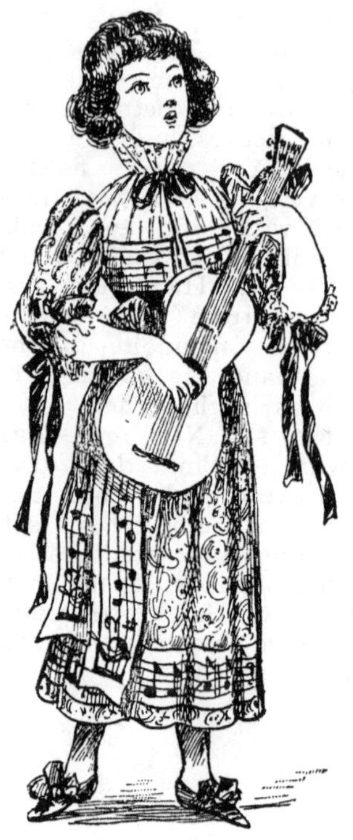

FIGURE No. 121.—MUSIC.

FIGURE NO. 121.—MUSIC.—Dress of black-and-white wool goods trimmed with white bands on which lines of music are printed. White chemisette, black velvet ribbon bows, white stockings and black slippers complete the costume.

FIGURE NO. 122.—REVOLUTIONARY GENTLEMAN.—White coat and vest trimmed with pale-blue cord and silver buttons. Dark knee-breeches and silk stockings, and shoes with silver buckles. White hat, white wig and lace cravat.

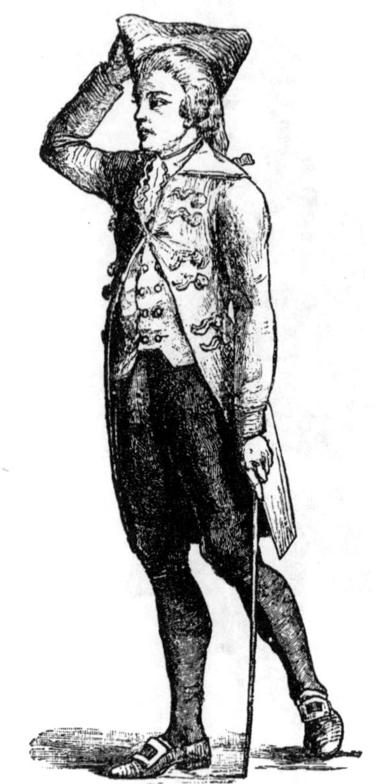

FIGURE No. 122.—REVOLUTIONARY GENTLEMAN.

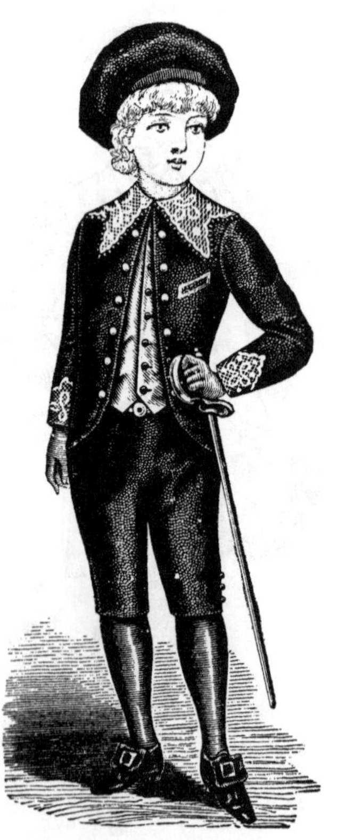

FIGURE No. 123.—COURT COSTUME.

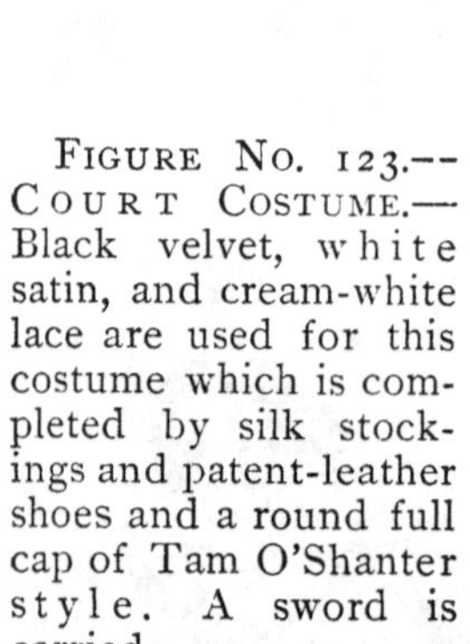

FIGURE NO. 123.—COURT COSTUME.—Black velvet, white satin, and cream-white lace are used for this costume which is completed by silk stockings and patent-leather shoes and a round full cap of Tam O'Shanter style. A sword is carried.

FIGURE NO. 124.—ASTROLOGER.—Gown and cap of black satin silk or cambric on which are pasted or sewed figures of animals, symbols, signs, etc., etc., which are cut from smooth white paper. Carries a telescope for studying the stars and wears large spectacles.

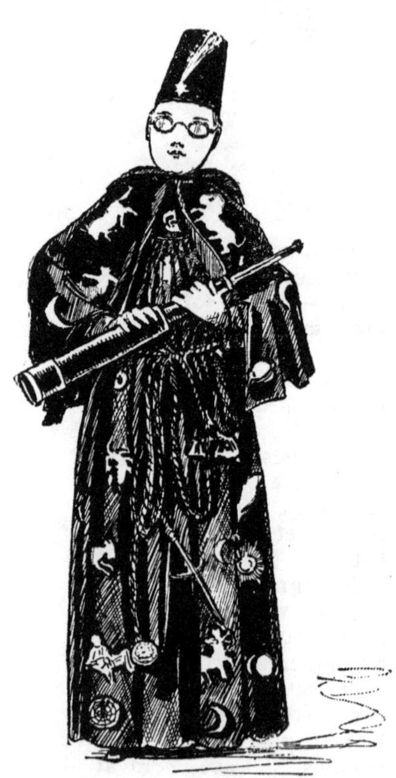

FIGURE No. 124.—ASTROLOGER.

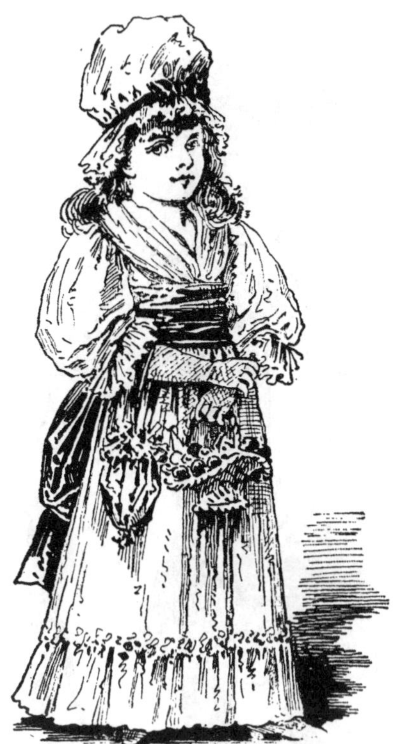
Figure No. 125.—CHERRY RIPE.

Figure No. 125.—Cherry Ripe.—Gown and cap of white made as represented. Cherry-red sash, bag, mitts and ribbons. Carries a basket filled with large red cherries.

Figure No. 126.—Cavalier.— Red velvet doublet and trunks; silver-gray cloak and hose. Red hat with silver colored plumes; and red shoes with silver buckles.

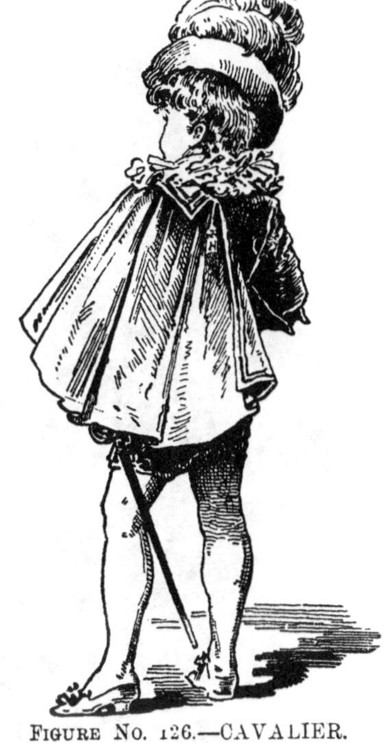
Figure No. 126.—CAVALIER.

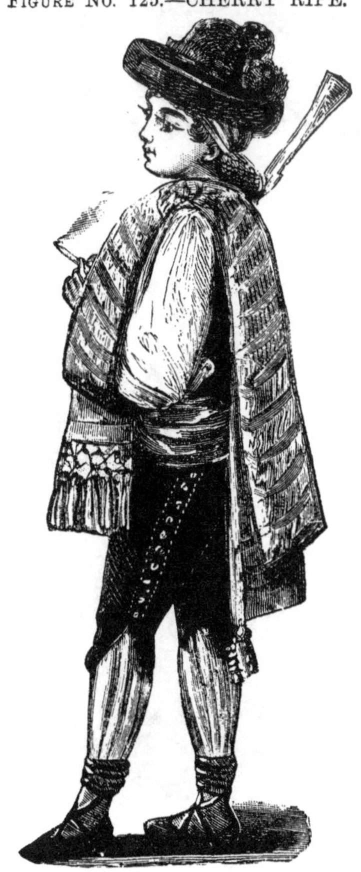
Figure No. 127.—MEXICAN BOY.

Figure No. 127.—Mexican Boy.—White shirt, red velveteen jacket and trousers trimmed with gilt braid and buttons; yellow sash around the waist. Roman - striped scarf thrown over the shoulders. Brown hat with red pompons; fancy-striped stockings, brown shoes. Hair in net. Carries a shepherd's horn, knives and pistols.

Figure No. 128.—Rosalind.—Chemisette or blouse of white; full sleeves banded with green velvet. Dress of green velvet; cloak of same lined with golden-brown. Golden-brown stockings banded and trimmed with white ribbon and fur; green slippers. Velvet hat with gray plume. Leather belt with silver buckle. Silver spear.

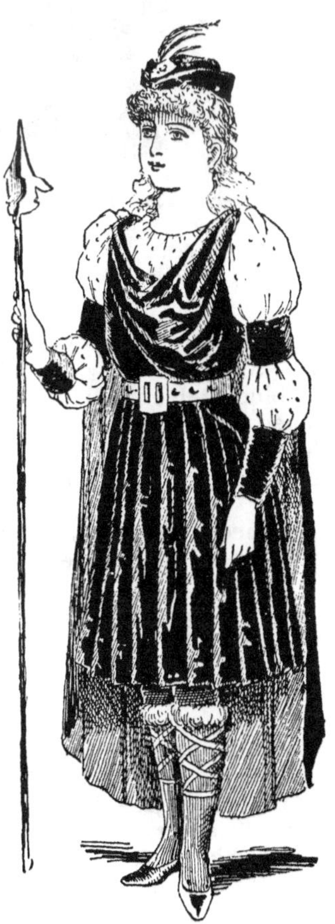
Figure No. 128.—ROSALIND.

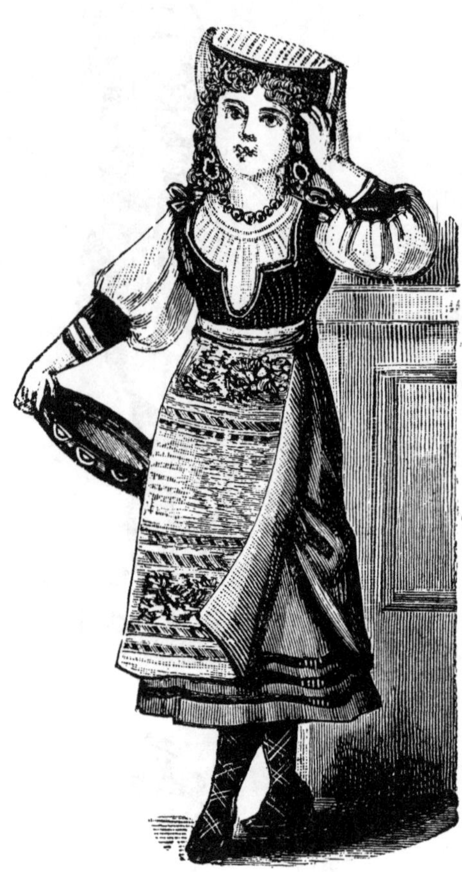

FIGURE No. 129.—ITALIAN PEASANT.

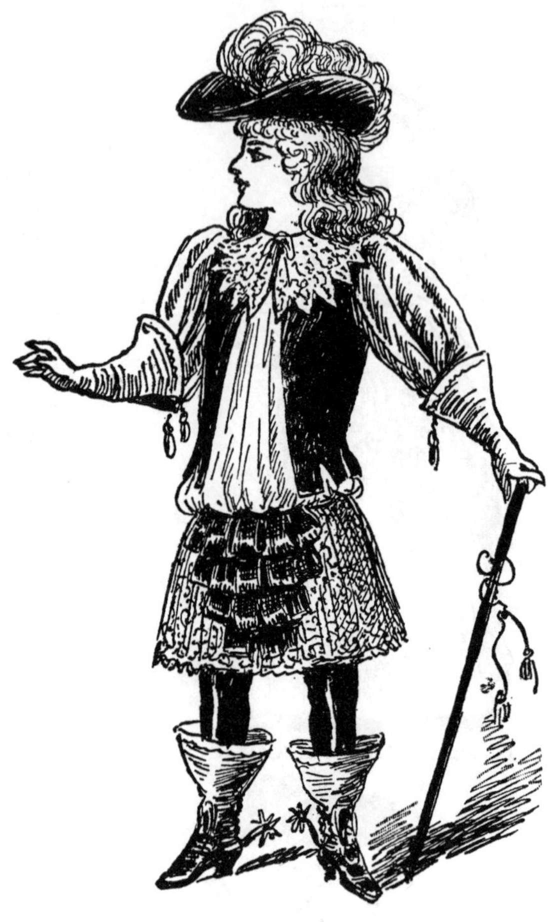

FIGURE No. 130.—KING CHARLES CAVALIER.

FIGURE No. 129.—ITALIAN PEASANT.—Skirt of brown wool trimmed with blue velvet. Blue velvet bodice trimmed with silver. White chemisette with sleeves finished with blue velvet and silver braid. Apron and head-dress of fancy-striped goods. Gold ear and neck ornaments. Fancy stockings, leather shoes. Real or imitation tambourine.

FIGURE No. 130.—KING CHARLES CAVALIER.—Red velvet sleeveless jacket, cream-white shirt with full sleeves; lace skirt and collar. Red hat with cream-white plumes. Red stockings; cream-white gauntlet gloves; and patent-leather boots with cream-white tops.

FIGURE No. 131.—JACK, THE SAILOR.—Blouse, trousers and cap of blue flannel, with blue silk tie. "America" in silver letters on the cap-band. Trousers may be of white duck; or, the whole suit may be of white flannel.

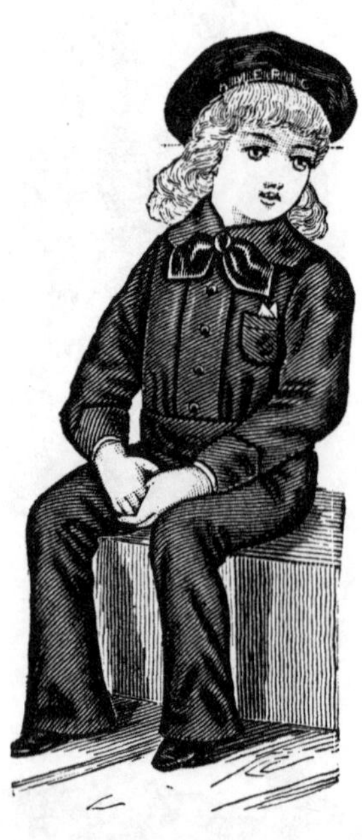

FIGURE No. 131.—JACK THE SAILOR.

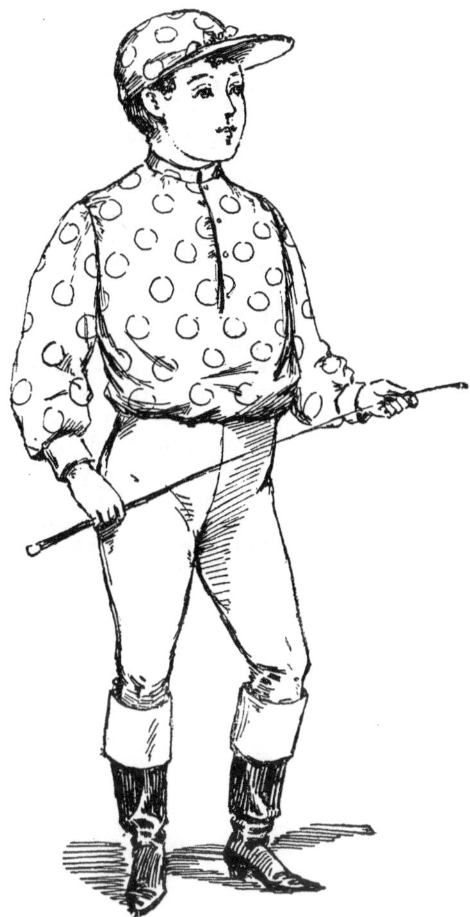

FIGURE No. 132.--JOCKEY.

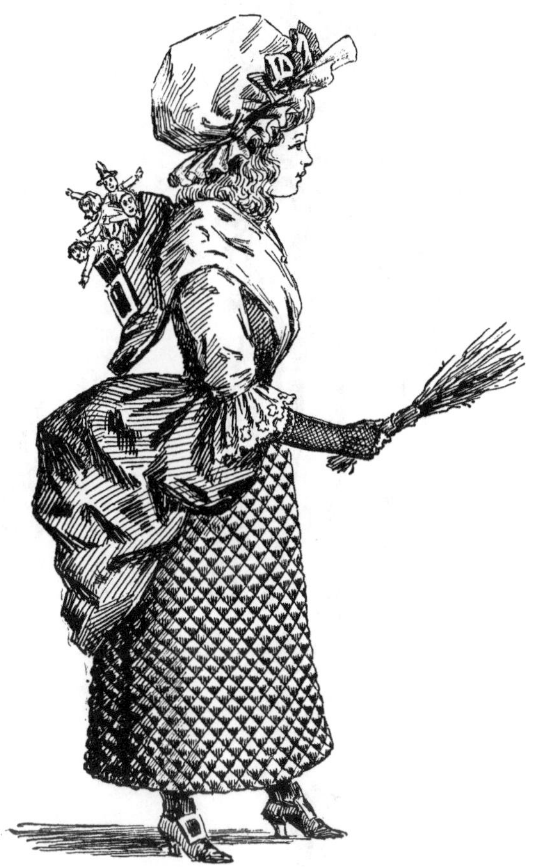

FIGURE No. 133.—THE OLD WOMAN WHO LIVED IN A SHOE.

FIGURE No. 132. — JOCKEY.— Blouse may be of any fancy colors preferred. Cap with white peak, to match. White breeches; black boots with white tops.

FIGURE No. 133.—THE OLD WOMAN WHO LIVED IN A SHOE.—Skirt of blue or brown quilted stuff. Overdress of blue or red wool goods. White cap, fichu and elbow-flounces. Black mitts, stockings and shoes. Large shoe filled with dolls fastened on her back. Bunch of switches in her hand.

FIGURE No. 134. — SAILOR LAD. — Suit of blue, gray or white flannel, decorated with silver or gilt ornaments. Silk tie; lettered cap-band. Silver whistle suspended from neck.

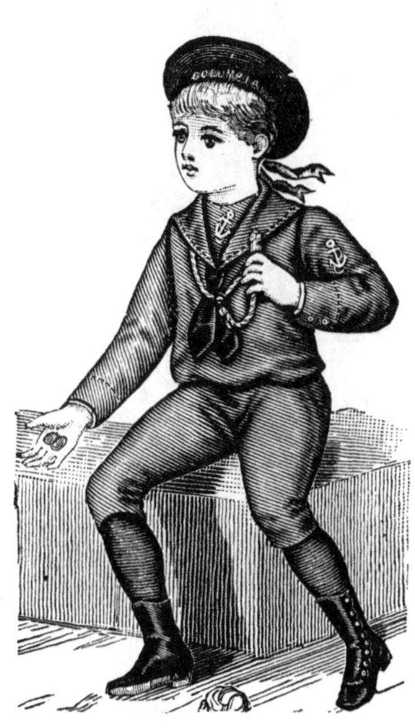

FIGURE No. 134.—SAILOR LAD.

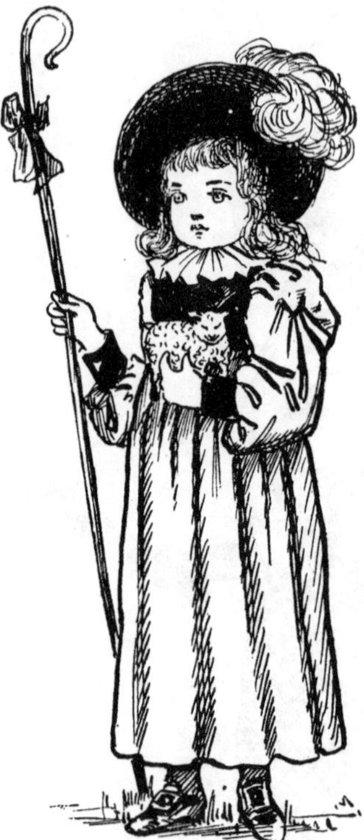

FIGURE No. 135.—LITTLE SHEPHERDESS.

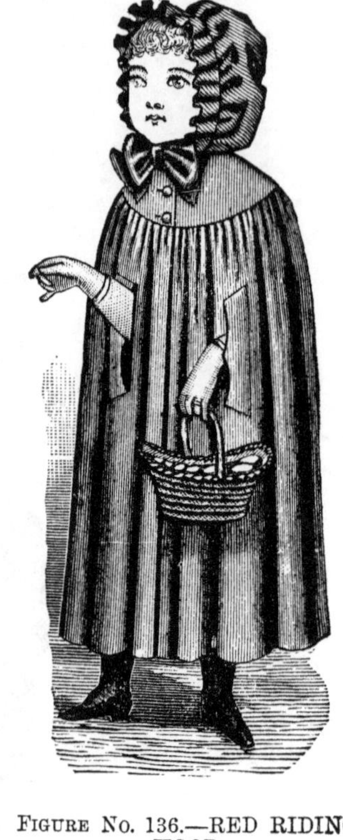

FIGURE No. 136.—RED RIDING HOOD.

FIGURE No. 135.—LITTLE SHEPHERDESS.—This costume is made of fawn-colored cashmere and brown velvet. The full skirt hangs gracefully from the short body. The sleeves are puffed and a small frill is about the neck. A large, black felt hat trimmed with a fawn-colored ostrich feather is worn.

FIGURE No. 136.—RED RIDING HOOD.—Under this cloak may be worn any fancy or evening dress desired; but the costume is a great favorite as represented. Scarlet flannel or cloth is used for the cloak. The basket may contain bread or cake covered with a napkin.

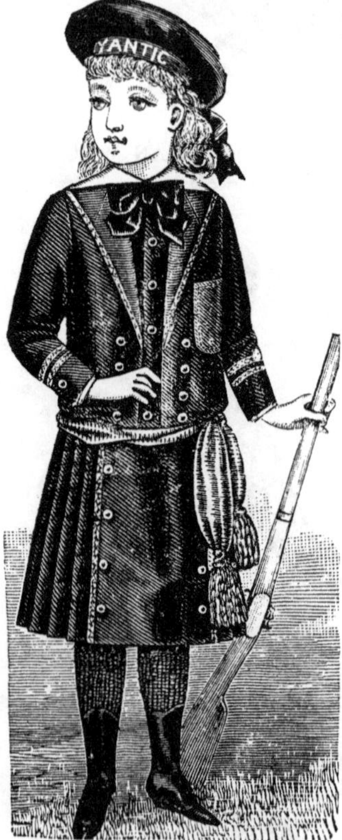

FIGURE No. 137.—THE LITTLE HUNTSMAN.

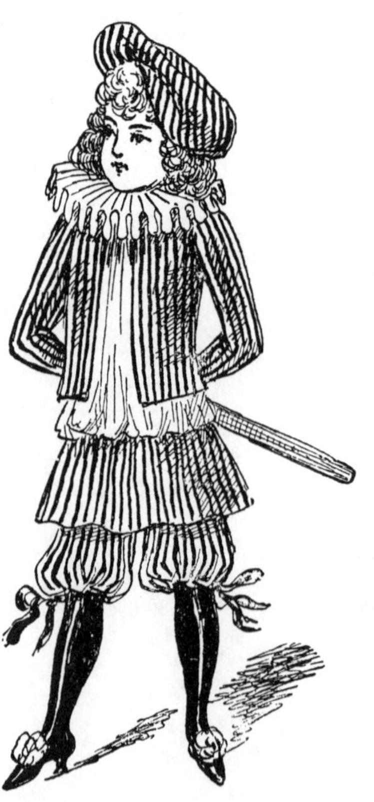

FIGURE No. 138.—FANCY DRESS COSTUME.

FIGURE No 137.—THE LITTLE HUNTSMAN.—Costume of dark-green cloth trimmed with gilt braid and buttons. A green silk sash tipped with tassels is about the waist, and a Tam O'Shanter cap is on his head. A gun or bow and arrows should be carried.

FIGURE No. 138.—FANCY-DRESS COSTUME.—Scarlet and white fabric and white mull are used for this costume, which is finished with a stiff muslin ruff, and scarlet stockings and shoes. Carries a short sword or a small club.

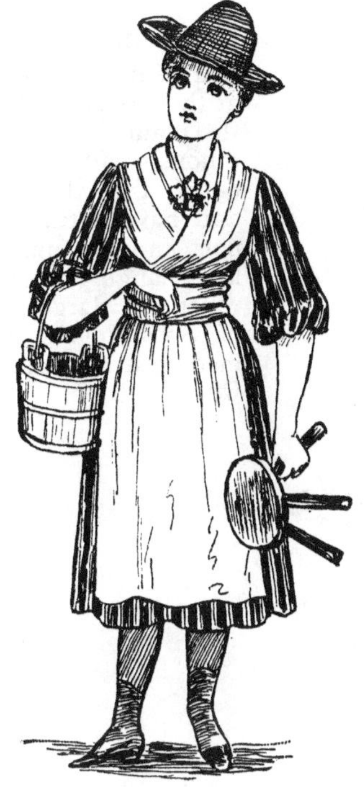

FIGURE No. 139.—MILKMAID.

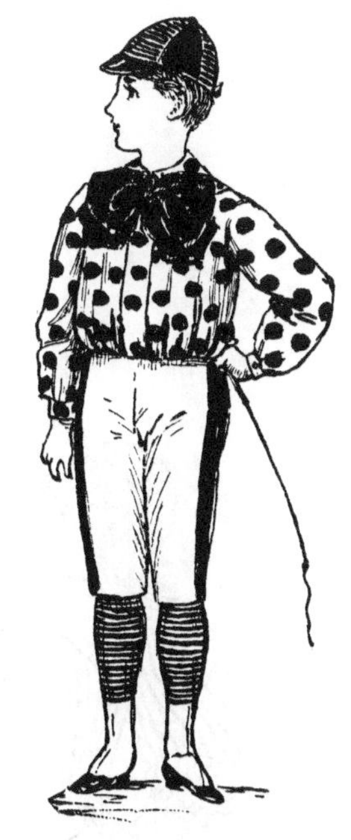

FIGURE No. 140.—JOCKEY.

FIGURE No. 139.—MILKMAID.—The material here used is blue-and-white striped calico. A fichu of white mull with its ends tucked under the top of a plain mull apron is worn; a bunch of flowers is at the throat. In the left hand is carried a wooden milking-stool, and a wooden milk-pail is hung over the right arm. An untrimmed straw hat with a rolling brim and a sugar-loaf crown is worn.

FIGURE No. 140.—JOCKEY.—Short trousers of white flannel trimmed with red. White blouse polka-dotted with blue; red windsor scarf. Cap of orange and orange-and-white striped flannel. Fancy stockings, white gaiters, black shoes.

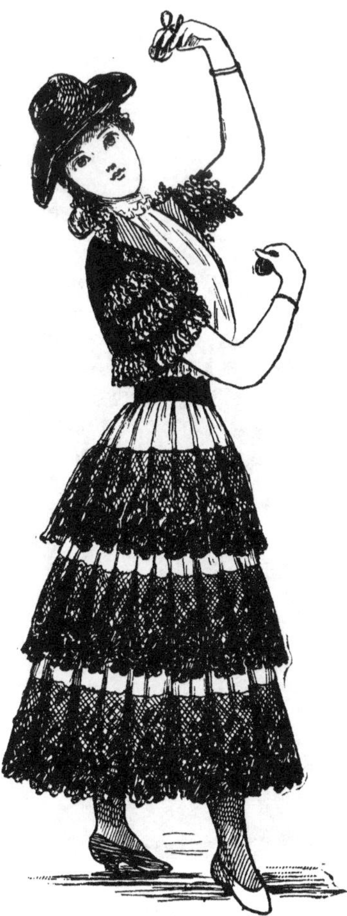

FIGURE No. 141.—SPANISH DANCER.

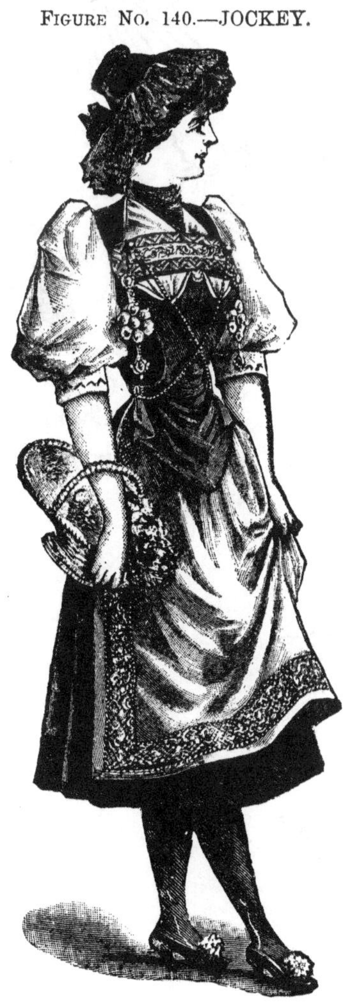

FIGURE No. 142.—SWISS PEASANT.

FIGURE No. 141.—SPANISH DANCER.—Yellow skirt, black lace flounces. Yellow blouse, black velvet Spanish girdle ; velvet jacket faced with yellow and trimmed with lace. Black hat and hose, yellow slippers. Gold ornaments; castanets.

FIGURE No. 142.—SWISS PEASANT.—The short skirt of this pretty costume is made of blue merino. The jacket is of black velveteen, with full vest of white veiling, and trimming of blue merino cut in three points at the top and buttoned on to the bodice with silver buttons. Band of embroidery, with silver chains and ornaments. Sleeves of veiling. Apron of linen, finished with a band of insertion. Cap of velveteen, edged with lace.

folded about the neck and Vandyke lace is at the wrists. The little maiden may wear a housemaid's cap and carry a small broom, and have a tiny dust-pan and a bunch of keys hanging from her waist. A large apron of Swiss muslin trimmed with lace may be worn.

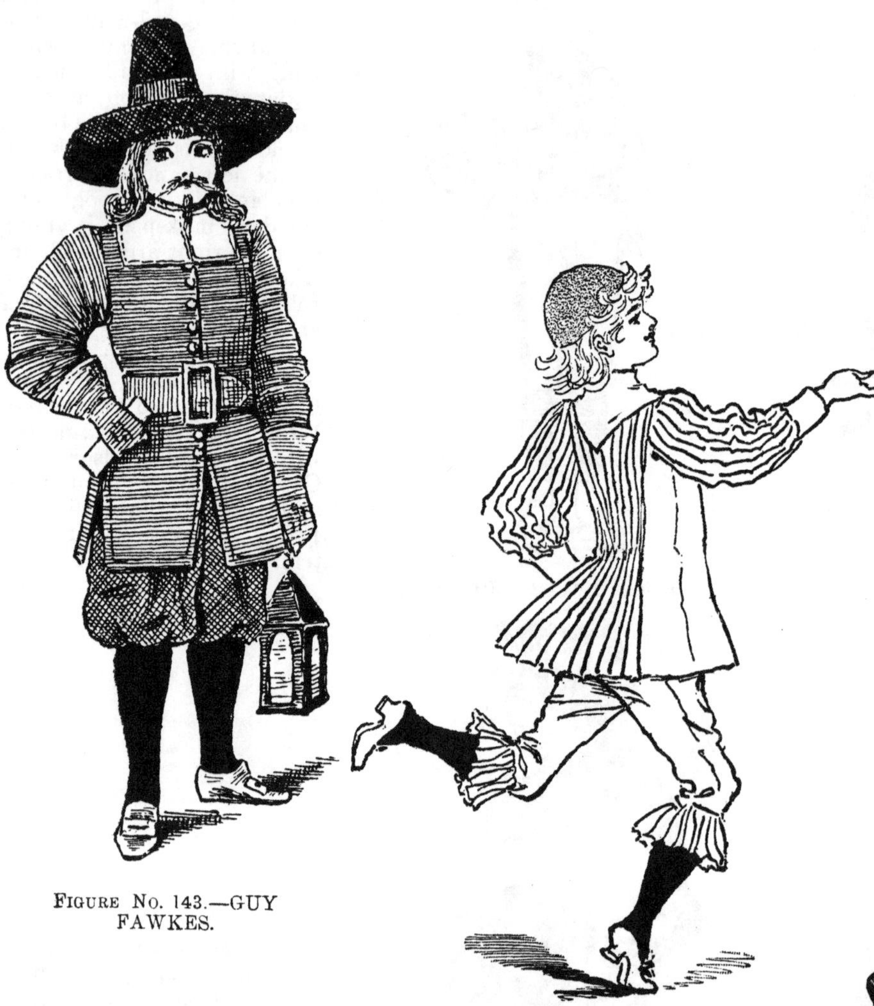

FIGURE No. 143.—GUY FAWKES.

FIGURE No. 144.—TOM, THE PIPER'S SON.

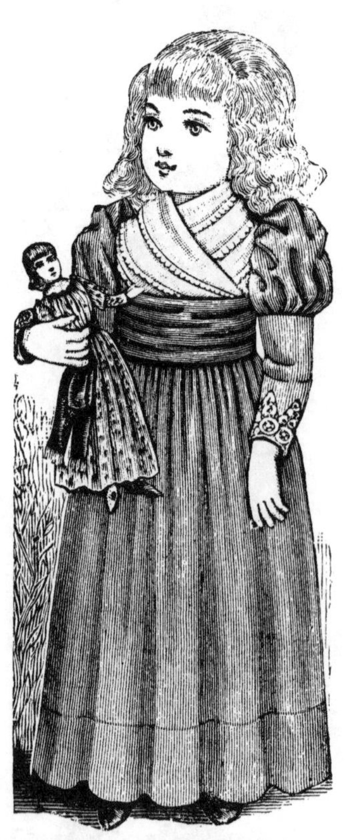

FIGURE No. 145.—THE LITTLE MATRON

FIGURE No. 143.—GUY FAWKES.—Doublet and trunks of brown stuff, with horn buttons. Leather belt with horn buckle. Red hat with leather band, red hose and brown shoes. White stiff collar and gauntlet gloves. Carries a scroll of paper and a lantern.

FIGURE No. 144.—TOM, THE PIPER'S SON.—Costume of pink or blue satin, with red or black stockings and blue or pink shoes and cap. He may carry a toy pig under his arm.

FIGURE No. 145.—THE LITTLE MATRON.—The dress is made of soft gray cashmere, and is finished with a deep hem. A white cambric kerchief is goods, with an embroidered decoration about the bottom; sash of striped silk carried about the waist in front, crossed at the back and carried forward again, its ends being knotted low at one side and trimmed with deep fringe. Wing sleeves of dotted muslin; metallic crescents. Turkish trousers of dotted muslin gathered to velvet bands studded with beads. White stockings; slippers embroidered and decorated with crescents. Bracelets of metal; necklace of beads; Turkish cap with tassel and crescent.

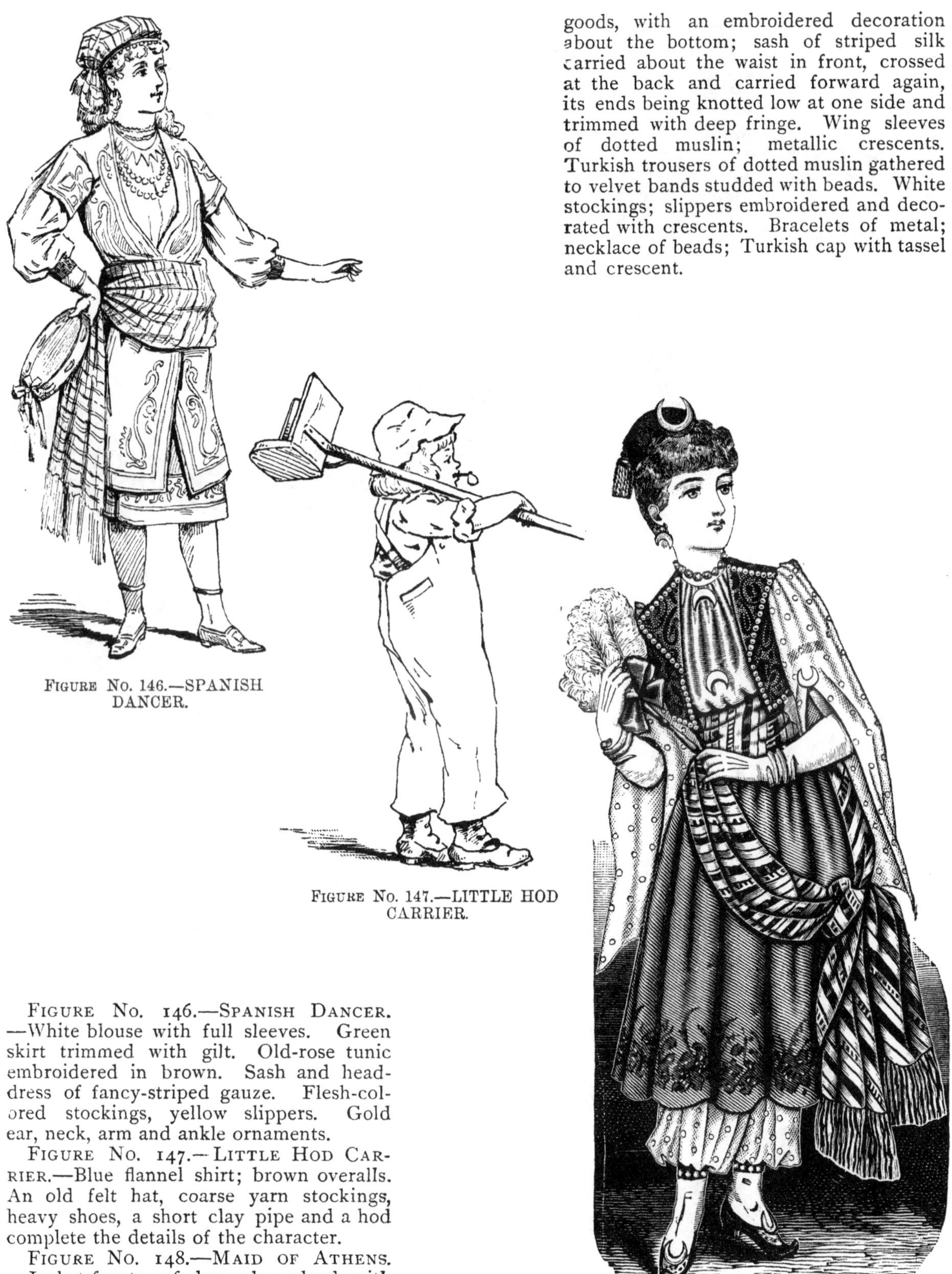

FIGURE NO. 146.—SPANISH DANCER.

FIGURE NO. 147.—LITTLE HOD CARRIER.

FIGURE NO. 148.—MAID OF ATHENS.

FIGURE NO. 146.—SPANISH DANCER.—White blouse with full sleeves. Green skirt trimmed with gilt. Old-rose tunic embroidered in brown. Sash and head-dress of fancy-striped gauze. Flesh-colored stockings, yellow slippers. Gold ear, neck, arm and ankle ornaments.

FIGURE NO. 147.—LITTLE HOD CARRIER.—Blue flannel shirt; brown overalls. An old felt hat, coarse yarn stockings, heavy shoes, a short clay pipe and a hod complete the details of the character.

FIGURE NO. 148.—MAID OF ATHENS.—Jacket fronts of brocade edged with beads; between them a puffed vest of soft muslin or silk. Skirt of silk or wool

NURSERY-RHYME COSTUMES

The Queen of Hearts,
She made some tarts,
All on a Summer's day;

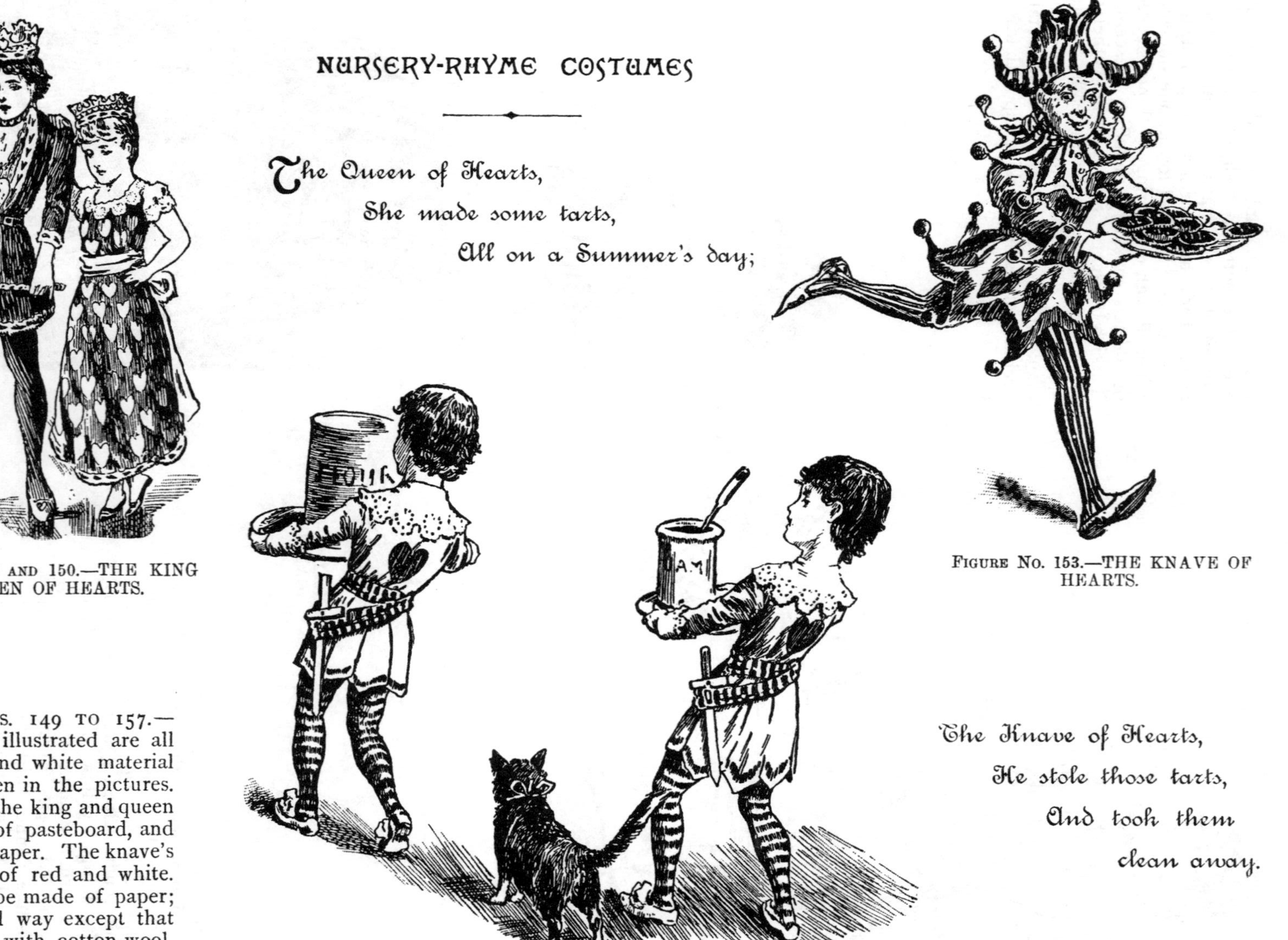

Figures Nos. 149 and 150.—THE KING AND QUEEN OF HEARTS.

Figures Nos. 151 and 152.—THE QUEEN OF HEARTS' SERVANTS.

Figure No. 153.—THE KNAVE OF HEARTS.

The Knave of Hearts,
He stole those tarts,
And took them
clean away.

Figures Nos. 149 to 157.—The costumes illustrated are all made of red and white material arranged as seen in the pictures. The crowns of the king and queen may be made of pasteboard, and silver and red paper. The knave's hat should be of red and white. The tarts may be made of paper; or in the usual way except that they are filled with cotton-wool.

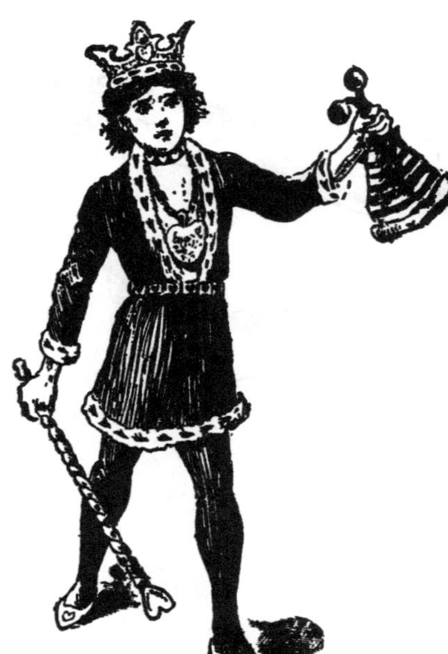

FIGURE No. 154.—THE KING OF HEARTS.

The Knave of Hearts
Brought back the tarts
And vowed he'd steal no more.

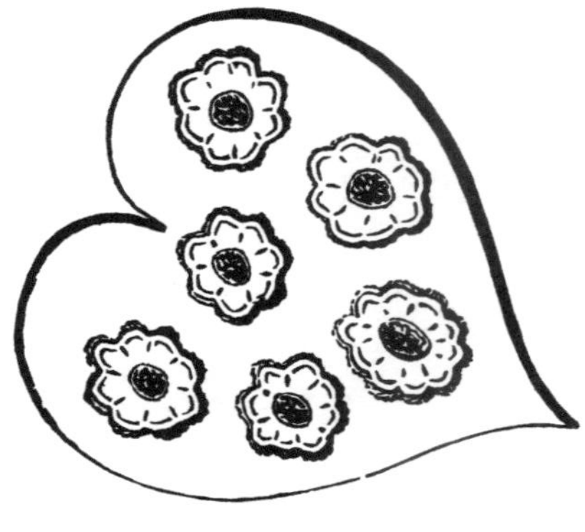

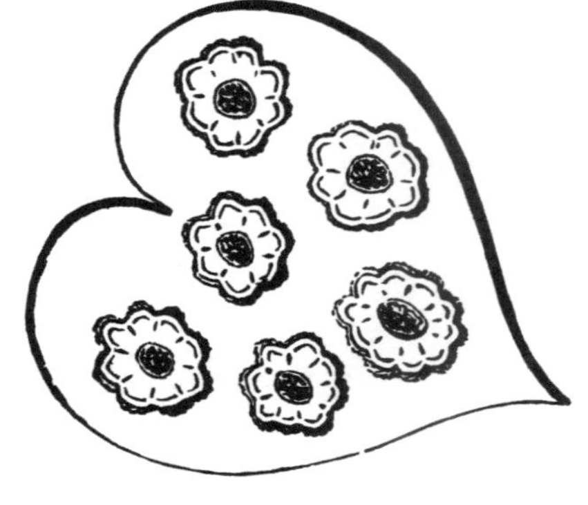

The King of Hearts
Called for the tarts
And beat the knave full sore.

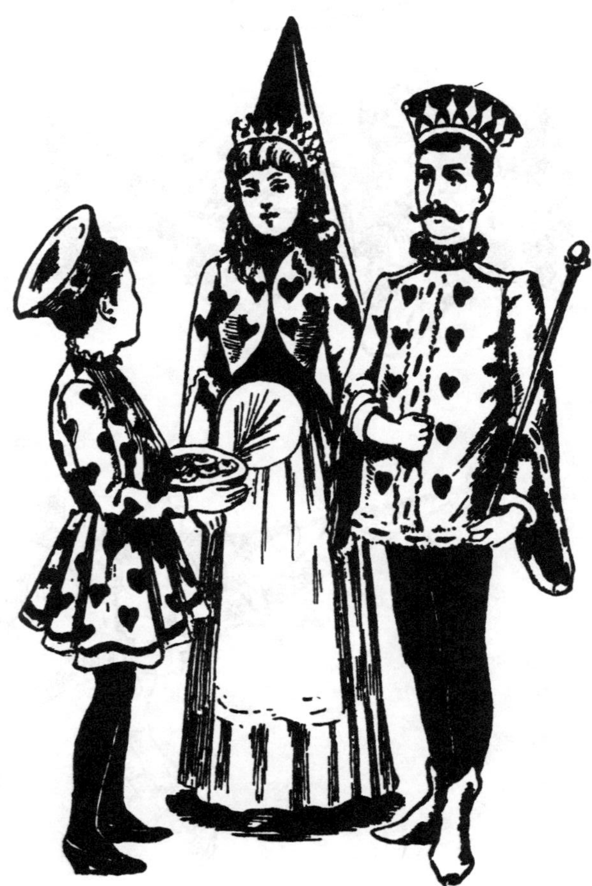

FIGURES NOS. 155, 156 AND 157.—THE KING AND QUEEN OF HEARTS AND THE PENITENT KNAVE.

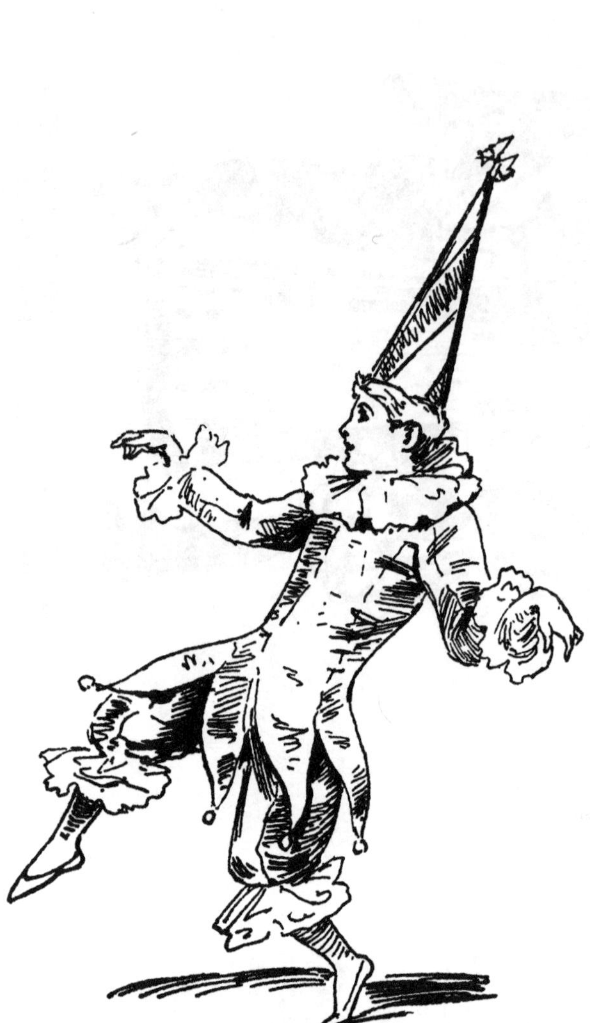

FIGURE No. 158.—JESTER.

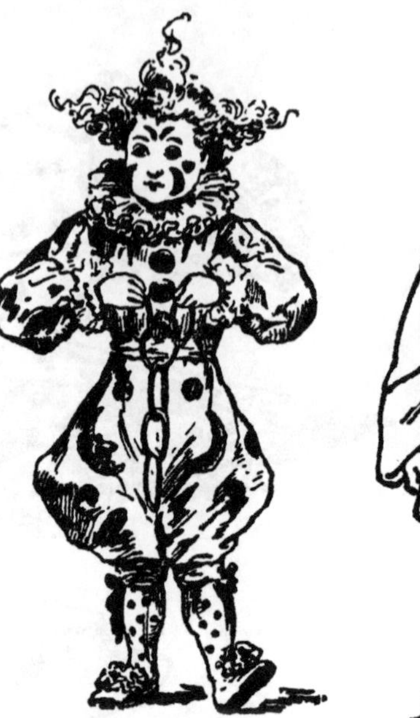

FIGURE No. 159.—
MECHANICAL TOY.

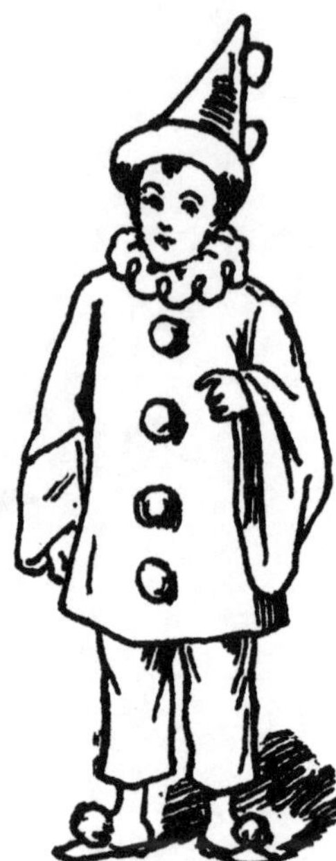

FIGURE No. 160.—
CLOWN.

FIGURES NOS. 158 TO 161.—GROUP OF FRENCH CLOWNS.—In making up these costumes great license in the matters of color and fabric is allowed. Two colors, blue and yellow, or red and yellow are usually chosen for the jester. White is most generally used for the remaining costumes on this page, with bright yellow, red or blue intermingled as decorations, etc., etc. The faces and hair should be whitened. When a wig is worn it is usually of a brick-red color.

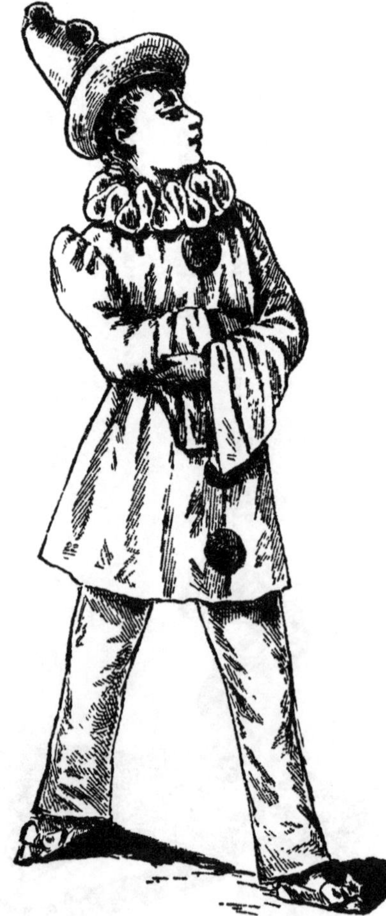

FIGURE No. 161.—PIERROT.

FIGURES NOS. 162 TO 165.—The Harlequin is dressed in black and white; the Clown in red and white; the Poodle Dog in black tights trimmed with astrakhan to represent the coat of a French poodle shaved as fashion dictates; while Punchinello is costumed in white with a red pompon, and lace-frill decorations; red and white stockings, and white shoes with white rosettes.

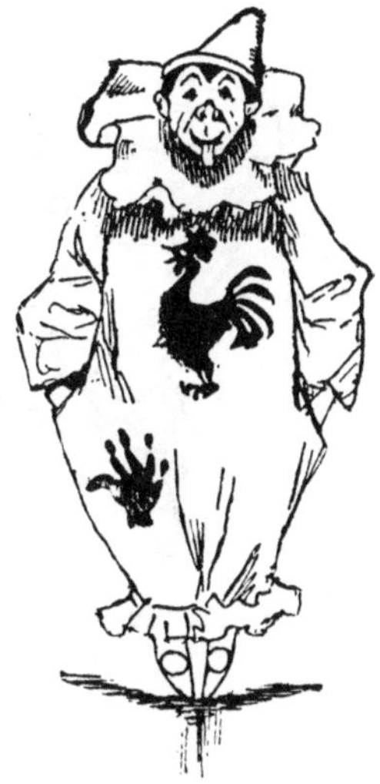

FIGURE NO. 162.—CLOWN.

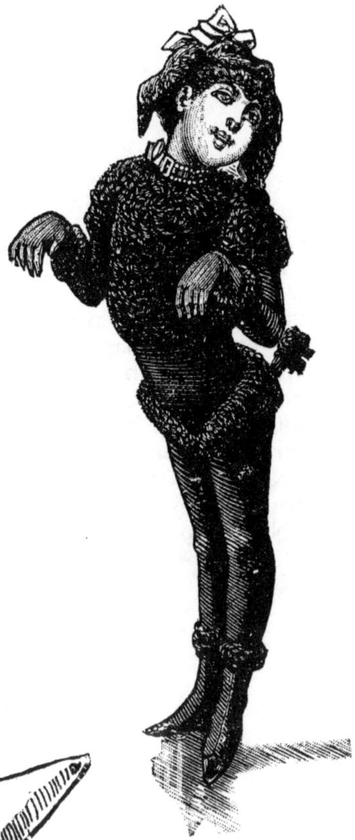

FIGURE NO. 163.—POODLE DOG.

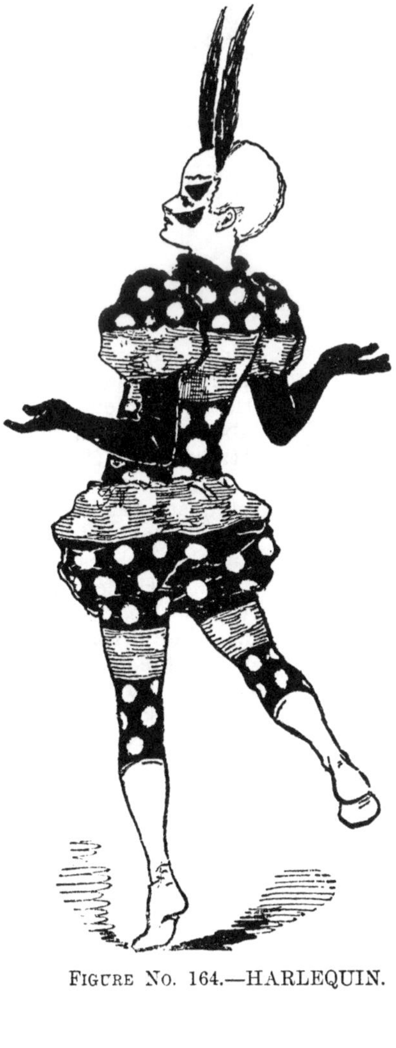

FIGURE NO. 164.—HARLEQUIN.

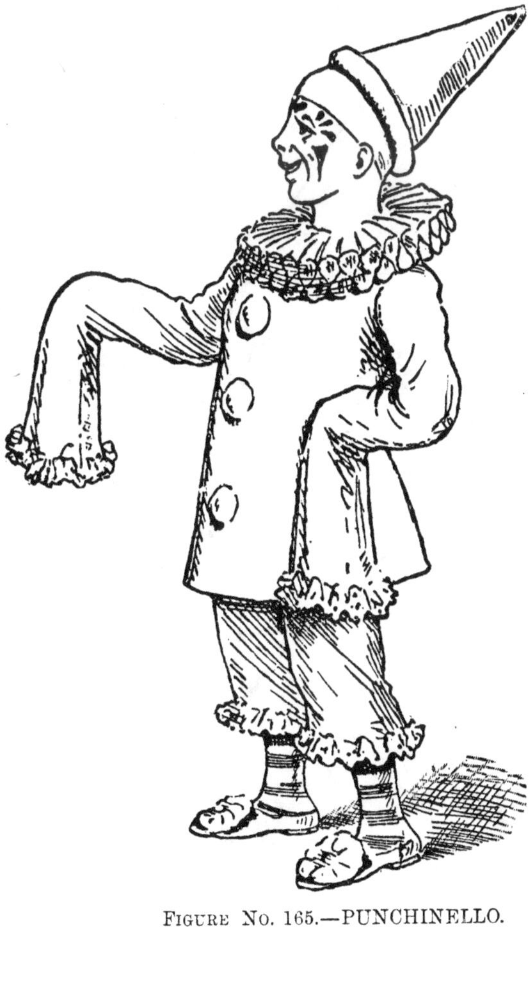

FIGURE NO. 165.—PUNCHINELLO.

FIGURES NOS. 166 TO 169.—GROUP OF CLOWNS AND HARLEQUINS.—The two clowns on this page are dressed as follows: Figure No. 166, white garment, hat and hair; blue pompons, and red and yellow stockings and white shoes. Figure No. 169, white jersey body and tights with yellow decorations; yellow ruche about the waist, ruffles at the knees and pompons on the shoes; blue face-patches; blue and yellow stockings and blue shoes.

The Harlequin at Figure No. 168 is all in white with a black visor; the one at figure No. 167 in yellow and black plaid; black hat and visor. Carries a magic wand.

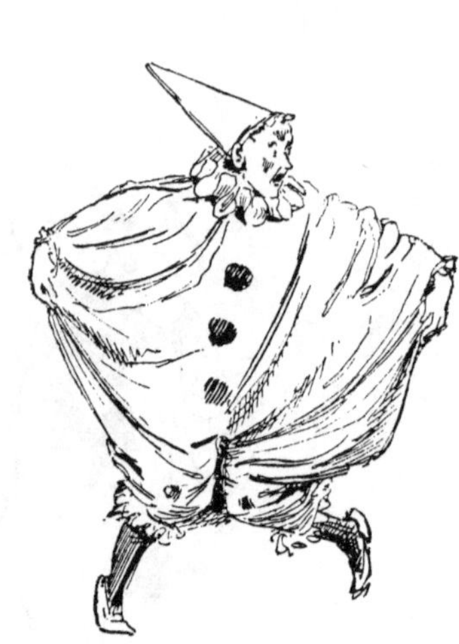

FIGURE NO. 166.—CLOWN.

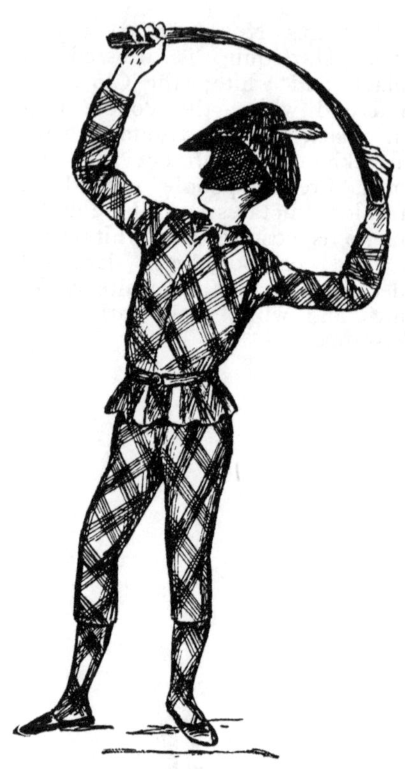

FIGURE NO. 167.—HARLEQUIN.

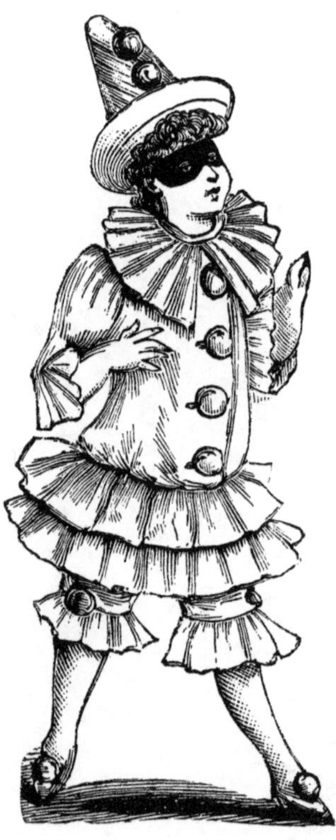

FIGURE NO. 168.—HARLEQUIN.

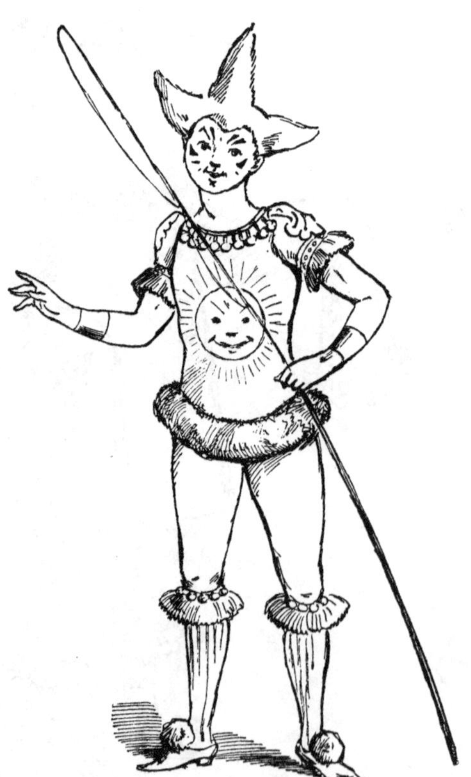

FIGURE NO. 169.—CLOWN.

FIGURES NOS. 170 TO 174.—GROUP OF CLOWNS, DEMON, FOOL AND IMP.—The two clowns are dressed in white with red or blue intermingled in the fabric or decorations as seen in the pictures of the costumes. The Demon may be dressed in red or black, with red or black wings. He may carry an imitation spear or fork, if desired.

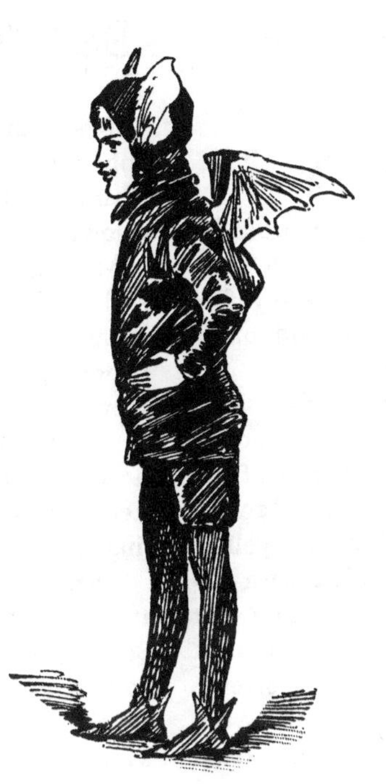

FIGURE NO. 170.—DEMON.

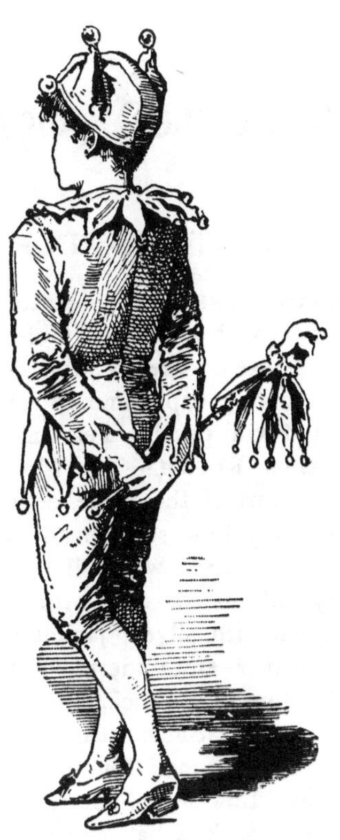

FIGURE NO. 171.—FOOL.

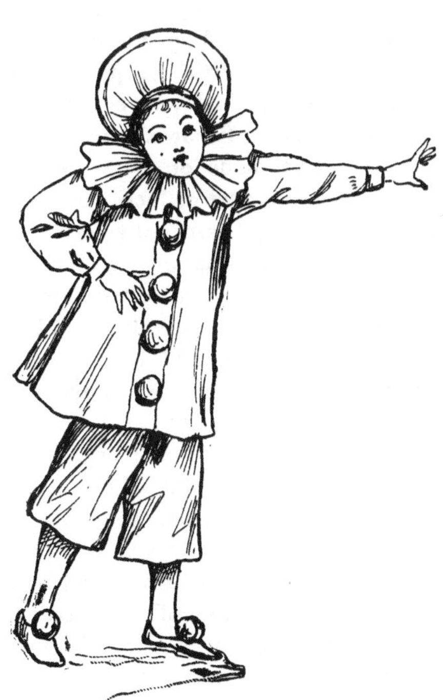

FIGURE NO. 172.—PANTOMIME CLOWN.

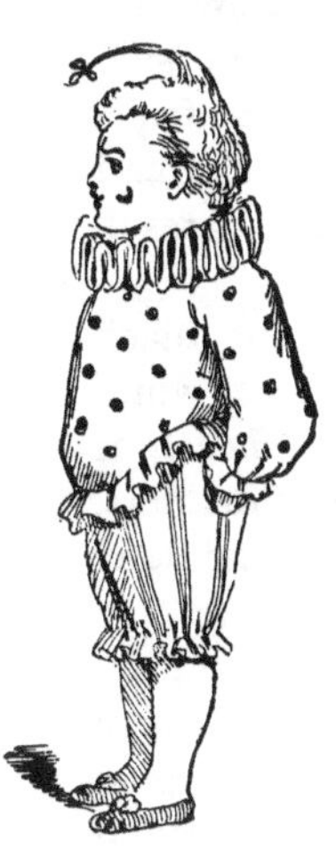

FIGURE NO. 173.—CLOWN.

The Fool may be dressed in blue and yellow, yellow and black, or red with yellow or black. Tiny bells are on his costume.

The Imp may be dressed in brilliant green, red, brown, yellow or bronze, and have wings of silver or gilt gauze.

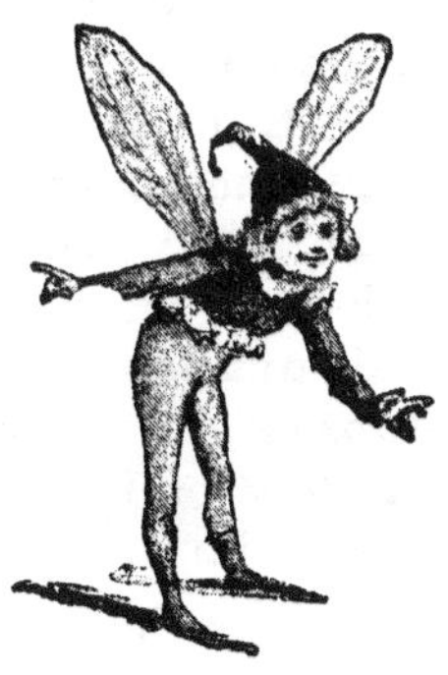

FIGURE NO. 174.—IMP.

SUGGESTED COSTUMES FOR ADULTS AND YOUNG FOLK.

COSTUMES FOR LADIES.

Lady Jane Grey.—Petticoat of gold brocade, trimmed with a train of violet velvet. High body with sleeves puffed at the shoulder. Lace ruffle. Close fitting cap trimmed with a veil and ornamented with pearls. Pearl necklace.

Lalla Rookh.—Turkish trousers of blue satin. Short skirt of the same, edged round with a deep band of yellow satin headed by two bands of the same, trimmed with silver ornaments. Jacket-body full on the hips with a vest front of yellow trimmed with silver; jacket also braided with silver; silver embroidery in the corners and cut rather low at the neck, being filled in with a muslin chemisette. Short satin sleeves and Greek sleeves of muslin. Small blue cap trimmed round with muslin. Low shoes, pointed and turned up. Gold necklace with a half-moon pendant, earrings and bracelets.

Marie Antoinette. — Skirt of white silk, trimmed with a flounce. Loose train forming a point made in blue satin and edged round with deep lace or ruching. Pointed body cut low and square, with a pointed stomacher of white silk. Elbow sleeves, trimmed with deep lace frills. Powdered hair in curls, trimmed with a cap and feathers. Long gloves. Walking-stick parasol. Pearl ornaments.

Marie Stuart.—Plain trained skirt of black satin. Pointed body trimmed with a yoke of white silk quilted in sequins and beaded with pearls at the points. Coat-sleeve puffed at the shoulders. Lace ruffle and cuffs. Pointed lace cap and long veil. Rosary at the side.

Persian Lady.—Loose under dress of embroidered silk, made with tight sleeves and open V-shape at the throat. Sleeveless paletot of pink brocade, edged round with fur, and tied around the hips with an amber silk sash. Cloak of pink brocade trimmed also with fur. Muslin turban.

Madame de Pompadour.— Poudré costume of the time of Louis XV. Petticoat of white silk trimmed with two plaited flounces. Train skirt of blue satin, open in front to show the petticoat, and edged down each side with lace and bows of ribbon. Body cut high at the back and square in front, and trimmed with a stomacher of pink ribbon bows and edged with lace. Elbow-sleeves trimmed with lace. Powdered hair trimmed with a flower.

Alsacienne.—Kilted petticoat stitched with red. Red woolen short skirt, showing about two inches of the petticoat. Apron of black silk, edged with a ruching. High linen chemisette with full sleeves, over which is the dress-body, cut very low, square in the front, strapped across the shoulders, and laced. Large black ribbon bow in the hair. Black lace scarf worn round the throat. Gold hoop-ear-rings.

Anne Boleyn.—Petticoat of white silk, edged at the bottom with a deep band of gold braid. Body and train in ruby velvet, quite plain. The body is cut square, edged with a band of gold, and jeweled. Long sleeves, puffed and fastened round with bands of braid edged with gold. Gilt coronet jeweled with pearls, over a veil. Pearl necklace and ear-rings ; girdle composed of pearls and jewels.

Madame du Barry.—Poudré costume. Petticoat of pink silk trimmed with rows of pearls, hung in festoons suspended on roses. Low pointed body of white silk trimmed with a berthé of pearls and lace. Watteau train of blue striped silk, edged with lace and festooned with roses. Elbow sleeves which are joined to the train and made of the same material, trimmed with deep flounces of lace. Flowers on the shoulders. Powdered hair, entwined with pearls. Bracelets, and pendant at throat.

Basque Peasant Woman.—Short kilted skirt of red woolen material. Short jacket-body of velvet trimmed round with a band of gold braid. Vest of embroidered material cut V shape. Lace cap with a blue long hood. Short gaiters.

Bretonne.—Short kilted skirt of black cashmere. Body of black with plastron of blue, cut low at the neck, trimmed with buttons and laced across with gold braid. Close sleeves of blue, trimmed round the wrist with an embroidered bow. High chemisette with deep linen collar. Red silk handkerchief around the head, over which is worn a full linen cap with pointed ends turned up over the crown.

Charlotte Corday.—Petticoat in plain material. Dress made in stripes, open down the front of the skirt and turned back to show the petticoat. Pointed body low at the neck and turned back with coat revers. Muslin fichu and cap, the latter ornamented with a ribbon and a tri-color rosette. Black scarf thrown over the shoulders.

CHINESE MANDARIN'S WIFE.—Very full green silk underskirt just escaping the floor and trimmed with black rouleaux. Tunic of silk, striped in two shades of blue and embroidered in patterns picked out with green, scarlet and saffron. Overdress of deep blue silk braided with gold and trimmed on the breast in a square pattern. Deep collar of saffron silk braided in black. Very wide hanging sleeves of crimson silk. Head-dress of saffron silk embroidered in blue and green. Gold ear-rings.

CIRCASSIAN GIRL.—Loose robe of scarlet, square at the neck and fastened round the waist by a scarf. Long, loose sleeves. Paletot in amber cloth, trimmed round with fur. Fur caftan. Pointed shoes turned up at the toes.

COLOMBINE.—Short plain skirt in rainbow-striped silk. Pointed body cut square at the neck, and made of blue silk with amber sleeves; pointed plastron of rainbow silk edged at each side with a plaiting. Frill around the neck. White felt hat trimmed with blue. Deep lace round the sleeves.

DOLLY VARDEN.—Short skirt of white quilted silk. Tunic of green cretonne flowered with red and turned back from the front, lined with pink and edged with a ruching. Plain body, cut in V shape at the throat. Short full sleeves turned up with white. Straw hat. Low buckle-shoes. Gold chain about throat.

DAUGHTER OF THE REGIMENT. — Moderately short skirt of dark green wool or silk, trimmed with three bands of wide, gold braid. High body with a plastron of white, braided across with gold braid; sleeves also trimmed some distance up with gold braid. Large white apron with pockets. Low cap with a French peak, trimmed with a band of gold braid. A small barrel is slung at the side by a leather belt. Hessian boots with a gold tassel. Gold ear-rings.

QUEEN ELIZABETH.—A full-trained skirt of gold-and-black brocaded velvet or velveteen, a bodice of plain black velvet and a large Medici collar of black velvet overlaid with white lace. The corners of the collar should be rounded, and a crown should be worn.

CAPTAIN.—Scarlet box-plaited skirt, and black basque with scarlet vest; skirt and basque trimmed with gold or silver braid. Scarlet-and-black cap, pouch, sword and black boots.

COLLEEN BAWN.—Black Irish peasant wrap lined with red. Under the cloak may be worn an evening gown or an Irish-peasant costume.

THE WILD WEST.—A brown blouse and skirt; collar and sleeves of red, and a broad band of red surrounds the skirt at the foot. The skirt may be short and chamois or brown leggings or over-gäiters worn. A heavy stick or a light gun is carried, and a large brown or red soft felt hat is worn.

PAULINE (LADY OF LYONS).—White, cream or rose-colored dècolleté gown. A sash, which may be tied at the front, side or back, as preferred, may be of ribbon or silk. Slippers and stockings the color of the gown.

AURORA.—Rose-colored low-necked gown in soft goods. A large scarf of pale-blue or pink tulle or some gauzy fabric is draped about the head, face and arms, and a sun's-rays crown is worn.

PROSERPINE.—Scarlet robe with wing sleeves lined with black, and a full, wide ruff of scarlet lined with black high about the neck. A large poppy for a head-dress, and poppies on the toes of the black slippers; red stockings.

VENUS.—Skirt of some white goods, and low-necked waist to match. The skirt is trimmed at the foot with a broad band of azure-blue showered with stars cut from silver paper, and all over it are strewn hearts, cupids, bows and arrows and doves. The cupids, etc., may be cut from cretonne or may be in decalcomania; or scrap pictures may be pasted on. A gauzy veil sprinkled with diamond dust is thrown about the head, face and shoulders, and a metal star is fastened in the hair in front.

LUNA.—Azure-blue skirt and a bodice to match. Moons, crescents, half moons and, indeed, all phases of the moon are cut in silver paper and pasted all over the bodice and skirt. A large crescent is also fastened in the hair, which is powdered with diamond dust; and from the back of the head a veil of tulle sprinkled with diamond dust hangs to the foot of the skirt and is caught up on one hip.

FRENCH WAITING-MAID.—A petticoat of plain bright satin; and a polonaise of brocaded goods opening on the front of the petticoat, cut low in the neck, but slightly draped, and with elbow sleeves. Neck draped with folds of muslin, a torsade of muslin about the head, high-heeled shoes. The colors should be bright but becoming.

A TYROLESE PEASANT.—A woolen dress, with square, low velvet bodice having straps of velvet over the shoulders; a white guimpe with sleeves trimmed with hemmed ruffles; and a large fringe-edged kerchief arranged about the shoulders and crossed in front. A Tyrolean hat with one side turned up and trimmed with a long feather, and a flowered print apron.

THE GHOST OF A BELLE.—Any style of costume in white. Powdered hair, white slippers and stockings. The face should also be powdered to look very white, or a white mask may be worn.

RAINBOW.—A gown with the skirt made of stripes in the seven colors of the rainbow. These stripes may be joined to run up and down the skirt or around it, as preferred.

The waist may be of the most becoming color, or of stripes running into the corresponding stripes of the skirt. A sun's-rays crown should be worn and a very thin gauzy veil of a silvery shade falling from the head to represent rain.

Another rainbow costume is made as follows: Sky-blue waist and skirt with drapings of tulle in the seven colors of the rainbow; viz., violet, indigo, blue, green, yellow, orange and red.

QUAKERESS.—A long, full skirt, a full, round waist with full sleeves, and a small sun-bonnet, all of soft gray goods. White mull kerchief about the neck, and white cuffs.

Costumes for Gentlemen.

RICHELIEU.—A robe of cardinal-red goods made in domino style and trimmed with ermine, and worn over a lace gown. A red mitre is worn, and a scepter is carried.

PIED PIPER OF HAMELIN.—Black spotted gown; short trousers, white stockings, low shoes and a red liberty cap with tassel. A horn, and some mice are carried.

KNIGHT TEMPLAR.—Black frock coat and trousers; scarf of white bordered on each side with black, and having a strip of very narrow navy (gold) lace along the inner edge of the black, and a large star enclosing a cross on the center of the front, the scarf being draped from the right shoulder to the left hip; sword-belt of red enamelled or fine patent-leather fastened with a button or clasp; and bright-red silk velvet shoulder straps bordered with a row of gold embroidery and ornamented with the Templars' cross in gold; gauntlets of buff leather, and military hat trimmed with one white and two black plumes and a cross.

IRISHMAN.—Black coat, light trousers, buff waistcoat and boots; a rather worn-looking high hat, a pipe, a knotty stick, a green scarf or kerchief tied about the neck, and a bandanna.

RIP VAN WINKLE.—Tattered trousers and coat of brown cloth, old shoes, long gray wig, red handkerchief and a soft felt hat.

NEPTUNE.—Pale-green flowing gown trimmed all over with grasses, shells and glistening sea-treasures; a trident in the hand and a crown on the head.

MERCURY.—Pale-pink trunk-hose, tights and close-fitting blouse; silver belt, pink heelless slippers with wings fastened on like spurs, and pink cap with a wing on each side.

JUPITER.—White flowing robe sprinkled all over with spangles; an electric or other light is carried to represent lightning, and a crown and a long white wig are worn.

ATLAS.—Bright-blue close, short trousers and coat, light-blue stockings and slippers and a blue cap; carries a globe representing the world on his shoulders.

BUFFALO BILL.—Large, loose-fitting coat, buckskin trousers, top boots, large soft felt hat, fur girdle, hunting bag and rifle.

HIGHLANDER.—Plaid kilt, single-breasted coat of cloth or velvet; belt, sporran on kilt, plaid scarf draped over shoulder; plaid stockings, low shoes, and Scotch cap with eagle's wing-feather and thistle pin.

EARL OF ESSEX.—Pale-blue trunk-hose, pale-blue tights, close-fitting crimson velvet coat, sleeves extending to wrists and gathered to form a series of encircling puffs, Elizabethan ruffs, jeweled belt with sword, and short crimson mantle, lined with pale-blue and bordered with gold galloon, hanging at the back; low shoes with jeweled buckles and a crimson Tyrolean hat with pale-blue feathers.

POWHATTAN.—Buckskin breeches with fringe down outside seams; tan-colored, low-necked, sleeveless blouse, belted and cut to form a fringe at the bottom; moccasins, hunting bag strapped across shoulders, bow and arrows, feather head-dress, blanket draped about figure.

YEOMAN OF THE GUARD.—Long-skirted scarlet Tudor coat trimmed with black velvet and gold, crown and Tudor rose embroidered on breast; close plaited muslin ruff at the throat; full sleeves to wrist; low-crowned black velvet hat, with blue, red and white ribbons around it; rosettes of the same on black shoes and at the knees of breeches; red stockings; sword in belt, halberd carried in hand.

DICK TURPIN.—Scarlet coat and waistcoat, with gold braid and buttons; high jack-boots; leather breeches; three-cornered hat and flowing wig; belt and pistols.

Dutch Fisher-Boy. — Wooden shoes; full breeches, coarse knitted stockings; striped blouse; red tie and cap.

Irishman.—Black coat, light trousers, buff waistcoat and boots; a rather worn-looking high hat, a short, stumpy pipe, a blackthorn or some other knotty stick, a green scarf or kerchief tied about the neck, and a bandanna.

The Two Obadiahs.—Two boys dressed exactly alike in some odd costume, such as monks, clowns, king's fools, etc.

Saconi or Italian Mute.—Monk's dress of plain white muslin; pointed cap with holes for the eyes and mouth, over head and face.

Ghost.—Costume composed of a sheet draped about the figure from neck to heels. Skull and crossbones cut from black cloth and sewn on at the middle of the back; cross-bones also in front where the sheet is draped up. Close-fitting cap of white muslin tied or pinned under the chin, and decorated with black to represent a skull.

George Washington.—Yellow knee-breeches, flowered waistcoat; army-blue coat, short across the front and with long tails; white cravat, black stockings, black slippers with buckles, white wig, and a Continental hat.

Prince.—Pale-gold, full, silk breeches gathered in Turkish fashion above the knees; light-blue velvet coat, trimmed all about with an embroidered band and belted in at the waist; a light-blue velvet cape with high collar, fastened so as to hang only at the back, and lined with pale-gold; lace collar; long coat-sleeves, with full, silk puffs at the top, striped with embroidered bands; blue silk stockings drawn well up under the breeches; black slippers with large buckles; a sword in the belt; and a cap with a brim and soft crown, and trimmed at one side with a drooping ostrich tip.

Hindoo Prince. — Choga of amber silk embroidered in squares, and a flower in each square; broidered over the breast with strings of pearls. Crimson-and-white silk sash around the waist from which a sword is suspended. The sleeves are close fitting, and trimmed with gold armlets, three on each arm. The leggings are of amber silk, slashed up the front and puffed with crimson. Scarf thrown over the shoulder, embroidered and edged with gold fringe. Turban richly jeweled. Pointed shoes turned up at the toes.

Peter The Great.—Military coat of green cloth with deep cuffs of scarlet, trimmed with braid and buttons. Long vest of scarlet cloth. Breeches to match. High boots. Various orders on the breast.

Huguenot (Saint Bris.)—Black silk doublet and trunks striped with velvet. Cloak with a high collar made of similar material. Lace ruffle. High hat with plume and also ornamented with a double cross in the front. High boots reaching nearly to the hips. Black embroidered sword belt. Gauntlet gloves. The fatal white handkerchief is carried in the hand.

William Tell.—Jacket of slate-colored satin fastened round the waist by a brown leather belt, and tied down the front with ribbons, with a small puffing of white between each tie. The sleeves are slashed and puffed at the shoulder and elbow. Scarlet satin trunks slashed with white. Crimson satin tights. Long cloak of brown cloth. Crimson satin cap with a feather in it. Cross-bow carried on the shoulder. Low shoes, strapped across the instep.

Algierian Costume. — Short open jacket of brown cloth edged round with black braid. Close vest of pink silk. Bag trousers fastened at the knee. White gaiters, and low shoes. Striped silk scarf around the waist. Red fez, with a silk scarf wound round it to form a turban.

Bandit.—A fancy Italian costume. Jacket of blue cloth braided with gold and fastened around the waist with a crimson silk scarf tied in a bow at the side and hanging in long fringed ends. The sleeves are opened up the inner side to the shoulder, exposing the shirt sleeves, and are lined with pink and braided with gold. Brown cloth breeches. Blue stockings, latticed with crimson ribbon. Low shoes. Wide felt hat.

Bohemian or Gypsy.—Short Spanish jacket of black velvet braided with gold, showing the white shirt at the waist. The sleeves are slit up and lined with pink, showing a pink undersleeve. Pink satin breeches. Striped scarf around the waist. Striped stockings. Gaiters. Cloak fastened around the throat with a cord and tassel. Tyrolese hat trimmed with a feather.

Circassian.—Tunic of scarlet cloth. Large overcoat of white sheepskin bound with red and yellow braid, and fastened round the waist with a belt into which is thrust a large knife. Sleeves, short and loose. High fur hat. High boots. Rifle slung at back.

Louis XV. Courier.—Short jacket of white cloth faced with crimson, and braided with gold and trimmed with bows of blue ribbon. Lace ruffles. Shoulder-knots of blue ribbon. Waistcoat of blue satin, braided with gold and fastened round the waist with a belt. Lace cravat. Crimson plush breeches, with a stripe of blue and gold down the sides. Long, white stockings, brought up over the breeches and fastened with blue ribbon garters tied in bows. Three-cornered hat, braided with gold and trimmed with a feather. Gold-headed stick.

DON JUAN.—Doublet of white silk, quilted, and braided with gold. Sleeveless jacket of black velvet trimmed with gold braid and made with epaulets. Trunks of white silk trimmed with bands of black satin and gold braid. White silk tights. Low shoes. Waist-belt with gold clasp.

FALCONER.—Short tunic of brown velvet trimmed with a plastron of gold cloth and bound with gold braid, fastened round the waist with a leather belt. Loose knickerbockers, gartered at the knee, and tied with a ribbon bow. White stockings with calf-pieces of velvet trimmed with gold braid. Leather shoes. Lace neck-frill. Soft, round hat of velvet, trimmed with two eagle's feathers.

COSTUMES FOR MISSES, GIRLS AND CHILDREN.

BOHEMIAN GIRL.—Double skirt of green sateen, the under one being trimmed with a flounce and a band of amber, and the upper with a band embroidered with hieroglyphics. Corsage body of amber sateen, ornamented around the bottom with coins, bound round the top with velveteen, and studded with gold stars. Striped cotton or muslin chemisette with elbow sleeves. Striped muslin cap trimmed with sequins in front. Sequin necklace.

FRENCH PEASANT.—Flower girl. Short skirt of pink-striped cotton, trimmed with a plaited flounce. Polonaise of pink-striped cotton with a vest-front of plain pink sateen. Elbow sleeves. Basket of flowers on the arm.

VIVANDIERE.—Short skirt of Turkey red trimmed with a band of blue twill. Military jacket of blue twill or cloth, ornamented with gold. Three-cornered felt hat. White muslin apron. Wood flask.

FISHER GIRL.—Skirt of blue twill, trimmed with two rows of red braid. Loose body with sailor collar and short sleeves, trimmed with red braid. White cotton apron with anchors at the corners.

GYPSY CHILD.—Red dress and black velvet bodice. A white kerchief about the neck and crossed upon the front; spangles all along the edges of the girdle; sleeves cut off at the puffs; tinsel bands about the skirt; red stockings and black slippers.

DAFFY-DOWN-DILLY.—A green skirt made to stand out well at the bottom and touch the floor; a low-necked red waist cut in leaf tabs at the bottom, and a pink bonnet rising high in a point in front and tied with long ribbons, one of which flies to the back and the other to the front. A bunch of the flowers is carried.

BUY-A-BROOM.—A full yellow skirt; a low white waist shirred round the neck and with full puff-sleeves reaching to the elbows; a closely fitting black peasant bodice cut in square tabs at the bottom; a close white cap with narrow front and full crown; white stockings and black slippers. The little masquerader carries several small brooms and sings "Buy a Broom."

QUEEN MAB.—Long-trained, low-necked, sleeveless gown of some clinging goods in a rose-pink shade, trimmed with silver tinsel; pink stockings and slippers; rose-colored gauze wings; a wreath of wild flowers on the head, and a wand decorated with pink ribbons in the hand.

POPPY.—A full skirt and bodice of pale-green. Bodice cut Pompadour in front with short puff-sleeves. A wide belt of poppy-red reaching well up under the arms, and a short, full vest shirred at the top to form a ruffle and placed on the belt in front. A deep flounce of poppy-red is joined to the edge of the bodice, which should extend only to the waist. From under the flounce extend ribbons of a different shade of green, having each a wide section of poppy-red gathered up close to its ends, and falling with the effect of poppies all round the bottom of the skirt. A large hat with full poppy-red brim and green crown; black stockings and poppy-red slippers; and a bunch of poppies or a green fan in the hand.

TELEGRAPH MESSENGER.—Full skirt and double-breasted jacket of dark-blue. Jacket closed with gilt buttons and bound with red braid. Skirt trimmed about the bottom with telegraph poles simulated with red braid, and wires simulated with gold or silver braid. On the wires at intervals are fastened slips of paper, with telegrams written on them. A messenger-boy's cap, and a note-book and high boots.

THE SOOTHSAYER.—A dove-gray kilted skirt, with panel of black on the sides. A closely fitting black bodice reaching only to the waist, opening over a low-cut dove-gray waistcoat, and having angel or wing sleeves lined with dove-gray. A white tucked and ruffled shirt front; a deep, fluted ruff about the neck and standing out well about the lower edge of the bodice; long black gloves, black stockings, and slippers with bows; eye-glasses, and a high black hat with pointed crown and a closely-rolled brim.

NEAPOLITAN GIRL.—Bright blue-and-red, blue-and-yellow or black-and-red costume, with short full skirt. The jacket and short sleeves trimmed with tinsel braid.

ZULEIKA.—Red Turkish trousers, blue skirt, white muslin waist, and a red zouave-jacket. No sleeves are used and a very wide sash is arranged about the waist and tied at one side. The jacket and skirt are edged with galloon or embroidered bands, and a close red cap similarly edged is worn.

COLUMBINE.—A low-necked, pointed bodice and full skirts of rose-colored tarletan. Several skirts should be made and all gathered to a belt so as to stand out well. Folds of pale-blue tarletan are arranged about the neck above a garland of leaves; the edge of the bodice is outlined with leaves, and a wreath is placed in the hair. Long pink gloves, blue stockings, pink slippers with blue bows on the toes, and a pink fan.

LADY-BUG.—A dull-blue plain dress, a bright-red circular cloak or long cape tied about the neck and thrown back of the arms, a red bonnet with poke brim, and irregular twigs standing out from the dress and hair in front to produce the effect of the bug's legs. The dress and cloak should touch the ground.

MAID MARIAN.—Cashmere skirt, plain. Polonaise of same fabric, trimmed with gold, and with wide sleeves. Jeweled belt around the waist. Long cloak of white cashmere. Fillet of gold around the hat.

GOODY TWO-SHOES.—Quilted petticoat of red satin. Bunched tunic of cretonne. Cretonne body laced across the front. Elbow sleeves edged with a frill of muslin.

FAIRY GODMOTHER.—Skirt of amber cashmere or veiling. Apron of white silk trimmed round with the eyes from peacock plumes. Pointed body of satin with a basque skirt cut in points. The body is trimmed with strips of white silk tied across and fastened in bows. Hanging sleeves, cut round in points. Cloak of green cashmere or satin. Deep, white linen collar. Sugar-loaf hat trimmed with a peacock plume.

BEAUTY.—Skirt of white silk embroidered in front with foliage. Train of pink silk embroidered or trimmed with silver braid. Square-cut, embroidered body. *Moyen âge* sleeves trimmed to match and lined with white silk. Jeweled girdle. Pearls around the neck and in the hair.

Costumes For Boys.

BEAST.—Silk tights. Trunks of satin slashed with white silk. Green velvet tunic cut square at the throat and trimmed round with fur. Short wide sleeves with undersleeves of sateen slashed with white. White cambric shirt. Jeweled necklace; belt and dagger. Should wear a donkey's-head mask.

ALADDIN. — Under-skirt of maize ornamented with a trimming of black cloth. Tunic of blue cloth or sateen, embroidered in front and on the sleeves. Over this is worn an open jacket of cretonne or any fabric of an Oriental character, with a deep collar. Chinese hat and a brass lamp.

KING ARTHUR.—Long-sleeved tunic of white cashmere or satin trimmed at the bottom with imitation mail. Cuirass of imitation mail. Worsted or silk tights. Long cloak of blue cloth, trimmed round with gold braid.

ROBIN RED-BREAST.—Short brown skirt covered with marabout feathers; round body with point at the back like the tail of a bird, made of feathers or plush; red waistcoat with high collar and red necktie; yellow or brown tights and feather-trimmed slippers; cap with peak as nearly as possible like a bird's head.

ALSATIAN BOY.—Knee-breeches of brown cloth, with buckles. White cotton stockings and shirt. Green jacket, without sleeves, of sateen or velveteen, trimmed with ornaments of gold. Fur cap.

IRISH CAR DRIVER.—Green coat patched with cloth; brass buttons. Brocaded waistcoat. Drab breeches with patches. High collar; red tie. Blue darned stockings, leather shoes. Hat trimmed with green and sprigs of shamrock.

KNIGHT OF MALTA.—Jacket with ruff; black puffed trousers. Red round cloak to waist, bordered with gold braid; and a cross on either side. Silk shoes and stockings. Feather in hat. Flowing hair. The cloak, with a ruff, might be worn over a boy's ordinary dress, as a saving of time and trouble.

DUKE OF MARLBOROUGH.—Full wig. Large lace neckcloth. Square-cut coat and long-flapped waistcoat; hanging cuffs and ruffles. Sash over the right shoulder. Blue or scarlet silk stockings with gold or silver clocks, drawn high up over the knee; square-toed shoes with high heels and small buckles.

PRINCE. — Crimson velvet knee-trousers and cutaway coat, frilled shirt, wide lace collar, lace ruffs in sleeves, black stockings, black slippers with large buckles, and a large crimson Gainsborough hat with long, white ostrich plumes.

Paul Pry.—High boots, with trousers of red-and-white striped calico tucked into them; waistcoat to match, with large watch and chain, powdered bag-wig; blue tail-coat with brass buttons. Umbrella under arm.

Puss in Boots. — Cat's head and bodice. Groom's coat made of white fur, with leather belt. Top boots.

Robin Hood.—Worsted hose, and high boots of untanned leather. Doublet of green cloth. Short cape with collar of scarlet cloth. Leather belt and girdle, with horn and bow.

Dick Whittington.—Tunic of cashmere ornamented with gold braid. Sleeves of a different color to match the hose. Carries a cat.

NURSERY-RHYME COSTUMES.

Polly Put the Kettle On.—Underskirt of black sateen trimmed with rows of colored braid. Loose polonaise of pink cashmere tucked up in front and bunched up at the back. Short sleeves turned up with white and edged with lace. Lace tucker round the throat. White bib-apron and white mob cap.

Old King Cole.—Loose tunic of cashmere fastened round the waist by a jeweled belt and trimmed round the bottom with amber satin. Cloak of green velveteen bound round with fur and clasped with gilt chain and brooch. Crown set with jewels. Worsted or silk hose.

Mother Hubbard. — Plain skirt of amber sateen. Tunic of black sateen, bunched at the back; headed by an amber puffing round the waist. Low, plaited body of black sateen with white plastron. Muslin chemisette and apron. Cloak of blue cashmere. Sugar-loaf hat trimmed with ribbon. Colored hose and low shoes.

Jack.—Cloth or cashmere jacket. Amber satin or sateen vest, and cashmere cloth or plush breeches.

Jill.—Under skirt of white, made with three tucks. Upper skirt and body of pink. Body cut square, back and front, and sleeves turned up with white. Straw hat.

Tom Tucker.—Costume of the time of George II. Blue cloth with square skirts trimmed with braid and buttons Sleeves with wide cuffs, trimmed to match. Long vest of silk or satin, embroidered. Plush or cashmere knee breeches. Silk stockings; low shoes.

Humpty Dumpty.—Doublet of striped silk falling over the hips. Baggy breeches made of plush or sateen. Short cloak of black satin trimmed with roleaux of amber satin and a collar with facings of rose silk. Amber silk hose. Low shoes trimmed with bows and small eggs. Lace ruffle at throat. The front of the blouse is covered with the representation of an egg made of white satin, with the back smaller than the front, and stuffed out with cotton. Felt hat turned up at one side and ornamented with an egg and a plume.

Margery Daw.—A pink dress under a white apron. A little kerchief about the neck, and a pink sunbonnet with very narrow front.

Little Miss Muffet.—A low-necked green waist, a full red skirt, very short white stockings, black slippers, a large-brimmed red hat and a yellow sash. A large spider-pin is fastened to the back of the skirt, and a cup or mug is carried.

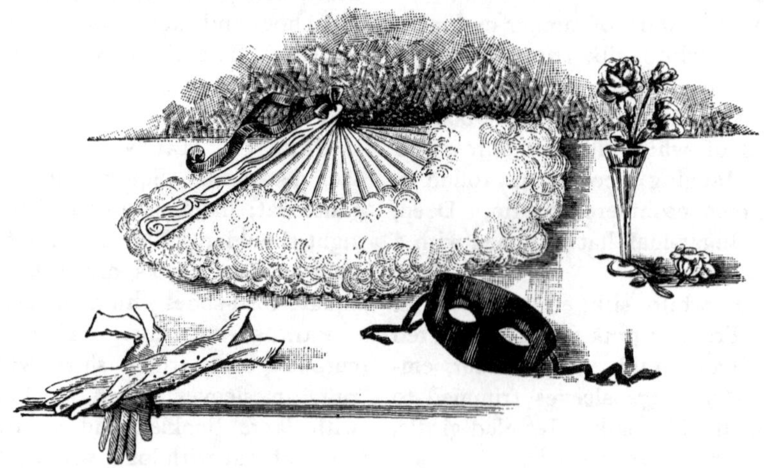

www.ingramcontent.com/pod-product-compliance
Lightning Source LLC
LaVergne TN
LVHW081403110826
845149LV00010B/1649
9781410103864